# 101
# Design Methods

## A Structured Approach for Driving Innovation in Your Organization

## VIJAY KUMAR

WILEY

JOHN WILEY & SONS, INC.

Published by John Wiley & Sons, Inc., Hoboken, New Jersey.

Published simultaneously in Canada.

Limit of Liability/Disclaimer of Warranty: While the publisher and author have used their best efforts in preparing this book, they make no representations or warranties with the respect to the accuracy or com-pleteness of the contents of this book and specifically disclaim any implied warranties of merchantability or fitness for a particular purpose. No warranty may be created or extended by sales representatives or written sales materials. The advice and strategies contained herein may not be suitable for your situation. You should consult with a professional where appropriate. Neither the publisher nor the author shall be liable for damages arising herefrom.

For general information about our other products and services, please contact our Customer Care Department within the United States at (800) 762-2974, outside the United States at (317) 572-3993 or fax (317) 572-4002.

Wiley publishes in a variety of print and by print-on-demand. Some material included with standard print versions of this book may not be included in e-books or in print-on-demand. If this book refers to media such as a CD or DVD that is not included in the version you purchased, you may download this material at http://booksupport.wiley.com. For more information about Wiley products, visit www.wiley.com.

*Library of Congress Cataloging-in-Publication Data:*

Kumar, Vijay,
  101 design methods: a structured approach for driving innovation in your organization / Vijay Kumar.
    p. cm.
  Includes index.
  ISBN 978-1-118-08346-8 (pbk.); 978-1-118-33024-1 (ebk); 978-1-118-33088-3 (ebk); 978-1-118-33306-8 (ebk); 978-1-118-39218-8 (ebk); 978-1-118-39219-5 (ebk)
  1. Technological innovations. 2. Organizational change. I. Title. II. Title: One hundred one design methods. III. Title: One hundred and one design methods.
  HD45.K827 2012
  658.4'063—dc23
                                    2012009778

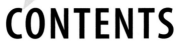

# CONTENTS

# FOREWORD

The company I have the honor to lead is 100 years old this year. In the same 100 years, many companies had come and gone. So as we prepared to embark upon a celebratory year; we started thinking—why did so few companies thrive and why had so many faded away? The truth is, it isn't companies that survive against the odds—its ideas and innovation. Ideas and the nonlinear, iterative process of innovation have made the world a better place—and that's something to celebrate.

What we can observe by looking back is that very thoughtful moments in the company's history played a vital role in future decades' success. And with this introduction I want to describe how Professor Vijay Kumar catalyzed in me and our company the power of solving very complex problems.

First, let me emphasize that I am happy to call Professor Kumar a great friend, and second that I am excited he has now published his life's work in *101 Design Methods*. Vijay is a well-respected teacher, author, and true thought leader about the "design of innovation". I hold him in special reverence because he has made his mark in a very specific arena of building frameworks to spool innovative thinking and influence. Think of these frameworks as a toolkit for the deep thinking that is needed to solve the most vexing problems inside a business.

I appreciate the thesis of Professor Kumar's work and see many parallels between what he has spent a lifetime studying and what he has written about in this book. I also see parallels with what I learned from him during my decade of serving on the Board of Advisors for the IIT Institute of Design.

My career with Steelcase is more than 30 years and I have been in the CEO seat for 18 of those years. In that span, Steelcase has transformed from a traditional manufacturer and the largest in its industry globally, to industry innovator around the world. We believe we are known as much for the insights behind our furniture as for the products themselves.

Many businesses aspire to be innovative. It is the key variable in profitable growth of most enterprise and a must-have for those in very competitive arenas.

In my early years in the CEO position I was allowed to sit in on a number of Professor Kumar's lectures to our Board of Advisors at the IIT Institute of Design. I recall suggesting after one of these lectures that if we could get his thinking translated to the C-suite of organizations, they would flock to his perspective and these tools of how to solve very complex problems in their businesses. In fact this led me to develop an internal course at Steelcase called the "Critical Thinking Model" which was used as a tool for our employees to hold "deep thinking" in higher reverence and was later detailed in a Harvard Business Review article in April 2007. It is a common and shared platform we use to bind individuals and teams around the world in a common language and process for critical thinking. From this perspective we saw that we were becoming more than just good business people...we were becoming design driven. With Vijay's perspective, among others, I can say it was a key step as part of our mission to cultivate a culture of innovation. When the link is made between the traditional quantitative world of the MBA

and design thinking, I am certain that we are making unique progress in the world of innovation. It might be my proudest moment in this role.

These steps are broadly discussed and heavily focused on in the remaining pages of this book.

We are in a moment of highly publicized anguish about whether the future will be as promising as what the world had in its past. Books like *101 Design Methods* become essential building blocks to getting the innovation mechanisms to work.

I suspect the methods will surprise and delight you just as they did me. And no greater endorsement can be given to a friend who rather than take me fishing, taught me to fish.

JAMES P. HACKETT
President and Chief Executive Officer,
Steelcase Inc.

# ACKNOWLEDGMENTS

I had a wonderful group of people helping me with this book and I thank them all for their sincere support.

*Hugh Musick* (Associate Dean of the IIT Institute of Design) has been a partner to me throughout the book publication process. Knowing that this book with content like it will be a tremendous help for the design community, Hugh took early initiatives to provide me with the most helpful support system at the Institute of Design that let me start down the path of making quick progress. I am thankful for Hugh's guidance on all aspects of the process—administration, coordination with the publishers, conducting research to fine tune the various methods covered in this book, and writing help.

I am deeply thankful to two of my students at the Institute of Design, *Leticia Baiao* and *Youna Choi,* who were with me going through all the challenges of this book project. They were amazing in their efforts to coordinate all the key activities leading to the successful implementation of the book. I am deeply thankful for their help in doing research, reviewing initial drafts for all the chapters, providing constant feedback, selecting example projects, creating all supporting images and illustrations, and managing the whole process. Their strong competencies in structured thinking, careful analysis, and visual communication steered the content and design of the book in the best possible direction.

*Traci Thomas, Reena Patel,* and *Derek Tarnow* were very helpful in carefully going through all the example projects used in the methods pages and drafting short descriptions about how teams effectively applied design methods in their projects. In particular, I appreciate Traci's initiatives in leading this effort by talking with various project teams, going through the project reports, drafting descriptions, and coordinating with everyone on the book team.

I am very thankful for the wonderful support I got from a very dedicated team of students—*Diba Salimi, Gretchen Kelly, Chia-ling Yu, Hyunjoo Lee,* and *Francesca Passoni*—who contributed tremendously to reviewing various chapters, envisioning images, getting permissions, and managing the operational details of assembling information from various sources. I express my sincere thanks to *Graham Tuttle, Farid Talhame,* and *Luis Eduardo Dejo* for providing feedback and for creating and testing prototype pages with prospective readers especially in the beginning stages of the book.

I am also grateful for the help I got from the Institute of Design PhD students *Yadira Ornelas,* and *Amanda Geppert,* and our friends from the *Danish School of Design*. for their contributions in defining some of the specific methods and projects included in this book.

I thank *Vince LaConte* (the former Director of Marketing and Communications, IIT Institute of Design) for his support in coordinating the early efforts of pushing forward the book proposal, coordinating with the publisher, and writing the drafts for the book prototypes. I am also grateful to *Brandon Schauer* for helping me define the outline of the book through many conversations we had and for helping me prepare a strong book proposal.

I am tremendously thankful to the *students* of the *Institute of Design*. They have provided me the greatest experiences in how to apply the design processes and methods for conceiving vastly valuable innovations. They taught me much about how teams work on innova-

tion challenges and how activities happen in harmonious ways while wading through complex and ambiguous situations. Such efforts ultimately produce synergic solutions. I thank the students whose team projects do such a wonderful job illustrating the application of many of the methods discussed in this book.

I am also greatly thankful for the continuous support I got from the *faculty* at the *Institute of Design* during my entire time at the school. I am particularly thankful to those who contributed their projects as examples to be included in the book. I am also very thankful for the support and encouragement I got from the *Institute of Design staff* for making the book preparation process easy and comfortable.

*Patrick Whitney,* the Robert C Pew Professor and Dean of the IIT Institute of Design, has been a friend, co-thinker, and an advisor to me for more than two decades. I am very thankful for his encouragement and guidance through all those years while I was building up the content for the book. I am indebted to *Professor Charles Owen* and late Professor *Jay Doblin* for teaching me the importance of structured approaches to make design process credible, formalized, and collaborative.

I learned a lot about the power of structured innovation planning methods, while I was the Chief Methodologist at *Doblin Inc*. (now a member of Monitor Group), working with *Larry Keeley, John Pipino,* and a brilliant team of people who pioneered many of the leading practices in design innovation. My experiences working with my Doblin colleagues and client organizations gave me a high level of confidence that structured processes and rigorous methods can make a big difference in the real world.

My work as a consultant and advisor to *client* and *sponsoring organizations* and working with innovation leaders taught me a great deal about innovation practices over the years. The experience showed me how they successfully addressed the big challenges organizations and markets faced. I learned a lot about how to effectively manage challenging and complex real world processes and I am grateful for these opportunities.

It was a great pleasure to work with my editor at John Wiley & Sons, *Margaret Cummins,* and her publishing team, who made this book a reality. I am also thankful to *Amy Yates* for her legal advice and support for making the publication process work.

Finally, it was my family that continuously provided me with the care and support that I needed to think through challenging ideas every day in my life. I thank my parents and my designer/architect/engineer/planner/educator brothers and sister for having a great influence on my life early on. I am blessed to have the care and support every day from my wife *Aisha,* my daughter *Darshana,* my son *Gautam,* and my daughter-in-law *Sruthi*.

VIJAY KUMAR

# INTRODUCTION

## Innovation (n): a viable offering that is new to a specific context and time, creating user and provider value

As firms like Apple and Google top the headlines and grab the attention of executives everywhere, just about every professional magazine, journal, conference, and meeting room today is awash with the term "innovation." Innovation has arrived, and it has made a huge splash in the world of business. Except that it hasn't. Despite the fact that there is so much attention on the strategic value of innovation, very few organizations know how to make it a reliable and repeatable practice. Business history speaks for itself. Research shows that less than 4 percent of the innovation projects undertaken by businesses are proven successful according to a source from Doblin Inc. The remaining 96 percent of the projects fail.

If innovation is so important, why aren't more organizations better at it? Why are innovation failure rates still this high? To begin with, there are four major assumptions organizations make that prevent them from achieving systemic innovation. Let's examine each of these assumptions one by one, and discover why they are incorrect and why there might be a better way of reliably achieving major innovation.

**Assumption**: Innovation as it is currently practiced is good enough.

**Reality:** Current innovation practices don't reliably deliver breakthroughs. There is a lack of a set of reliable tools and methods for creating real breakthroughs rather than incremental or random improvements.

When an innovation team is asked to do more than develop incremental improvements to an offering, but rather develop leapfrog or disruptive innovations, many of their existing practices and tools simply no longer apply. The realization of a need for new ways of working is likely to make teams feel directionless. For example, a simple $2 \times 2$ position matrix is a widely used tool to plot a market or opportunity space; but how should a team use this tool when the innovation sought is so radical that competitors have yet to emerge, the problems aren't fully understood, and the opportunities are still undefined?

**Assumption:** Innovation is for executives.

**Reality:** Practitioners "on the ground" are most often the source of breakthrough ideas, but they need structures and processes to help them plan and define innovation.

Most of the current thinking about innovation serves as a reminder to business executives that innovation is a necessary part of strategy, goading them to keep innovating with well-known inspirational examples like the Apple iPod. While general theories, strategies, and market approaches can be seen as critical steps toward innovation, they are hardly the only steps. Once an innovation initiative is defined, teams of managers, designers, researchers, marketers, and engineers must figure out how to act on it. The team must create a plan for bringing to market something that no one has ever done before. What new and different path should it follow? What stages, activities, and skills will be needed? Innovation must be mastered at the level of "how do we do it?" as well as the level of "what do we do?"

**Assumption:** Innovation is for practitioners.

**Reality:** Innovation isn't just for practitioners. Practitioners need to work with executives to be able to integrate innovation tactics into a larger strategy.

Innovation requires a much broader scope of understanding than other business practices. The designers and technologists developing new offerings must not only know how to innovate on a tactical level, they must also comprehend the strategic objectives and wider implications of their work. In the old model of incremental innovation, strategy was conveyed to practitioners in the form of business requirements, objectives, and specifications. Documents clearly outlined the boundaries of the solution, described the end result, and set out criteria for success. But, in the emerging world of leapfrog and disruptive innovation, practitioners must be empowered to question previously held assumptions, invert and transcend the tenets of their disciplines, and explore unaddressed market needs and opportunities. This requires them to possess a deep understanding of the business strategies behind their work, of where and why the company is trying to innovate in the first place.

No existing approaches draw connections between what practitioners do and how their actions affect strategy. This disconnect results in a situation in which practitioners change boundaries and reverse assumptions either without regard, or without comprehension, of whether their ideas fit with a rational, profitable strategy. Practitioners need an encyclopedia of tools and activities; they also need a guidebook that integrates these tools and activities into the theory and strategy of innovation.

**Assumption:** "Innovation planning" is an oxymoron.

**Reality:** Measured, scientific approaches to innovation do exist, and can make it a systematic process.

When organizations think of management, they think of control, of processes that can be forecasted, planned, systematized, and guided to yield predictable results. When they think of innovation, however, these attributes are not likely to come to mind. It is a common belief that innovation is about simply "doing things differently," or "thinking outside the box" where the normal rules of management don't apply. Few organizations, however, can afford to invest in a practice that defies control and

produces valuable breakthroughs in a random, nonlinear, often untimely fashion. Innovation represents a new and important capability, much too important for managers not to understand how it can be systematized and structured. Elusive and complex business practices can be reinvented when approached as a science. For innovation to become more widely successful, organizations require a new approach to practicing it.

The practice of innovation needs to be mastered by organizations attempting to harness its power. Innovation is a discipline. It is not magic. It is something organizations can choose to practice, improve, and excel at. This book is about how to engage in that practice.

# Four Core Principles of Successful Innovation

Analyzing some of the most innovative companies in the world, and studying hundreds of successful innovations, there emerge four principles successful innovators tend to follow. With these principles as a foundation, organizations can begin to develop mastery of a new, effective innovation practice.

## PRINCIPLE 1: Build Innovations Around Experiences

Experience can be defined as "the act of living through events." Although the term "user experience" (or UX) has become associated with the software and information technology industries, user experience is a key factor in the success of any type of offering. Every company and organization in some measure creates or affects peoples' experiences. Focusing on the nature of those experiences provides the perfect starting point for innovation.

Imagine yourself as an employee of a shoe company charged with creating successful new innovations in running shoes. You would normally start by studying shoes and thinking about how to improve their performance, comfort, and style in order to produce a better product. Since competing companies do exactly the same thing, their improvements more or less match your own. However, by looking at the larger context of "running shoes," the wider range of activities your customers engage in related to running, innovation opportunities are greater which in turn afford new ways of competing.

*experience*

*product*

Athletic shoe giant Nike maintains a market-leading competitive position not by focusing on creating a better shoe, but by designing a better athletic experience. Beyond innovations in materials, aesthetics, and performance, the company has developed innovations that extend the runner's experience. Embedded sensors in shoes enable runners to capture, monitor, and upload data about their running to measure their progress over time. Similarly, Nike provides online tools to help runners plan runs and choose routes. The result of these kinds of innovations has helped Nike remain a market leader against intense competition. In short, Nike's innovations have extended beyond just a better shoe to supporting peoples' activities, in running, sports, or regular use, giving people an engaging experience around wearing shoes.

In most organizations, innovation does not work this way. Instead, it starts with a focus on their offerings. Organizations try to understand why consumers purchase their current product and how they use it. The typical methods used to find this information are surveys, focus groups, interviews, home visits, and usability tests. Consumer researchers seek to answer a host of questions that are primarily about the product. What improvements can be made to it? Why did people buy this product over another? What additional features would cause them to pay more for it? As a result, innovations center on the product itself.

Experience-focused innovation uses a different approach. Emphasis is not on the product, but on its users. The focus shifts from the things people use, to what they do—their behaviors, activities, needs, and motivations. The most successful innovations are built not only on detailed knowledge of a product or technology, but also on what the organization learns from studying peoples' overall experience. In studying peoples' experiences, innovators should focus not only on the obvious experience of "using the product," but on the host of activities that surround the context in which it is used including: recognizing a need, discovering a product or service to meet that need, learning about it, using it, and extending its use (e.g., sharing, customizing, servicing, upgrading). Organizations need to expand their concept of product performance beyond understanding the attributes, functions, and features of an offering, to understanding its users' motivations, needs, and beginning-to-end experience.

Thinking about and understanding the extended user experience can lead to great innovations; but it's far from easy. Design innovation employs the social science of ethnography—the collection of data about people through direct observation and interaction with them—to develop a deeper understanding of people. While innovation should not ignore traditional market-research methods like focus groups and surveys, ethnographic observation puts a premium on the valuable and often unexpected insights about people that result from observing them directly in the context where the organization's offering (product, service, message) will be used. This approach changes the focus from what people say to what they actually do.

## PRINCIPLE 2: Think of Innovations as Systems

An offering, whether it is a product, a service, or media/message, naturally belongs to a larger system of offerings, organizations, and markets. A "system" can be defined as any set of interacting or interdependent entities that form an integrated whole which is greater than the sum of its parts. Innovators who understand how this larger system works can better create and deliver offerings with high value.

A traditional approach to designing a healthcare-related product would be to focus on product performance. By placing the product in the context of the overall healthcare system, we can develop a greater understanding of the product's value in relation to all the components of the system, such as the patient, doctor, hospital, home, pharmacy, medical device manufacturer, medical supplier, insurance company, pharmaceutical company, government, and so forth. The attributes that define these components can also be described; for example, the patient's health condition, treatment plan, and other information similar to what is found in the patient's electronic health record. Further, we can also think about the flows that happen between components, such as a patient's payments to the insurance company or the information that patients and doctors exchange. Thinking about your product in relation to the healthcare system not only helps understand system-level implications for the design of the product, but also reveals new opportunities for innovation that otherwise you would not have considered.

Going even further, organizations can pursue simultaneous innovation in several parts of the system. Offerings based on integrated innovation of multiple parts of a system are likely to have greater value, and tend to confer massive competitive advantage for the company creating them. The classic example of this principle is Apple. The iPod and iTunes, the iPhone, the App Store, and later the iPad, all reflect Apple's intentional systems innovations. In addressing innovation at a systems level, the company reinvented the music business, the mobile devices sector, and the tablet computers industry.

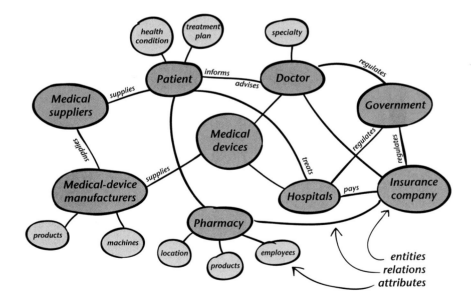

## PRINCIPLE 3: Cultivate an Innovation Culture

The story of Apple's successes through design innovation is well known, and not very surprising. Apple is a relatively young company, founded and built on the idea of user-centered design of technology. Although now an established Fortune 500 firm with 60,000 employees worldwide, it has inherited and maintained much of its organizational culture from its days as a Silicon Valley start-up. Its founder-CEO, Steve Jobs, was a natural innovator and showman who knew that design is one of the company's primary differentiators. In short, a company like Apple has many built-in organizational and cultural advantages that allow it to pursue a design innovation strategy.

Less well known than Apple, but equally important, are the stories of large, long-established companies that have not historically relied on a design innovation strategy, but find themselves needing to adopt one. Procter & Gamble's transformation of its innovation strategy under the leadership of A.G. Lafley is a prime example. In 2000, the household products giant's stock was collapsing as it faced alarming declines in growth and threats from a plethora of private-label brands with increasing access to the same production technologies and markets. Facing the decision of whether to cut costs to compete head to head with private-label brands or pour additional resources into R&D and marketing to rebuild margins, Lafley boldly chose to do both. One of his key strategies was to inject user-centered design innovation into P&G's organizational "DNA."

This principle is about cultivating a mindset among people in an organization that everyone is actively engaged in innovation on a daily basis and that everyone's actions can add up to the overall cultural behavior of the organization.

Innovation practice is a collaborative process and people with competencies in different fields need to come together to make the process thorough, inclusive, and valuable. Engineers, technical experts, ethnographers, managers, designers, business planners, marketing researchers, and financial planners, all need to come together in a shared mental space. Most recently, even end users and community members are also brought into the innovation process. Although achieving this level of collaboration is a huge challenge, organizations can take small steps that eventually can lead to big positive changes in the innovation culture of organizations. One such step is to conduct frequent interactive work sessions and brainstorming activities among people with diverse expertise.

## PRINCIPLE 4: Adopt a Disciplined Innovation Process

To reiterate: "innovation planning" is not an oxymoron. Successful innovation can and should be planned and managed like any other organizational function. It is possible to create innovations using well-developed processes and repeatable methods, all in the service of supporting and extending the other three principles of successful innovation—understanding experiences, thinking in terms of systems, and fostering an innovation culture. A high degree of discipline is necessary for these processes and methods to work, but when they do, the probability of creating successful innovations can increase dramatically. Simply recognizing and understanding that innovation can and should be planned is the first, critical step.

It is important to note that the innovation process exists in parallel to many other equally important processes in an organization and needs to integrate well with them. Innovators need to synthesize processes from design, technology, business, and other areas. For example, typical technology- and business-driven innovations start with the identification of a business opportunity or a technology possibility followed by concept development and then offering them to users. Design-driven innovations start by understanding people, developing concepts, and then conceiving businesses around those concepts. Knowing when and where all these processes touch and interact is key to successful collaboration in organizations.

Companies need to understand effective and compatible design methods to practice design innovation collaboratively, reliably, and repeatedly. Innovations conceived by carefully integrating design processes with business and technology have a better chance of achieving high user value and economic value, leading to greater adoption and market leadership.

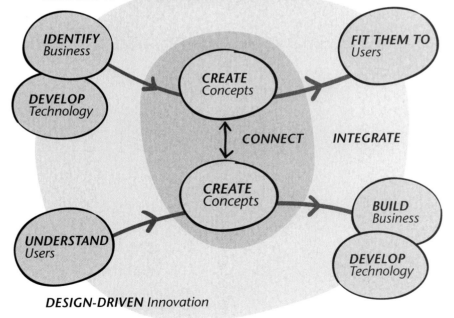

# A Model of the Design Innovation Process

The reasons why organizations need a reliable innovation process, and some of the general principles that underlie successful innovation, were discussed earlier. In the remainder of this book, a model design innovation process is presented with discussion of 101 design methods innovators can apply throughout that process. These design methods evolved out of many years of studying cases of innovation projects and successfully applying the four core principles discussed earlier—building innovations around experiences, thinking in systems, cultivating an innovation culture, and adopting a disciplined process.

## The Design Innovation Process

The design innovation process starts with the real—we observe and learn from the tangible factors from real-world situations. Then we try to get a full understanding of the real world by creating abstractions and conceptual models to reframe the problem in new ways. Only then do we explore new concepts in abstract terms before we evaluate them and implement them for their acceptance in the real world. This requires fluidity in our thinking between the real and the abstract.

Just as with nearly any creative or exploratory process the design innovation process moves back and forth through modes of activity, oscillating between poles of Real versus Abstract and Understanding versus Making. A 2 × 2 map illustrates the design innovation process. The lower left quadrant represents "research," about knowing reality. The upper left quadrant stands for "analysis," since this is where we process the information about reality in abstract terms and try to come up with good mental models to drive innovation. The top right quadrant is about "synthesis," during which the abstract models developed during analysis are taken as a basis for generating new concepts. And lastly, the lower right quadrant defines the "realization" of our concepts into implementable offerings. All these four quadrants—

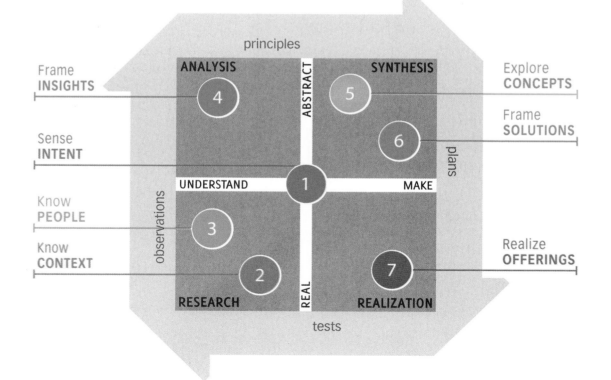

research, analysis, synthesis, and realization—combined together is a well-formalized process model with which to drive innovations in your organization.

Within this framework reside seven distinct modes of activity for design innovation: Sense Intent, Know Context, Know People, Frame Insights, Explore Concepts, Frame Solutions, and Realize Offerings. (These seven modes, incidentally, form the structure not only of the innovation process, but also of the rest of this book.) Understanding the outlines of the innovation process can greatly help innovators, by providing a guiding structure and sequence for any given project, and ensuring that the team has the right information and knowledge at the right time.

## Process Is Nonlinear

Although the idea of a process implies a linear sequence of events, this can be misleading. Many projects are actually nonlinear. For example, a project may begin with a sudden brainstorm (Explore Concepts) and then proceed "backwards" to research and analysis to validate and improve the idea, followed by further exploration and iteration.

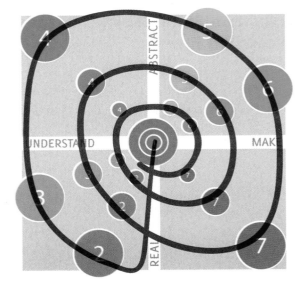

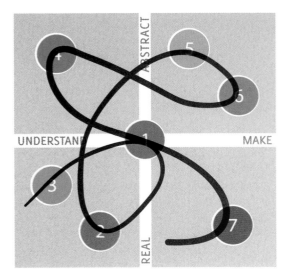

## Process Is Iterative

The process is also iterative, requiring many cycles through the process, and often through one or more modes (cycles within cycles), rather than being a direct sequential push. A project might start with an intent and some contextual research; then follow several consecutive rounds of user research and analysis, with initial insights being fed back to users for validation; then several rounds of concept exploration, user feedback through prototype testing, refinement of analysis, and then further exploration, further prototyping, and so forth. The number of repetitions and loops in any given innovation project is largely a function of the project's budget and scope. In some cases, multiple loops may be necessary, in others merely desirable, and in still others totally unfeasible. Doing more iterations generally leads to higher-value, more successful innovations—although not if pursued for too long or without discipline.

# Seven Modes of the Design Innovation Process

As discussed previously, there are seven distinct modes of the design innovation process, each with its own goals and activities. Each mode will be introduced, and then covered in detail in its own separate chapter

## Mode 1: Sense Intent

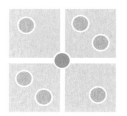

Early on in the process we are in this mode of figuring out where to start. Before jumping straight into a project we take a pause and consider the changing world around us. We look at all the changes happening in business, technology, society, culture, policy, and the like. We gather the latest happenings, cutting-edge developments, and latest news. We study the trends that can affect our topic area. We look at the overall effects of these changes. All these offer us a way to reframe our initial problem and look for new innovation opportunities. It helps us think of an initial intent about where we should be moving.

- Gathering the latest: Searching for the latest happenings, cutting-edge developments, and the latest thinking going on in the field

- Mapping overviews: Taking a step back from details and creating high-level views of the changes going on in the topic area

- Mapping trends: Getting high-level overview of relevant trends in business, technology, society, culture, and policy

- Reframing problems: Framing-up challenges differently based on the associated trends and conditions and finding opportunities where the organization could create high-value innovation

- Stating initial intent: Outlining hypotheses of how the organization could take advantage of innovation opportunities

## Mode 2: Know Context

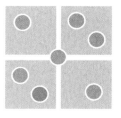

In Know Context we study the context—the circumstances or events that affect the environment in which our innovation offerings (products, services, experiences, brands, etc.) exist or could exist. We study how our offerings perform in the market. We focus on offerings that are similar to ours and see how they perform. We study our organization. We look at all the competitors and their evolving strategies. We learn about our organization's relationship to our complementors in the industry. We find out if government policies and regulations have an effect on our innovation topic. Broadly, in this mode, we pay attention to what is transforming our innovation context including society, environment, industry, technology, business, culture, politics, and economics.

- Planning for research: Creating a work plan for understanding the context based on available time, resources, methods, and expected deliverables

- Searching knowledge base: Searching through large quantities of data from existing sources to find emerging patterns

- Mapping evolution: Creating overviews of key industry developments, eras, timelines, and likely futures

- Doing comparisons: Creating overviews showing organizations in relation to industry networks, competitors, and analogous organizations

- Diagnosing conditions: Gaining perspective on the organization's capabilities, their performance, and industry patterns of innovation

- Asking experts: Communicating with experts in the field and understanding their analytics, opinions, and recommendations

## Mode 3: Know People

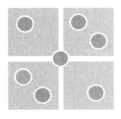

In this mode our goal is to understand people (end users and other stakeholders) and their interactions with everything during their daily lives. In this mode traditional market research techniques are most useful when a new offering is already defined. But to explore a person's unmet or unspoken needs we must have more powerful methods and tools. We use observational and ethnographic research methods to learn about people in ways that are different from interviews or focus group studies. A key objective in this mode is to extract the most valuable insights from our observations. An "insight" here is defined as an interesting revelation or learning that emerges out of observing peoples' actual behavior. Insight is an interpretation of what is observed, and is often the result of asking the question "why?"

- Planning research: Deciding on research objectives, target users, fieldwork protocols, budgets, and timeframes
- Observing people: Recruiting participants, doing fieldwork, documenting people, their activities, and interactions with objects and environment
- Asking people: Conducting surveys, discussing findings with users, and gathering feedback and validation
- Engaging people: Having users participate in activities, conversations, and interactions with researchers
- Organizing finding: Collecting observations and research data, tagging with keywords, and identifying gaps in research

## Mode 4: Frame Insights

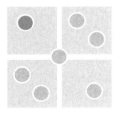

After conducting research, the next challenge is to bring structure to what has been found and learned from the previous modes. We sort, cluster, and organize the data gathered in the previous three modes and begin to find important patterns. We analyze contextual data and view patterns that point to untapped market opportunities or niches. Finding insights and patterns that repeatedly emerge from multiple analyses of data is beneficial. Therefore in this mode we use a mix of different kinds of methods in order to gain multiple perspectives of the context for a fuller understanding. Guidelines or principles that are generated in this mode help us move to the next mode for exploring concepts and framing solutions.

- Finding insights: Identifying patterns in research results about people and the context and looking for insights
- Modeling systems: Diagramming the context as a system showing its components, relationships, attributes, and value flow
- Finding clusters: Sorting data in different ways, finding groupings, and revealing high-level insights
- Finding patterns: Visualizing research findings as diagrams and revealing hot spots, gaps, and overlaps
- Making profiles: Defining attributes of key stakeholders and other parts of the system
- Mapping flows: Visualizing how value flows in networks of producers, consumers, suppliers, and other stakeholders
- Mapping experiences: Diagramming user journeys in space and time, discovering pain points, and showing opportunities
- Making frameworks: Summarizing insights and translating them into frameworks and guidelines to drive concept generation

# Mode 5: Explore Concepts

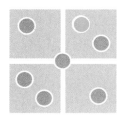

In this mode we do structured brainstorming to identify opportunities and to explore new concepts. We use the insights and principles framed earlier as the starting places to generate concepts. We ensure that fresh and bold ideas are generated through collaborative sessions. Team members build on each other's concepts while carefully postponing critical evaluation. Further, by basing our concepts on the results from previous modes, we ensure that the concepts are defensible and grounded in reality. Concepts for products, services, communications, environments, brands, and business models and others are typically explored in this mode. Even at this early stage of exploration, we construct rough prototypes, either to focus team discussions or to get early user or client feedback.

- Framing concept space: Converting insights to design principles, reframe assumptions, and making hypotheses for concept generation

- Defining concepts: Brainstorming concepts within the widest solution space permitted by design principles, gaining inspiration from metaphors, and visualizing concepts

- Organizing concepts: Sorting, recombining, and dividing concepts into logical systems and groups; collecting and archiving concepts for future reference

- Communicating concepts: Sketching, diagramming, prototyping, visualizing, and narrating concepts to understand, validate, and convey their value

# Mode 6: Frame Solutions

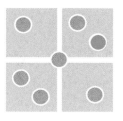

In this mode, we build on the large set of concepts that have been developed earlier by combining them to form systems of concepts, named "Solutions." We evaluate concepts and identify the ones that bring the most value to stakeholders (primarily users and businesses). The most valuable concepts are combined into systems of concepts that work together well and reinforce each other's value. We also evaluate concepts based on their compatibilities to help form holistic solutions. We ensure that the concepts and solutions are organized into useful categories and hierarchies. We iteratively prototype solutions, and test them in real-world settings. In this mode descriptions of solutions are turned into depictions to give the team, the users, and the client(s) a visceral sense of "what could be."

- Generating options: Combining the many point-concepts explored in Explore Concepts mode into a set of solution options for further selection

- Systematizing concepts: Clustering and synthesizing concepts into coherent systems, planning lifecycles of offerings, and creating roadmaps

- Evaluating concepts: Scoring, voting, and ranking concepts against design principles, cost/benefit, viability, and feasibility

- Communicating solutions: Refining sketches, diagrams, prototypes, visualizations, and narratives of proposed solutions

- Organizing solutions: Sorting, collecting, and archiving solutions for easy access, including use by other teams and projects

## Mode 7: Realize Offerings

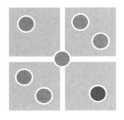

Once potential solutions are framed and prototypes tested, they need to be evaluated to move to implementation. In this mode, we ensure that the solutions are purposefully built around peoples' experiences and can provide real value. It is also important to make sure these solutions add economic value for the organizations producing them. Once we establish high-value solutions, implementation plans follow. For this, design and business innovators collaborate to define viable strategic directions. We create roadmaps to show the speculated progression of solutions in distinct phases. These roadmaps are shared with the stakeholders, showing everyone involved the steps necessary to implement the solution. A business case is prepared for prompting further action with clearly defined and specific initiatives the organization will follow to facilitate implementation.

- Building prototypes: Developing prototypes to test details, feasibility, viability, and technical specifications
- Defining strategies: Determining market positioning, platforms, partners, and business plans key to the innovation's success
- Defining tactics: Identifying capabilities necessary to achieve strategies and plan development trajectory
- Developing initiatives: Gathering resources, constructing budgets and schedules, hiring teams, and creating plans for pilots and launches

## Understanding Methods

Understanding the entire design innovation process and life cycle is an initial requirement to achieving reliable innovation. However, an organization also must understand the specific activities and methods it can deploy at different points throughout the process. This may include things as simple as a 2 × 2 position map, like the images shown in this Introduction, or as complex as a proprietary software system for analyzing and sharing innovation insights and protocols. Just as a master carpenter will expertly select a different set of tools depending whether he is building a house or a chair, the master innovator needs to be familiar with a variety of methods in order to choose them effectively for a given project.

The seven modes of the design innovation process form the structure for the remainder of this book. Chapters 1 through 7 elaborate on the key activities in each mode, and describe in detail over 100 different simple, powerful, highly flexible methods innovators can use to progress through the innovation process. Each method description includes an example illustrating how that method was used in that project during the process. These example illustrations range from exploratory class projects to well-known corporate cases, highlighting the broad applicability of this process to many different types of innovation projects.

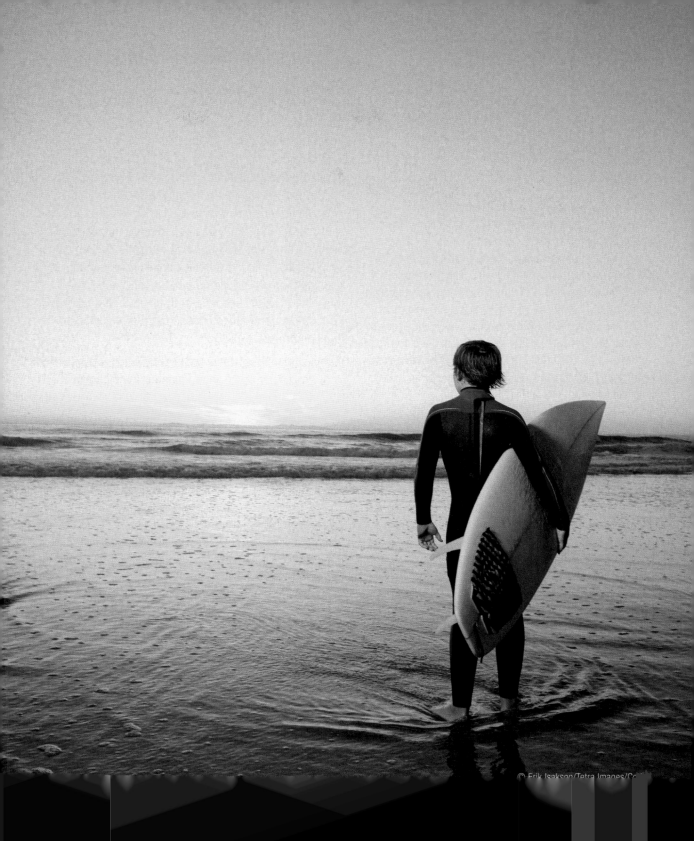

# mode 1
# SENSE INTENT

WHERE TO PLAY? WHAT TO OFFER? HOW TO WIN? These three questions are at the heart of organizational strategy. Answering them is one of the chief goals of innovation. While the majority of the innovation process in this book is intended to help us answer the last two questions—the what and how—the concept of "Sense Intent" is more about the first—the where. Where is the world moving? In which sector, industry, and market does our organization intend to innovate? In which areas of people's changing life patterns will our innovation fit? Being in this mode helps us take a pause before jumping into a project and consider the changing world around us. We study the trends causing changes in technology, business, culture, people, markets, and the economy. We frame the problem space through a quick diagnosis of the situation, both inside and outside the organization. We rethink conventions and seek new opportunity areas for innovation. This leads us to set an initial direction and ask where our organization should be moving.

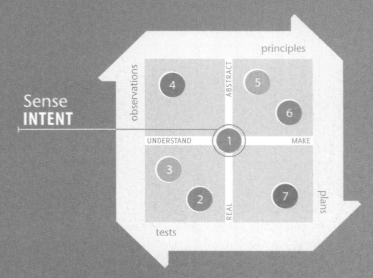

# SENSE INTENT *mindsets*

The Sense Intent mindset is about continuously detecting the **latest changes happening in the world today** and forming speculations about what new situations may be looming on the horizon. It is about recognizing what is new or in flux, and identifying hotspots of potential growth. This mindset helps us identify potential opportunities for innovation and form our initial hypotheses. While these hypotheses will be explored and tested in the modes that follow, the goal in this mode is to provide sufficient early direction for research and exploration.

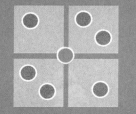

**Mindsets**
- Sensing Changing Conditions
- Seeing Overviews
- Foreseeing Trends
- Reframing Problems
- Forming an Intent

*Search engine developers like Google have been sensing change patterns and creating powerful tools to search through millions of sources and produce desirable results in fractions of seconds. Equipped with such tools, it is easier to be in the mindset of continuously sensing changing conditions.*

## Mindset: Sensing Changing Conditions

As creators of the new, innovators need to have the mindset of continuously keeping up with the pace of change whether political, economic, social, cultural, scientific, or technological. Changes, especially in areas where others have not yet fully explored, often indicate fertile ground for innovation. But, in our information-intensive world the challenge of finding new and unexplored opportunities is huge. The torrent of news and data can be overwhelming, and we must think about where to gather information, how to categorize it, and how to relate it to the goals and strategies of the organization. We should actively monitor various information sources—periodicals, websites, books, broadcasts, podcasts—and opinions of leading experts and thought leaders. We should regularly debrief about what these sources and experts are saying, and discuss what trends we see emerging. It is important not only to spot changes in trends but also to understand how those changes have occurred over time, so that we can foresee how changes might happen in the future and tell us something about how our innovations will fit.

Courtesy of photographer Stefan Nilsson and www.gapminder.org.

*Gapminder is a visualization system that shows context overviews as dynamic and interactive diagrams. Data about context are plotted as scatterplots to show their distribution patterns. Through interactive animations, Gapminder shows changing patterns in powerful and easy-to-understand terms.*

## Mindset: Seeing Overviews

While in an unfamiliar place, observing surroundings and getting information on the ground helps us navigate in that place. Cues in the environment, landmarks, and street signs are all helpful sources of information for guidance. Also valuable are "overviews," like street maps, navigation systems that show GPS location, and radio broadcasts about traffic and weather patterns. These big pictures help provide a broader understanding of the place compared to detailed perspectives on the ground. Innovators searching for opportunities greatly benefit from such overviews as well. Parts, relations, patterns, and dynamics that are visualized as overviews help us better understand the changing context in which we intend to innovate.

The insights that we gain from close-proximity and ground-level observations about people and context are a good source for incremental innovations. Often radically new and disruptive innovations emerge from our overview mindset, the ability to see big pictures.

*Amazon's Kindle e-book reading device was the result of foreseeing significant trends in the field and quickly and effectively responding to them. Drastic improvements in digital ink technologies, declines in traditional publishing, environmental concerns about traditional printing, and readers' growing comfort and familiarity with mobile devices all led to the development of Kindle in 2007.*

## Mindset: Foreseeing Trends

Trends show us general directions in which something is developing or changing. They emerge in our daily life all the time. For sensing innovation opportunities the most common trends that we track relate to technology, business, culture, people, markets, and the economy. Some trends are short-lived, like subprime mortgage lending, while others signal lasting changes in our daily life. We should identify and understand trends early on so that we are in a better position to quickly and positively respond to their impact on the future. Recognizing trends is a skill that can be cultivated by carefully learning to discern patterns of activities taking place around us. Simply being able to recognize which sectors of the economy are growing and which are in decline can help us develop a provisional sense of the economic opportunity. Staying on top of the latest technology developments and seeing patterns of their adoption, we can begin to foresee how technology trends may shape the types of products and services that will be required in the future.

We also ought to cultivate a mindset for recognizing "megatrends" (e.g., aging of the population in the United States and Europe) and thinking about the implications such big changes will have on innovation opportunities.

*In 2001, Proctor & Gamble introduced its Crest Whitestrips, a product that reflected P&G's reframing of the idea of oral care. Instead of limiting the meaning of oral care to cavity prevention, it broadened its meaning to include personal care and looking good. Crest Whitestrips took the brand from cavity prevention to whiter smiles and in the process introduced a product line with significantly higher margins than the commodity toothpaste category.*

## Mindset: Reframing Problems

Being able to recognize and understand the "conventions" that operate in an organization can help us think about how things might be approached differently. For example, in industries governed by Six Sigma practices, minimizing variability in manufacturing becomes a primary driver of business decisions. This practice makes sense for established processes, but may not be the appropriate mindset when pursuing new-to-the-world businesses. As conditions change, what was once true may no longer be so. To be truly innovative, new problems and opportunities need to be thought through differently. Challenging conventional wisdom requires an understanding of how it came to be in the first place and thinking about how best to reframe it to be appropriate for a future possibility. Just as it is important to question prevailing conventions, it is equally important to question how innovation challenges are framed. Is the innovation challenge about making a better mobile phone, a better mobile communication device, or creating a compelling remote communication experience? Moreover, mindsets for reframing problems broaden possibilities and help us arrive at nonobvious solutions.

*In 2006, when Nintendo introduced the Wii, the gaming industry's convention was that success of new consoles mainly depended on more "power." Nintendo, instead of following this model to compete with Sony and Microsoft, focused their intent on how many more people they can get to play games. It was on the basis of this intent, supported by a deep understanding of technology trends, that Nintendo innovators were able to simplify the game interface, do away with the multibutton controller, and develop the wireless Wii remote that anyone could use with gestures and spatial movement. Urban condo-dwellers, country ranchers, parents with children, and even grandparents started enjoying the Wii.*

## Mindset: Forming an Intent

After we develop a good understanding of the latest news, developments, trends, and conventions, we switch to a mindset of consciously forming an early intent for innovation. By consciously stating the prevailing and emerging conditions, it becomes easier to define the type of innovation that should be conceived. For instance, if a long-range trend indicates an aging population that is expected to live longer than any prior generation, then our innovation intent will prominently factor in the needs of people with potentially limited mobility.

Continuously keeping up with latest events and trends helps us develop hunches about where the world may be headed and gut feelings about the kinds of innovations that can be built on those trends. Many businesses operate according to such hunches. But such an intuitive approach may be wildly off the mark and can lead to unnecessary expenditures and failed products. More than asserting an intent based on best guesses, grounding an initial intent statement in a fact-based context makes it both reliable and credible. It is ok to lead with a hunch but then qualify it with supporting evidence so that the emerging goals are reasonable and logical. The intent statement becomes even stronger if it can reference historical precedents.

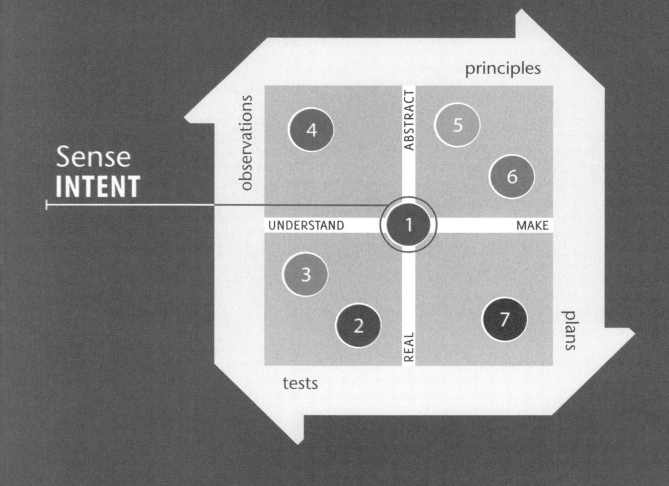

Sense
**INTENT**

principles

observations

ABSTRACT

4

5

6

UNDERSTAND  1  MAKE

3

REAL

2

7

plans

tests

20

# SENSE INTENT *methods*

# 1.1 Buzz Reports

Collecting and sharing information about the latest "buzz" from a wide array of sources

Shared Knowledge Base

## EXAMPLE PROJECT:
### Learning Apps—Peapod Labs (2010)

A team of three graduates from the IIT Institute of Design, who were former engineers, founded Peapod Labs to create playful, educational apps for children. They rigorously applied the process described in this book to develop innovative learning apps. Their philosophy was rooted in the belief that learning should be collaborative between parent and child and, above all, fun. Children share what they learn on their apps, making it easy for parents to contribute to the learning process as well.

Following the same collaborative approach, the founders of Peapod Labs used *Buzz Reports* to build an internal culture around sharing and active discussion. Buzz Reports, which comprise e-books, articles, and journals, were shared informally among all the team members. When a team member disseminated information, a comment was also included about the relevance of the article to the team's goals. This helped to keep everyone on the same page and brought structure to the meetings where the reports were discussed and topics debated. This method helped them keep abreast of the current trends and news in their relevant industries such as education, technology, and mobile devices.

**BENEFITS**
- Captures the latest
- Organizes information for easy access
- Promotes shared understanding
- Inspires possibilities

**INPUT**
- Latest information (news and opinions) from formal and informal sources

**OUTPUT**
- Evolving central repository of latest information

**WHEN TO USE**

## WHAT IT DOES

Understanding patterns of change and new developments in our daily life that can drive innovation often comes not only from the core research done for a project, but from tangential, peripheral, or unexpected sources. The "buzz" that goes on around the world that catches everyone's attention today, even though seemingly unrelated to a project, is a good source of inspiration for finding innovation opportunities. Buzz Reports are a way to collect such information about changes on a regular basis and share it among team members to have a broad understanding of what is currently significant. Buzz Reports function like a self-generated news aggregation service. They encourage curiosity about the latest developments and inspire new directions for innovation.

## HOW IT WORKS

### STEP 1: Allocate regular time to explore the latest in various sources.

Regularly schedule time to seek out the buzz from any possible source. This can include news broadcasts, websites of note, television broadcasts, library searches, technology reviews, lectures posted on sites like Ted. com, book reviews, or anything else that seems new and noteworthy. A valuable insight for innovation might come from anywhere when you are constantly on the lookout for inspirational directions for the project. Cast a wide net.

### STEP 2: Browse through sources of information for the current buzz.

Keep an open mind and browse through a variety of sources of information. Look for buzz directly and indirectly related to the project—anything that covers the dynamics of the world, whether they are technological, cultural, political, or economic. Try to avoid only looking for information closely related to the project. A broad perspective at the start of the project can help identify larger patterns at play, reveal nonobvious connections, and inform a possible direction to pursue.

### STEP 3: Aggregate and share findings.

Aggregate findings into a collection of shared documents (Buzz Reports) that is easily accessible to all members of the team. A compelling headline and a brief synopsis of each submission allows for a quick scan of the information. Set submission dates to ensure that this becomes a formal part of innovation activities. Tag these submissions with keywords that are easily understood by all team members. In this way, the shared document grows into a compendium of information that can be searched by date or tagged words at a later time by different team members. It is very useful to add comments about how ideas discussed in the submissions can impact your project.

### STEP 4: Have discussions in group sessions.

Have discussions around Buzz Reports among your team members. Share thoughts on how these latest developments would have an impact on your project. Use these discussions for shared understanding and inspiration.

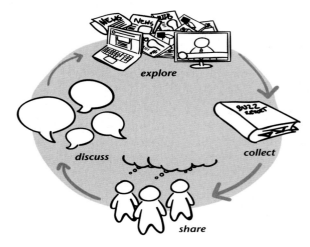

explore

collect

share

discuss

1.1 BUZZ REPORTS

# 1.2 Popular Media Scan

Understanding key cultural phenomena through a broad look at what is published and broadcasted in popular media

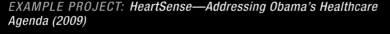

News Clippings

Popular blogs

SHOULD YOU BE A VEGETARIAN

Daily paper and latest magazines

### EXAMPLE PROJECT: *HeartSense—Addressing Obama's Healthcare Agenda (2009)*

The year 2009 marked an important year for healthcare reform under the Obama administration because it aimed to change U.S. healthcare by providing coverage to the uninsured, reducing healthcare costs, improving patient safety and quality of care, holding insurance companies accountable for the services they provide, and investing in prevention and wellness. Professor Larry Keeley asked his students at the IIT Institute of Design to create a platform that addresses Obama's national healthcare agenda using design innovation methods.

To better understand the issues, the team performed a *Popular Media Scan* to learn about the current and evolving healthcare landscape by going through books and articles from leading authors such as Clayton Christensen's *The Innovator's Prescription*. They also visited popular media websites like the *New York Times, The Economist*, and the Fast Company and blogs like HelloHealth.com. These sources revealed different perspectives of the healthcare crisis, ongoing innovations, and future possibilities. They found key trends in telemedicine, open source platforms, and social and cultural medicine. The team designed HeartSense, a platform that helps to reduce heart disease in low-income African American women using culturally sensitive outreach programs, targeted subsidies for healthy foods, and easily identifiable claim labels supported by mobile technology aiding better consumer choices in the grocery store.

**BENEFITS**
- Shows cultural context
- Reveals patterns
- Provides direction

**INPUT**
- Project's topic
- Sources in popular media

**OUTPUT**
- Areas for further research
- Opportunity areas for innovation

**WHEN TO USE**

## WHAT IT DOES

Popular media scans act as a kind of cultural barometer registering what is happening or emerging on the cultural landscape. The method scans popular media like broadcast news, magazines, and TV programming to find out anything that seems like a noteworthy cultural activity. Just as satellite images show changing weather patterns, a survey of popular media can be used to identify cultural currents that could indicate hot spots of noteworthy activity. Popular media scans provide a high-level understanding of the latest trends, what is on peoples' minds, and what cultural trackers find new and noteworthy. They help innovation teams articulate the cultural currents that can influence the formation of an initial intent for the project.

## HOW IT WORKS

### STEP 1: Identify broad topics related to the project.

Whether stated in a client's design brief or self-determined, conduct a mind-mapping session to lay out broad

topics related to the project. Use identified topics, and perhaps subtopics, as a guide to further explore.

### STEP 2: Seek out information related to the topics.

Look for what is being written about on blogs and websites, and in magazines. Use screen captures, scans, photocopies, or pages to build a library of findings. Scan television programming, advertisements, events, and movies for content that may relate directly or indirectly to the topic. Collect these references as notes or samples that can be placed into the library of findings.

### STEP 3: Look for patterns.

Sift through the information accumulated in the collected documents to reveal patterns of activity. These patterns provide a general sense of the current and emerging cultural trends.

### STEP 4: Look at adjacent topics as well.

Sometimes emerging trends in a different topic can influence what may happen in your area of primary interest. For example, the evolution of the mobile phone applications market have given rise to a number of health and wellness offerings that enable people to more easily monitor their food consumption, thereby influencing how people eat.

### STEP 5: Summarize findings and discuss opportunities.

Add your point of view about what is happening in culture and what is possible. Discuss and articulate how the patterns of cultural currents can point to opportunity areas for innovation and influence the initial statement of intent. Use these discussions to guide your activities for deeper exploration.

1.2 POPULAR MEDIA SCAN

## EXAMPLE PROJECT: *New options for Out-of-School Youth (2008)*

A nonprofit foundation and a philanthropic organization dedicated resources to address the lack of opportunities for out-of-school youths. A team of design planners from the IIT Institute of Design worked with the foundation to propose a solution that would connect out-of-school youths with sustainable and satisfying careers. The high school dropout rate is commonly referred to as the "silent epidemic" and it prompted the team to uncover the causes behind the epidemic and its overall impact to the individual and society.

The team researched white papers and educational sites to find *Key Facts* about the drivers behind the nation's elevated high school dropout rate. They discovered that while this epidemic crosses economic and ethnic backgrounds, the situation is more dire in minority populations with almost as much as 50 percent of African American, Hispanic, and Native American youth leaving high school without a diploma. They also found that many of these out-of-school youths were smart, but they were dropping out due to boredom, lack of motivation, and misaligned interests relative to the curriculum. Understanding these key facts allowed the team to build a supportive platform that would connect the skills of out-of-school youths with businesses and communities in which everyone would benefit.

|   | A | B | C | D | E | F | G |
|---|---|---|---|---|---|---|---|
| 1 | TOPIC | Sub-topic | Relevancy | Data Type | KEY FACTS | SOURCE | FURTHER RESEARCH |
| 39 | Risk Factors for Dropping Out | factors | relevant | statistic | Nearly half (47 percent) said a major reason for dropping out was that classes were not interesting. These young people reported being bored and disengaged from high school. Almost as many (42 percent) spent time with people who were not interested in school. These were among the top reasons selected by those with high GPAs and by those who said they were motivated to work hard. | "The Silent Epidemic: Perspectives of High School Dropouts", by John M. Bridgeland, John J. DiIulio, Jr., Karen Burke Morison, A report by Civic Enterprises in association with Peter D. Hart Research Associates for the Bill & Melinda Gates Foundation, March 2006 | What are the other drivers that impact the youth to drop out other than the individual/social factors (ex. family & community factors, economic status, etc.)? |
| 40 | Risk Factors for Dropping Out | suggested solutions | relevant | opinion statistic | Improve teaching and curricula to make school more relevant and engaging and enhance the connection between school and work: Four out of five (81 percent) said there should be more opportunities for real-world learning and some in the focus groups called for more experiential learning. They said students need to see the connection between school and getting a good job. | "The Silent Epidemic: Perspectives of High School Dropouts", by John M. Bridgeland, John J. DiIulio, Jr., Karen Burke Morison, A report by Civic Enterprises in association with Peter D. Hart Research Associates for the Bill & Melinda Gates Foundation, March 2006 | Are there any solutions, improvements suggested by the other institutions? What are the main consensus/alternatives currently discussed about this topic? |
| 41 | Who Drops Out? | graduation rate, ethnicity | related | statistic | The Alliance reports that approximately 1.23 million students fail to graduate from high school each year, and more than half of those represent minority groups. Nationally, about 70% of dropouts graduate on time with a regular diploma, more than half of African Americans and Hispanics earn diplomas with their peers. In some states the difference in percentages can be as much as 40-50 percentage points. About 2,000 high schools or 14% produce more than half of the country's dropouts. In these "dropout factories," the number of seniors is 60% or less of freshman from four years earlier. These dropout factories produce 81% of all Native American dropouts, 73% of African American dropouts, and 66% of Hispanic dropouts. | Alliance for Excellence in Education. (2007). High school dropouts in America. Fact Sheet. Washington, DC: Author. |  |
| 42 | Risk Factors for Dropping Out | factors | relevant | opinion | The researcher identifies primary reasons for dropping out from a review of relevant literature about youth dropout views. The reasons are a) dislike of school and the felling that school is boring and not relevant to their needs, b) low | Beekman, N. (1987). The dropout's perspective on leaving school. ERIC/CAPS Digest. Retreived from |  |

+ ≡ Summer 2008 ▾ Spring 2008

## WHAT IT DOES

Key Facts are concise pieces of information from credible sources that indicate the state of a given topic. For example, if the project is on "high school education," a key fact might be that 40 percent of high school students in the United States do not complete their program. Key Facts can be statistical in nature, or expert opinions summarized in brief statements, organized in shared documents for discussion. Aggregating many different bits of information as Key Facts helps teams to create a good fact-based rationale for their initial innovation intent. They are also starting points, indicating where to go to find additional information.

## HOW IT WORKS

### STEP 1: Define the general topic.

This may come from a client brief or it can be self-determined. Establish boundaries within which most important aspects of the topic reside. However, be flexible to extend these boundaries as new research findings emerge.

### STEP 2: Identify sources of credible information about the topic.

As you begin your search for information, identify domain experts, research organizations, government and private agencies that collect and compile statistical data, and other places where relevant information may be found.

### STEP 3: Cast a wide net and conduct research.

Conduct research as if it is detective work to gather reliable information on the topic. Library searches and online searches are effective ways to get an initial sense of pertinent information on a topic. Articulate what makes them Key Facts, how they are relevant, related, or tangential to the topic.

### STEP 4: Organize information by type.

Once Key Facts are sorted as relevant, related, or tangential, they can be further categorized by type, such as statistic, opinion, or summary. Facilitate team members to place their individual Key Facts into a single organizing structure. This helps build a shared understanding of the topic.

### STEP 5: Summarize the Key Facts into a coherent rationale.

Use this as a starting point for molding the primary objective for innovation. Let the Key Facts also point to additional research needed.

1.3 KEY FACTS

Finding inspiration from studying innovative offerings, companies, and people

## EXAMPLE PROJECT: *Home-Life Strategic Platform (2010)*

A group of consumer home products companies worked with the IIT Institute of Design to seek innovations in the area of home-life using platform strategies. Recent trends show that industries related to home-life, just like most other industries, are converging and becoming increasingly connected. Value is no longer being created by single entities, but through the collaboration of multiple players.

The team began exploring the evolution of platforms from modular product platforms to more recent open and collaborative knowledge-sharing platforms. They studied successful platform examples such as Facebook, eBay, Yelp, Groupon, LinkedIn, and Wikipedia. All examples were then added in a database that served as the *Innovation Sourcebook*, with the organization name, description of how the platform works, platform attributes, and the stakeholders. The database served as a valuable resource for the team to keep track of a number of innovative platform examples. Actively discussed, compared and contrasted, the examples yielded a good understanding of platform strategies and even frameworks for platform types. This formed the foundation for the team to design platforms in four areas of home-life: Work-at-home, Eating/Cooking, Retirement Planning, and Home Budgeting.

| | A | B | C | D |
|---|---|---|---|---|
| 1 | **Example** | **Platform Description** | **Platform Attributes** | **Stakeholders** |
| 30 | yelp | A a social networking, user review, and local search website that allows people to share reviews of restaurant/store experiences in major cities. Yelp has more than 31 million monthly unique visitors as of early 2010. | - Provides standardized format for users to post/read reviews<br>- Encourages users to participate more for more reliable data<br>- Allows users (buyers) to share information<br>- Helps users to make better purchasing decision<br>- Allows sellers (store owners) to advertise | - 150+ employees<br>- Local retailers/advertising clients<br>- Users (reviewers) |
| 31 | Kickstarter | A crowdfunding initiative. As stated by themselves: A new way of funding and following creativity (online threshold pledge system for funding creative projects). They use social networking to fund art and creativity projects. Kickstarter takes 5% of the funds raised; Amazon charges an additional 3-5%. | - Gathers multiple stakeholders to fund a cause.<br>- It has been the base for different types of innovation: Business Model, Enabling Process, Networking, Customer Experience and Service<br>- Unlike many forums for fundraising or investment, Kickstarter claims no ownership over the projects and the work they produce. However, projects launched on the site are permanently archived and accessible to the public. | - Artist<br>- Funders<br>- 22+ Kickstarter staff<br>- Community<br>- Amazon Payments |
| 32 | Facebook | A social networking website, currently has more than 500 million active users in July 2010. Users can add people as friends and send them messages, and update their personal status, upload pictures, play games, follow brands/companies/organizations on facebook. | - Provides a place to communicate/keep in touch with friends<br>- Users can create profiles with photos, lists of personal interests, contact information, and other personal information.<br>- Users can also create and join interest groups and "like pages" (called "fan pages" until April 19, 2010), some of which are maintained by organizations as a means of advertising.<br>- Facebook enables users to choose their own privacy settings and choose who can see specific parts of their profile.<br>- The Web site is free to users, and generates revenue from advertising, such as banner ads.<br>- Facebook launched a new portal for marketers and creative agencies to help them develop brand promotions on Facebook. | - Users<br>- Investors/shareholders<br>- Advertisers<br>- 1400+ employees |
| 33 | Google | Internet and software corporation specialized in Internet search, cloud | - Enable the proliferation of a wide variety of internet-based services.<br>- Information management platform that searches the internet quickly, | - Shareholders<br>- 20000+ employees |

+ ≡    **Defining Platform** ▾    Class Discuss 9/9    Era Analysis    Trends        Wikipedia

## WHAT IT DOES

The Innovation Sourcebook is a structured approach to assembling best practices embodied in a wide range of innovation successes. The method helps find and organize successful examples of offerings (products and services), organizations, and people. Comparing and contrasting them helps understand the reasons behind their successes as platforms. Delving deeper to understand the strategies employed by these innovations is even more valuable to teams. The Innovation Sourcebook becomes a source of inspiration for teams tasked with tough innovation challenges. The generic platform strategies in the Sourcebook can serve as a reference throughout the innovation process and teams can build on them for their own platform solutions.

## HOW IT WORKS

### STEP 1: Establish an agreed-upon definition of innovation.

Discuss and reach a team alignment about what they consider as innovation. For example, the team might consider the definition *something new made real in a marketplace that provides both customer value and provider value.* Ensure that there is alignment and a good shared understanding.

### STEP 2: Search for examples of successful innovations.

Scan the popular media and other sources for examples of noteworthy new offerings (products, services, experiences, etc.) organizations, and people. In general, examples should follow the agreed-upon definition of innovations. Feel free to look for examples not just from the present, but also from the near past.

### STEP 3: Create an Innovation Sourcebook table.

Each example innovation is entered as a row under one of the categories—Offerings, Organizations, and People. The three columns in the table have titles for the name of the innovation, description of the innovation, and strategic advantage created by the innovation. Fill in the table cells for each innovation example.

### STEP 4: Review the many examples in the Sourcebook table.

Compare innovations to one another. What do the examples have in common? How do they compare in terms of strategic advantage? Look for common innovation strategies that cut across many examples.

### STEP 5: Use the Sourcebook for inspiration.

Think of how the common strategies found in the examples could be adopted. Refer to the Innovation Sourcebook throughout the design process to gain inspiration for innovation opportunities.

**1.4 INNOVATION SOURCEBOOK**

**EXAMPLE PROJECT:** *Convivial Food Platform (2010)*

A group of consumer products companies worked with the IIT Institute of Design on the topic of home-life. One of the projects was to innovate around the topic of food, especially using platform strategies. The student team working on this project developed Convivial—a food and wellness platform—that takes a comprehensive and integrated approach to how people engage with food, with whom they eat, and how to build a path toward healthy living.

The team thought there was an abundance of information in this opportunity space. However, they found it best to conduct *Trends Expert Interviews* that could quickly give them a broader picture of what was happening in the home and new approaches to food/meal management. They identified experts who were consultants to food manufacturing companies, who partnered with healthcare organizations, and who were involved in creating wellness programs. The team engaged these experts with questions about wellness trends and home-living dynamics. Interviews were conducted at the beginning of the user research phase, and the findings helped the team plan individual family research. Moreover, even after the interviews, the teams continued to have follow-up dialog with the experts to test assumptions and conduct additional research

## BENEFITS

- Facilitates quick and early discovery
- Brings in new perspectives
- Captures knowledge

## INPUT

- Project's topic
- Pool of trend experts

## OUTPUT

- Understanding of trends and growth factors
- Areas for further research

## WHEN TO USE

## WHAT IT DOES

A Trends Expert Interview helps one quickly learn about trends related to a topic. Speaking with experts like futurists, economists, professors, authors, and researchers, who stay on top of what is happening in a specific topic area, can very quickly reveal valuable insights. Speaking with them also provides guidance for where to look for additional information. It is very helpful to use frameworks during the interviews to guide the conversation and to comprehensively cover the topic. For example, the conversations may proceed in a structured way by focusing on various types of trends—technology, business, people, culture, policy, or others.

## HOW IT WORKS

### STEP 1: Determine the topics to be understood.

The prompts for this often come from the project brief. However, review the topics and types of trends that you are interested in learning more about. Which topics should we focus on—technology, business, people, culture, policy, or other project-specific topics?

### STEP 2: Identify experts.

Through a combination of Internet searches, conversations with colleagues, literature searches, or other means, pull together a list of people who are recognized experts in the identified topics. Ask people working in those topics for their recommendations of experts. Look to conduct interviews with more than one expert in each topic.

### STEP 3: Make preparations for the interview.

Read articles, books, or anything the expert might have authored to understand his or her point of view. Prepare a set of questions to help guide the interview session. For example, you might use a "plant" metaphor as a way to ask questions during the interview and structure the conversation: (1) Seeds—What are the early, emerging trends and innovations? (2) Soil—How are the fundamentals af-

fecting growth? (3) Atmosphere—How are the surrounding conditions affecting growth? (4) Plant—How do innovations grow to become robust? (5) Water—How are the catalysts affecting growth?

### STEP 4: Conduct the interview.

Carefully thought-through interviews make the most of limited time available with the expert. Use prepared questions to guide the conversation and perhaps not ask them directly. From references during the conversation remember to list resources that you can tap into for additional interviews.

### STEP 5: Listen, capture, and follow up.

Interviewing requires active listening. If allowed, use a recording device to capture the conversation. As the conversation unfolds take copious notes and keep track of clarifying questions you may want to ask later.

### STEP 6: Transcribe and summarize.

Have the recorded conversation transcribed so that key phrases or interesting insights can be extracted. Summarize the findings and add them to documents to be shared with the rest of the team.

1.5 TRENDS EXPERT INTERVIEW

# Keyword Bibliometrics

Using keywords for researching spread of ideas among publications and databases

**EXAMPLE PROJECT:** *Innovations for Medical Devices Company (2007)*

A medical devices company worked with Dob[l]... member of Monitor Group) to identify opportu[nities]... innovation beyond the focused, clinical oppor[tunities]... typically surfaced by its traditional R&D proce[sses].

Doblin used *Keyword Bibliometrics* as the pri[mary]... method to uncover innovation opportunities f[or]... this client company. Combining search terms [in]... healthcare context such as health conditions,... technologies, regulations, and policy, the tear... performed searches in health-specific, as we[ll as]... popular, journals and newspaper databases t[o find]... instances of concepts, products, services, ev[ents or]... businesses. Thousands of article excerpts ca[me from]... this broad range of published literature that t[he team]... analyzed for emerging themes in health and e[veryday]... life. For example, one theme was "patient-ce[ntered]... primary care/patient-centered medical home[/virtual]... medical home." Conversations about these th[emes]... helped the team reveal innovation opportunit[ies. Based]... on such opportunities, the client went on to f[urther]... explore them and create innovation agendas, [including]... multiyear initiatives and investment.

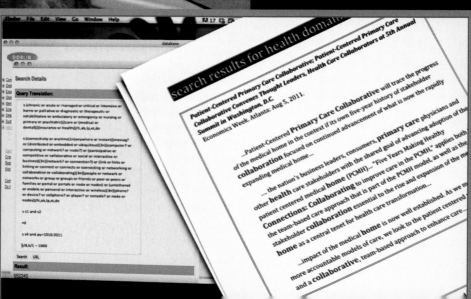

**BENEFITS**
- Processes large sets of data
- Reveals patterns
- Encourages comprehensiveness

**INPUT**
- Set of keywords related to specific topics
- Identified specialized database

**OUTPUT**
- Insights and patterns revealed by the search on specific topics

**WHEN TO USE**

## WHAT IT DOES

Keyword Bibliometrics is a method adapted from library and information sciences used in researching the spread of ideas among publications and databases in fields such as science, medicine, economics, and technology. Keyword Bibliometrics operate like search engines. It uses keywords to search through huge databases to find relevant articles and writings. The list of documents generated through a search is analyzed to understand the nature of what is being written about the topic or uncover emergent nonobvious relationships. Bibliometric searches are generally done within specialized databases so that the results directly relate to a specific interest. These specialized databases can be found through Web or library searches or through consultation with an academic library or research service.

## HOW IT WORKS

### STEP 1: Determine keywords that will be searched.

These words should be as context-specific as possible. Broad terms will return undifferentiated information, but context-specific and narrowly defined words will return results likely to be more valuable for your area of interest.

### STEP 2: Consider the time period that will be searched.

A survey of writings from the last 50 years may help in constructing a historic era analysis, but one that looks at publications from the last 24 months will be more pertinent for understanding what thought leaders are concerned about today.

### STEP 3: Combine keywords to find overlaps.

It is valuable to combine words using "and, or, not" logic to find out if ideas happening in one area have influences on others or not. For example, combining keywords "nanotechnology" and "biomedical engineering" might return articles about how nanotechnology is being used in biomedical engineering.

### STEP 4: Review returned results and reiterate if needed.

Look for publication patterns. Trace the influence of an idea. What is the article in which it first appeared? In what publications has it been referenced since then? How have the ideas transformed as it is incorporated into other publications? Moreover, be prepared to reiterate searches if needed. If the publications in the search result appear to be either too general or not directly related, then modify your keywords and search again.

### STEP 5: Summarize findings.

Share the summaries with team members and engage in conversations to find insights about the topic. Visualizing the results from bibliometrics based on the occurrences of keywords using diagrams can reveal patterns to better understand what is being written about in the topic.

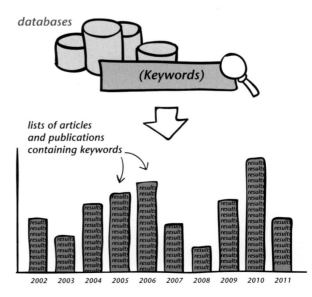

1.6 KEYWORD BIBLIOMETRICS

# 1.7 Ten Types of Innovation Framework

Understanding the nature of different types of innovations in industries

**EXAMPLE PROJECT: Innovations for a Car Rental Company (2000)**

In 2000, Doblin (a member of Monitor Group) worked with a car rental company to provide customer-centered innovation for its business. As a leading innovator, the company had built a strong competitive position in the car rental industry. But it began to lose ground due to changes such as increased airport taxes and decreased partnerships with automakers that left them as a low-cost brand with a high-cost structure.

Using the *Ten Types of Innovation Framework,* Doblin mapped out the innovations within the car rental industry and revealed that the industry was stuck in "feature warfare." Most of the activities from the competitors were concentrated within the "offerings" type of innovation; for example, ensuring availability of specific car models, rapid-pick and rapid-return, and a service system ensuring the prompt return of lost cell phones. The framework also indicated areas weak in innovation such as "brand" and "customer experience." Based on the insights from the framework and customer research, Doblin recommended that the company reposition itself to meet the unique needs of leisure travelers. As a result, they would be able to remove its commodity, low-price status by differentiating themselves through their brand and customer experience, and provide a premium position for their offerings, something that they could not do before.

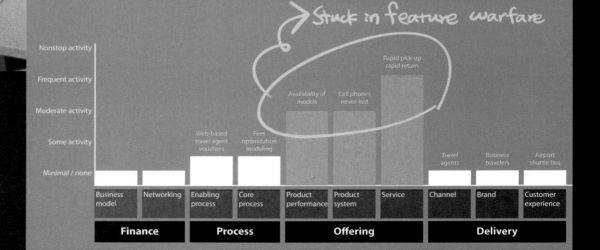

**BENEFITS**

- Broadens mindset
- Encourages comprehensiveness
- Shows best practices
- Facilitates comparison
- Provides organizing structure

**INPUT**

- Identified industries, organizations, and their innovations relevant to the project's topic

**OUTPUT**

- Understanding of how the different types of innovation are playing a role in the studied industries

**WHEN TO USE**

## WHAT IT DOES

The Ten Types of Innovation Framework, developed by Doblin, is a method for surveying an industry (or sometimes an economic sector or an individual organization) to understand and plot different types of innovations. The method also helps us with what to look at more closely, where the innovation trends are in the industry, and where to direct forthcoming research efforts.

The framework proposes that regardless of industry, innovations happen in one of four areas: finance, process, offering, and delivery. Among the four areas can be found ten distinct types of innovations. In the finance area, there are business model and networking innovations. Process innovations include both core processes and enabling processes—an organization's new ways for developing their offerings. Innovations in the offering area are product performance, product systems, and service. Delivery includes innovation types like channel, brand, or customer experience.

## HOW IT WORKS

### Step 1: Gather information about the industry.

Conduct library and/or database searches, review published reports, and contact industry experts to get a sense of the key players in the industry and the business landscape.

### Step 2: Search for innovations in the industry and organize them.

Document the industry's innovations according to the ten types of innovations organized under four categories—finance, process, offering, and delivery.

1. *Finance*: How do the most successful organizations generate revenue through *business model* innovations? How are they effectively *networking* with partners?

2. *Process:* What are the successful *core processes* for making offerings with competitive advantage? How do companies innovate in *enabling processes* that provide support for employees and operations?

3. *Offering*: What are the innovations in *product performance* that offer distinctiveness? How do companies successfully link their offerings as *product systems*? What are the *service* innovations that provide assistance to prospects and customers?

4. *Delivery*: What are the industry's innovations in managing *channels* of distribution and getting offerings into the hands of end users? What are the industry's notable *brand* innovations? What are the most distinctive *customer experiences* in the industry?

### Step 3: Make a visual diagram of innovations.

Gather all of your findings from Step 2 and write brief descriptions that can be input into the Ten Types of Innovation Framework. Ensure that the research covers a wide spectrum of the industry. Make a diagram (bar chart or line chart) showing high and low innovation activities for each of the ten types.

### Step 4: Find insights, share, and discuss opportunities.

Review the ten types of innovation. Are the reasons for abundant or scarce innovations obvious? Document your insights, share them with the team, and discuss finding innovation opportunities and further explorations.

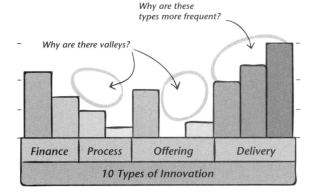

**1.7 TEN TYPES OF INNOVATION FRAMEWORK**

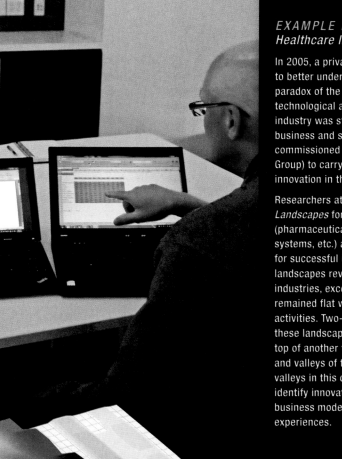

*EXAMPLE PROJECT: Innovations in Healthcare Industry (2006)*

In 2005, a private healthcare foundation sought to better understand the reasons behind the paradox of the healthcare system: Despite many technological advancements, the healthcare industry was still operating on antiquated business and service models. The foundation commissioned Doblin (a member of Monitor Group) to carry out a detailed analysis of innovation in the healthcare sector.

Researchers at Doblin created *Innovation Landscapes* for eight key healthcare industries (pharmaceuticals, health insurance, hospital systems, etc.) and to explore where opportunities for successful innovation might lie. What the landscapes revealed was that most of these industries, except the pharmaceutical industry, remained flat with little evidence of innovation activities. Two-dimensional patterns from these landscapes were then overlaid one on top of another to collectively view all the peaks and valleys of the innovations. Looking at the valleys in this combined view helped the team identify innovation opportunities in the areas of business models, product systems, and customer experiences.

## WHAT IT DOES

The Innovation Landscape is a diagnostic method that applies Doblin's Ten Types of Innovation Framework to understand the broader patterns of innovations in industries over time. The method creates a three-dimensional terrain map by plotting the type of innovation on the X-axis, time on the Y-axis, and number of occurrences of innovation activities as the height dimension. The ten types of innovations plotted are in finance (business models, networking), process (enabling, core), offering (product performance, product system, service), and delivery (channel, brand, customer experience). The landscape shows the intensity of innovation activities by the height of the peaks, the diversity by the number of peaks, and the pace of change by how many new peaks form and by the change of their slopes. These patterns are useful for facilitating discussions about where most innovations are happening and for drawing attention to areas where opportunities for creating innovations may be found. The change in patterns over time also helps spot trends that can point to innovation opportunities.

## HOW IT WORKS

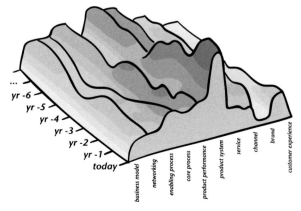

## STEP 1: Select the industry and identify databases to be searched.

Ensure that the selected databases (e.g., ProQuest and EBSCO) are about latest news and innovation activities happening in the sector including the industry you have selected for mapping.

## STEP 2: Specify keywords and the time period to be searched.

Select keywords that are related to the ten innovation types and are commonly used in recognized journals and publications of the industry. Decide on the time period to be searched; a ten-year period is most often used.

## STEP 3: Search the databases and compile results.

Send keywords about types and time periods as queries to the databases. While sending queries, specify that search results should provide the number of occurrences of innovation activities for each of the ten types for each year in a ten-year period. Compile these numbers in a spreadsheet.

## STEP 4: Visualize the results as a terrain map.

Create a three-dimensional terrain map with innovation types as the X-axis and time period as the Y-axis. Plot the number of occurrences of innovation activities as height on the terrain landscape. There are peaks and valleys distributed across the terrain where innovation is occurring and where it is not.

## STEP 5: Discuss the patterns and explore opportunities.

Discuss the nature of the terrain. Are the peaks oversaturated areas for innovation in the industry? Do the valleys offer opportunities for innovation? Do the rising new peaks indicate trends and offer innovation opportunities? These questions and others offer valuable directions for further exploration.

**1.8 INNOVATION LANDSCAPE**

# 1.9 Trends Matrix

Summarizing changes happening today that lead to a future direction

*CityFriends* is a concept for a company developed by a team of IIT Institute of Design students. It provides cultural travelers with unique and local travel experiences by using local guides and a compelling online presence.

The team's research through a *Trends Matrix* indicated that changes within the travel industry are leading to an emerging new group of travelers called "Venturers," who demand more authentic and off-the-beaten-path travel experiences. The team saw an opportunity to provide tailor-made services to this group of travelers. The Trends Matrix bolstered the team's understanding of how travel was evolving across the areas of technology, market, people, culture, and business. It also helped to isolate the emerging trends that would be important in concept development. The emerging trends highlighted reliance on technology such as mobile Web applications and virtual tour guides and that creating memorable cultural experiences are becoming an increasingly important differentiator for travel companies. In the concept stage, the team created a *CityFriends* system that gave travelers a compelling experience by directly connecting them to local guides or service providers through a friendly online site.

|  | Formerly | Currently | Emerging |
|---|---|---|---|
| **Technology** | Auto travel<br>Paper maps/travel<br>books 35mm | Online booking/price<br>Mobile communication<br>Audio guides<br>3G applications/GPS<br>Digital cameras/movie | Mobile Web revolution<br>Real-time interaction<br>Virtual tour guides<br>RFID |
| **Market** | Brand<br>Holiday travel<br>Sightseeing | Price and perks<br>Weekend getaways<br>No frills mass travel<br>Single travelers<br>L.O.H.A.S. | Experience<br>More sporadic travel<br>Segmented/customized<br>Medical tourism |
| **People** | Travel as a luxury<br>Family travel<br>Camping-car traveler<br>Unique local shopping<br>9-5 work life | Travel as routine<br>Style-lifers; cities to rural<br>Thrill/companion seekers<br>Shopping traveler<br>Flexible working conditions | Travel as escape<br>Cultural travel<br>Unusual destinations<br>Secondhand nostalgia<br>Flexible work life |
| **Culture** | Homogeneous culture<br>Car culture | Hybrid culture<br>Globalization<br>Urbanization<br>Hassle of travel | Less cultural shock<br>More comfortable with<br>world cultures |
| **Business** | Travel agencies<br>Traditional packaged-<br>tour AAA<br>Motels | DIY online travel<br>A la carte<br>American Express<br>All inclusive mega resorts<br>Eco-tourism/Voluntourism | Personal concierge<br>Network/local<br>Delivery service<br>Book buy back |

## WHAT IT DOES

A trends matrix presents a high-level summary of how trends and forces of change affect technology, business, people, culture, and policy. The matrix offers an at-a-glance understanding of how trends impact your project. For a project on cultural travel, one might study travel tools, travel-related services, travel experiences, travel information, and other similar aspects. Sometimes the aspects we study are time-related and structured: where we've been (formerly), where we are (currently), and where we may be headed (emerging). The Trend Matrix can also show how changes happening in one area, for example technology, may have influenced others, for example culture or business.

## HOW IT WORKS

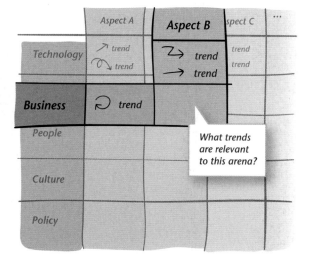

## STEP 1: Set up the dimensions for the Trends Matrix.

The vertical axis is usually shown as technology, business, people, culture, and policy. The horizontal dimension shows the aspects of the project that you are interested in tracking, for example, types of users, topics, and components of a system that you are considering. Sometimes it is valuable to define the horizontal dimension as "formerly," "currently," and "emerging."

## STEP 2: Fill the matrix with relevant trends.

Conduct research to identify trends in technology, business, people, culture, and policy that will have an effect on the project. Describe these as trend statements in the matrix cells. A trend statement is usually a short sentence that describes how something is significantly changing. An example of a trend statement is "travelers have an increased interest in unusual travel destinations and cultural travel experiences."

## STEP 3: Take a step back and discuss the matrix as an overview.

Remember that the purpose of the Trends Matrix is to offer a high-level overview of changes. Compare the trends to others to see how they are related. Recognize patterns of similar trends developing together. These might help you speculate on future directions and see how certain trends might affect your project.

## STEP 4: Capture insights as overlays on the matrix.

Discuss and document your team's insights about trend patterns, how leading trends are affecting major changes, and speculations about how things might develop. Highlight these insights as overlays on the matrix for easy reading and sharing.

## 1.9 TRENDS MATRIX

Visualizing converging fields and seeing opportunities for innovation at the overlaps

## EXAMPLE PROJECT: *FOOD-WELLNESS-DIABETES CONVERGENCE (2008)*

Industries are not only transforming at accelerating rates, but they are converging and providing unique areas for businesses to innovate. Professor Larry Keeley, innovation strategist and co-founder of Doblin (a member of Monitor Group), used the *Convergence Map* to illustrate the healthcare convergence. The map demonstrated how food production, wellness, and diabetes have increasingly become overlapped over time. Some of the innovations happening at the intersection of food, wellness, and diabetes came from Mayo Clinic and the Joslin Diabetes Center, who were providing integrated solutions for healthy eating, cooking, food guides, and tools to give people more control over their health.

Professor Keeley's students at the IIT Institute of Design used this high-level understanding about convergence to build a platform strategy addressing the diabetes epidemic in the United States. Using the premise that healthcare is not one size fits all, the team built a local community-based strategy by integrating ideas from all three converging fields—food, wellness, and diabetes.

*Better Choices*
*Good health habits*
*Healthy living choices*

### Food Production ($1581B)

Weather insurance

Green collar workers

Agriculture highschools

Drought resistant seeds

Heritage varieties

Composting

Seed banks

Food-tracking systems

Microfinancing

Locavores

Mobile data delivery to BoP (Base of the Pyramid) farmers

Safe food

Vertical agriculture

cooperatives

Community gardens

Farmers markets

Rooftop farms

Food warehouses

Hygienic food packaging

Home garden

Farm to school

Food aid

Portion controlled foods

Food desert

Door-to-door food delivery

Locavores

Hydroponics

Organic foods

Nutritional labels

Functional foods

Healthy vending

Pesticide free

Diabetes awareness

Eating well, eating right

Online health websites

Uneven healthcare delivery

Work-life balance

Weight control

Multiple medication management

Green cleaning

Reduce, reuse, recycle

Self diagnosis tools

Yoga

Meal timing

Monitoring conditions/ symptoms

Meditation

Insulin pens

Active leisure

Moderate eating

### Diabetes ($92B)

### Wellness ($118B)

**BENEFITS**

- Visualizes data
- Reveals opportunities
- Reveals relationships
- Promotes shared understanding

**INPUT**

- Data from research about trends and innovations in selected topics

**OUTPUT**

- Visual map showing where topics are converging and the related trends affecting them

**WHEN TO USE**

## WHAT IT DOES

The Convergence Map makes visible how areas of daily life (work-life, home-life, mobile communications, etc.) or industries are beginning to overlap more and how new behaviors are emerging because of this dynamic. Using visualizations that show these overlapping areas, we can have focused conversations about how people's activities are changing in these areas and consider them as fertile grounds for innovation opportunities.

## HOW IT WORKS

### STEP 1: Identify topics for creating the Convergence Map.

Based on your research about latest developments, discuss and identify topics that are overlapping most with your project topic. For example, if "diabetes" is the project topic, your research might suggest that "food" and "wellness" are topics that most overlap with it.

### STEP 2: Identify trends and innovations in these topics.

If you have already written trend statements in any of the other methods, use them to help build the Convergence Map here. Otherwise, look for trends in your topic that relate to technology, business, people, culture, and the market. Summarize trends in brief statements, for example, "diabetic patients are increasingly using mobile technology to monitor their food habits." Using this understanding of trends, identify key innovations (and key players) in these topics.

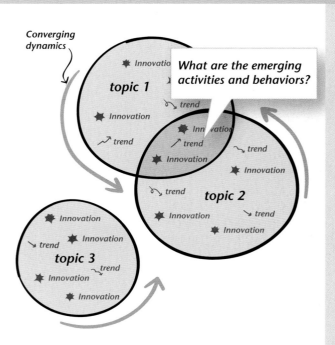

### STEP 3: Build a Venn diagram showing overlapping regions.

Each circle in this Venn diagram represents a topic. Show these circles as overlapped based on common trends and key innovations. Add descriptions about how new behaviors or activities are emerging in these overlapping regions.

### STEP 4: Discuss and identify opportunities.

Speculate on potential innovations that could support the trends or emerging behaviors in these overlaps. Describe opportunities for innovation emerging from these convergences.

1.10 CONVERGENCE MAP

# 1.11 From...To Exploration

Moving from a current perspective based on conventions to a new perspective based on trends

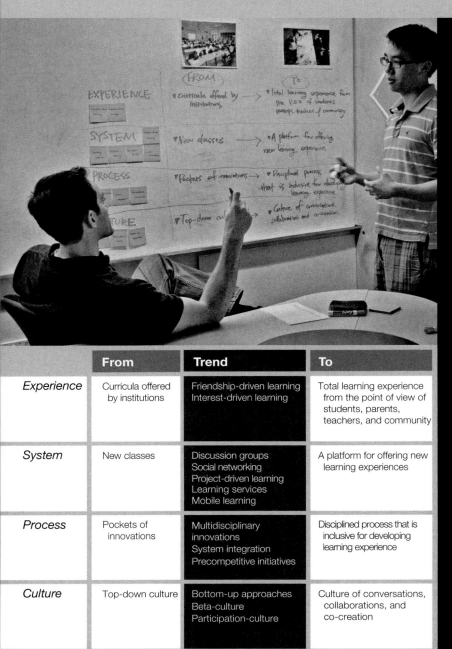

## EXAMPLE PROJECT: *Reframing Education—Singapore Polytechnic (2009)*

In 2003, Singapore set out to steer its economy toward design to incubate new levels of creativity, innovation, and ideas. Fueling this sentiment was the increased competition in the global markets from the likes of the United Kingdom, China, and Taiwan, who were creating national design policies as a way to drive economic growth. This meant Singapore needed to bring design to the national forefront. Education was one area targeted to encourage and nurture the design approach. One of its leading educational institutions sought recommendations on how to transform its education to promote the design approach with the help of Professor Vijay Kumar.

To facilitate transformation, *From. . .To Exploration* was done to help the institution think about how to reframe its new direction. For example, from viewing education as a top-down, Socratic approach, the institution will move to providing education through a culture of conversations, collaborations, and co-creations. Likewise, the institution will move from viewing curricula as merely a set of classes to a platform of offerings with project-driven learning, discussion groups, and social networking. As an initial step to implement this new perspective, the institution has kicked off initiatives such as training sessions to create competencies for this new approach and prototyping design-driven innovation labs with ongoing collaborative projects.

|  | From | Trend | To |
| --- | --- | --- | --- |
| *Experience* | Curricula offered by institutions | Friendship-driven learning<br>Interest-driven learning | Total learning experience from the point of view of students, parents, teachers, and community |
| *System* | New classes | Discussion groups<br>Social networking<br>Project-driven learning<br>Learning services<br>Mobile learning | A platform for offering new learning experiences |
| *Process* | Pockets of innovations | Multidisciplinary innovations<br>System integration<br>Precompetitive initiatives | Disciplined process that is inclusive for developing learning experience |
| *Culture* | Top-down culture | Bottom-up approaches<br>Beta-culture<br>Participation-culture | Culture of conversations, collaborations, and co-creation |

**BENEFITS**
- Challenges assumptions
- Identifies opportunities
- Gives focus to the process

**INPUT**
- List of key aspects of the project
- Understanding of key trends related to the project

**OUTPUT**
- Table with conventions, trends, and possibilities
- Innovation opportunities

**WHEN TO USE**

## WHAT IT DOES

*From . . .To Exploration* is a method that helps turn a current perspective into a new perspective for solving problems. It is about challenging orthodoxies, questioning why things are the way they are, exploring possibilities, and making suggestions. Based on a good understanding of the latest trends, the method proposes how the current context may be changed for the better. The method helps participants think about the goals of the project. It also suggests directions for further research.

## HOW IT WORKS

### STEP 1: List the key aspects of the project.

Speculate on which aspects of the project have the most need for innovation. For example, the aspects of a project on educational innovations might be "learning environments," "curricula," and "research programs," among others.

### STEP 2: Identify trends related to project aspects.

Identify the latest trends affecting the various aspects of the project. For example, for a project on educational innovations, a trend related to "learning environment" might

be "learning environments are becoming distributed due to developments in communication technologies."

### STEP 3: Describe current perspectives based on conventions.

Describe the current conventions about each project aspect. For example, a convention for a "learning environment" is a physical classroom. Describe this current perspective under the "From. . ." section.

### STEP 4: Describe new perspectives based on trends.

Based on your understanding about trends from Step 2, speculate about what could be possible. Think of how current conventions may be reframed. For the learning environment example, can physical classrooms be reframed as virtual learning environments? Describe the new perspective under the ". . .To" section.

### STEP 5: Discuss innovation opportunities.

Discuss how these new perspectives can lead to potential innovations. Think of how the innovation intent could be framed up based on these new perspectives. Think about which of these new perspectives your organization has the greatest potential to deliver.

1.11 FROM...TO EXPRORATION

# 1.12 Initial Opportunity Map

Speculating on an opportunity space to move to in relation to the current position

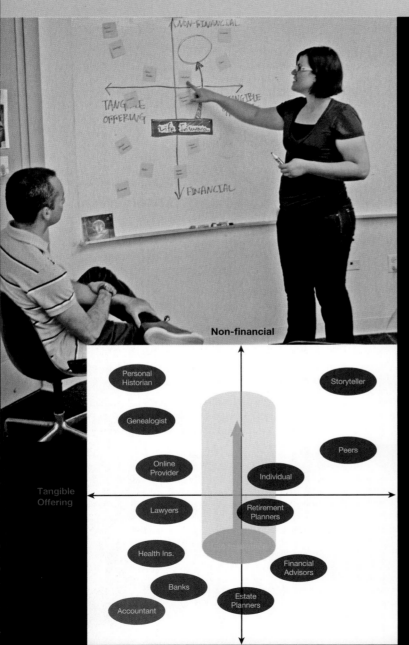

*Non-financial*

*Tangible Offering* ← → *Intangible Offering*

- Personal Historian
- Storyteller
- Genealogist
- Online Provider
- Peers
- Individual
- Lawyers
- Retirement Planners
- Health Ins.
- Financial Advisors
- Banks
- Estate Planners
- Accountant

*EXAMPLE PROJECT: Legacy Planning—Opportunity for a Life Insurance Company (2007)*

In 2007, a life insurance company was seeking strategic recommendations to innovate its business. Life insurance is an economies-of-scale industry that offers various financial-related products and services, but these offerings lack strong emotional value. The project team identified that legacy planning is an emerging area in which this company could expand its offerings and strengthen the emotional connection with its customers.

Legacy planning is primarily about passing on four types of possessions: values and life lessons, wishes to be fulfilled, personal possessions of emotional value, and financial assets or real estate. This understanding led the team to determine two key dimensions that formed the *Initial Opportunity Map*—tangible versus intangible and financial versus nonfinancial. People and service providers who practiced in that space were plotted on this 2 × 2 map. This indicated a possible opportunity where the company could innovate, particularly where the company could provide emotional value to its customers. For example, rather than simply getting an impersonal check after a loved one passes away, their customers would receive a customized bundle of memories, lessons, and values that the deceased collected and saved throughout his or her life.

## WHAT IT DOES

The Initial Opportunity Map helps you explore possible opportunities for your organization's innovations on a 2 × 2 map. The map uses two key dimensions that are found to be strategically significant to the project based on a deep understanding of the trends and other changes taking place. Plotted on the map are various participants operating in that space. The map shows your organization in relation to others and can support speculations on where opportunities exist for your organization to move. During the early stage of an innovation project, this method helps explore the fundamental question of strategy: Where to play?

## HOW IT WORKS

### STEP 1: Identify key dimensions.

List trends that may potentially influence the direction of the industry you are considering. Identify a few strategically important dimensions prompted by these trends. For example, if a trend in the insurance industry is about insurance companies increasingly delivering nonfinancial support to their customers, the key dimension to be considered is "financial services versus nonfinancial services."

### STEP 2: Create a map and plot industry participants.

Create a 2 × 2 map using the two identified key dimensions. Plot the industry participants on the map. Decide as a team what can be included under "participants" for the most useful analysis—practitioners (people), organizations, offerings, or services?

### STEP 3: Discuss the map and identify opportunity spaces.

Identify opportunity spaces where no participants currently play a major role. Assess whether these spaces are in fact opportunities based on the trends and other dynamics of the industry. Assess existing participants' proximity to these opportunity spaces as well for making decisions.

### STEP 4: Speculate on innovation opportunities.

Discuss the possibilities for your innovation (or organization) moving into the identified opportunity space. Consider how your innovation will successfully fit in that space. Can that be a position you can take as initial innovation intent?

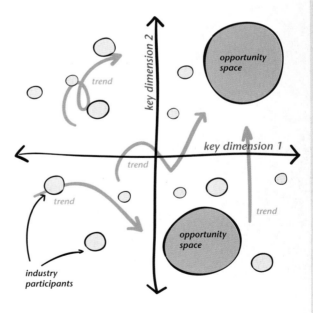

**1.12 INITIAL OPPORTUNITY MAP**

# 1.13 Offering-Activity-Culture Map

Exploring innovation opportunities by shifting focus on offerings, activities, and culture

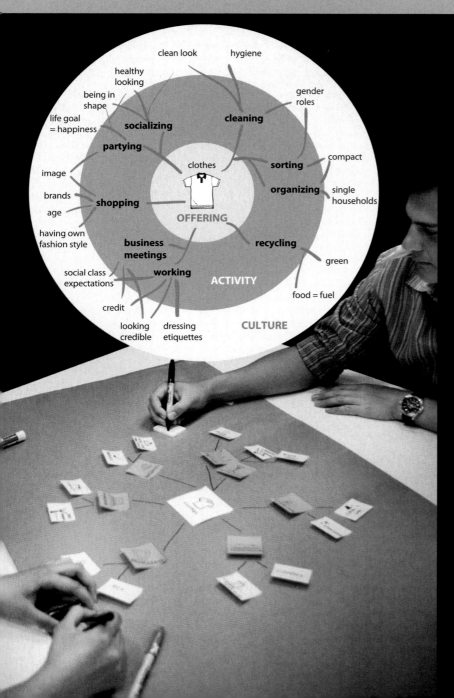

**EXAMPLE PROJECT:**
*Maintaining Clothes (2011)*

How people maintain their clothes was a topic selected by a design analysis team at the IIT Institute of Design. Their initial research indicated that maintaining clothes was largely viewed as a chore. The average person spends six hours a week doing laundry, and people typically wear only 20 percent of the clothes they have. These data indicated to the team that, for innovation, a fuller understanding of the context is needed, going beyond just "clothes" or "laundry."

Using the *Offering-Activity-Culture Map*, the team quickly went beyond just studying clothes. They mapped out activities such as shopping, organizing, cleaning, socializing, recycling, and working. They analyzed how individual and social norms had influenced these activities. Activities about personal shopping habits and style preferences were driven by individual norms, whereas social norms influenced activities such as shopping together, and gifting, in families and in communities. They studied further the cultural context that included aspects like age, image, gender roles, and certain established dressing etiquettes. Through this holistic exploration the team was able to identify a set of rich insights that helped them move to supporting the needs of a specific user-type—single male professional.

**BENEFITS**
- Broadens mindset
- Identifies opportunities
- Visualizes information

**INPUT**
- Offerings to study and their attributes
- Understanding of cultural context around chosen offering

**OUTPUT**
- A mapped set of activities and influencing cultural factors relevant to the product
- Speculations on innovation opportunities

**WHEN TO USE**

## WHAT IT DOES

The Offering-Activity-Culture Map uses three ways to look at innovation opportunities: the "offerings" (products, services) with their functions and features, the "activities" people do with those offerings, and the "cultural context" in which people use those offerings. In thinking about opportunities this way, the method provides a high-level view that broadens explorations. Moreover, this method helps us think about an innovation not just as an offering with improved functions and features but as something that connects with people, what they do, and how they live. By expanding thinking from offerings to activities to cultural context, it opens up the opportunity space at the onset of a project.

## HOW IT WORKS

### STEP 1: Describe the offering and its attributes.

Make a diagram showing the offering in a central circle. Describe its functions, features, and other attributes.

### STEP 2: Describe activities related to the offering.

In a circle surrounding the offering in the diagram, describe people's activities driven by individual and social norms. If the offering is a "book," an example of an activity driven by individual norms will be "writing notes while reading a book." An activity driven by social norms will be "discussing the book content as a group" or "giving the book as a gift."

### STEP 3: Describe the cultural context.

Describe the cultural factors that influence people's activities in the outer circle of the diagram. How do different groups use the offering differently? What are the shared beliefs about the offering? What are the accepted norms, customs, and practices? What are the prevailing cultural trends? What meanings and values are attached to the offering?

### STEP 4: Discuss and speculate on innovation opportunities.

Use this diagram to discuss your team's overall thoughts about offerings, activities, and cultural context. Speculate on opportunities for innovation that touch on many parts of the diagram. How can these be translated into the innovation intent for the project?

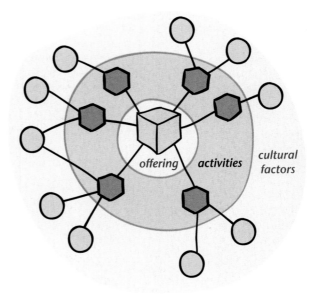

offering   activities   cultural factors

# 1.14 Intent Statement

Stating an initial innovation intent based on an identified opportunity

**Problem:** Change the thinking about and the approach to the violence problem from one of suppression, punishment, and incarceration, to one of changing behavioral and social norms associated with violence.

**Audience:** Prioritize not only on the high-risk, but also on the low-risk, those whose lives have been directly or indirectly impacted by violence.

**Failures:** Prior efforts to contain violence have been based on the principal of punishment: incarceration, gun control, dry state, etc.

**New Value:** The idea that violence is a behavior that can be changed: an interesting parallel between epidemiology and the spread of violence that uses top down as well as bottom up processes to reduce violent incidents.

**Opportunity:** Inspire and change behavior through the use of a unique campaign that communicates a radical ideology by bridging the communication gap between the low-risk and the high-risk groups.

**Risk:** The creation of a campaign lacking in energy/gets a negative media response/unanticipated backlash.

1. Fundamentally change the thinking about and the approach to the violence problem from one of suppression, punishment and incarceration, to one of changing behavioral and social norms associated with violence; and,

2. Impact the violence problem nationally and internationally (e.g., Reduce homicide United States by 25% b

*EXAMPLE PROJECT:*
*Reducing Violence—CeaseFire Chicago (2009)*

Gun violence in the United States is an epidemic, especially in large urban cities like Chicago, where many youth are shot or killed before they reach age 25. A team from the Institute of Design worked with CeaseFire Chicago, a violence prevention program, to develop a communications strategy.

Defining an *Intent Statement* that would guide the project going forward required more than understanding CeaseFire's organizational model, core competencies, strengths, and weaknesses. It also required addressing the thinking that underlies the behaviors perpetuating the transmission of violence at the individual and community level. Through many collaborative sessions and observations, the team recognized CeaseFire's strength is in working with high-risk individuals— who may shoot or are likely to get shot—but not with the low-risk—those whose lives have been directly or indirectly impacted by violence. Seeing violence as a behavior issue, the team defined their intent as bridging the communication gap between low-risk and high-risk groups, and creating a shared sense of community building and dialog for change.

**BENEFITS**

- Defines direction
- Supports transition
- Gives structure to the process
- Promotes shared understanding

**INPUT**

- Research findings, trend statements, and maps produced in previous methods

**OUTPUT**

- A clear and concise statement of the innovation intent for the project

**WHEN TO USE**

## WHAT IT DOES

Getting a good sense of what the opportunities are for creating something new is the main focus during Sense Intent mode. These opportunities are identified by understanding latest developments, seeing big pictures, recognizing current trends, and by reframing problems. The *Intent Statement* method builds on this understanding to speculate on an initial point of view to guide the innovation efforts. Usually the statement takes the form of a few sentences that capture the key aspects of a desired innovation. The Intent Statement is only preliminary, and therefore you should be ready to reframe it as you go through the process. A well-thought-out Intent Statement presents a good rationale for the work that is to follow. It is an important means for building support for innovation initiatives in your organization.

## HOW IT WORKS

### STEP 1: Review innovation opportunities identified by other methods.

Go through the findings from other methods that helped you understand latest developments, recognize trends, see overview patterns, and reframe problems. Review the identified innovation opportunities, and focus on those with high potential.

### STEP 2: Define and state innovation opportunities.

Further define the opportunities since they may be boundless in your early explorations. Define the opportunities based on the following framework for clarity:

Limitations—What are the constraints?

Intentions—What should be the goals?

Aspirations—What will be nice to have?

### STEP 3: Have a point of view.

Discuss possibilities among your team members. Which opportunities can be built as a strong initial position to move your innovation efforts forward? Take an initial stance. Create a shared point of view with which to start.

### STEP 4: Frame the initial innovation intent.

Use a structured framework for stating the innovation intent. This should help project stakeholders to have a shared understanding of the goals and wishes.

Who is the customer?

What are their needs?

What are the opportunities?

What new values can be created?

What are the risks?

### STEP 5: State the innovation intent.

Draft a statement that describes the aforementioned aspects in clear, easy-to-understand, and sharable form. Creating a one-paragraph (or a few sentences), concise statement is a common practice. Alternatively, you might state it as bullet points or a storyline, or write a detailed statement in two to three pages.

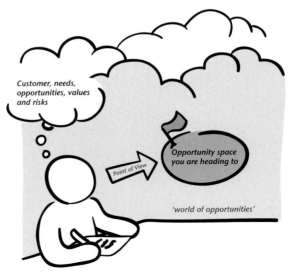

Customer, needs, opportunities, values and risks

Point of View

Opportunity space you are heading to

'world of opportunities'

1.14 INTENT STATEMENT

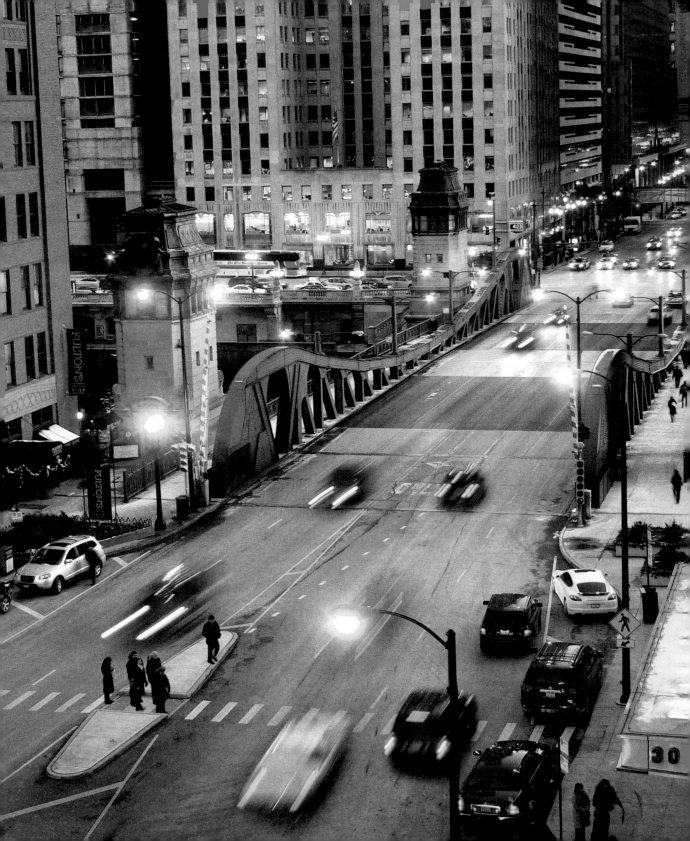

# mode 2
# KNOW CONTEXT

In the "Sense Intent" mode, we focus on the trends and changes that happen around us so that we can sense an initial direction for our innovation. In the Know Context mode, we move to gain a full understanding of the surrounding conditions in which those changes happen. This is what we call the context. It is in this changing context that our innovation offerings (products, services, experiences) need to work to be successful. The question is: How do we understand this context well enough for us to be confident about our innovations? How do we study the components in the context such as products, services, organizations, competitors, markets, industries, governments, policies, environments, and technologies? How do we study their relationships? How do we understand our current offering's performance in the market relative to the competition? How do we sense our competitor's evolving strategies? How do we diagnose the conditions of our own organization? How strong are our relations with our industry partners? How do we find out what effects government policies and regulations have on our innovation? All these and similar questions are good to ask when we are in this mode. Overall, the goal is to gain as many insights as possible about the context, get prepared to confidently explore opportunities, and begin to see directions for the future.

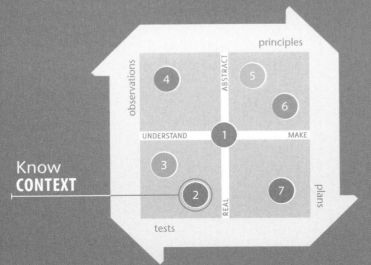

Know
**CONTEXT**

# KNOW CONTEXT *mindsets*

In Sense Intent mode, we were in the mindset of scanning broadly and widely, looking for promising places to go with our ideas. Now it is time to shift the mindset to one of focus and depth, geared up for a full understanding of the context. In this mode, part of our focus is to understand what in the past has led us to where we are now. The mindset is also about constantly being aware of the state-of-the-art and the cutting-edge developments. We visualize interconnected components of the context in flux, including stakeholders, as broad overviews for a full understanding. Moreover, we constantly try to understand this flux moving back and forth, local to global, and narrow to broad, always seeking a different perspective. Clear mental models and frameworks are helpful in understanding the complexity of the context we are studying.

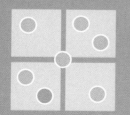

**Mindsets**
- Knowing Context History
- Understanding Frontiers
- Seeing System Overviews
- Understanding Stakeholders
- Using Mental Models

*For example, the history of innovations in the automobile industry reflects far more than just styling changes. In the 1950s in the United States, oil and gas were subsidized and plentiful. This condition gave rise to the development of an interstate highway system. Increasing economic prosperity produced more automobile owners. Automobile manufacturers responded by producing more models. Car designs tended toward the large and ample. Over the next 50 years conditions changed. Today, dwindling world oil reserves have pushed up the gasoline price. At the same time, greater concerns about the environment are changing social behaviors. As a result, automobile manufacturers today focus on fuel efficiency. Gas-guzzlers are being pulled out of the current context. Developing small cars that use hybrid energy technologies has become a primary focus for innovators in the automobile industry.*

## Mindset: Knowing Context History

Anyone who has ever started following a television series that has been already running for a few seasons knows the experience of trying to understand the story that is unfolding before them. Viewers who have been watching since the beginning of the series have an advantage over latecomers: historical context—knowledge of what has already happened and why things are happening now the way they are.

Learning the historical context expands our understanding of change, explains why things are the way they are, and sometimes indicates what might be.

*In 2008, the organizers of Senator Barack Obama's presidential campaign leveraged their knowledge of the state-of-the-art technologies to create a groundswell of national support. They used tools at the frontiers of Web-based applications at that time like Twitter, Facebook, and Google Maps to build a community of support and communicate with voters in ways that had never been possible before. Deploying these technologies to engage with voters in real time gave the campaign a significant advantage over opposing candidates, and especially resonated with young voters who were beginning to embrace the idea of social networking.*

## Mindset: Understanding Frontiers

Just as looking to the past helps understand the present, learning about the latest offers glimpses of possible future. We continually seek out the latest news and stories about the most advanced development, technique, or level of knowledge achieved in the topic. We look out for cutting-edge work. We look for innovations that are on the frontiers. We probe to identify the underlying forces and conditions that cause the formation of these frontiers. We learn from thought leaders whose latest thinking drives those innovations. All this is a great way to foresee what might happen next and what promising opportunities are ahead.

Understanding the latest developments at the frontiers helps us see the near-future context in which our innovations should work.

SimCity Societies image used with permission of Electronic Arts Inc.

SimCity Societies image used with permission of Electronic Arts Inc.

*SimCity is a simulation game that challenges the players to make decisions at all levels, whether about building a local structure or maintaining the resources of the city as a whole. As you are building structures, you can look at the overall behavior of the city over time with the help of diagrammatic overlays like population, traffic density, or crime rate. Easy switching between local and system views of the context is what helps you succeed in building a prosperous city.*

## Mindset: Seeing System Overviews

At one time or another everyone has become so deeply focused on the details of a problem that they've lost sight of the "big picture." Stepping back to get some perspective can be enormously beneficial. This is how we reveal some of the things that we may have missed when we were deeply immersed in all the details.

The context—the circumstances and events in a situation in which something happens—has numerous components that we must understand. For example, the things that people use, services they subscribe to, the brands that surround them, the markets that they are part of, the policies that govern their transactions, and a number of other components relate to each other in some way as a system. In addition, we need to understand how all these are changing over time because of forces like trends, people's changing preferences, availability of resources, and so forth. In short, the context that we need to understand is complex and dynamic.

The goal is to shift our focus at times to visualize the context as overviews so that we holistically understand its components, relations, and dynamics.

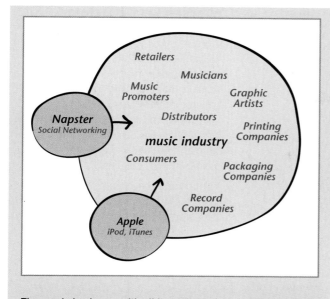

## Mindset: Understanding Stakeholders

Contexts have stakeholders (individuals or organizations) that have an investment, whether personal, financial, or otherwise. Among them are companies, partners, competitors, regulatory agencies, trade associations, and similar entities. It is valuable to map out all the stakeholders involved in the context so that their relationships can be better understood. It is also useful to understand how stakeholders derive value from the context. This helps explain their motivations and interactions. It also helps us think about how stakeholders may be affected when changes happen to the context when new innovations are introduced.

*The music business, with all its stakeholders, in the '90s went through an interesting transformation. At the time, the music business included primary stakeholders such as musicians, record companies, distributors, retailers, and consumers, but also a host of less obvious ones, like graphic artists, printing companies, packaging companies, music promoters, and others. The entire industry was structured around the sale of album-length recordings sold as CDs. In 1999, Napster entered the mix, a peer-to-peer file-sharing service that allowed people to freely share music with one another, well supported by the emergence of social networking. The recording industry stakeholders in peril reacted strongly to this change. But, record companies in their efforts to regain their position, in some sense, failed to embrace the need for change and capitalize on it. When Apple stepped forward with its iPod and iTunes store, the context was again transformed; a world in which the stakeholders' roles became very different.*

*A framework (a set of ideas or principles that are used as a basis for understanding an external reality) is another good mental model. For example, a social science–based framework such as "Cues, Signals, and Messages" is a good tool to design communications in a space. Cues passively indicate the current state—for instance, a visible kitchen in a restaurant providing a sense of food preparation activities. Signals, unlike cues, are active indicators that explicitly show that something has changed—for instance, a device with a flashing light programmed to indicate that the order is ready. Messages are explicit communications meant to direct an activity, for example, a visual menu board.*

## Mindset: Using Mental Models

One of the ways in which we can get comfortable with the complexity of the context that we are trying to understand is through the use of clear mental models. Fundamentally, a mental model is an internal representation we use to understand an external reality, and it is particularly useful to comprehend complexity.

Keeping a collection of mental models as a repository helps us retrieve the most appropriate ones to understand specific contexts as needed.

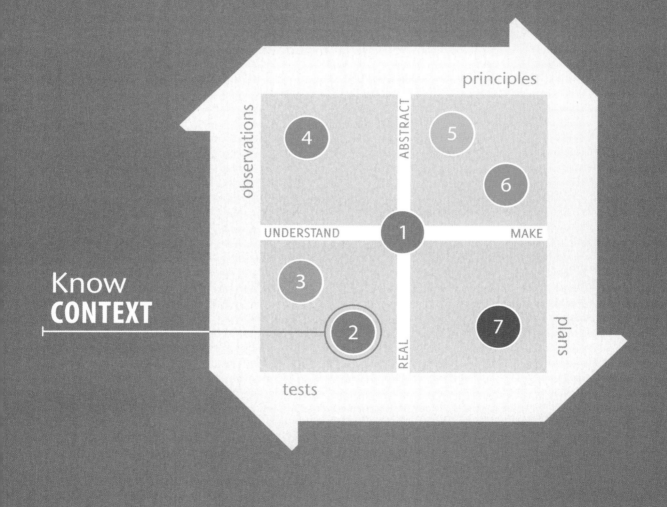

Know
**CONTEXT**

# KNOW CONTEXT *methods*

# 2.1 Contextual Research Plan

Making a schedule and plan for researching the innovation context

## EXAMPLE PROJECT: Automobiles in India Research (2008)

A group of Japanese automakers approached Daishinsha, a Japanese consulting firm, to gain insights into the automobile market in India and get strategic recommendations on how to penetrate that market. To execute the research, Daishinsha worked with Professor Vijay Kumar's innovation consultancy firm in the United States.

The U.S. team did initial background research on the Indian automobile market to gain a general grasp of the project scope. The team reconvened to share and discuss their learning, assumptions, and questions that would help shape the *Contextual Research Plan, such as sources of information they could access, appropriate methods to use, meeting schedules, major deadlines, and specific deliverables. The team had six months to work on the four modes—sense intent, know people, know context, and frame insights. Because of the tight timeframe they chose methods that were less time-intensive, for example, publications research, expert interviews, field visits, and ethnographic interviews. The resulting research plan organized dates, activities, resources, methods, milestones, and deliverables in a spreadsheet format and was shared with all team members and the client. Taking the time to seek input and alignment from the outset helped team members have clarity of their tasks and deadlines, which minimized multiple check points and helped overall time management throughout the process. It also helped to create transparency with the client who had a chance to review the plan and see that the efforts of the team were aligned with their expectations.*

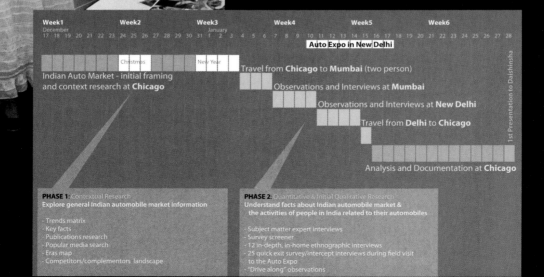

| | Week1 | | Week2 | | Week3 | | Week4 | | Week5 | | Week6 |
|---|---|---|---|---|---|---|---|---|---|---|---|
| December | 17 18 19 20 21 22 23 | 24 25 26 27 28 29 30 | 31 | January 1 2 3 | 4 5 6 7 | 8 9 10 11 12 13 | 14 15 16 17 | 18 19 20 21 | 22 23 24 25 26 27 28 | | |

Auto Expo in New Delhi

Christmas — New Year

Indian Auto Market - initial framing and context research at **Chicago**

Travel from **Chicago** to **Mumbai** (two person)

Observations and Interviews at **Mumbai**

Observations and Interviews at **New Delhi**

Travel from **Delhi** to **Chicago**

Analysis and Documentation at **Chicago**

1st Presentation to Daishinsha

**PHASE 1:** Contextual Research
Explore general Indian automobile market information

- Trends matrix
- Key facts
- Publications research
- Popular media search
- Eras map
- Competitors/complementors landscape

**PHASE 2:** Quantitative & Initial Qualitative Research
Understand facts about Indian automobile market & the activities of people in India related to their automobiles

- Subject matter expert interviews
- Survey screener
- 12 in-depth, in-home ethnographic interviews
- 25 quick exit survey/intercept interviews during field visit to the Auto Expo
- "Drive along" observations

**BENEFITS**

- Defines direction
- Manages resources
- Promotes shared understandings

**INPUT**

- Project goals
- Potential sources of information

**OUTPUT**

- Research plan with timeline, teams, and choice of methods to be used

## WHAT IT DOES

The Contextual Research Plan is a method to develop a general plan and schedule for what we want to research about the context and how it will be accomplished. It brings a degree of rigor and clarity to exploratory activities at the beginning of projects. What methods should we use? Should we speak with industry experts? Survey publications? Conduct an online survey? How will the research activities be divided among the team? What resources are needed? What will be the timeframe for gathering and reviewing information? How can the findings be summarized for sharing? Working with these questions early on as a team builds a shared understanding about the context to be studied and helps manage time and resources effectively. The process of drafting the plan in teams also allows for team alignment. The key components to be discussed are research teams, activities, dates, duration, resources, methods, milestones, and deliverables.

## HOW IT WORKS

### STEP 1: Define areas for research.

Given that time and resources are limited, focus on the most relevant areas related to your context for study. Discuss the selection of these general areas and articulate why they are relevant to the project. Discuss what is known, assumed, and unknown and define areas for further research.

### STEP 2: Define sources.

Identify the kinds of information you need to gather. Will you speak with industry experts? Survey available literature? Visit key organizations involved in the context? Identify where the information can be obtained. If it is not readily available, how might you go about accessing key information—people, publications, media,

databases? Make an initial assessment of the amount of effort required to gather the information you seek.

### STEP 3: Define methods.

Decide on the specific research methods you want to use. Refer to the methods in this chapter to determine which ones align with the kinds of information you hope to collect.

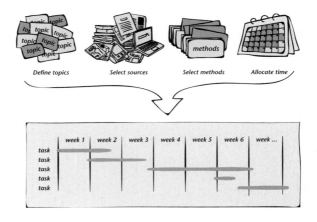

### STEP 4: Create a research plan timeline.

Clearly define the start and end dates. Determine how work will be accomplished during this time period. Lay out when the key pieces of information will be gathered. Include intermediate check-in dates for the team to come together to review collected data and discuss.

### STEP 5: Create an overview diagram of the research plan.

Prepare a visual overview of the Contextual Research Plan, and review it as a team. Use this overview as the basis for discussion about roles and responsibilities. Address any concerns team members might have about what they will be doing and when the work must be completed.

2.1 CONTEXTUAL RESEARCH PLAN

*EXAMPLE PROJECT:*
*SHIFT Platform (2010)*

Successful innovation strategies build platforms that integrate multiple offerings beneficial to all the stakeholders involved. A team of designers working with Larry Keeley (president of Doblin) in 2010 chose the topic of recycling and designed a platform called SHIFT (the name suggests a combination of SHARING and GIFT). The concept emphasized environmental consciousness and community building through object-exchange activities—finding new homes for items that no longer have value for their current owners.

The *Popular Media Search* method informed the team about the ways in which recycling activities were evolving. One emerging area of interest was local sharing. To become more versed in the topic, the team searched for and gathered information about collaborative consumption and the sharing economy from online sources like Fast Company and BusinessWeek. They also sought to identify companies promoting a local sharing culture to reduce waste and found examples such as freecycle.org, bookcrossing.com, and pass-the-baton.com. This process not only engaged the team in active discussion, but also enabled them to develop deeper knowledge of the topic that helped discover opportunity spaces. As a final concept, SHIFT uses the Waste Management Company and Greenopolis as its main sponsors and connects donors with donees for specific items. Rewards are also built into the platform that provides donors with redeemable points to buy products at local shops.

**BENEFITS**
- Captures knowledge
- Reveals cultural patterns
- Promotes shared understanding

**INPUT**
- Topics relevant to the project
- Popular sources of information around those topics

**OUTPUT**
- Set of documented observations about the context of the project

**WHEN TO USE**

## WHAT IT DOES

Popular Media Search is a method to find out anything new being said about the context in the media landscape. During this search, we survey a wide array of media sources, such as newspapers, broadcast media, Web content, bookstores, popular magazines, and movies, to find references to new developments related to the context in which we are interested. We gather different kinds of information through scouting, Web-based searches, or library scans. We try to understand companies, industries, trends, competitors, the state-of-the-art, or other such aspects of the context. The goal is to look for results that are particularly insightful and revealing about interesting developments taking place. When taken as a whole, the results of a Popular Media Search summarize the range of opinions, ideas, and influences tied to the context.

## HOW IT WORKS

### STEP 1: Identify topics most relevant to the project.

Segment your topic to bring focus to the areas of greatest interest to you. For example, if looking at the organic food industry, topics for research might be "scalability in organic farming," "agri-business's response to organic farming," or "managing supply chain with local producers of organic foods."

### STEP 2: Identify sources of insightful information.

Who are the industry experts or people within an organization who can provide informed and thoughtful input on what is happening? Who are the bloggers writing about the context in a way that is insightful and timely? What are the publications that cover specifics about context?

### STEP 3: Conduct searches.

Conduct a Web-based search, or library search, or scout around for information that may be available anywhere. Collect search results like articles, interviews, notes, photographs, and so forth into a single sharable space for all team members to work together.

### STEP 4: Review, extract, and document observations.

As you accumulate information, write notes summarizing key points, record your distinct points of view, and capture any other information that can lead to insights. Discuss, extract, and document your observations in a sharable space for all team members to participate.

### STEP 5: Cite sources.

Every observation that makes its way into a final report or presentation should include a citation as to where it came from, who wrote it, and any credentials of the writer. Citing sources is a way to anchor a point of view and demonstrate rigor and credibility.

*Topic Focus*

**2.2 POPULAR MEDIA SEARCH**

# 2.3 Publications Research

Finding out what is being written and published about aspects of the context

### EXAMPLE PROJECT: *Points of Arrival in Emerging Markets (2005)*

An information systems firm offering a range of productivity tools and business-to-business intelligence to the architecture and construction industry found itself struggling against the rapid advances in information technology amid a severe economic downturn. With easier access to information via the Web, customers no longer had to rely on this firm as the primary provider for information and data on the construction industry. The project team saw viable potential in the emerging markets sector, particularly India because of its growing middle-class population, increased migration to urban centers, foreign capital investments, and policy changes that were increasing the demand for residential and commercial construction.

The team did *Publications Research* to understand India's demographics and construction industry. They initiated the research using a Publications Research survey to find the most relevant and reliable sources from construction websites, journals, and government publications. These sources were studied and then annotated in a table with the information capturing the key points regarding people, culture, markets, government, and technology—how things are currently structured and any changes that are happening. This served as an evolving reference document for the remainder of the project. Any new resources that were essential to understanding relevant aspects of the Indian construction industry were added to this document. This became a strong basis for the team to build concepts and strategies for the firm.

| Title | Author | Category – Aspects of the Market | Category – Source of Change | Rating | Summary | Source |
|---|---|---|---|---|---|---|
| Social Capital as a Product of Class Mobilization and State Intervention: Industrial Workers in Kerala, India | Patrick Heller, Professor of Sociology and International Studies, Columbia University | Dynamics | People | ★★★ | Cooperatives. In the state of Kerala, India, mutually reinforcing interactions between a programmatic labor movement and a democratic state have created the institutional forms and political processes required for negotiating the class compromises through which redistribution and growth can be reconciled. | World Development, Vol. 24, Issue 6, 1055-1071, June 1996 |
| The Contradictions in Enabling Private Developers of Affordable Housing: A Cautionary Case from Ahmedabad, India | Prof. Vinit Mukhija, Department of Urban Planning, UCLA | Structures | Culture | ★★★★★ | Formal and Informal Networks. Enabling informal developers can be trickier because public support can reduce their flexibility and incentives, as well as impact the expectations and opportunities of the homebuyers. | Urban Studies, Vol. 41, Issue 11, 2231-2244, October 2004 |
| India's Quiet Revolution | Shailaja Neelakantan | Elements | Markets | ★★★★ | Increase Ownership Earlier. The growing popularity of mortgage financing in India will do more than just enable millions to become first-time homeowners. It will deepen the financial market, boost the housing and construction industries and spur economic growth. | Far Eastern Economic Review, Vol.167, Issue 24, 50, June 2004 |
| Sustainable Practices to Meet Shelter Needs in India | Piyush Tiwari, Institute of Policy and Planning Sciences, University of Tsukuba | Dynamics | Government | ★★★★ | Crowding Out of Private Investment. The private financial sector has played a very conservative role, and the share of the formal finance sector has never been more than 20%. | Journal of Urban Planning and Development, Vol. 129, Issue 2, 0733-9488, June 2003 |
| Prefabrication Building Methodologies for Low Cost Housing | Shri P K Adlakha, Shri H C Puri | Elements | Technology | ★★★ | Low Cost and Environmentally Sustainable Construction Technologies. New technologies can help the Indian construction industry save money and become more environmentally efficient. | IE (I) Journal, Vol 84, April 2003 |

Publications Research   Research Questions   Contextual Research Plan

## WHAT IT DOES

Publications Research is a method for understanding what is being written about a topic of interest related to a project. Often this topic of interest comes directly from the definition of the innovation intent that we establish at the beginning of the project. By searching through key publications, we get a good sense of how thought leaders and industry professionals are thinking about the topic. We also analyze search results to find prominent patterns about trends and new developments in the context. Moreover, Publications Research creates a comprehensive list of relevant readings that can go into our growing reference library.

## HOW IT WORKS

### STEP 1: Define the topic of interest.

Publications Research is most effective when targeted and narrowly scoped. Use your project brief and project goals to help you define topics that you need to deeply understand.

### STEP 2: Search for publications.

Conduct a search for publications that are related to your topic of interest in public and university library collections; most of them are now available online. Search through news reports, academic journals, company reports, books, trade publications, conference publications, government publications, and encyclopedias. Use keywords and search terms that are related to your topic.

### STEP 3: Study relevant publications and extract insights.

Review the titles and summaries returned by your searches. Try sorting in several ways—by title, topic, and author—to get a sense of broad categories.

Identify and select a manageable number of publications for further review and study. Extract insights from what is written, include your ratings based on their relevance to the project, and add your comments.

### STEP 4: Create and manage a repository.

Create a Publications Research findings repository. The repository should have a basic structure that organizes findings in the form of a spreadsheet with basic columns like titles, ratings, and summaries. This basic repository should be treated as an extensible document in which details such as authors, excerpts, and insights can be added as needed and can be commented upon throughout the course of a project.

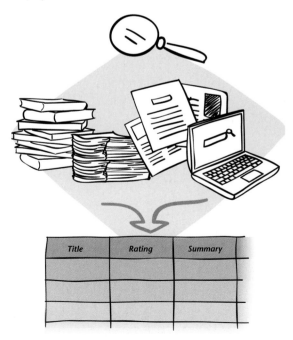

| Title | Rating | Summary |
|-------|--------|---------|
|       |        |         |
|       |        |         |
|       |        |         |

# 2.4 Eras Map

Mapping distinct eras in the context and describing them across topics of interest

| | Era 1 — In the Dog house — 1920–1948 | Era 2 — Dog Boom — 1949–1970 | Era 3 — On the Move — 1971–1994 | Era 4 — Living the Good Life — 1995–Present |
|---|---|---|---|---|
| Relationship to Owner | Outside Pet | Family Member | Companion Best Friend | Parent Child |
| Owner Type/ Location | Workers, Families Urban-Rural | Families with Kids Suburban | Urban Dwellers Suburban Families with Kids | Singles, Empty Nesters Couples with no kids |
| Product Trends | Mass Produced Dog Food Homemade Toys | Accessories, Grooming | Health, Exercise, Containment Recreation, Nutrition | Designer, Eco Friendly, Luxury Convenience, Organic |
| Service Trends | Animal Welfare Clinics Pet Photography | Health, Training | Grooming Rescue & Placement | Luxury, Health Travel, Social |
| Retail | Feed Stores, Sporting Goods | Feed Store, Grocery Stores Pet Stores | Neighborhood Pet Stores Big Box Pet Stores | Mass Market Retailer Designer Boutiques (Niche) |
| Activities | Working, Playing, Sporting Hunting | Grooming, Playing, Training | Exercising, Socializing Walking, Showing, Competing | Traveling, Styling, Partying |
| Brands | Hartz, Ralston Purina Milk Bone | Alpo | Iams, Eukanuba, Hills Science Diet, Petco, Petsmart | Target Old Mother Hubbard |
| Cultural Icons | Rin Tin Tin, Toto | Lassie, Benjy, Belka Shaggy Dog, | Spuds McKenzie, Scooby Doo Turner & Hooch, Millie | Taco Bell Chihuahua Frasier-Moose, Air Bud, Marley |
| Cultural Moments | First Dog in movies WWII, Athletic Competitions | First dog in space - Sputnik | Dogs in Advertisements | Best Seller Marley & Me Celebrity Owners |

## EXAMPLE PROJECT:
## Dog Ownership (2007)

An IIT Institute of Design team that did a project on dog ownership in the United States applied design analysis methods to uncover opportunities for innovation. To study the context the key topics they covered included understanding the dog industry and the events that fueled the industry's growth, identifying the different types of pet owners and their values, assessing marketplace dynamics by looking at current product and service innovations, and lastly, delving into the overall experience of owning a dog according to different pet owners.

The team used the Eras Map to analyze the growth of the industry in four distinct eras starting from the 1920s through to the current time—"In the Dog House" period, when pets were primarily kept outside to the present day "Living the Good Life," where pets are cared for as children. One of the key insights that emerged from the Eras Map was that dogs' lives are now parallel with those of their owners. They can now travel, socialize, and exercise in the lap of luxury. Another insight highlighted the shift of dog ownership from suburban to urban environments, a phenomenon called urbananimalization, which resulted in new standards for taking care of dogs. The Eras Map analysis helped the team pinpoint the human nature of the dog/owner relationship as an area to explore design concepts, particularly among affectionate dog owners who expect the same standards, products, and services for their dogs as they do for themselves.

**BENEFITS**
- Maps change over time
- Creates overview
- Organizes information for easy access

**INPUT**
- Attributes of the project topic
- Timeframe of interest

**OUTPUT**
- Distinct eras showing how different attributes of the project topic have evolved over time

**WHEN TO USE**

## What It Does

The Eras Map provides historical perspective to the context being studied. Understanding how things change over time offers a fuller picture of the context and helps teams think about where things may be headed in the future and where opportunities might exist. The Eras Map highlights the key characteristics of each relevant period, shows how each era is different, and indicates how much they have changed over time. Constructing this as an overview map helps us see the larger patterns of change in the context being studied.

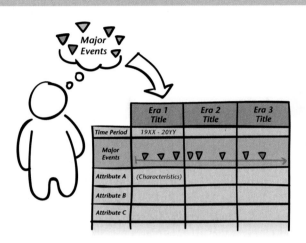

## How It Works

### STEP 1: Define the attributes and time periods to track.

Define which attributes of your project topic that you want to capture in the Eras Map. Behavioral changes over time, developments in technology, and key influential people who played major roles at various times are some examples of attributes that are useful to track and segment into eras. Determine the time period that will be captured in the map. Decide how many years back you want to go for recognizing clearly distinguishable eras.

### STEP 2: Research the historical context.

Find historical information about the events that have occurred during the selected time period. Study how the selected attributes have changed over time. Seek out industry experts, historians, professors, and others who could help contribute information about the historical context. However, keep in mind that an Eras Map is an overview map used to compare eras and, therefore, look for the right level of information—not too detailed, not too general.

### STEP 3: Visualize the map.

Map the information collected from the research on a horizontal timeline. Consider what an appropriate division of time is. For example, dividing time by years as opposed to decades may be appropriate for areas that experience rapid change, such as social networking. Lay out the different attributes identified in Step 1 as horizontal bands to include descriptions of changes over time. Look for patterns that can be reliably used to segment the timeline into eras.

### STEP 4: Define and label eras.

Identify distinct eras on the timeline and show them as clearly marked vertical segments. Describe and label each segment with defining characteristics of that particular era. For example, a project on communications might summarize eras as "the age of telegraphy," "the age of telephony," and "the Internet age."

### STEP 5: Look for insights.

Step back and study the overview map as a team. Discuss and extract interesting insights about the eras identified. What can be learned about the clear distinction between eras? What are the high-level characteristics of each era that can point to future possibilities? Summarize all insights as an additional information layer on the Eras Map.

**2.4 ERAS MAP**

Mapping how innovations of the organization and industry have evolved over time

### EXAMPLE PROJECT: *The Future of Play (2006)*

A leading U.S. manufacturer of traditional toys was faced with an innovation dilemma as a result of a shift in children's preferences from traditional to technology-focused toys and games. The project team at the IIT Institute of Design identified new innovation opportunities for the company to shift away from its primary focus on the traditional toy segment for kids up to eight years and build on the new trends in technology-focused toys. The team also saw opportunities in content creation and community building because of their importance to today's kids. Physical activity immersion was also a possible opportunity because of its potential for engaging play and wellness in the future.

To generate concepts the team first needed to understand the company's innovations and their impact on the industry. The Innovation Evolution Map provided the structure to visualize the evolution of prominent product innovations in key time periods. The team also paid attention to indications that could lead to future possibilities. Emerging from the analysis were areas of ups and downs indicating where the company did and did not do well. The team also tracked their stock price in parallel. In the early '90s the company enjoyed stock price increases because of their acquisitions. They then suffered a significant decline in the late '90s because of the growing popularity of video and online gaming, one of the areas in which the team thought they had promising opportunities.

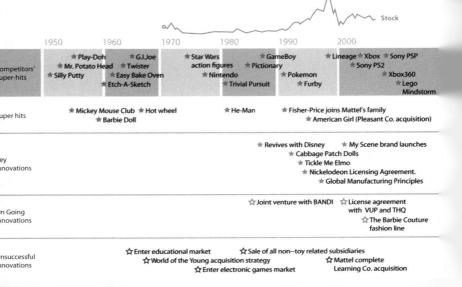

| | 1950 | 1960 | 1970 | 1980 | 1990 | 2000 | |
|---|---|---|---|---|---|---|---|
| Competitors' Super-hits | ★ Play-Doh ★ Mr. Potato Head ★ Silly Putty | ★ G.I.Joe ★ Twister ★ Easy Bake Oven ★ Etch-A-Sketch | ★ Star Wars action figures ★ Nintendo | ★ GameBoy ★ Pictionary ★ Trivial Pursuit | ★ Lineage ★ Pokemon ★ Furby | ★ Xbox ★ Sony PSP ★ Sony PS2 ★ Xbox360 ★ Lego Mindstorm | |
| Super hits | ★ Mickey Mouse Club ★ Barbie Doll | ★ Hot wheel | | ★ He-Man | ★ Fisher-Price joins Mattel's family ★ American Girl (Pleasant Co. acquisition) | | |
| Key Innovations | | | | | ★ Revives with Disney ★ Cabbage Patch Dolls ★ Tickle Me Elmo ★ Nickelodeon Licensing Agreement. ★ Global Manufacturing Principles | ★ My Scene brand launches | |
| On Going Innovations | | | | ☆ Joint venture with BANDI | | ☆ License agreement with VUP and THQ ☆ The Barbie Couture fashion line | |
| Unsuccessful Innovations | | ☆ Enter educational market ☆ World of the Young acquisition strategy ☆ Enter electronic games market | | ☆ Sale of all non--toy related subsidiaries | | ☆ Mattel complete Learning Co. acquisition | |

Stock

## BENEFITS
- Maps change over time
- Helps understand best practices
- Facilitates comparison
- Reveals relationships

## INPUT
- Timeframe relevant for study
- Historical data about innovations in your company and industry

## OUTPUT
- Visual map of innovations over time
- Observations about the relationships between innovations and quantitative measures

## WHEN TO USE

## WHAT IT DOES

The Innovation Evolution Map shows how innovations in the company and in the industry as a whole have evolved over time. The ups and downs of the organization's innovation evolution are compared to other players in the industry. It is a visual aid that facilitates side-by-side comparisons for gaining insights. The map also can be overlaid with other information, for example, stock price, revenue, market capital, or market share. These attributes analyzed together with the innovation evolution can reveal interesting correlation insights. Overall the map serves as a comprehensive historical overview of innovations in the given industry.

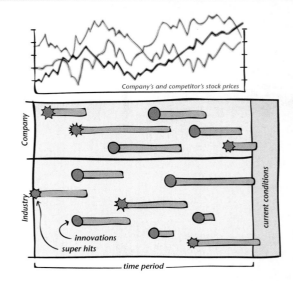

## HOW IT WORKS

### Step 1: Determine the time period to study.

Consider the most relevant period for understanding your project context. Tracking long periods, say the last 30 years, likely will yield useful historical patterns. A shorter period, say the last 3 years, may be more meaningful to understand what is currently happening in the context.

### STEP 2: Compile the innovation history of the organization and the industry.

Conduct an audit of your organization's innovations as well as industry-level innovations. Pay particular attention to super-hits—those innovations that have resulted in marked and significant increases in revenues, market share, or industry leadership.

### STEP 3: Gather data for key quantitative measures to be compared.

Identify key quantitative measures that can be compared against the evolution of innovations by the organization and industry. For example, growth (or decline) in revenue, market share, return on investment, profitability, and stock price. Gather data for these key measures during the selected time period.

### STEP 4: Create a visual map.

List years across the column headings. List your bases for comparison as row headings such as innovations, super-hits, revenue, or market share. Plot the innovations by the organization and the industry for each of the two rows titled Innovations and Super-hits. Distinguish between organization and industry information using color codes. Use line graphs to show revenue or market share.

### STEP 5: Look for insights.

Discuss the map as a team and look for insights. What impact does your organization's innovations and super-hits have on the industry? What is the correlation between your organization's innovation patterns and stock prices or market share? Ask questions like these to find insights and describe them on an additional layer of the map.

2.5 INNOVATION EVOLUTION MAP

# 2.6 Financial Profile

Profiling and comparing financial performances of organizations and industries

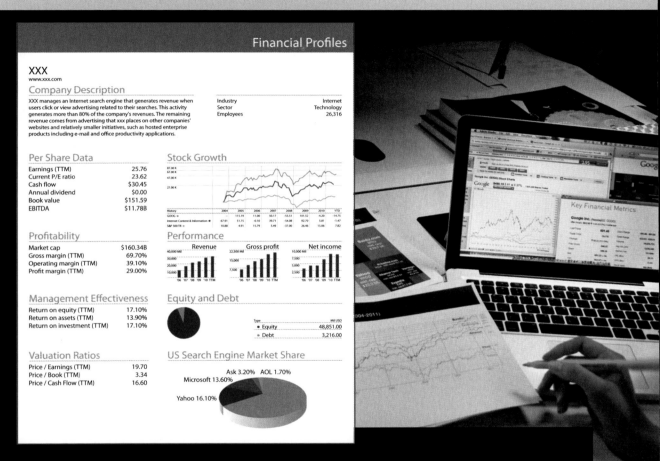

## Financial Profiles

### XXX
www.xxx.com

#### Company Description

XXX manages an Internet search engine that generates revenue when users click or view advertising related to their searches. This activity generates more than 80% of the company's revenues. The remaining revenue comes from advertising that xxx places on other companies' websites and relatively smaller initiatives, such as hosted enterprise products including e-mail and office productivity applications.

| | |
|---|---|
| Industry | Internet |
| Sector | Technology |
| Employees | 26,316 |

#### Per Share Data

| | |
|---|---|
| Earnings (TTM) | 25.76 |
| Current P/E ratio | 23.62 |
| Cash flow | $30.45 |
| Annual dividend | $0.00 |
| Book value | $151.59 |
| EBITDA | $11.78B |

#### Profitability

| | |
|---|---|
| Market cap | $160.34B |
| Gross margin (TTM) | 69.70% |
| Operating margin (TTM) | 39.10% |
| Profit margin (TTM) | 29.00% |

#### Management Effectiveness

| | |
|---|---|
| Return on equity (TTM) | 17.10% |
| Return on assets (TTM) | 13.90% |
| Return on investment (TTM) | 17.10% |

#### Valuation Ratios

| | |
|---|---|
| Price / Earnings (TTM) | 19.70 |
| Price / Book (TTM) | 3.34 |
| Price / Cash Flow (TTM) | 16.60 |

#### Stock Growth

| History | 2004 | 2005 | 2006 | 2007 | 2008 | 2009 | 2010 | YTD |
|---|---|---|---|---|---|---|---|---|
| GOOG % | | 115.19 | 11.00 | 50.17 | -55.31 | 101.52 | -4.20 | -14.75 |
| Internet Content & Information ● | 67.91 | 51.75 | -0.10 | 39.71 | -54.08 | 92.70 | 5.81 | -1.47 |
| S&P 500 TR ≈ | 10.88 | 4.91 | 15.79 | 5.49 | -37.00 | 26.46 | 15.06 | 7.82 |

#### Performance

Revenue  Gross profit  Net income

#### Equity and Debt

| Type | Mil USD |
|---|---|
| ● Equity | 48,851.00 |
| ≈ Debt | 3,216.00 |

#### US Search Engine Market Share

Ask 3.20%  AOL 1.70%
Microsoft 13.60%
Yahoo 16.10%

---

*EXAMPLE PROJECT: e-Wallet—Creating Mobile Service for Financial Management (2010)*

Shaping new product and service innovations is a process that requires a good understanding about the company's business and the potential opportunity space in the industry in which it can participate. The e-Wallet project looked at new product innovations for an Internet search engine company in the personal finance industry. e-Wallet was positioned as a product that makes on- and offline purchases quick, easy, and seamless through a mobile device.

Through the use of a Financial Profile, the team gained a good understanding of this company's current business environment including the company's strategic focus, core competencies, business lines, strengths and weaknesses, and industry dynamics, including competition. After constructing a picture of the company's business, the team began to define its opportunity space within the e-commerce, smartphone, and Android markets due to their exponential growth and complementary alignment to search engine business. e-Wallet, targeting customers with a high-paced and frugal lifestyle, was one of the ideas conceived from the opportunity space. In addition to providing quick and easy purchases, it also offered customer rewards programs, personal finance management, and enhanced security providing customers with peace of mind against breaches and identity thefts.

**BENEFITS**
- Facilitates comparison
- Builds credible foundation
- Reveals patterns

**INPUT**
- Sources of financial data for your organization, other organizations, and industry

**OUTPUT**
- Financial profiles of companies and industries
- Insights about the financial conditions of companies and industries

**WHEN TO USE**

## WHAT IT DOES

This is a method to map out financial attributes of an organization to create its profile. Understanding the full financial profile of an organization and comparing it with others in the industry often reveals new opportunities. The common financial measures used for profiling are market capital, revenue, profit/loss, market share, stock performance, equity, debt, and R&D spending. Financial information about organizations, industries, and even economies are combined into unifying maps for gaining broad insights.

## HOW IT WORKS

### STEP 1: Identify relevant financial information and find sources.

Identify the most pertinent type of financial information for understanding your organization and other organizations in the industry that you want to compare. For example, if the scope of your project is broad and you are looking for meta-level insights, then it is appropriate to look for broad economic indicators. Assess whether or not the financial information you are seeking is readily available. If looking at industries dominated by privately held companies, financial statements may not be easily available, and you may need to use available market data to estimate a profile.

### STEP 2: Search for financial information.

Conduct searches on sources like annual reports, government reports, trade journals, company websites, and other publicly available databases. Some of the key data to search for are market capital, rev-

enue, profit/loss, market share, stock performance, equity, debt, and R&D spending.

### STEP 3: Organize profiles for comparisons.

Create an overview table or diagram in which you can enter the financial data you have found for your company, other companies, and the industry overall. Lay them out for easy comparisons; compare with other company profiles, compare with the industry profile, and compare with broader financial indicators like the Dow Jones Industrial Average, S&P 500, and the like. Create sharable repositories with this information.

### STEP 4: Look for insights.

Discuss the profiles as a team and look for insights. What are the financial growth patterns of your company in relation to competition? What is your organization's financial impact on the industry, compared to other players? Show your insights on the profile diagram.

**2.6 FINANCIAL PROFILE**

# 2.7 Analogous Models

Looking at similar models in the world for inspiration, abstraction, and guidance.

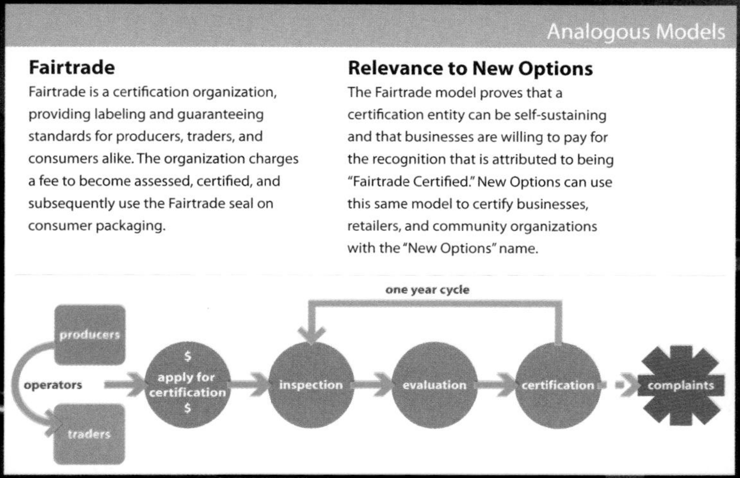

Analogous Models
Fairtrade
Fairtrade is a certification organization, providing labeling and guaranteeing standards for producers, traders, and consumers alike. The organization charges a fee to become assessed, certified, and subsequently use the Fairtrade seal on consumer packaging.
Relevance to New Options
The Fairtrade model proves that a certification entity can be self-sustaining and that businesses are willing to pay for the recognition that is attributed to being "Fairtrade Certified." New Options can use this same model to certify businesses, retailers, and community organizations with the "New Options" name.
one year cycle
producers
operators
traders
$ apply for certification $
inspection
evaluation
certification
complaints

*EXAMPLE PROJECT: **New Options for Out-of-School Youths (2008)***

A significant problem affecting today's youth is the high school dropout epidemic. It is estimated that in the United States as many as 4 million youth aged 16 to 24 do not possess a high school diploma and are not actively taking steps to achieve one. The IIT Institute of Design worked with one of the world's largest private foundations on a project that specifically focused on connecting out-of-school youths with sustainable and satisfying careers. The proposed solution was a system that brought together out-of-school youths, businesses, the community, and individual volunteers with the underlying goal to provide these youths with new options to develop their skills and find promising careers.

To better understand the problem space, the project team researched ***Analogous Models*** across different aspects of the project, including certification/accreditation—how New Options could provide credibility to these youths; alternative value systems—how to mitigate the risk for businesses who hire out-of-school-youth; and group dynamics—how these youths can develop professional and social networks. These Analogous Models inspired many of the solutions, including the *Entry Level Partnership* that provided youths entry-level jobs that served as the starting point to a career path; the *Interaction Space*, which offered potential employers a safe and welcoming place to interact with these youths; and the *Alternative Value Network*, which offered alternatives to monetary currency such as loyalty programs and points.

**BENEFITS**
- Reveals opportunities
- Helps understand best practices
- Facilitates comparison
- Challenges assumptions

**INPUT**
- Aspects of your project to compare to Analogous Models

**OUTPUT**
- Set of Analogous Models and descriptions of how they are relevant to the project's topic
- New ways to think about opportunities for the project

**WHEN TO USE**

## WHAT IT DOES

Sometimes breaking out of the current project space to see how similar contexts operate elsewhere can spark new insights. Analogous Models are behaviors, structures, or processes present in other domains that bear some similarity to the context being examined. The method is also effective for studying what makes for success or failure and understanding how they might be embraced or avoided. For applying the method, we first identify key aspects of our project that are then modeled as abstractions of behaviors, structures, and processes. These abstract models are then used to seek similar models working in adjacent or even remotely related industries. We then look for inspiration by studying and comparing these Analogous Models and even using them to guide our thinking about our own context.

## HOW IT WORKS

### STEP 1: Identify project aspects for analogous thinking.

Identify important aspects of your project that can benefit from analogous thinking. For example, if doing a project on "brand loyalty," the idea of "affiliation" will be important and it may be selected for finding analogous contexts in which the idea of affiliation is successfully applied.

### STEP 2: Find Analogous Models.

Analogous Models can be related to organizations, products, services, or even individuals. Look at varied types of Analogous Models. For example, if trying to understand "affiliation," look at formal organizations like professional societies, less formal groups like alumni associations, or loosely affiliated social groups like skateboarders.

### STEP 3: Create descriptions and diagrams of the Analogous Models.

Write a brief description of how these Analogous Models can be relevant to your project. Create diagrams showing how the selected Analogous Models work. Include participants, relationships, and processes in these diagrams.

### STEP 4: Compare the Analogous Models for insights.

Discuss these diagrams as a team and compare them to learn about how successfully they work. Compare your project context with these analogous models and discuss what implications they have on your own project. Build on these thoughts as a way to guide your search for opportunities.

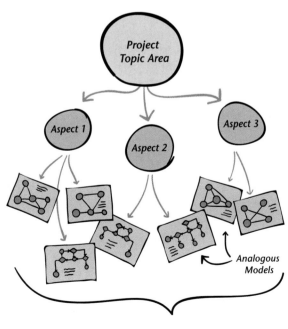

*Compare and analyze models*

2.7 ANALOGOUS MODELS

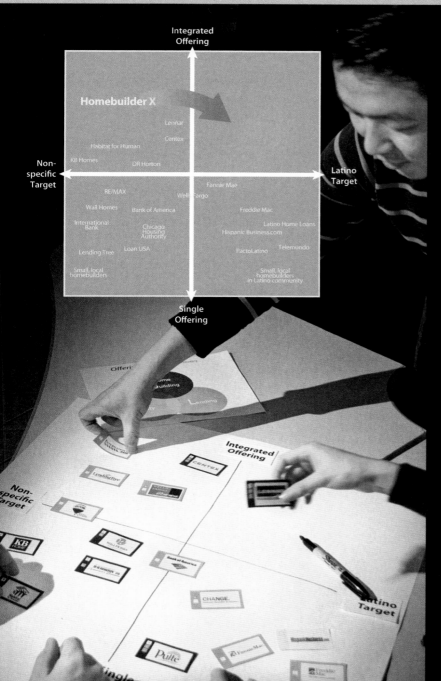

Integrated Offering

Homebuilder X

Lennar

Centex

Habitat for Human

KB Homes

DR Horton

Non-specific Target

Latino Target

RE/MAX

Wells Fargo

Fannie Mae

Wall Homes

Bank of America

Freddie Mac

International Bank

Chicago Housing Authority

Latino Home Loans

Hispanic Business.com

Lending Tree

Loan USA

PactoLatino

Telemundo

Small, local homebuilders

Small, local homebuilders in Latino community

Single Offering

**EXAMPLE PROJECT:**
*Homebuilder—Addressing the Needs of Underserved Markets (2006)*

The leadership position of one of the nation's largest homebuilders was threatened due to a bad economic climate causing its strongest competitors to follow close behind. The IIT Institute of Design team found that the company had great opportunities to innovate in the Latino market, as it would give the company first-mover advantage in an underserved, rapidly growing market of 40 million people.

Developing a new strategy meant first surveying the company's core competencies and its competitors. Using the *Competitors-Complementors Map* method, the team formed a good initial understanding by mapping the competition on a 2 X 2 position map with two defined scales: companies with single versus integrated offerings and companies that have a Latino customer target versus a nonspecific customer target. The quadrants of the 2 X 2 map revealed that competitors had similar attributes and there existed a significant gap in which there were no current integrated offerings tailored to Latinos. Identifying this gap provided an opportunity to uniquely position the company to respond to the needs of the underserved and growing Latino market. What resulted were two strategic plans: Strategy Verde and Strategy Rojo. Strategy Verde is based on a possible low Latino population growth in the future and Strategy Rojo on a possible accelerated growth. Both plans offered a four-step approach including financial advisement, community empowerment, culturally relevant communications, and a longer-term offering as the family grows.

**BENEFITS**

- Visualizes information
- Facilitates comparison
- Reveals opportunities
- Reveals relationships

**INPUT**

- List of competitors and complementors

**OUTPUT**

- Visualization of the competitor-complementor landscape
- Opportunity areas for further exploration

**WHEN TO USE**

## WHAT IT DOES

A top view of an industry map can effectively show how the various organizations in that industry compete or complement one another. This method maps an organization and its competitors to key business dimensions such as price, quality, revenue, market share, or type of audience. The resulting map picture shows how each company's performance stands relative to others. A broader view of the map allows for the inclusion of complementors as well—companies that benefit the organization, giving them strategic advantage over the competition.

A Competitor-Complementor Map can take a number of forms—a 2 × 2 map, scatterplot, or a network. These kinds of visualizations translate numeric data into graphic forms that can be understood at a glance without the need for time-consuming analyses.

## HOW IT WORKS

### STEP 1: Identify competitors and complementors in the industry.

Competitors are organizations that go after the same customers as your organization. Complementors are organizations that support each other in the same industry but may compete in another, or they can be organizations in a complementary industry. For example, the tire industry is complementary to the automobile industry in the sense that sales in the latter have a direct impact on what happens in the former.

### STEP 2: Establish dimensions for comparison.

These can be market share, profitability, types of customers, or any other dimensions you are interested in for comparisons. Make sure dimensions are broad enough so that they can be applied to all organizations you have identified in the earlier step.

### STEP 3: Map the competitors and complementors.

Use the dimensions to create visualization; a 2 × 2 map is most commonly used. Plot all the competitors and complementors in this map by placing them according to their position on the dimensions and according to their relative positions.

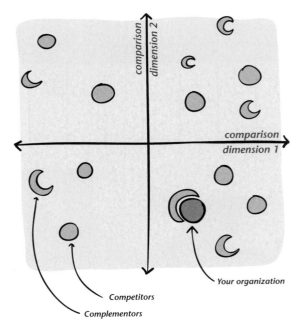

### STEP 4: Review the map, reflect, and look for insights.

Discuss the map as a team. What are the relationships between competitors? How does the existing configuration define or characterize what is happening? Does the map point to potential opportunities that have not been explored? What sorts of changes happening in the technology, the economy, or other sectors might impact the current map? Document these insights on the map.

**2.8 COMPETITORS-COMPLEMENTORS MAP**

Mapping the innovation portfolios of organizations and industries

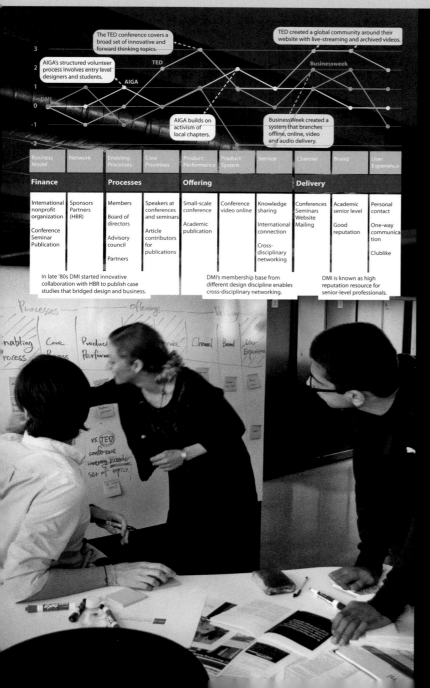

The TED conference covers a broad set of innovative and forward thinking topics.

TED created a global community around their website with live-streaming and archived videos.

AIGA's structured volunteer process involves entry level designers and students.

TED

Businessweek

AIGA

DMI

AIGA builds on activism of local chapters.

BusinessWeek created a system that branches offline, online, video and audio delivery.

| Business Model | Network | Enabling Processes | Core Processes | Product Performance | Product System | Service | Channel | Brand | User Experience |
|---|---|---|---|---|---|---|---|---|---|
| **Finance** | | **Processes** | | **Offering** | | | **Delivery** | | |
| International nonprofit organization | Sponsors Partners (HBR) | Members | Speakers at conferences and seminars | Small-scale conference | Conference video online | Knowledge sharing | Conferences Seminars Website Mailing | Academic senior level | Personal contact |
| Conference Seminar Publication | | Board of directors | Article contributors for publications | Academic publication | | International connection | | Good reputation | One-way communication |
| | | Advisory council | | | | Cross-disciplinary networking | | | Clublike |
| | | Partners | | | | | | | |

In late '80s DMI started innovative collaboration with HBR to publish case studies that bridged design and business.

DMI's membership base from different design discipline enables cross-disciplinary networking.

DMI is known as high reputation resource for senior-level professionals.

**EXAMPLE PROJECT:** *Long-Term Strategy for a Professional Organization (2008)*

Design Management Institute (DMI), a nonprofit organization founded in 1975, credited for being the first professional organization to address design as an essential part of business strategy, later found itself in a saturated industry with several similar services being offered. In light of this change, coupled with increased competition, the project objective was to assess how the organization could build on its current strengths to become a more relevant and innovative service to the design community.

The IIT Institute of Design project team reviewed the organization's core innovations using Doblin's *Ten Types of Innovation* method to diagnose which ones had the most impact for the organization. The team found that the most outstanding innovative initiatives were the organization's partnership with HBR (*Harvard Business Review*), cross-disciplinary design reach, and strong brand as an expert in design leadership for senior professionals. The team also mapped out its innovations relative to those of its competitors and ranked them on a high-low scale. They found that the organization ranked considerably lower in both their offerings and service delivery systems compared to TED (Technology, Entertainment, Design) a company that has created a global online community via live streaming and videos, and AIGA (American Institute of Graphic Arts) an organization that has organized local chapters. The analysis also highlighted key challenges to be addressed such as the organization's reliance on a U.S.-centric and one-size-fits-all approach, not quickly adapting to the changes and trends in the marketplace, and having a limited target audience on senior management.

**BENEFITS**

- Helps understand best practices
- Helps understand context
- Reveals opportunities
- Broadens mindset

**INPUT**

- List of relevant innovations from your organization and industry

**OUTPUT**

- Understanding of different types of innovation in your organization in comparison with others
- Innovation opportunities for further exploration

**WHEN TO USE**

## WHAT IT DOES

This is a diagnostic method that uses Doblin's Ten Types of Innovation framework for understanding the organization's innovations and identifying new opportunities. The ten types include business model and networking innovations in finance; enabling and core processes in process; product performance, product systems, and service in offering; and channel, brand, and customer experience in delivery. The Ten Types of Innovation framework provides a structure for assessing the innovations the organization has developed in each type. As descriptions of innovations get put into the framework, what emerges is an innovation profile that is useful for identifying the strongest innovations as well as points of weakness. The method also helps compare the organization's innovations with those of other organizations.

## HOW IT WORKS

### STEP 1: Identify organizations to study and find experts.

Make a list of organizations whose innovations you want to compare with yours. Find experts from within and outside your organization who can assess different types of innovations.

### STEP 2: Understand innovations by organizations.

Study innovations by your organization as well as others' in the following types: business model, networking, core processes, enabling processes, product performance, product system, service, channel, brand, and customer experience.

### STEP 3: Assess the quantity and quality of innovations.

Consult with the experts and score the identified innovations based on a low and high scale, considering quantitative (revenue generated or growth in market share) and qualitative (attention given in media/publications or recognition) success measures.

### STEP 4: Compare and look for insights.

Discuss the map and its patterns and extract insights. What are the big differences between your organization's profile and others plotted? What can be done to the low points on the map? What opportunities exist for raising certain types of innovations in your organization? Document your insights on the map.

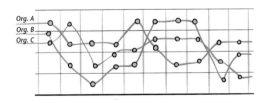

Conduct multidimensional assessments of an industry's innovations

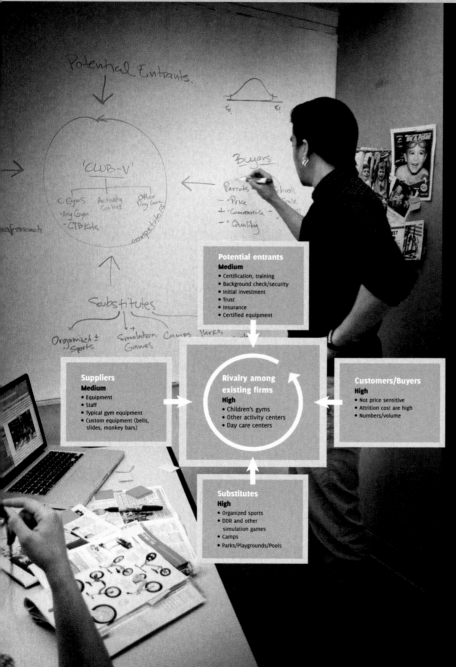

Potential Entrants.

'CLUB-V'

C Gyms    Activity    Other
- My Gym   Centred    Day Care
- CTB Kids

Buyers
Parents        Schools
- Price
+ Convenience
- Quality

Substitutes

Organized +    Simulation  Camps  Parks
Sports         Games

**Potential entrants**
**Medium**
- Certification, training
- Background check/security
- Initial investment
- Trust
- Insurance
- Certified equipment

**Suppliers**
**Medium**
- Equipment
- Staff
- Typical gym equipment
- Custom equipment (bells, slides, monkey bars)

**Rivalry among existing firms**
**High**
- Children's gyms
- Other activity centers
- Day care centers

**Customers/Buyers**
**High**
- Not price sensitive
- Attrition cost are high
- Numbers/volume

**Substitutes**
**High**
- Organized sports
- DDR and other simulation games
- Camps
- Parks/Playgrounds/Pools

*EXAMPLE PROJECT: Club V: A Strategic Venture (2006)*

Club V is a strategic venture for a leading branded venture capital organization that combines entertainment, learning, and exercise into a unique experience for kids. The IIT Institute of Design team working on this strategic design project did background research to understand the opportunity space for the organization entering the U.S. market with a focus on activity centers for children. A key issue driving the opportunity space was the need for engaging, convenient, and high-quality childcare for modern professional parents due to the growing number of both parents in the workforce.

To assess its viability into the children fitness industry, the team performed *Industry Diagnostics* using Michael Porter's Five Forces framework. The analysis showed the relative degree of threats coming from potential market entrants and the bargaining power from suppliers to be low to medium. In contrast, the threat of substitutes and rivalry among competitors were fairly high. Examining the strengths and weaknesses of substitutes for childcare such as organized sports, camps, and public park facilities helped them to identify solutions for children's gyms as an area of unmet needs and in which competition was low. Solution concepts incorporated design principles for brand differentiation by creating a "cool" culture around diverse programs; promotion of a healthy lifestyle, technology, and connectivity to facilitate multitasking; enriching environment staffed with mentors; and convenience in accessing locations.

**BENEFITS**
- Reveals opportunities
- Captures current conditions
- Identifies challenges

**INPUT**
- Industry information from contextual research

**OUTPUT**
- Understanding of the forces at play in an industry

**WHEN TO USE**

## WHAT IT DOES

Industry Diagnostics employs frameworks to identify key aspects of an industry and clarify its current state of health. One framework that is particularly effective for understanding the competitive intensity of an industry is Michael Porter's Five Forces. The Five Forces include: the threat of potential entrants to the market, the threat of substitute products or services, the bargaining power of customers/buyers, the bargaining power of suppliers, and the intensity of rivalry among competitors. An extension of Porter's framework, called Six Forces, added the concept of "complementors," who strategically align with the organization. This method is helpful in seeing early opportunities for the organization's innovations and strategic positioning in the industry.

## HOW IT WORKS

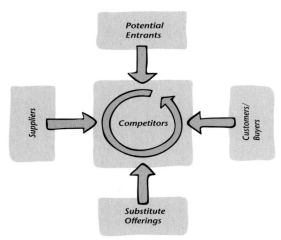

### STEP 1: Gather information about the industry.

Prepare to assess the impact of all the Five Forces in your industry: potential entrants, substitutes, buyers, suppliers, and competitors. Review information that you may have already gathered that relate to any of these Five Forces and be prepared to do additional research if needed.

### STEP 2: Assess the impact of the Five Forces on the industry.

1. *Potential entrants:* Using industry information, ask who might be new entrants to the market. How high are the barriers to their entry? How vulnerable is the industry to threats from these new entrants?

2. *Substitute offerings:* Ask how readily customers may switch to alternative or substitute offerings. How vulnerable is the industry to the threats from such substitute offerings?

3. *Customers/buyers:* Ask how much control customers have in dictating the kinds of products and services available in the industry. How much influence do customers have in pricing or other attributes of the offering?

4. *Suppliers:* Ask how suppliers exert their demands. How reliant is the industry on the suppliers? How much control do suppliers have in determining the kinds of products and services the industry produces?

5. *Competitors:* Understand the nature of rivalry among competitors. Is it technology driven, price driven, or service driven? Is the rivalry consistent across competitors or variable?

### STEP 3: Identify the organization's response mechanisms.

Mechanisms are organization's activities that can respond to these Five Forces. Examples include policies, procedures, plans, budgets, controls, and protocols. What mechanisms are in place to monitor changes and make corrections as required?

### STEP 4: Discuss the findings and look for insights.

Put together all the findings from previous steps in a presentational form. Discuss this as a team. What are the opportunities for your organization to play a new role in the industry?

**2.10 INDUSTRY DIAGNOSTICS**

# 2.11 SWOT Analysis

Evaluate an organization's strengths, weaknesses, opportunities, and threats

### Strength

- Diversified parent company
- Strong localism
- Biggest brand newspaper in the Midwest
- Chicagoland market dominance in circulation, distribution, local reporting presence, community connections
- Wide range of media channels in portfolio
- Owns three of the largest circulating papers in the US
- Still represents an authoritative news institution
- Publishes a Spanish language daily

### Weakness

- Lack international and national clout like the *New York Times*
- As *The Tribune* tries to offer more news, people become oversaturated, and information becomes less relevant
- Focus on personal relevant
- Customer-created content
- Overburdened staff whose journalistic role has taken on many more responsibilities
- Low-website traffic
- Fail to understand how people use website

### Opportunity

- Has only about 1/3 the circulation size as *USA Today*
- Can become the authoritative voice on Chicago
- Empowering readers through digital media and mobile accessibility
- Diversification of advertising channels
- Tailored newspaper or new delivery channel for specific users
- Hyper-local newspaper
- Embrace citizen journalists
- Change biz model for customized news and delivery

### Threat

- Burdened down by the capital of its printing business
- Heavily invested in a nondynamic, labor-intensive, and shrinking newsprint industry
- Struggling to understand the online medium
- Lots of other smaller online competition
- More advertising money is still spent in the print arena, growth is flat, and advertisers are shifting into the online arena as the cost of entry is very low
- The authority of newspaper institutions is being challenged by citizen journalists in the online world

## EXAMPLE PROJECT: *The Future of News Media (2007)*

The changing landscape of print news media has galvanized news organizations such as a large Midwest media conglomerate into thinking about how to move forward in an environment where new technology and reader behavior are changing the way news fits into people's lives. A team from the IIT Institute of Design saw an opportunity for this organization by delving deep into its readers' behaviors and translating those insights into actionable strategic plans and solutions.

One of the tools the team used was **SWOT** (strengths, weaknesses, opportunities, and threats) to define the organization's position within a highly competitive industry. A clear strength for the organization was its dominance in the Midwest region and its diversified parent company with multiple media channels. These strengths pointed to opportunities in building on these diversified channels and becoming an authoritative "local" voice through digital media. Weaknesses were driven by the internal organizational changes, dependence on its printing business, low website traffic, and an overall lack of international presence compared to its competitors. Because readers are actively creating and engaging with content online, new competition is growing in the online space, leaving advertisers to abandon print media for online, where cost of entry is low. In understanding these industry forces and through participatory user research, the team designed an innovation strategy comprising four main concepts: (1) *Raw News*, which offers news content in a raw and customizable format across different media; (2) *Tribazon*, which offers content tagging and recommendation technology; (3) *Gap Map*, which visualizes where gaps in news coverage exist; and (4) *The News Place*, where the organization can welcome and engage the public's support.

**BENEFITS**

- Creates overview
- Provides direction
- Identifies challenges
- Reveals opportunities

**INPUT**

- Formal statement of the project objective and understanding of its context

**OUTPUT**

- Diagram showing the project's strengths, weaknesses, opportunities, and threats

**WHEN TO USE**

## WHAT IT DOES

The SWOT Analysis, a method widely popular for decades, is used to evaluate an organization's strengths, weaknesses, opportunities, and threats. The analysis begins with studying the organization and its innovations and seeks to understand how the organization performs in relation to competitors in the market. A high-level assessment is made of the strengths and weaknesses of the organization, the opportunities available as well as competitive threats. It looks at factors inside and outside the organization to determine whether defined business objectives are achievable or not. Because of its general nature, a SWOT Analysis can be done with relative ease and speed in the early part of knowing the context.

## HOW IT WORKS

### STEP 1: Describe the initial innovation intent.

Define the basic goal that you are considering for your innovation, and clarify the reasons for pursuing that direction. Think of the benefits from doing so.

### STEP 2: Assess the organization's strengths, weaknesses, opportunities, and threats.

*Strengths:* What about your organization gives your innovation an advantage over competitors in your industry? What are the organization's capabilities in technology, operations, people, brand, user experience, and other areas?

*Weaknesses:* What aspects of your current organization will make it difficult for the innovation intent to be realized? Examples may include: financial constraints, unproven technologies, or an unreliable supply chain. How do your weaknesses put you at a disadvantage relative to your competition?

*Opportunities:* What is happening in the marketplace that indicates the likelihood that your innovation intent will succeed? Where are the gaps

in offerings that you can fill? Why aren't they currently being met?

*Threats:* What are the external threats to realize your innovation intent? What elements exist in the current environment that will be barriers? What is the nature of rivalry in the industry?

### STEP 3: Organize findings into a 2 X 2 SWOT diagram.

Summarize findings into brief statements that can be listed in each of the four quadrants, no more than seven or eight statements per quadrant.

### STEP 4: Review, discuss, and analyze the SWOT diagram.

Involve key team members to discuss the findings. What does the unified presentation of the different elements suggest about the opportunity space? Is the innovation intent worth pursuing? Is the level of risk acceptable to you? Do your strengths outweigh your weaknesses? Do the opportunities outweigh the threats? Discuss these questions and summarize them for sharing. Involve key decision makers to determine the directions to pursue for the project.

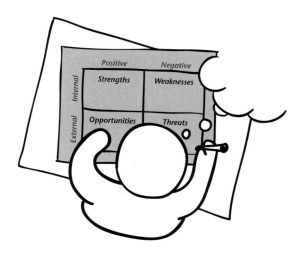

**2.11 SWOT Analysis**

# 2.12 Subject Matter Experts Interview

Speak with subject matter experts to understand the most advanced and potential developments

### EXAMPLE PROJECT:
### Schools in the Digital Age (2007)

The U.S. school system has largely remained unchanged since the Henry Ford model of the Industrial Age. Despite the revolutionary changes of the Digital Age in how we live and work, schools have not responded in the same manner. A new model for learning requires transformational change—one that considers new technological capabilities and socioeconomic context. Through the sponsorship of one of the nation's largest independent foundations, an IIT Institute of Design project team undertook the challenge of identifying how schools can respond to the disruptive effects of digital media.

To reframe the issues faced by an ailing school system, the team conducted *Subject Matter Expert Interviews* and reviewed literature in the areas of organizational transformation, disruptive technology, and education. Interviewees were professional executives, lecturers, and pioneers in their fields. The result was a long list of insights relating to four broad categories of problems: schools' failure to respond to change in social and economic contexts, change in the culture and experience of schools' audience, change in the knowledge and learning environment, and the growth of schools' bureaucratic structures. Workshops were conducted with some of the expert interviewees to generate a list of research ideas that were then developed into concepts. Many of the new concepts focused on more flexible areas of social networks and digital technology as the experts suggested. The concepts also related to capital expenditure and other longer-term elements of schools, including the physical facility and computer networks.

**BENEFITS**
- Defines direction
- Captures the latest
- Brings in new perspectives

**INPUT**
- Subject areas relevant to the project
- Pool of experts in subject areas

**OUTPUT**
- Understanding of essential information, latest developments, and varying opinions in a subject area

**WHEN TO USE**

## WHAT IT DOES

The Subject Matter Experts Interview is a method for getting up to speed quickly on your area of interest. Speaking with experts in a given field accelerates general understanding about it, offers information about the most advanced developments, and provides guidance for where to look for additional information. Using frameworks as a reference is useful for getting the most out of conversations with experts, for example, a framework organized around time—the past (how did we get here?), present (what is happening today?), and future (where are things going?). It is beneficial to understand the topic from the expert's specific point of view. The interview works as a guided conversation during which a combination of essential information, facts, expert opinions, and interesting insights are gathered and shared.

## HOW IT WORKS

### Step 1: Define the subject to be covered.

The type of information you seek will guide how to find the appropriate experts. If the subject area is broad like economics, define the appropriate branch you want to understand: micro, macro, behavioral, and so forth.

### Step 2: Identify experts.

Through a combination of Internet searches, conversations with colleagues, literature searches, or other means pull together lists of people who are recognized as experts in the given subject. Survey people working in related fields for their recommendations of the subject matter experts. Look to conduct interviews with more than one expert in each area. Compare several experts' views on a given subject to get a full picture of the context. Highlight points of alignments and differences that may merit further exploration.

### Step 3: Come prepared.

Read articles or books written by experts to familiarize yourself with their points of view. Prepare questions you hope to have answered during the course of the interview.

### Step 4: Conduct the interview.

Interviews are about making the most of someone's limited time and building a resource network that you can hopefully tap into in the future. Use prepared questions to guide the conversation. The conversation should focus on essential information, facts, or the expert's opinions as needed.

### Step 5: Listen, capture, and follow up.

Interviewing requires active listening. If allowed, use a recording device to capture the conversation. As the conversation unfolds, take copious notes and keep track of clarifying questions you may want to ask later.

### Step 6: Transcribe and summarize.

Have the recorded conversation transcribed so that key phrases or interesting insights can be extracted, written as summary documents to be shared with the team.

2.12 SUBJECT MATTER EXPERTS INTERVIEW

# 2.13 Interest Groups Discussion

Immerse with interest groups to learn about what is being discussed in a topic

*EXAMPLE PROJECT:*
*Peapod Labs (2010)*

Founded in 2010 by three IIT Institute of Design students who were also former engineers, Peapod Labs is a Chicago-based start-up that makes playful learning apps for children and has quickly become a leader in media literacy for preschoolers. The mission behind Peapod Labs' apps is to create an engaging and collaborative learning process between parents and children. As children share what they learn, parents are able to contribute.

With their target market focused on children and parents, Peapod Labs turned to the opinions, thoughts, and impressions of groups like Mom with Apps as part of their *Interest Groups Discussion* research. Mom with Apps is an online forum of family-friendly developers seeking to promote quality apps for kids and families. It is a forum for learning the approaches of other developers and also obtaining best practices information like subsidiary rights, licensing agreements, and strategies for product launch. It also serves as a place for the team to gain visibility and traction by being able to upload their app to the forum for feedback. Leveraging the information shared on the discussion boards, Peapod Labs is able to build greater agency in their apps and company. Though a young company, Peapod Labs' successes rivals those of larger, more mature companies. They currently have seven apps in the iTunes app store and three main product channels: *ABC Series* for content delivery, *Boxing* for curriculum-based learning, and *Firehouse Adventures* for "edugaming."

**BENEFITS**

- Brings in new perspectives
- Captures the latest
- Facilitates quick and early discovery
- Reveals patterns

**INPUT**

- List of interest groups around topics of interest to your project and ways to access them

**OUTPUT**

- Understanding of latest developments, variety of viewpoints, and trends in a subject area

**WHEN TO USE**

## WHAT IT DOES

Groups often form around shared interests in particular subject matters. Whether the groups are affiliated with a professional organization or come together in an informal structure, their shared interests fuel active dialog about what is happening around a given context. Spending time on online forums or at planned gatherings and engaging in discussions is a way to find out about the latest developments. The key to gaining the most from interest group discussions is to be an active listener of conversations, or if online, an active follower of forums. By following what is being discussed among interest members, we can learn a lot about themes, points of view, news items, forthcoming changes, extreme user behaviors, and other content that can be captured easily and shared with team members.

*Subject matter relevant to project topic*

*capture findings*

## HOW IT WORKS

### STEP 1: Seek out interest group forums.

Conduct online searches, visit professional association websites, and scan social networks for interest groups organized around the subject of interest to you. Find out when and where groups get together, how forums are organized, and what forthcoming topics will be addressed.

### STEP 2: Find out what is being discussed in interest forums.

Scan interest forum directories for the topics being discussed. This will give you a high-level view of what matters to people organized around the subject matter.

### STEP 3: Dive in.

If you are entering an online forum, read recent postings to get a sense of what people are discussing. Read further back to understand how the conversation has changed over time. Participate and post questions and comments.

### STEP 4: Capture your findings.

Write brief statements that capture what is discussed in these forums. Record what you see as the various points of view on the topic, the latest developments being discussed, trends mentioned, extreme contexts and behaviors that emerge, and similar types of information that is valuable to you. Collect these findings in a form that can be shared with others.

### STEP 5: Review and summarize.

Review your findings to look for larger themes or patterns that may be emerging. Try to identify what is driving these themes. This may suggest opportunities for additional research. Summarize.

### STEP 6: Share and discuss.

Share your summary with stakeholders and/or subject matter experts to get their opinions of the findings.

**2.13 INTEREST GROUPS DISCUSSION**

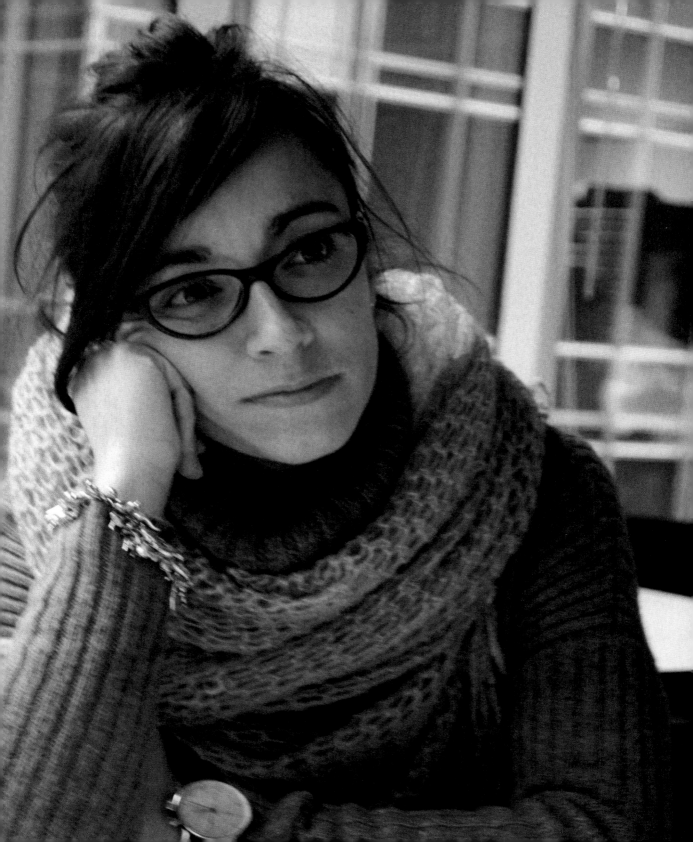

# mode 3
# KNOW PEOPLE

The concept of "user-centered" or "human-centered" design is not exactly new. In fact, most definitions of design include some reference to crafting things that people use. However, as an antidote to the one-size-fits-all, mass production age of 19th and 20th century design, it has become important to re-emphasize the centrality of users to the process. Design that is sensitive to and based on people's needs and patterns of behavior will be good design. As such, the mode of Know People, with its focus on empathy, observation, personal engagement, and problem solving, is an indispensable phase of the design process.

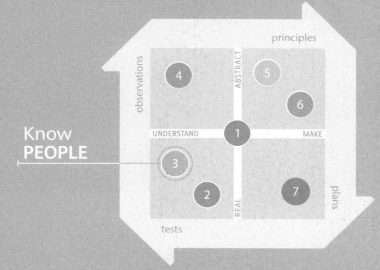

Know PEOPLE

# KNOW PEOPLE *mindsets*

Knowing people is about gaining an empathic understanding of people's thoughts, feelings, and needs by listening, observing, interacting, and analyzing. Immersing yourself in people's daily lives and keenly listening to their stories can reveal very valuable insights, sometimes quite surprising and nonobvious. To get to such valuable insights we should focus on everything that people do, say, and think; we should be in the mindset to deeply understand people's activities, needs, motivations, and overall experiences, just as well as we study our products when we do a product development project. We should be on the lookout for understanding the problems they face, the workarounds they do, challenges they overcome, and the needs they express and those they do not express. Knowing people well can lead us to entirely new categories of products, services, or business strategies that fundamentally address people's needs and desires, create significant new value, and are very hard to copy.

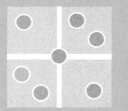

**Mindsets**
- Observing Everything
- Building Empathy
- Immersing in Daily Life
- Listening Openly
- Looking for Problems and Needs

## Mindset: Observing Everything

Observe everything in the context of study, not just the people or the products in use. Notice places, notice other people, notice inconsistencies between what people say and what they do. Be prepared to consider innovations that address these seemingly external factors. Even more importantly, look at who and what is not in the field of study. Who and where are the nonusers or nonparticipants, and why are they missing? Good innovators notice not only what's there, but what's not there.

Photo by Shin Sano.

*A study of the automobile market in India unexpectedly revealed that, unlike Americans, only 10 percent of Indians eat or drink in the car. On the other hand, 80 percent display religious symbols near the dashboard, and in India, cars are a common wedding present. All of these observations were at the periphery of the central study—how do Indians buy cars?—but were invaluable in designing better cars for the market.*

## Mindset: Building Empathy

Is it possible to go beyond just knowing about people's experiences and feelings, to the point of actually sharing them? Spend a day with a busy mom as she struggles to organize the family's day, share and identify with her daily experiences, frustrations, and challenges. If we make a deep, direct emotional connection with end users' needs, we will be in a far better position to develop new ideas in tune with the customer.

*A Jump Associates innovation team gave executives at Mercedes-Benz an assignment: Sit down and have a conversation with a group of young, upwardly mobile drivers for whom they were trying to innovate, and then go out and buy a gift for them. What would be a gift they would value? The best innovations should feel like a gift from a knowing friend, according to Jump.*

## Mindset: Immersing in Daily Life

Spending time with people in their everyday lives can be eye opening. Use the ethnographer's approach to live with and learn about the behaviors, practices, and motivations that form the context in which people will use the tools, artifacts, messages, and services that you intend to create. Spending a day in the life of people for whom you are designing will be revealing. We can learn a lot by shopping along with people to learn about how they make decisions where to go and what to buy, how they plan for it, how they coordinate their other life activities simultaneously, and how they overcome hauling and transportation challenges. Immersing yourself in these contexts will produce immensely valuable insights about people and their needs, even about needs that remain unmet by our current systems. With immersion, be the first in your industry to understand how consumers' patterns of life are changing, and what they will be like in the future, and you could be in for big success.

*Immersive ethnographic research is frequently used by companies like consumer product companies trying to create new products and services. Only by immersing into the daily lives of their new customers can they hope to understand the vastly different behaviors and values. Margaret Mead, an American cultural anthropologist, pioneered the idea of immersive ethnographic research. In a study she conducted among a small group of Samoans, she got to know, live with, observe, and interview 68 young women between the ages of 9 and 20 to frame-up classic revealing insights about behaviors during the passage from childhood to adulthood.*

## Mindset: Listening Openly

We should not just prepare and follow a script for our interaction with research participants. We should let them guide the discussion toward what's important to them; we have to be students, not teachers. Likewise, it is not a good idea to go into the field to prove a hypothesis or test a preexisting idea, and avoid judging people's behaviors or motivations. We ought to think of open-ended questions, suggest general solution alternatives, and be prepared to hear things that will help us reframe our approach to the problem in a way that our competitors can't—because they weren't really listening.

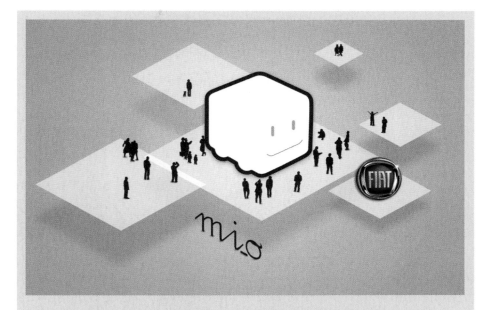

*Fiat Brazil developed the design of their car, Fiat Mio FCC III, by adopting an open source approach through a dedicated website, listening to about 10,000 ideas and suggestions coming from about 17,000 members of the community viewed by 2 million people from 160 countries. This approach, based on large-scale "listening," was a challenge for the company, but they successfully established both physical and virtual collaborative environments among the online community and the company's various departments.*

## Mindset: Looking for Problems and Needs

What's not working well in the current situation and why? How are people facing challenges in their daily lives? How are they working around the problems? Or are they just giving up since there is nothing that can support their needs? These are great questions that we should ask to reveal opportunities for new products or services. But, let us not just ask people what is wrong and expect them to know how to tell us. As Henry Ford is supposed to have said, if he had asked people what they wanted, they would have said, "Faster horses." Can we extend our thinking to not only look for problems but also to sense unstated needs?

*How many people would have intentionally asked for a microblogging service that limited their posts to 140 characters? Probably none, but as of 2011, Twitter had more than 300 million users and counting. The microblogging service satisfied a completely unstated need for a way for friends and strangers to exchange quick, 140-character updates. Despite the lack of a stated need, Twitter is now handling over 1.6 billion search queries per day.*

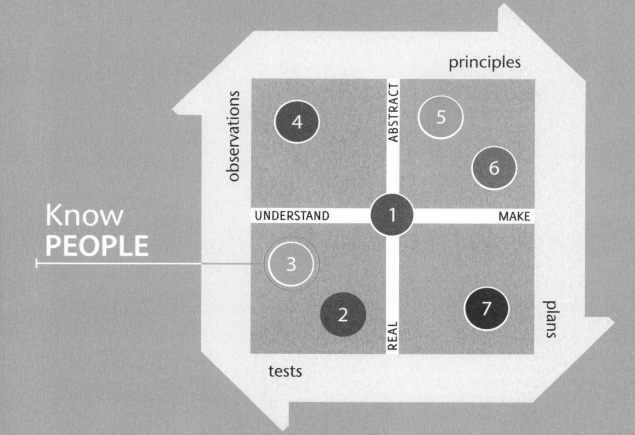

Know
**PEOPLE**

observations

principles

ABSTRACT

UNDERSTAND

MAKE

REAL

tests

plans

94

# KNOW PEOPLE *methods*

Mapping people in relation to the project's topic and selecting candidates for research.

**Free-form** → **Standardized**

**Multiple Locations** (top) / **Single Location** (bottom)

Private Investigator
Photo Journalist
Tourist
Surveyor
Paramedic
Police
Social Worker
Fire Fighter
**Student**
Real Estate Sales
Power Line Repairman
Actor
Parole Officer
Auditor
Independent Courier
Traveling Salesperson
**Lawyer**
Interpretor
Geologist
Accountant
Locksmith
Sheet Metal Worker
Archeologist
Musician/Singer
Construction Manager
Public Relations Agent
Painter/Artist
OTR Truck Driver
Corporate Management
Civil Engineer
**Doctor**
Fisherman
Mail Courier
Aerospace Engineer
Delivery Driver
Guidance Councelor
Carpet Layer
Carpenter
Aircraft Mechanic
Veterinarian
**Nurse**
Flight Attendant
Welder
Drywall Installer
Plumber
Court Reporter
Construction Electrician
Waiter/Waitress
School Principal
Respiratory Therapist
Car Mechanic
Hotel/Building Manager
Funeral Director
Pipe Fitter
Auctioneer
**Landscaper**
Crop Duster
Airline Load Manager
Livestock Worker
Crane Operator
Pilot
Commercial Artist
Teacher
Jeweler
Auto Parts Clerk
Pharmacist
Receptionist
Broadcaster
Travel Agent
Bank Manager
Butcher
Baker
Child Care Worker
Dentist
Librarian
Air Traffic Controller
Preschool Teacher
Factory Worker
Short Order Cook
Hairdresser
Bus Driver
Bank Teller

## EXAMPLE PROJECT:
### Mobile Computing—Doblin (1995)

As part of a research project on mobile computing, the innovation consulting firm Doblin wanted to look at the various opportunities for and requirements of mobile devices across different professions. One of the first steps the team took was to use a *Research Participant Map*.

The Doblin team began by brainstorming a wide range of occupations that interacted with mobile devices, from lawyers to livestock workers. They then plotted these occupations on a map with two attributes deemed important to the project. The first attribute was level of protocol; boundaries between live, learn, work, and play. The second was the uniformity and number of environments each occupation typically encountered. The team then selected at least one occupation from each quadrant to explore further, thus providing a more complete picture of the different needs of workers. Selecting one occupation from every quadrant was important to ensure coverage of a broad set of perspectives and insights. The team then spent several months performing comprehensive ethnographic research (such as interviewing and shadowing) on the individuals in the chosen occupations. By creating a Research Participant Map at the beginning, Doblin quickly narrowed down who would be included in the research (lawyers, doctors, nurses, students, and landscapers) while ensuring coverage across occupations and minimizing redundancy. It served as an invaluable tool to kick-start the team's research.

**BENEFITS**

- Encourages comprehensiveness
- Facilitates comparison
- Facilitates discussion
- Helps select options
- Structures existing knowledge

**INPUT**

- Project's area of study
- List of people as possible participants in the project

**OUTPUT**

- Selection of participants that covers the full range of the project space

**WHEN TO USE**

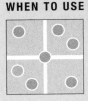

## WHAT IT DOES

Research Participant Maps help us see an overview of all the people involved in the project topic, based on their roles and activities, in order to ensure that the right people are researched for a given project intent. A Research Participant Map begins with a consideration of the kinds of people we want to study and the aspects of their daily lives or activities we want to understand. This will allow us to think of at least two attributes of the project topic that are important for understanding the full range of people involved. A simple 2 × 2 map allows a variety of people to be plotted along these two attributes. The resulting map provides an overview of the kinds of participants to be included in the study and how they differ in relation to one another. This overview can help us make decisions about where the focus of the research efforts should go.

## HOW IT WORKS

### STEP 1: Identify target participants.

Brainstorm a broad, unstructured list of the types of people who could be selected as participants in a research study to gain knowledge of a well-defined topic for innovation (developed during Sense Intent).

### STEP 2: Create a map that defines the project topic.

Identify one or more attributes, based on the innovation intent, that are important to the project—these will get converted into defining scales for a 2 × 2 map. Create the map that defines the participant space of your research.

### STEP 3: Plot participants on the 2 × 2 map.

As a group, populate the map with the list of people from Step 1. One good way to begin is by identifying

which people fall in the extremes of the map: Who is at each corner? Other people can then be plotted relative to these "anchors."

### STEP 4: Analyze the plotted map.

Identify the people on the map who come closest to your ideal range of participants. Assess the ease with which you can access them and engage them in your study. Frequently, at least one representative participant is selected from each of the quadrants of the map to ensure coverage based on the project topic.

### STEP 5: Share your findings and discuss.

Write a brief summary that can be shared with the team to explain why you have chosen specific participants over others and how their selection will contribute to the project.

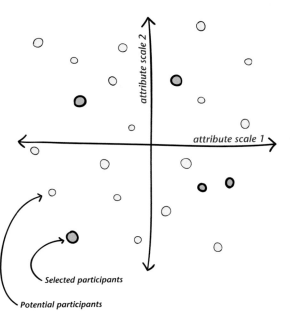

Selected participants

Potential participants

Conducting preliminary surveys to select candidates and identify areas for further research

## EXAMPLE PROJECT:
### Gen Y and the Future of Retail (2007)

The future of shopping is a topic of interest for many corporations. In 2007, a design team worked with a large retail discount chain to explore the relationship between Generation Y and the future of retail. The team sought to answer the questions: How will Generation Y relate to the company over time? What does the company need to do to stay relevant?

Based on these overarching questions, the team developed and distributed an initial *Research Planning Survey* composed of 32 closed and open-ended questions. Sent to more than 50 Generation Y participants using Survey Monkey, the survey provided information on shoppers' demographics and shopping preferences, behaviors, and trends. The participants were asked to provide specific information on aspects such as their age, location, shopping preferences, and average expenditures. After analyzing the responses, the team identified one core user group and two extreme user groups. These three user groups represented the right mix of participants that the team could focus on for further, deeper research. The Research Planning Survey served as a valuable method, allowing the team to choose 12 primary research participants based on their responses to the survey and their fit into one of the three user groups.

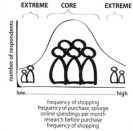

frequency of shopping
frequency of purchase, splurge
online spendings per month
research before purchase
frequency of shopping

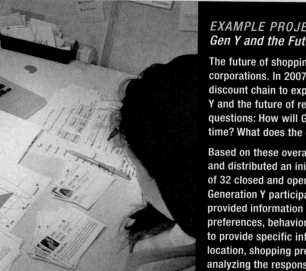

**BENEFITS**

- Facilitates quick and early discovery
- Provides evidence
- Reveals patterns
- Supports decision making

**INPUT**

- Project's topic area and the innovation intent

**OUTPUT**

- Understanding of participants' behaviors and interesting patterns to guide further research
- Identified participants that can be contacted for further research

**WHEN TO USE**

## WHAT IT DOES

Unlike traditional market research surveys, Research Planning Surveys are short, quick, loosely constructed questionnaires used at the early phase of a research project to understand peoples' activities, behaviors, and attitudes about a particular topic of interest. They provide quick overviews of a topic, identify interesting trend patterns, and help the team decide where to focus their detailed research. Simultaneously, Research Planning Surveys can be used to screen and select the participants for later ethnographic research. The initial results from the survey may also prompt a modification of research plans, if the results differed greatly from what was expected.

## HOW IT WORKS

### STEP 1: Develop survey questions.

Based on the innovation intent, develop questions that probe for broad patterns of behavior, values, or needs. For example, if the intent is to innovate in the area of retail, ask questions like: "What resources do you use when shopping?" or "Do you shop more in stores or online?"

### STEP 2: Create survey.

These days, it is very quick and easy to set up online surveys using tools like Google Docs or SurveyMonkey.

com. However, in particularly complex projects, a market research firm may be used.

### STEP 3: Distribute survey.

Identify a group of people, either through the team's personal contacts or via a market research firm. Send them the survey through channels like e-mail, bulletin board, or Web postings. Be sure to set a closing date for the survey.

### STEP 4: Identify patterns.

Analyze the results to see common patterns of behavior, or, just as important, extremes of behavior, or "fringe" behavior. For example, notice that most people use a wide variety of different resources and decision-making tools when shopping, or that a minority of people are beginning to use mobile phones to do online price comparisons while in a physical store.

### STEP 5: Select candidates and plan additional research.

Plan what deeper research to conduct on people representative of the interesting patterns identified by the survey. Determine a good mixture of representatives from the patterns for further research such as majority core users, some extreme users, and some nonusers.

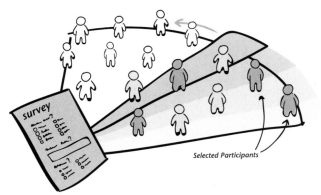

*Selected Participants*

**3.2 RESEARCH PLANNING SURVEY**

# 3.3 User Research Plan

Detailing the type of people to be researched, and when and how the research will be conducted

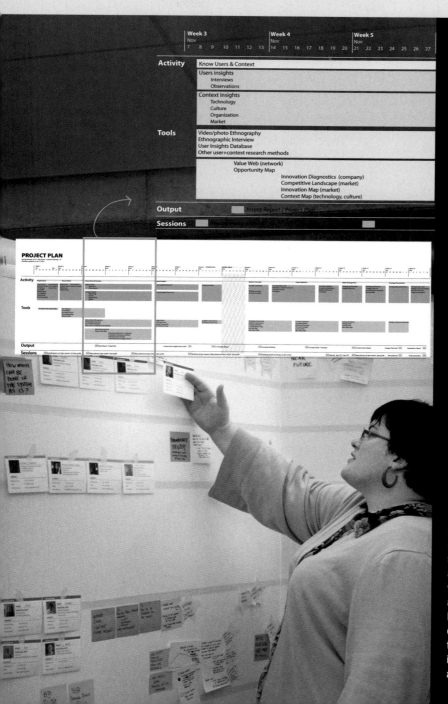

**EXAMPLE PROJECT:**
*Residential and Commercial Renovations (2010)*

A design team working together with innovators from a 3D design, engineering, and entertainment software company, developed a user-centered framework for Customer Engagement Experiences for the discovery, selection, and recommendation of products and services during residential and commercial renovation projects. This framework was the result of a variety of design methods, but most importantly the product of an early-stage, carefully crafted *User Research Plan*.

The User Research Plan outlined the three types of users that would be studied: professional designers like architects, consumers, and manufacturers. Three subteams did the research on these three user types simultaneously because of tight time and resource constraints. The research schedule (part of the User Research Plan) detailed the types and number of people to be studied, the team's activities, tools to be used, output produced, and collaboration sessions as parallel bands of information in conjunction with a timeline. The activities included both observations and interviews for generating user insights as well as doing trend research for context insights. The tools to be used like video/photo ethnography and ethnographic interview were described in parallel. The output produced at various stages of the process, like reports, as well as collaborative sessions with the client, were also planned in parallel with other activities. As a benefit of the User Research Plan, the team was not only able to stay organized and on task, but was also able to generate insights and concept directions in a short amount of time with limited, available resources.

**BENEFITS**
- Defines direction
- Manages resources
- Promotes shared understanding
- Supports transition

**INPUT**
- Project topic and innovation intent
- Time and resource limitations

**OUTPUT**
- Detailed plan defining schedule, methods, and participants for research

**WHEN TO USE**

## WHAT IT DOES

A User Research Plan is a method for organizing the research portion of a project. The method is a disciplined approach to define all aspects of the work to be done. It sets forth the stated goals of the research including, types of people to be studied, the desired number of participants required, what is hoped to be learned, a protocol for interacting with participants, a statement about methods used to collect user information, the possible output at various stages, work sessions, a timeline, and a budget.

## HOW IT WORKS

### STEP 1: Choose the types of people to study.

Depending on the nature of your project, focus the study on different types of users, such as core users, extreme users, experts, nonusers, or some other type. Besides the majority of core users to study, make sure that you include extreme users and nonusers since they can provide unconventional and nonobvious insights.

### STEP 2: Choose participants based on screening criteria.

State the criteria you will use to select research participants. What are the attributes that you will be looking for in the types of participants? What kind of participants can provide the most valuable information you seek?

### STEP 3: Decide on research methods.

Based on the time and resources available, choose the research methods most well suited to your goal. For example, Video Ethnography yields large amounts of rich data but is time- and resource-intensive; quick Field Visits with a notebook can be done much more quickly and cheaply, though with a corresponding reduction in the richness of data. Which methods to

use depend not only on budget and time, but also on the people being observed, their context, availability, desire for privacy, and other factors. Describe protocols for interacting with participants.

### STEP 4: Create a budget.

Based on the plan, determine how much it will cost to conduct the various activities. Develop a budget to be shared with your client or within your organization that can be used to justify anticipated spending.

### STEP 5: Create a timeline and show activities.

Gantt charts, spreadsheets, or other common project-planning tools can be used to show the activities and estimate the amount of time required to complete tasks and to order them in a sequence that meets your stated goals.

### STEP 6: Share the plan and discuss further actions.

Share the research plan with your team and other relevant stakeholders, such as clients or research contractors, to discuss the next steps of starting the research process.

Select participants — Select methods — Allocate time and resources

**3.3 USER RESEARCH PLAN**

# 3.4 Five Human Factors

Studying physical, cognitive, social, cultural, and emotional factors that drive overall user experience

*items remaining on the shelf.*

*lots of magnets! front or refrigerator not magnetic?*

een Party Disc D / Party Date: Sept. 30, 2005 / Recorded by Doug Wills & Taylor Lies on October 11, 2005

## EXAMPLE PROJECT: *Entertaining at Home (2005)*

A top household products company worked with a design team to learn more about how to integrate the design-thinking process into their core business activities. The scope of the research addressed entertaining at home, an area indirectly related to the company's core business. Directing the research focus away from an area targeting one of the company's products to a focus on an analogous activity was deliberately decided upon as a way to better steer the company's attention to the design process than content during the project.

For primary research, the design team recruited five participating families and asked each of them to throw a party and take pictures before, during, and after the party ended. The team then organized the photos in a field notebook to conduct a follow-up interview with each participant. To ensure observations were captured in a comprehensive and organized manner, the notebook included annotation space for the *Five Human Factors* framework. The framework template helped the team look for particular issues across the five factors—physical, cognitive, social, cultural, and emotional—and probe for hidden insights during the interview. Some observations brought to light were the emotional frustrations in trying to find room for leftovers in the fridge, social aspects highlighting the fun participants had with food preparation in a social setting, and their preference to do clean-up individually. All the observations gleaned from the research were uploaded to the user observations database, where the photos were tagged and data organized and preclustered for further analysis.

| Activity *after party* Time *night of party* | | Insights |
|---|---|---|
| *putting away food: organizing refrigerator she got away food* / *clean up* / *leftovers* | | *making room in the refrigerator is time consuming* |
| **Interview** | | |
| *"It's hard to find room in the refrigerator."* | | |
| | | **Need Statement** *need way to... organize and create space in refrigerator.* |

| People | Objects | Environments | Messages | Services |
|---|---|---|---|---|
| *Mother (adult female)* | *refrigerator tupperware bag aluminum foil bowls corn hamburger* | *kitchen* | | *cleaning food storage* |

| User Experience | |
|---|---|
| Physical | *difficulty holding / controlling what she wants to put in refrigerator* |
| Cognitive | *confused by how to make everything fit. as she moves them to make space* |
| Social | |
| Cultural | |
| Emotional | *frustrated trying to make room in refrigerator.* |

Workshop-Party Observation/Teams/Institute of Design / IIT / Chicago/ Fall 2005

**BENEFITS**
- Broadens mindset
- Encourages comprehensiveness
- Focuses on details
- Focuses on experience
- Gives focus to the process

**INPUT**
- Project's area of study
- Identified situations for user observation

**OUTPUT**
- Organized observations about each of the five factors that drive user behavior

**WHEN TO USE**

## WHAT IT DOES

The Five Human Factors is a method for supporting observation in the field, prompting researchers to look for the physical, cognitive, social, cultural, and emotional elements present in any situation to understand how they affect peoples' overall experiences. Understanding five factors of a person in a structured way and thinking about all these factors together will give us a rich, deeper understanding of the experience of that person. The resulting holistic assessment can bring focus to the various elements that need to be considered when developing concepts and solutions. In this way, this research method breaks down a person's experience into its constituent parts to understand each in detail, and then reassembles our findings to understand how they form an overall experience.

## HOW IT WORKS

### STEP 1: Prepare to go into the field.

Create a note-taking template where you can record and categorize your observations according to the Five Human Factors. Carry tools (notebooks, cameras, pens, recorders, etc.) that will support user observation or interviewing.

### STEP 2: Go into the field.

Observe or engage people in a conversation. Observe or ask about peoples' activities, the objects they use, their environments, the information they interact with, and similar aspects. Take down notes based on your observations or the responses from people.

### STEP 3: Look through the lens of the Five Human Factors.

*Physical:* How do people experience their physical interaction with things and other people? What do they touch, push, pull, open, close, lift, carry, control, and so forth?

*Cognitive:* How do people associate meanings to things they interact with? What are the various interactions that require people to think? What do they read, research, process, assess, and decide?

*Social:* How do people behave in teams or in social settings? How do they formally and informally interact, make decisions, coordinate actions, make schedules, and work together?

*Cultural:* How do people experience shared norms, habits, and values? What, if any, shared values seem present? How are they manifest?

*Emotional:* How do people experience their feelings and thoughts? What in the environment is triggering these emotions? Are people sad, aggravated, frustrated, or happy?

### STEP 4: Describe peoples' overall experience.

Look for problems as well as surprisingly positive observations about each of the five factors. Describe your high-level sense of peoples' experiences in the situation that you have observed. Discuss and document.

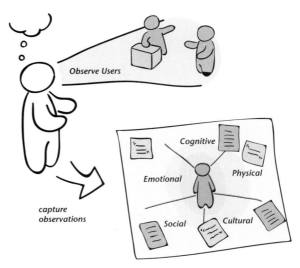

Observe Users

*capture observations*

Cognitive

Emotional

Physical

Social

Cultural

3.4 FIVE HUMAN FACTORS

# 3.5 POEMS

Studying people, objects, environments, messages, and services in a context.

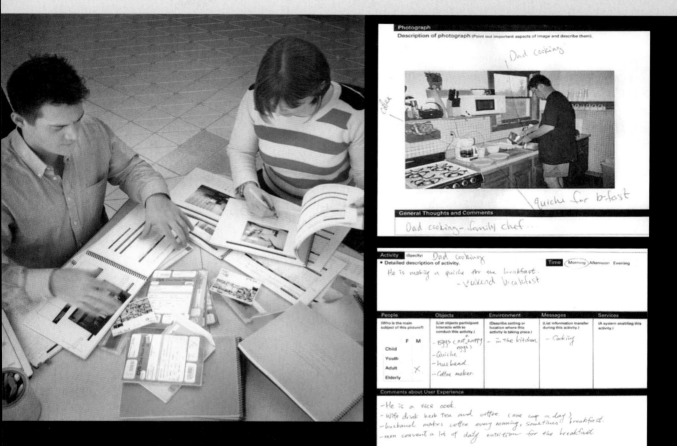

**EXAMPLE PROJECT: Kitchen Activities (2005)**

The kitchen design is a complex process with many different aspects to consider. A large audio systems manufacturer partnered with a design team to gain a better understanding of what physical design and aesthetic considerations people engage in when buying existing kitchens, remodeling, or building new homes.

The design team conducted research on the activities that take place in the kitchen, focusing primarily on middle-to-upper class families living in Chicago who have lived in their homes for at least five years. Each family was in different phases of the kitchen redesign process, from planning, executing, and finishing to completion. A range of ethnographic methods was used to conduct the research, including photo ethnography in which participants were asked to take photos both within and outside the home whenever they were making a kitchen redesign decision. The team then conducted follow-up interviews after the photo ethnography. All data were entered into standard field books that included the *POEMS* framework, which helped them structure the data relating not only to people, but also to what they were using and doing in the kitchen environment. In addition to providing structure, the POEMS framework helped to generate data on the participants' motivations and needs, things that dissatisfied them, their desire to customize their space to meet personal preferences, and the importance of validating time and monetary investments. At the conclusion of this study, the team recommended that the company focus on large families, people who pursue extreme activities in the kitchen such as entertaining multiple times a week, and cooks with professional cooking skills.

**BENEFITS**
- Broadens mindset
- Encourages comprehensiveness
- Gives focus to the process
- Helps understand context
- Focuses on details

**INPUT**
- Project's topic
- Identified situations for user observation

**OUTPUT**
- Organized observations about aspects of a context

**WHEN TO USE**

## WHAT IT DOES

The POEMS framework is an observational research framework used to make sense of the elements present in a context. The five elements are: People, Objects, Environments, Messages, and Services. Application of the POEMS framework encourages researchers to examine these elements independently as well as an interrelated system. For example, a team researching a specific product using the POEMS framework would look beyond object (the product) to services, messages, environments, and people that have a relationship with the broader context in which that product is used. In broadening perspective, the framework helps teams think about contexts as systems of related elements

## HOW IT WORKS

### STEP 1: Prepare for going into the field.

Create a note-taking template where you can record and categorize your observations according to the POEMS framework. Carry tools (notebooks, cameras, pens, recorders, etc.) that will support user observation or interviewing.

### STEP 2: Go into the field.

Observe or engage people in a conversation. Observe or ask about peoples' activities, the objects they use, their environments, the information they interact with, and similar aspects. Take down notes based on your observations or the responses from people.

### STEP 3: Understand the context through POEMS.

**People:** Who are the different kinds of people in the context? Mother? Repairperson? Customer? What appear to be their reasons for being there? Try to capture the full range of types of people present. Record them on your note-taking template.

**Objects:** What are the various objects that populate the context? Phones? Dining table? Newspaper? What are the broader categories of objects? What is their relationship to one another? Record them.

**Environments:** What are the different settings where activities take place? Kitchen? Store? Meeting room? Determine the distinct environments within the context. Record them.

**Messages:** What messages are being communicated in the context, and how are they being transmitted? Conversations? Package labels? Signs? Record the messages.

**Services:** What are the distinct services offered in the context? Cleaning? Delivery? Media? Note the types of services available and record them.

### STEP 4: Describe your overall observations.

Describe the overall context you have understood through POEMS from your observations or responses from interviews. Collect all your notes and share your observations with team members for discussion.

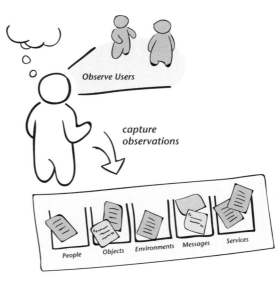

Observe Users

capture observations

People    Objects    Environments    Messages    Services

**3.5 POEMS**

# 3.6 Field Visit

Bringing researchers into direct contact with people, places, and things they are studying

### EXAMPLE PROJECT: *Learning through Play (2009)*

The "Learning through Play" project in partnership with a children's museum offered a design team an opportunity to design an exhibit around the theme of learning and play within a 1,500 square foot exhibit space.

To immerse themselves in the areas of learning, doing, and playing in the context of children, the team did *Field Visits* at the children's museum and other museums frequently visited by parents and their children. Providing a mix of different museums gave the team an opportunity to explore different environments, people, and behaviors instead of focusing on one location. They drafted research plans to pinpoint the area(s) of the visit that would be most valuable to them and questions to ask when they were speaking with museum staff and/or visitors. The research plan provided high-level guidance and structure, but the team took a true exploratory approach taking many pictures of things that were interesting, whether it was physical artifacts or a child engaged in an activity by himself/herself, with others, or with his/her parents. Photos and notes were taken for further discussion. The field visits later helped to define the design principles for the five design concepts they identified, some of which targeted hide-and-seek behavior and lights to evoke a sense of open-endedness, novelty brilliance, and mystery.

**BENEFITS**
- Focuses on details
- Focuses on experience
- Provides evidence
- Promotes learning in context

**INPUT**
- Project's topic
- List of important/relevant locations for understanding the topic

**OUTPUT**
- Rich observations about users' activities and behavior in context

**WHEN TO USE**

## WHAT IT DOES

The field visit is the most direct means of building empathy with people. Spending time with people engaged in real-world activities helps innovation researchers understand relevant behaviors firsthand. Unlike surveys or focus groups, where researchers' questions dictate the conversation, a field visit emphasizes observation and inquiry about what is being observed. Researchers ask participants to talk about specific activities and things they use. Conversations are guided by simple open-ended questions such as "Can you tell me about what you're doing?" and "Can you tell me more?" The method is a way to get acquainted with users in an unbiased fashion and frequently provides glimpses of nonobvious or surprising behaviors and insights about unmet needs.

## HOW IT WORKS

### STEP 1: Plan field protocol.

A field protocol is a detailed plan of where the team will visit, who they will observe and interact with, how long they will be there, what they plan to explore (general themes and/or specific questions), and how the team will function—for example, who will take notes, who will guide the conversation with the people, and who will take photos/video or record audio.

### STEP 2: Assemble resources.

Put together a Field Visit kit, which may contain things like notebooks, cameras, sketchbooks, audio recorders, bags, or containers for artifacts taken back from the field. Prepare any *pro forma* documents like permissions or disclosure agreements.

### STEP 3: Go into the field.

Upon arriving at the site, establish relations and begin to build trust with the people there. Before going into the research, have people sign any necessary paperwork, make them comfortable, explain the process, and let them ask questions about it. It is essential to have conversations not formal interviews, and to let the subjects lead the discussion as much as possible. Remember to ask, "Can you show me?," to repeat back what you are hearing, and confirm that your observations are valid. Always be respectful of peoples' time, and, when appropriate, provide compensation.

### STEP 4: Capture observations.

Throughout a Field Visit, some members of the team should be dedicated documenters, taking notes, sketching, taking photos, making audio or video recording to capture conversations, collecting artifacts (always with permission), and, as much as possible, keeping this data organized for later analysis.

### STEP 5: Debrief with team.

As soon as possible after the visit, compare notes, discuss what was learned, what was important, what additional research is needed, and how it should be done.

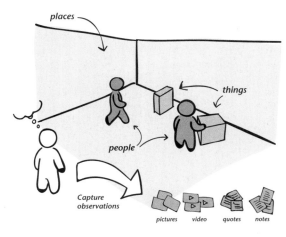

places

things

people

Capture observations

pictures    video    quotes    notes

**3.6 FIELD VISIT**

# 3.7 Video Ethnography

Video documenting people and their activities in their context to reveal insights

*EXAMPLE PROJECT:*
*Air Travel Experience (1996)*

Several years ago, an airline company was looking for opportunities to improve the experience of airline passengers throughout their journey, not just onboard. Getting enough information about the air travel experience from start to finish required studying people from their homes, to their cars, to airports, airplanes, car rental agencies, and all points in between. They and their partners at Doblin Inc. realized the only way to capture all this experiential data would be a series of *Video Ethnography* studies. So the team set up fixed-position cameras in public areas of airplanes and airport lounges; they videoed people on their way to and from the airport on ground transportation; they arranged dozens of visits and recorded interviews in homes, hotels, and other private areas. All this research fed into this innovation process that resulted in a plan encompassing better solutions for everything from reservations to check-in to gate areas to baggage claim, making this carrier one of the most customer-friendly airlines in the industry.

**BENEFITS**

- Captures information over time
- Facilitates storytelling
- Focuses on experience
- Provides evidence
- Reveals the unexpected

**INPUT**

- Project's topic
- List of locations for Video Ethnography

**OUTPUT**

- Video footage showing user processes and behavior over time
- Observations about user processes and behavior

**WHEN TO USE**

## WHAT IT DOES

Video Ethnography is a method adopted from the field of visual anthropology. The objective is to capture peoples' activities and what happens in a situation as video that can be analyzed for recognizing behavioral patterns and insights. The method is similar to photo ethnography, but has the ability to capture entire periods of time as well as audio recording. It is good for recording processes or dynamic situations such as public or group spaces, and for conversations or experiences in which sound is important. On the downside, video requires far more time to analyze than photographs. It is most effective for understanding time-bound activities, especially in instances where there may be many other adjacent activities happening simultaneously or in the background. Video Ethnography can be done by researchers or done by participants for purposes of self-documentation. Once guidelines for capturing are established and permission obtained, video is shot and collected for later analysis.

## HOW IT WORKS

### STEP 1: Determine what will be filmed.

Depending on the project you may choose to conduct "talking head" interviews, document activities, record changes in environments or the levels of activity over a span of time, or some other focus. Decide if you will set up a stationary camera and let it film, or have a researcher film using hand-held cameras. There are advantages of each. The former is effective for interviews or observing an environment over time, while the latter works well in environments where there may be many things happening that involve more than one or two people.

### STEP 2: Determine who will film.

Depending on the project, decide whether you want researchers to document users, have participants self-document, or use a combination of both.

### STEP 3: Obtain necessary permissions.

Prepare permission and release forms that will enable you to film or use video footage of participants who are self-documenting. The permission form should state the intended use of the footage and should indicate who will be able to view it.

### STEP 4: Shoot video.

Equip researchers and participants with easy-to-use cameras. They should have a clear understanding of how to use the cameras before going off to film. Then, have researchers or participants film their activities and related elements of the context. Provide a schedule to indicate when you will need to collect footage.

### STEP 5: Collect and analyze footage.

Spend time with participants reviewing footage and capturing their reflections as they view it. If it is footage shot by your team, review it together, analyzing small increments at a time. A general rule of thumb is to allow three hours for analysis for every hour of footage. Maintain a log to capture observations and, if possible, indicate where in the footage the insight was found. A well-organized log will help as a useful reference tool later in the design process.

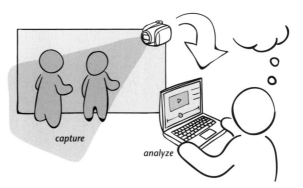

capture

analyze

3.7 VIDEO ETHNOGRAPHY

Having conversations with people about their daily lives and contexts.

### EXAMPLE PROJECT:
### Automobiles in India (2008)

To understand how people in India choose, use, and value their automobiles, Daishinsha, a Japanese consulting firm, collaborated with the author's design team to gain insights and strategic recommendations on how to penetrate that market. Participants were selected from a preselection survey and through family and friends networks producing a diverse group across age, sex, marital status, and professional background.

Over a two-week period, two members of the design team traveled to six different locations in India, including the major cities of New Delhi, Mumbai, and Bangalore to conduct research. This included going into the homes of nine participants to conduct in-depth *Ethnographic Interviews*. The interview protocol used was designed to be loose and flexible consisting of a few topics and questions to encourage engaging conversations. In addition to the in-home interviews, researchers also conducted interviews around their cars and, in some cases, were able to ride with the participants in their cars. This gave them a more intimate view into the behaviors, values, and preferences that the participants had about their automobiles.

The observations captured through these experiences led the team to interesting insights that later supported the final recommendations to the client. One of the recommendations presented was to build car experiences that emphasize family input and usage. The supporting insight demonstrated that car experiences are family-centric, where the purchase of a new car is both a memorable and significant event for all in the family.

ケイタイの充電器にステレオのリモコン、

| BENEFITS | INPUT | OUTPUT | WHEN TO USE |
|---|---|---|---|
| ■ Builds empathy<br>■ Focuses on experience<br>■ Promotes learning in context | ■ Project's topic<br>■ List of possible questions to initiate the conversation with the participants | ■ Observations about users' experience told from their point of view |  |

## WHAT IT DOES

A close companion to field visit observational research, Ethnographic Interview is concerned with understanding peoples' activities and experiences from their own perspectives and in their own places. It lets the researcher learn about people through their stories and in their own words, in an open-ended and exploratory fashion, with less risk for bias than interviews based on scripted questions. Typically, Ethnographic Interviews are conducted in the actual location or context where the activities being discussed occur. This makes the conversation much more directed and less abstract. It allows subjects to demonstrate activities and share their experiences with researchers. Discussing experiences in their actual context can often aid peoples' memory. Finally, people are usually more comfortable and talkative in their own environment than in an artificial or unfamiliar setting like a focus group.

## HOW IT WORKS

### STEP 1: Plan interview protocol.

An interview protocol is a detailed plan of whom you will visit, whom you will talk with, how long you will be there, what you plan to ask the participants, and how you will function; for example, who will take snapshots, who will take notes, and who will be talking with the participants.

### STEP 2: Assemble resources.

Put together an interview kit, which may contain things like notebooks, cameras, sketchbooks, and audio recorders. Prepare any *pro forma* documents like permissions or disclosure agreements.

### STEP 3: Conduct visit.

Upon arriving at the site, establish relations and begin to build trust with the participants there. Before starting the interview, have people sign any necessary paperwork, make them comfortable, explain the process, and let them ask questions about it. It is essential to treat the participants as equals, to have conversations, and to let the participants lead the discussion as much as possible. Remember to ask "Can you tell me more?," to repeat back what you are hearing, and confirm that your observations are valid. Always be respectful of peoples' time, and, when appropriate, provide compensation.

### STEP 4: Capture conversations.

Some members of the team should be dedicated documenters, taking notes, sketching, taking photos or short videos, recording conversations, and, as much as possible, keeping this data organized for later analysis.

### STEP 5: Debrief with team.

As soon as possible after the interview, the team should have a discussion about it to compare notes, decide what was learned, what was important, what gaps in their knowledge still need filling, what additional research is needed and how it should be done.

*user's context*

3.8 ETHNOGRAPHIC INTERVIEW

Having conversations with people about the photographs they have
taken of their activities

*EXAMPLE PROJECT:*
*Eating and Drinking On-the-Go (2010)*

In today's busy lifestyle, many people look
for convenience and speed, especially in the
home. Three large consumer goods companies
were interested in learning about eating and
drinking on-the-go from the user point of view. A
design team working on this project was able to
understand what, how, and why people eat and
drink on-the-go through structured, ethnographic
research involving eight extreme participants.

The *User Pictures Interview* was one of the
methods used in the ethnographic research.

Participants were given instructions with
examples of the types of pictures they should
take to self-document their eating and drinking
habits for one to two weeks. Using the POEMS
framework as a guide, the goal was to capture
the people, objects, environments, messages,
and services that were a part of the participants'
eating and drinking habits. This included, but
was not limited to, eating or drinking while in
the car, on the train, walking down the street,
playing with their kids, and shopping. Using an
iPad app to capture participants' responses, the
team asked participants to recall the details of
the events in each photograph during a two-hour,
face-to-face interview.

The method assisted participants to tell personal
stories and gave the team valuable insights from
which the themes of convenience, clean and
green, healthy, my way, efficiency, socializing,
and pleasure emerged. These themes led to
design principles that addressed fast and
healthy options, customized personal spaces to
the way people eat, and created opportunities
for personal interactions while purchasing or
consuming food. As a result, this analysis guided
the team's next steps and defined possible
opportunity areas for concept generation within
the realm of eating and drinking on-the-go.

## BENEFITS

- Builds empathy
- Captures users' points of view
- Grounds conversation with artifacts
- Promotes learning in context
- Reveals the unexpected

## INPUT

- Project's topic
- List of activities relevant to your study, especially the ones that are spontaneous and difficult to observe

## OUTPUT

- Photos and observations of situations that are important to participants

## WHEN TO USE

## WHAT IT DOES

The User Pictures Interview is a method that combines aspects of Photo Ethnography and Ethnographic Interview. The interview follows a period in which subjects have been asked to use photography to document their engagement in specific activities or experiences. An interview is scheduled and a researcher sits down with the participant to review the photographs. The method gathers information, through open-ended questions, about participants by getting them to talk in detail about the photographs they have taken. The narratives emerging from the interviews are sources of rich information and potential insights about the user's experiences and possible unmet needs.

## HOW IT WORKS

### STEP 1: Plan research protocol.

Decide who will be asked to take photos, where and when, roughly how many photos are desired, and choose any frameworks, such as POEMS, that they should use to guide them.

### STEP 2: Assemble resources.

Create diary templates (print or electronic) and instruction sheets; procure disposable cameras, if using them, or set up digital photo-sharing services.

### STEP 3: Brief participants.

Explain how to take photos—quickly, liberally, don't worry about artistic quality; what to take photos of (for example, POEMS, any and all people, objects, environments, messages, and services related to an activity); how many days the study will continue; and logistical details (where to send back disposable cameras or where to upload digital photos); provide disposable cameras, if using them; provide the diary templates.

### STEP 4: Give mid-course feedback.

Ideally, have a quick check-in with participants after they have shared an initial set of photos. Use this opportunity to give them feedback, correct any misunderstandings, answer their questions, debug technical difficulties, and possibly ask them to refocus on new or different things.

### STEP 5: Interview participants.

Ideally in the same location the photos were taken, have participants walk the team through the diary. Ask questions, get clarification, take additional notes, and don't forget to capture everything about the interview.

### STEP 6: Debrief.

Immediately after the interview, debrief the team about what was learned, and if necessary plan to follow up with participants for additional clarification.

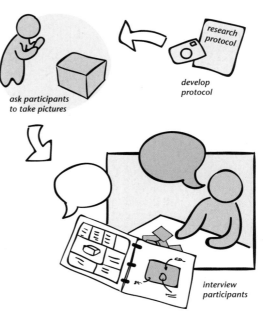

ask participants
to take pictures

research protocol

develop protocol

interview participants

Discovering perceptions of people using artifacts that are culturally relevant to sociocultural groups

### EXAMPLE PROJECT:
#### Comunidad Diabetes (2009)

Comunidad Diabetes is a project that explored community and wellness through a cultural lens. The project focused on diabetes in Chicago's Latino neighborhoods suffering from high prevalence rates. The goal was to rethink community health models to promote sustainable well-being and build a solution to prevent the disease and support those who are diagnosed. *Cultural Artifacts* was one of the research methods used by the project team to understand the Latino community's perceptions of health around food and community.

Lotería cards, a traditional Mexican board game, was used to establish a strong cultural and emotional connection to the research participants. Nine questions were developed in a kit containing these cards and given to each participant to be completed over a two-week period in their home and at their leisure. The idea was to make the activity fun, exploratory, and stress-free. Each question could be answered either by writing or using an image from one of the Lotería cards to illustrate how the participant felt about the question. After the two-week period, the kits were collected and analyzed for deeper meaning and insights based on the participants' responses. The team then did a follow-up interview to better understand the narrative behind the responses.

The research data from the Cultural Artifacts method and other research tools were then compiled for analysis and synthesis in Stage II of the project, where the team began to concentrate more on how they could contribute to a rollback of diabetes and obesity in specific Chicago neighborhoods as demonstration models for transformative social change.

**BENEFITS**

- Builds empathy
- Captures users' points of view
- Grounds conversation with artifacts
- Promotes playfulness
- Reveals the unexpected

**INPUT**

- Project's topic
- A relevant artifact significant to the group of users being studied

**OUTPUT**

- In-depth knowledge of users' activities and thought processes
- Kits and activities completed by users

**WHEN TO USE**

## WHAT IT DOES

This method leverages the emotional charge and cultural meaning artifacts have on people. The connotation of "culture" here is not restricted only to nationality or ethnicity. Sociocultural groups have particular customs, behaviors, traditions, thoughts, and practices of everyday life. In other words, every group has its own culture. The Cultural Artifacts method reappropriates a specific element of that culture, either tangible such as a physical object or intangible such as a specific belief the group has, into an artifact relevant to that group and uses that artifact to discover peoples' perceptions traditionally overlooked by other research methods.

## HOW IT WORKS

### STEP 1: Develop a kit with Cultural Artifacts and tasks.

Taking into consideration cultural nuances about the group of people particular to the project, develop a research kit containing a disposable camera, journal to record thoughts, voice or video recorders, and cultural artifacts. Artifacts are reappropriations of specific elements from that culture/group. The artifacts are intended to trigger the most emotional responses, allowing researchers for a deeper conversation with participants that would not be possible with a traditional Ethnographic Interview. The kit also includes some tasks that you want the participants to do. It could be a set of questions or requests for creating something for which you want the participants' response in the form of stories or interpretation of the artifacts in the kit.

### STEP 2: Brief participants.

Explain the artifacts and the tasks included in the kit to participants. All materials must include printed instructions and contact information in case participants need feedback.

### STEP 3: Provide time for participants to respond.

Allow ample time for participants to respond. The objective is to allow them to do this at their leisure in a stress-free environment.

### STEP 4: Collect kits.

Collect the kits in person or retrieve them by mail through a prepaid postage included in the package.

### STEP 5: Analyze information.

Once the kits are collected, analyze the information provided and prepare for a debriefing interview with participants.

### STEP 6: Interview participants.

Because the method's tasks are meant to be inspirational, a follow-up, semi-structured interview is conducted with participants to review and dig deeper into their responses.

### STEP 7: Frame inspirations.

Framing the participants' inspirations into insights helps the design team generate personas and scenarios.

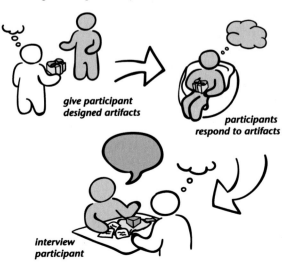

*give participant designed artifacts*

*participants respond to artifacts*

*interview participant*

3.10 CULTURAL ARTIFACTS

Having people sort symbolic images to find out their thoughts and attitudes about a topic

*EXAMPLE PROJECT: Reducing Violence—CeaseFire Chicago (2009)*

CeaseFire Chicago, a violence prevention program, worked with a design team to find solutions to curb neighborhood violence through transforming behaviors. Before designing any solutions to the problems facing neighborhoods deluged by violence, the team sought to understand the details of the current situation. Since the subject of violence is emotionally charged and the team was concerned that cultural differences would be a barrier during interviews, they designed a deck of *Image Sorting* cards to help elicit the personal narratives from residents about neighborhood violence.

Each card in the deck featured an image of an object or location that could help construct stories about the neighborhood. A member of the team would then ask the participant questions based on five randomly drawn cards such as: "Which pair of them has the most to do with each other? What is their relationship?" Used as conversation starters, these cards supported a series of insightful discussions into the kinds of beliefs and emotional and social connections that are prevalent within the culture. For example, the low-risk people in the community like to stay uninvolved, but like to form protection for family and friends. In an effort to not have these images play on racial stereotypes, they were selected with the help of CeaseFire outreach workers to form a set of symbols that covered the breadth of experience in and out of the neighborhood. The final deck included 59 cards, ranging from the kitchen table to the Daley Plaza and from textbooks to crack rocks.

**BENEFITS**

- Captures users' points of view
- Grounds conversation with artifacts
- Provides evidence
- Reveals relationships

**INPUT**

- Project's topic
- A comprehensive set of images to help users communicate abstract ideas

**OUTPUT**

- Observations about users' values and attitudes toward a topic

**WHEN TO USE**

## WHAT IT DOES

Image Sorting is a method used to find out peoples' associations and perceptions of particular topics. Engaging in activities in which people sort, discuss, and create stories using preprepared images is a powerful way of revealing the emotions, relationships, and values people associate with other people, places, and objects in a situation. For example, in the context of job searching, an image of money may correspond to feelings about success or advancement, whereas in the context of crime, money may represent vulnerability or corruption. This exercise sparks a conversation about abstract ideas and feelings that otherwise may remain undetected in a traditional Ethnographic Interview.

Image Sorting works by presenting participants with images of common objects, people, or places and having them sort according to particular themes or criteria. For example, you might ask participants to sort images according to community versus solitary activities to get a sense of how they feel about social responsibility versus individual ambition. This can be done one-on-one or with a group of participants. Several sessions with different individual participants are usually required in order for patterns to emerge and generalizations to be made. The Image Sorting exercise with a group of participants is effective for understanding shared beliefs and/or where people diverge on a given topic.

## HOW IT WORKS

### STEP 1: Determine what topics you want to explore.

Based on your project intent, decide what attitudes you want to explore that will help you understand how people think about a given topic. For example, if working on a service design initiative, you may want to understand peoples' attitudes and perceptions about what constitutes good and bad service experiences.

### STEP 2: Select an Image Sorting method.

Depending on what you want to explore, employ an appropriate sorting method. Use a *grouping* method for clustering images based on a particular criterion. For example, to understand attitudes about environments, you might ask participants to sort images according to notions of "welcoming" versus "unwelcoming." Use the *Top Tens* method and ask participants to express their personal values by ranking images from favorite to least favorite. Use the *Narrative* method to make participants use images to tell stories that reflect their perceptions or attitudes.

### STEP 3: Select images.

Search for images that can be used for sorting activities. When seeking out images, it helps to use the POEMS (people, objects, environments, messages, and services) framework to create a comprehensive set that will allow participants to express their values and attitudes in several ways.

### STEP 4: Invite participants.

Invite people to participate in the sorting activity. Explain what they will be doing and the reason why it is being done. Indicate where and when the activity will take place and how long they can expect to be there. In most cases, compensation is provided to participants for their time.

### STEP 5: Conduct Image Sorting exercises.

Provide instructions to participants at the start of each exercise. Allow time for them to do the exercise alone or in groups. At the completion of each exercise, photograph the resulting sort.

3.11 IMAGE SORTING

**STEP 6: Engage in conversations.**

Ask participants to explain why they sorted the images as they did. Have team members take notes to capture responses or, if participants permit it, use audio or video recordings. Often useful insights can be gained by asking participants to elaborate on their answers and talk more broadly about what informed their thinking, what associations the images brought to mind, and how they relate them to their daily lives.

**STEP 7: Document photos and responses.**

Gather photographs of image sorts and corresponding responses into documents that can be reviewed and analyzed by your team. Discuss the attitudes and perceptions participants have shown through the activity and gain insights.

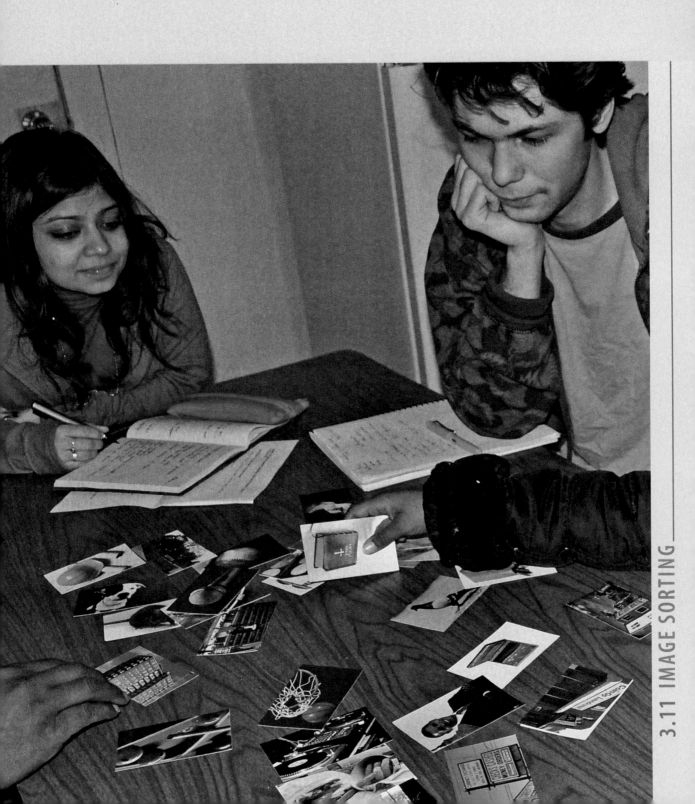

# 3.12 Experience Simulation

Engaging people in simulated experiences to understand what matters to them

## EXAMPLE PROJECT: Bus Rapid Transit (2008)

In 2008, a major urban transit authority planned to launch a high-speed bus service to reduce vehicle traffic and increase ridership. The new bus service is based on 60 feet of newly configured articulated buses. Key features of the system include improved fare handling through multiple entry points, select station service, and right-of-way signal prioritization electronics.

Through *Experience Simulation*, the project team provided key decision makers the opportunity to learn about passenger behaviors to change the design of the vehicle's interior. Through the simulation the team was able to study improved passenger flows by reducing bottlenecks, enhanced riders' experience, and improved bus operations. The full-scale, low-fidelity bus simulation took roughly a day and a half to build, using 61 stack chairs, 2 rolls of tape, 6 particle boards, 9 sheets of foam core, and graphic printouts. The simulated experience promoted a "learn by doing" approach, fostering communication between the members of the transit authority and project team, enabling them to make quick and informed decisions about better passenger experience.

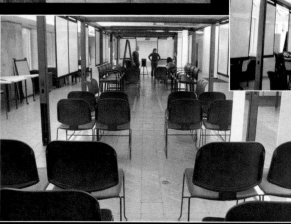

**BENEFITS**
- Captures information over time
- Facilitates comparison
- Focuses on experience
- Grounds conversation with artifacts

**INPUT**
- Research questions about behaviors or activities
- Selected experiences to simulate

**OUTPUT**
- Observations of how users might behave or interact in a situation

## WHAT IT DOES

Experience Simulation is a research method used to help researchers understand how people might behave or interact in a given situation. The method is useful for studying experiential offerings such as new services, environments, or interactions. For example, researchers might set up a food stand that provides consumers with detailed nutritional information delivered in a variety of ways such as labeling, signage, or in-person coaching in order to observe how different methods affect food choices and purchase decisions. The method allows us to explore what matters most to users in an experience. An environment is constructed and participants are invited into it to spend time engaging in an activity or activities. Researchers observe participants' interactions with elements of the environment and conduct follow-up interviews with them to understand both details and overall user experience.

## HOW IT WORKS

### STEP 1: Identify the research question.

Decide what behaviors or activities the team is interested in studying. How people choose to buy organic food in supermarkets? How parents teach children about physics by playing with blocks?

### STEP 2: Select a specific experience to simulate.

Determine which aspects of the experience need to be realistic and which can be "simulated." Does the "supermarket" need to be realistic or can it be constructed in a conference room?

### STEP 3: Design the simulation.

Build the environment, create the objects, develop the messages and services, find the people to run the simulation, and recruit the participants for it (this may be done beforehand, or, in the case of public simulations, people may be recruited onsite or passing by).

### STEP 4: Run the simulation.

Simulations could last anywhere from a few hours to a few weeks; in some cases they might be semi-permanent, as in a test store. Obviously, different scales and durations of simulation will require different levels of planning, staffing, and resources.

### STEP 5: Capture behaviors and insights.

Assign designated observers to take notes, capture video/audio/photos, and possibly identify gaps or flaws in the simulation or process that can be corrected. Document insights. Discuss them with your team and with participants to get more feedback.

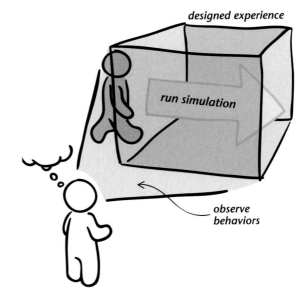

designed experience

run simulation

observe behaviors

**3.12 EXPERIENCE SIMULATION**

Engaging people in contextual activities, observing them, and later interviewing them

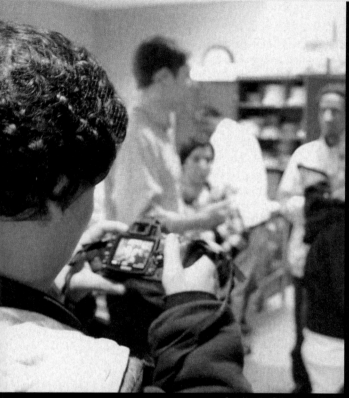

Seth Kutnik, IIT, Institute of Design

### EXAMPLE PROJECT:
### New Options for Out-of-School Youth (2008)

As many as 4 million youths aged 16 to 24 in the United States do not have a high school diploma and are not actively taking steps to achieve one. These out-of-school youths (OSY) struggle to find meaningful employment and often suffer a lower quality of life. A design team worked with a large philanthropic nonprofit organization on an initiative that would connect these youths with sustainable and satisfying careers. Insights from their primary research showed that the initiative should allow for self-discovery and reflection, connect with participants' strengths and interests, and involve a tangible, real-world experience.

As part of their research, the design team used *Field Activity* as a method that would connect and expose OSY to different businesses and work professions. The Field Activity took place over two days and involved four businesses and six youths and was conducted at different locations like an advertisement agency, real estate agent's office, a professional photography studio, and a performance theater, all located in Chicago. The Field Activity was used to understand how real-life exposure triggers interest for OSYs and to test the assumption that harnessing interest brings key strengths into focus. The activity also tested the assumption that OSYs would respond positively to having responsibilities given an exposure to those. After debriefing the OSYs and employers, the team learned that these youths felt they were able to relate to and saw future possibilities in the work to which they were exposed. The overall experience made them feel more connected, engaged, and inspired.

Seth Kutnik, IIT, Institute of Design

Seth Kutnik, IIT, Institute of Design

**BENEFITS**
- Builds empathy
- Focuses on experience
- Grounds conversation with artifacts
- Promotes learning in context

**INPUT**
- Behaviors and activities to be studied

**OUTPUT**
- Observations of how users engage in existing situations

**WHEN TO USE**

## WHAT IT DOES

Field Activities is a method designed to understand how people might respond to an actual situation by having them engage with it. The method involves taking targeted users into the field and engaging them in selected activities in a specific situation in order to observe their behaviors. Follow-up interviews are conducted with the participants to collect statements about their experiences. These statements are reviewed for the purpose of assessing our assumptions about user behaviors, identifying unmet user needs, and conducting additional research.

## HOW IT WORKS

### STEP 1: Identify user behaviors to study.

Based on the innovation intent, identify specific user behaviors that you want to study in an actual situation. The main objectives are to test early assumptions about user behaviors and/or to find unmet user needs.

### STEP 2: Identify research participants.

Select and invite users who you want to take to the field. Once invited, describe to them what you hope to learn by taking them to the field.

### STEP 3: Establish the activities for participants.

Make arrangements to engage users in selected activities. For example, engage users in office work situations where youths are engaged in hands-on activities in order to study their response to work situations. Determine whether you will be looking at specific activities or the entire experience.

### STEP 4: Take participants to the field.

Provide orientation documents to the participants telling them about what to expect while out in the field. When bringing subjects into the field, determine how prepared the environment will be to accommodate their activities. Provide guidance to the participants while activities are ongoing.

### STEP 5: Observe users engaged in Field Activities.

Decide how to capture observations—video, photographs, or field notes. Make sure that everyone in the field knows that they are being observed and documented for the purposes of research.

### STEP 6: Conduct interviews with participants.

After the Field Activities are over, engage participants in a conversation to learn about their responses, opinions, and viewpoints. Ask questions to clarify what you have learned from observations. Transcribe interviews.

### STEP 7: Summarize findings and discuss.

Create a summary of findings, from both observations and interviews. Share them with team members and other stakeholders and use them for later analysis.

*Guided Activity*

*Interview participants*

## Using online research tools for users' self-documentation studies

### EXAMPLE PROJECT: *Automobiles in India (2008)*

To understand how people in India choose, use, and value their automobiles, Daishinsha, a Japanese consulting firm, collaborated with the author's design team in the United States to gain insights and strategic recommendations on how to penetrate that market.

As part of the qualitative research, the design team conducted *Remote Research* with users from India about their activities in selecting, buying, financing, using, maintaining, and disposing of their automobiles. This part was done to supplement the ethnographic research that had been done for a week with preselected families in various parts of India. Participants selected for the Remote Research took photos of their daily life in the context of using their cars. Dozens of photos were submitted with a brief description of the activity on a Flickr account, set up and viewed only by the researchers. Using Skype, researchers had follow-up interviews to discuss why they took specific pictures and the meanings behind them.

The Remote Research not only produced additional insights, but also helped to validate some of the existing observations and added to others. A number of insights were categorized across three main themes—searching for cars and buying, car specifics, and car usage and activities. The insights included the family-oriented nature of car experiences, incorporating the opinions of women in a male-dominated activity, and the need for customizability and ergonomics due to cultural factors. Revealing these insights also yielded actionable design criteria to help design for this market.

## BENEFITS

- Accesses hard-to-reach user groups
- Builds empathy
- Captures information over time
- Captures users' points of view
- Organizes information for easy access

## INPUT

- Topic that would benefit from reflective responses from participants

## OUTPUT

- Users' documentation of attitudes, motivations, thought processes, and contextual stories around a topic

## WHEN TO USE

## WHAT IT DOES

Remote Research is a method of user self-documentation that employs Web-based tools. The method leverages Internet connectivity so that studies can be conducted simultaneously in multiple locations anywhere in the world without requiring researchers to be out in the field. Participants receive invitations to access online tools where they can log on and receive instructions about the study and what is required of them. Then, they can start to document their activities, upload photos and videos, and communicate directly with researchers online. Information uploaded by users flows into research documents that can be reviewed and analyzed on an ongoing basis. This continuous monitoring feature enables researchers to track findings in real time and communicate with users should new research questions arise.

## HOW IT WORKS

### STEP 1: Identify activities you want to study.

Based on the innovation intent, identify specific user activities that you want to study in Remote Research. Determine the scope of your study. Will you be looking at specific activities and interactions or the entire user experience?

### STEP 2: Identify users for Remote Research.

In preparing a study group, record why this group was chosen and what you hope to learn by studying them. Determine how you can gain access to them and how you will invite their participation in the study.

### STEP 3: Write a research protocol and upload it online.

Inform participants what is expected of them, how long the study will last, and how they will be compensated. Provide a detailed schedule indicating when partici-

pants are to upload materials, participate in online interviews, or attend online participant forums.

### STEP 4: Select the online tools you will use.

Study the online research tools available, and select the most appropriate ones for your use. Remote Research can be conducted using photo-sharing or video-sharing sites. When using such sites, it is important to create password-protected collections that cannot be accessed by anyone other than the research participants and the research team.

### STEP 5: Launch the study and monitor it.

Ask participants to upload photos and descriptions of their activities. Ask them to express their attitudes, motivations, thought processes, and contextual stories. Review information being uploaded by participants. If the information is incomplete or requires clarification, communicate via online tools to ensure adjustments are made or questions that arise are addressed.

### STEP 6: Compile findings and share them with the team.

If using online platforms, data may be aggregated into reports for analysis. Describe users' attitudes, motivations, thought processes, and contextual stories that you have learned from the process. Collect information into documents that will facilitate comparative analysis.

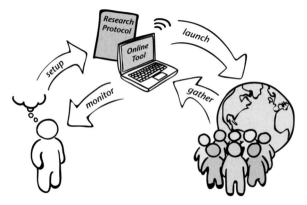

# 3.15 User Observations Database

Organizing and sharing observational data and insights from different projects

**EXAMPLE PROJECT:**
*Entertaining at Home (2005)*

A large household products company worked with an IIT Institute of Design team to understand the topic of Entertaining at Home. Primary research was conducted with five Chicago families who were requested to host a party in their homes and take photos during the whole process, including planning. After the event, participants were interviewed around the photos they had taken. Descriptive frameworks like POEMS and Five Human Factors provided structure for asking questions during the interview.

All user observations, including notes and photos, were transferred to the *User Observations Database*, an Excel-based research collection tool that manages large amounts of research data. The team entered a photo in each cell of the first column, and the subsequent columns were filled with its respective information corresponding to the fields from the field note template. Basic features in the spreadsheet allowed them to sort, group, and examine observations in different ways and quickly gain valuable insights; from the multiple stages participants use to manage the long cooking process to the multipurpose use of kitchenware. The database also served as a valuable tool and resource for other home-life-related projects.

**BENEFITS**

- Builds knowledge base
- Enables systematic analysis
- Handles large sets of data
- Organizes information for easy access
- Reveals patterns
- Supports transition

**INPUT**

- All previously generated user research data (observations, photos, videos, etc.)

**OUTPUT**

- Organized and searchable archive of user observations

**WHEN TO USE**

## WHAT IT DOES

The User Observations Database is a method for organizing data gathered during user observation. It contains data in many forms—videos, photos, field notes, diagrams, and others—captured during a research project. Each piece of data is tagged using frameworks like POEMS and Five Human Factors so that the data can be searched using these tag words. The database becomes more useful over time as it is populated with more data as new projects are completed. Moreover, the database is not only useful for searching for specific sets of observations but also useful for finding clustering patterns in observations. Despite the extra initial effort needed to enter data, the analysis we can do using a large collection of observations coming from many projects is valuable.

## HOW IT WORKS

### STEP 1: Identify data to be input.

Gather observations from various research methods, and write each observation as a uniform description to be input into the database. The observations to be input may be in the form of videos, photos, field notes, diagrams, transcripts, audio recordings, or other such media. Upload all the observations into the database.

### STEP 2: Inventory uploaded data.

For every unit of observation uploaded into the database, provide a project name, researcher's name, date, location, title of observation, description, relevant quotes, notes/comments, and any other relevant information.

### STEP 3: Tag data with frameworks.

Tag each observation with one or more frameworks such as POEMS, Five Human Factors, or another framework. Use predetermined generic tags (e.g., kitchen, mother, cookbook, television) as well as project-specific tags (Chicago, young mother, Martha Stewart).

### STEP 4: Conduct searches.

Use the keyword search function to compare the findings of your research with that of prior projects. Look for patterns among the findings and note new insights about the project.

### STEP 5: Summary search results.

Prepare a summary of search results. Describe the insights you gained by looking at the patterns you found through your searches. Do they reveal larger behaviors that you need to pay attention to for generating concepts? Likewise note differences among your findings and those of past projects. Share your summary with team members and discuss follow-up research or further analysis.

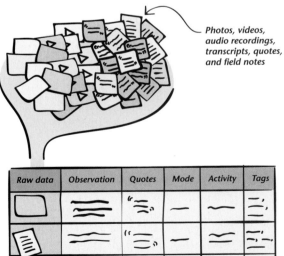

*Photos, videos, audio recordings, transcripts, quotes, and field notes*

| Raw data | Observation | Quotes | Mode | Activity | Tags |
|----------|-------------|--------|------|----------|------|
| | | | | | |
| | | | | | |
| | | | | | |

**3.15 USER OBSERVATIONS DATABASE**

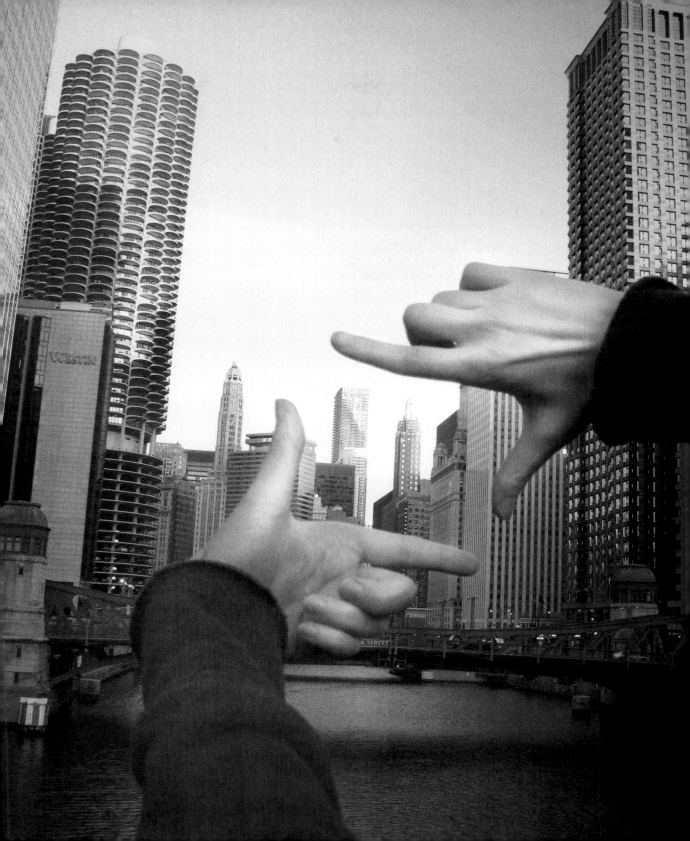

# mode 4
# FRAME INSIGHTS

In the Know Context and Know People modes, we discussed how to understand the context of an innovation project and how to uncover peoples' experiences and needs. We move from gaining such knowledge to clearly understanding that knowledge in Frame Insights. We move from researching and collecting data to applying various analytical frameworks to the data so that we can organize our thinking and gain a clear perspective. The methods and tools in this mode help us distill reams of research into a handful of key insights, and then turn those insights into concise, actionable principles for innovation.

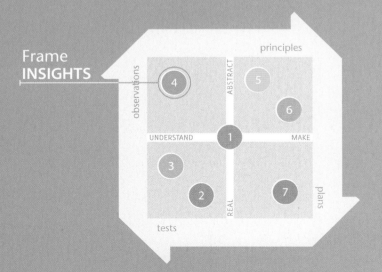

Frame
**INSIGHTS**

# FRAME INSIGHTS
## *mindsets*

As our mode shifts from knowing the context and the people to revealing insights and framing them up, we are actually moving from the very real world that we have researched to the very abstract world of insights, principles, systems, and ideas. In this mode we begin to make sense of all that we have learned from the real world and start to extract key insights out of large, fuzzy data sets. It is like "cutting cubes out of fog," in the words of Jay Doblin.

The people for whom we innovate have diverse behaviors and characteristics. The context in which our innovations need to function is complex; it is a dense network of interconnected parts. We actively seek to explore this complex system, we process the research data with rigor, and look at research findings from many different perspectives and angles. We face the many uncertainties our findings present and think through the ambiguity. We externalize our thoughts as visualizations or diagrams to bring clarity to our own individual thinking, collaboratively work with our colleagues, and effectively communicate with our stakeholders. With a certain level of clarity achieved we are in a position to identify new opportunities for innovation. We also ensure that our explorations generate reliable guidelines and principles that we can follow through for generating innovations. In short, the mindset in this mode should set us up with a robust foundation for later synthesis of valuable innovation concepts.

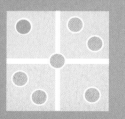

**Mindsets**
- Exploring Systems
- Looking for Patterns
- Constructing Overviews
- Identifying Opportunities
- Developing Guiding Principles

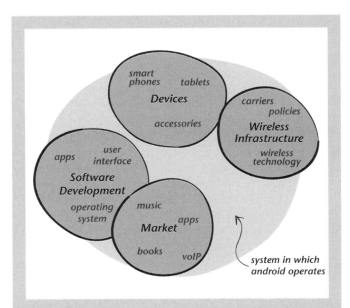

*system in which android operates*

*Google's Android mobile operating system, Honeycomb, is an open mobile platform with an intricately interconnected set of entities related in critical ways that make the operating system function well for a wide spectrum of users. Entities like user-interfaces, operating systems, apps, apps markets, music, books, VoIP, smart phones, tablets, wireless technologies, carriers, and policies are all interconnected in a complex hierarchical system, working in harmony to provide a compelling mobile experience. Moreover, the open nature of the system is what is helping Android grow rapidly.*

## Mindset: Exploring Systems

As we discussed earlier, one of the core principles of nearly every successful innovation effort is thinking in terms of systems. Although this principle applies to all modes of an innovation process, it is perhaps nowhere more evident than during Frame Insights. This is the mode in which we try to understand the complexity of our innovation challenges. This is when we create our own proprietary system views of this complexity. This is when we ensure that the concepts we will create have a better chance to fit well with complex real-world systems. Moreover, thinking in terms of systems helps avoid the classic pitfall of focusing too soon and too narrowly on just the offerings.

Systems are collections of entities. Some examples of entities that we most commonly use in our projects are people, offerings, organizations, and markets. Entities have relations between them, for example similarity, belonging, or complementing. Entities and relations have attributes like demographics, price, or brand. There are flows like transfer of money, goods, and information among entities. Systems also have hierarchy, the many levels in which the entities of the system are organized. We also recognize that systems have their own dynamics, changes happening over time. Although this way of defining systems is simplistic, it is a great start to fully understanding our innovation challenge.

In this mode we visualize systems as network diagrams, Venn diagrams, hierarchical tree diagrams, 2 × 2 position maps, a series of scenario sketches, and others. We examine the system from several different perspectives so that we can identify the most meaningful patterns and gain the most valuable insights.

*Developments in sharable databases and visualization technologies are allowing cities to open up data about the city's services, facilities, and performance to the public. New York City, San Francisco, and Chicago in the United States have portals providing a variety of tools for information visualization and pattern finding about the cities' contexts like budget, crime, housing, transportation, and employment. Seeing patterns in open sources of systemic data like this will increasingly support innovators' mindsets to visualize patterns and rapidly generate insights.*

## Mindset: Looking for Patterns

When dealing with large, complex, fuzzy sets of qualitative data about people and contexts, as is often the case with human-centered research, it's generally impossible to understand and represent every detail of the situation completely. There are too many pages of notes, too many hours of video, too many nuances of meanings to know everything about everyone. Fortunately, a perfect and complete understanding of the entire landscape is not necessary for successful innovation. What is important is to understand the most relevant patterns in the data, in order to reveal the general principles that should focus ideation.

One way to find patterns is by cataloging often-repeated words or phrases from interviews. Another way is by plotting data points in a scatterplot and studying the distribution. Scoring, sorting, and clustering related observations could also reveal patterns. The resulting visually represented patterns are a powerful analysis and communication tool, both while framing insights and later during concept exploration.

However they are found or represented, the key advantage of finding patterns is that they help us move from detailed, "messy" data, to general, abstract, easily grasped models of how a context works. From these models, we can readily form a point of view, generate insights, or develop innovation principles.

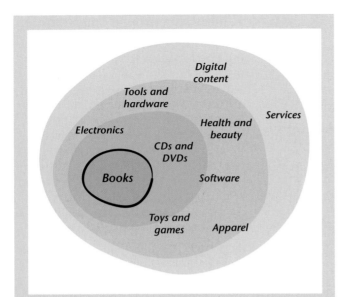

*In the early days of online commerce, Amazon.com's innovation framework was built on a good understanding of online retail, customer interaction, and the bookselling business. Providing a strong customer interface for browsing books, a large number of choices, reading reviews, information about similar books others bought, and one-click ordering all were parts of Amazon.com's bookselling framework. But the larger overview framework they constructed was a picture that their innovations in bookselling can be easily extended to a bigger retail footprint by providing other products and services (DVDs, CDs, MP3 downloads, software, video games, electronics, apparel, furniture, food, and toys) to become the world's largest online retailer.*

## Mindset: Constructing Overviews

Just as seeing patterns in fuzzy and complex data are helpful in getting insights, constructing overviews too is beneficial for getting a fuller understanding of the context. Challenging innovation projects produce large amounts of data from research methods. The rigors of these methods allow us to systematically reveal insights from complex data at numerous levels of granularity and in abundance. Moreover, while being immersed in the process, it is clear that intense focus is essential for uncovering rich insights. However, the challenge is to elevate the mindset to a higher comprehensive level in which overviews of patterns identified and insights generated are clearly visible and understood.

Good overviews function like a proprietary map—containing less detail than the actual territory they represent, but giving its audience, the innovation team and stakeholders, just enough information to generate discussion, ideas, and decisions. Good overviews also tell stories about real people and their experiences, often illustrating a process, a journey, or a situation in a way that helps the team broadly understand and empathize with the potential users of a new offering.

Overviews should be comprehensive, representing both the core aspects of the context, as well as its fringes. An overview of the context of pet ownership should not only contain information about how people acquire pets or buy pet supplies, but also about how they decide to own a pet in the first place, how they interact with their pet in extreme situations like air travel, and the process of remembering a much-loved pet that has passed away. Gaining insights at the "edges" of a context is of great help in the later modes, when the team is looking for new opportunities to develop concepts that others have missed.

*Innovators in one of the largest conglomerates in India, Godrej Group, in their continuous quest for excellence, sought new opportunities in "disruptive innovations," as suggested by Professor Clayton Christensen. They identified huge opportunities in offering an affordable and easily serviceable domestic refrigerator for the very large population of people in rural India. The team in Godrej actively sought out this opportunity, consciously set out to create a disruptive innovation, a refrigerator called "Chotukool," and dedicated their full attention to realize this successful innovation.*

## Mindset: Identifying Opportunities

Just as successful entrepreneurs continuously and actively look for opportunities for new ventures, innovators too seek out ways to define offerings that create new value for people and organizations. A key frame of mind during this mode is to be on the lookout for the most promising opportunities that are grounded on the needs of the people and the context. Just as with some of the other mindsets that we have discussed, like looking for patterns and constructing overviews, analyzing a context as a holistic system is an excellent approach to finding opportunities for innovation.

An innovator in the U.S. healthcare industry, for example, needs to think not only in terms of the valuable offerings for patients or doctors, but also the opportunities to create value for other stakeholders in the system such as hospitals, pharmacies, insurance companies, and drugmakers—all players with a huge financial stake in the system. Even a simple mental model to imagine how value flows between all the stakeholders in the system can be a good diagnostic tool for finding out where the most valuable opportunities for innovation might lie.

Most often opportunities for innovation that others might have missed are not at the core of your topic. Unexplored opportunities exist at the fringes, adjacent areas, and peripheries. Innovators should be paying attention to these areas for inspiration.

## Mindset: Developing Guiding Principles

The abundance of insights gained out of the many activities that we do in this mode will have to be somehow made actionable so that concepts could be explored based on a strong foundation. Here is where thinking about guidelines and principles will help us to think about what to create. Throughout the innovation process we ought to be on the lookout for extracting such principles from our learning about people and the context. We ought to use mental tools to "bubble up" insights and observations into a handful of key, significant clusters that can then be translated as our guiding principles to drive innovation generation efforts. The advantage of such a mindset is that we can be sure that the creative process that we use for generating concepts will be based on a set of principles solidly supported by learning about real-life challenges and opportunities.

Mahatma Gandhi was one man who turned everything he saw around him in the life of ordinary people into powerful guiding principles to affect people around him and create innovations in social reform. For example, nonviolence as a principle, very different from the conventional wisdom of any revolutionary fighting for freedom, had a powerful impact on social reform. With such guiding principles he was able to focus his energy on innovative initiatives for easing poverty, extending women's rights, building religious and ethnic unity, and enhancing economic self-reliance—and ultimately helping India achieve independence from foreign rule.

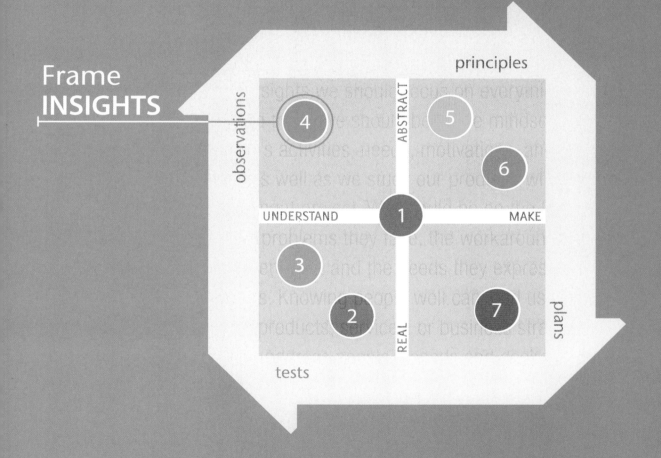

Frame
**INSIGHTS**

principles

observations

ABSTRACT

5

6

4

UNDERSTAND          1          MAKE

3

REAL

2

7

plans

tests

# FRAME INSIGHTS
## *methods*

# 4.1 Observations to Insights

Learning from what is observed in research by revealing nonobvious inner meanings

## EXAMPLE PROJECT: *Transaction Account of the Future (2011)*

Recent regulations limiting debit card swipe fees and the increased fees large banks impose on transaction accounts have created opportunities for small banks and credit unions to offer new products and services to their customers. Baker Tilly, an accounting and advisory firm, collaborated with a credit union–owned organization and the IIT Institute of Design to explore the next generation transaction account. A team comprising a project manager, consultant, and design analyst did research to understand the competition, current industry solutions, and trends. The team surveyed 89 banking and credit union customers online. Through prescreenings and 21 phone interviews, they identified 7 extreme customers, 18 to 65 years old, whose debit card transactions were extremely high or extremely low. The team then conducted in-depth interviews with these extreme customers to study their relationship with their banks, how they use technology, how they save, and how they use incentives and rewards programs.

Observations in the form of field notes and audio and video recording were organized and displayed on a project room white wall. By comparing and analyzing the responses of all participants the team generated six key insights. The insights were drawn from customers' behaviors and motivations. The insights were about the role of the family in banking and spending habits, knowledge as a key driver to use more products and services, adapting to customers' routines and behaviors, and customers desiring a uniform experience. More importantly, the team was able to map out these insights in a framework measuring avoidance, fear, anxiety, trust, responsibility, knowledge, and resolution.

**Insight :** Customer's adjust their behavior to adapt to their bank's policy and procedures.

Partitioning funds prevents users from taking responsibility of their spending.

>>If I keep a reserve set of funds- I don't have to control what I spend
>>I use my CC when I run low on cash so I don't have to control my spending and deny myself
>>I use a balance threshold to help me identify when I need to start monitoring my spending

EDUCAID
Partitioning of money
WACHOVIA

## PARTITIONING

Banking Routine (after change to bi-weekly pay)

Credit Union

W/D cash for expenses

also current method

TCF — Primary acct 1 week expenses

TCF (Secondary acct) business acct 2nd week funds on reserve

transfers as needed

Hayes 5.26

EDUCAID

**BENEFITS**

- Supports transition
- Builds knowledge base
- Encourages comprehensiveness
- Makes process transparent
- Promotes shared understanding

**INPUT**

- All observations captured during the Know People and Know Context modes

**OUTPUT**

- A collection of structured insight statements that can be traced back to corresponding observations

**WHEN TO USE**

## WHAT IT DOES

Research produces a number of observations about people and context. In this method we systematically think through all these observations and extract valuable insights. An insight, according to common definition, is the act of "seeing into" a situation or understanding the "inner nature" of what we observe. It is our learning from an observation through our interpretation by asking the question why. It encapsulates a point of view, a generally acceptable interpretation that we can somewhat objectively rationalize. The most useful insights are nonobvious and surprising.

An example description of an observation is: "People so often move a chair a few inches this way and that before sitting on it." An example insight description for the above is: "Before taking possession of things, people demonstrate their control over them as a declaration of autonomy to themselves."

## HOW IT WORKS

### Step 1: Gather observations and describe them.

Observations come from field notes, photos, video/audio recordings, facts, and the results of other methods. For each observation, write a small description as a factual statement of what is happening. No interpretations or judgments should be made at this point while describing observations.

### STEP 2: Ask why and find an agreed-upon rationale.

As a group, question why these observations are happening. Find out people's reasoning behind their actions and behaviors. Take a point of view or make a well-aligned interpretation. Document all "insights" and choose the most agreeable ones.

### STEP 3: Describe the insights.

Write a concise and objective statement for each insight. Insights should be written as a general statement since it represents a higher-level learning from a specific observation. The statement, "People move chairs before sitting on them as a demonstration of their control over it" is a good interpretation but still too specific. It is because this behavior is not only about moving chairs, but also about other things that people take possession of, for example, moving bagged items toward them on the checkout counter even before finishing the payment process and leaving the station. "Before taking possession of things, people demonstrate their control over them as a declaration of autonomy to themselves" is a more general insight statement.

### STEP 4: Organize the insights.

Organize all the observation statements and the corresponding insight statements in a spreadsheet. Note that many observations might lead to one insight or many insights could come out of one observation.

### STEP 5: Discuss and refine.

As a group, discuss the insights as overall learning from the research. How surprising or nonobvious are these insights? Is the collection of insights extensive enough to cover the whole topic? Is more research or validation needed?

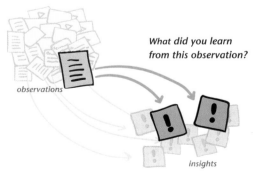

*What did you learn from this observation?*

observations

insights

Manually sorting insights from research to find clusters and hierarchies

Roles & Expertise

Promote accountability and trust among project stakeholders by helping them define roles and demonstrate expertise.

Common Context

Improve communication and understanding by helping stakeholders establish common ground.

Value Creation

Help stakeholders identify sources of value to better allocate resources and improve their overall experience.

Making It Real

Support discovery and decision making with tools that reflect real-world situations.

Project Transparency

Simplify information capture and access over the life of a project and beyond.

Personal Relationships

Incorporate empathy into the underlying architecture to build trust and support interpersonal relationships.

*insight clusters*

*insight cards*

## EXAMPLE PROJECT:
### Residential and Commercial Renovation (2010)

In 2010, a 3D design, engineering, and entertainment software company worked with the IIT Institute of Design team to understand how customers select products for residential and commercial construction and renovation projects. From research the team generated 40 insight statements. One of them, for example, was about access and it stated: "Quick access to real-world examples of product use and trusted product experts can be critical to validate product selection." Another insight was about experience: "Providing clients a way to experience the look and feel of the final design concept is important to convince them to pursue a design direction." At the end of the research phase, the IIT Institute of Design team invited the company representatives to participate in a work-session to present their early-stage research findings and to engage in a co-analysis of their collected insights.

One of the main exercises in this workshop was Insights Sorting in which the team and the company representatives together identified relationships among the insights and clustered them to find useful patterns. Some of the initial clusters dealt with customers' knowledge about renovation, their expectations of value, life of the renovation project, ownership, and trust among others. After many iterations of sorting, the team narrowed down their insight clusters into six themes: Value Creation, Roles and Expertise, Common Context, Personal Relationships, Project Transparency, and Making It Real. The theme of Making It Real, for example, showed that customers are reluctant to take a chance on new products, and this can be overcome with a tangible experience. Later, design principles were created for these themes. One of the design principles that came out of the Making It Real theme was, "Help homeowners understand spatial relationships and overall context of use." Each theme led to several such design principles that would provide a strong direction for concept generation, serve as an evaluation criterion to refine concepts, and further inform

**BENEFITS**

- Reveals patterns
- Reveals relationships
- Structures existing knowledge
- Facilitates discussion

**INPUT**

- All insights captured during Know Context and Know People modes

**OUTPUT**

- Clusters of insights showing patterns and relationships

**WHEN TO USE**

## WHAT IT DOES

The method starts with gathering all the insights we have generated from research. We write insight statements on sticky notes and start sorting them to find an agreed-upon clustering logic. Once the team agrees on this clustering logic, we resort all the insights to reveal interesting clustering patterns. Analyzing these clustering patterns not only gives us a better understanding of the topic but also provides a strong foundation for generating concepts. To get the most value out of this method, we should use a manageable number of insights—not more than 100 insights for a small project. This method is a quick and rough analog version of the digital spreadsheet-based matrix sorting.

## HOW IT WORKS

### STEP 1: Gather insight statements.

Gather all the insight statements you have generated from research. If you have not already generated insights, then go through your observations and other findings from research and generate them. Insights are interpretations of what you have observed in your research about people and the context that reveal something nonobvious, surprising, and valuable for your project. Write insight statements as one or two phrases or sentences.

### STEP 2: Do a sample sort and reach alignment on clustering logic.

Write insight statements on sticky notes. As a team, start clustering these insight statements on a wall or table surface. Discuss the logic you are using to cluster them. A common logic frequently used is how one insight is "similar" to another in terms of meanings they share. Reach alignment about this clustering logic.

### STEP 3: Cluster and recluster insight statements.

Complete the clustering activity based on the agreed-upon clustering logic. Discuss and gain a shared understanding about why all the insight statements in a cluster are grouped together. Cluster and recluster if necessary until you reach a stable clustering pattern.

### STEP 4: Define the clusters.

Discuss insight clusters and recognize why they are grouped that way. Define each cluster and describe its overall characteristics. Give each cluster a short title.

### STEP 5: Discuss next steps.

Document the patterns. Discuss among your team members how these clustering patterns can be made valuable to the later stages of the project. Are the insight clusters comprehensive enough to holistically address the project? Are there apparent gaps that need to be filled? Are the clusters defined well enough to generate design principles? Can the clusters be used as criteria to evaluate and refine concepts?

sort A sort B sort C sort D sort E

**4.2 INSIGHTS SORTING**

# 4.3 User Observation Database Queries

Making requests to databases containing observations and getting responses

| | Common to all | Unique |
|---|---|---|
| **Needs** | **Storage**<br>Dedicated storage<br><br>Temp dry and cold storage | **Energy Sources**<br>Specific cooking processes (e.g. grilling, frying, steaming)<br><br>Socioeconomic limitations |
| **Principles** | Modularity<br>Multifunctionality<br>Adaptability<br>Social/family use | Cultural Factors (e.g. keeping food kosher)<br><br>Volume and frequency of use |

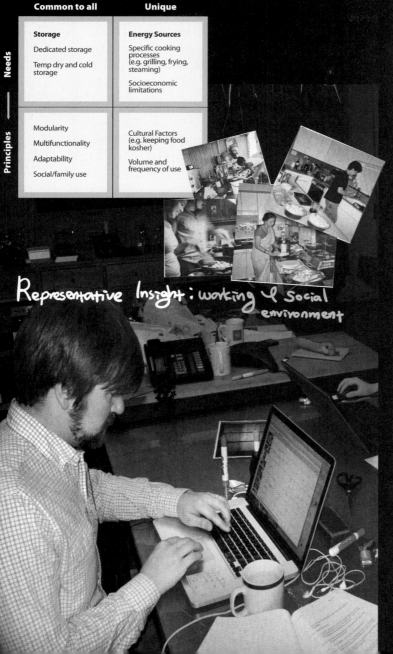

*Representative Insight: working & social environment*

*EXAMPLE PROJECT:*
## *Global Cooking Platform (2007)*

With all the cultural diversity across the globe, some basic activities, like cooking, are a common thread among all of us. A team at the IIT Institute of Design initiated a project with the goal of conceiving a global cooking platform, focused on the commonalities in cooking activities across cultures, while having the flexibility to be customized to adapt to local nuances. With only four months to complete the project with such a broad scope, the project team decided to draw insights from the IIT Institute of Design's proprietary User Observations Database, which had data from a number of completed research projects. From this comprehensive database, the team selected six discreet studies spanning 2 years, 3 countries, and 38 households that covered different areas of home-life activities, including healthy eating, activities centered in the kitchen, kitchen design/renovation processes, and entertaining. The final sample for analysis comprised research data from 12 different households in Chicago; 20 in Johannesburg and Cape Town, South Africa; and 6 in New Delhi and Mumbai, India.

The team searched through this segment of the database with several queries. Some of the queries were aimed at revealing commonalities or differences among cooking activities in different cultures. The team selected and compiled those insights most relevant to creating a global cooking platform. One of the insights they found common to all cultures was kitchen as a flexible and social environment and a space that's adapted to different tasks. They also uncovered insights about differences in these cultures. For example, the need for dedicated and temporary storage was common to all. But the need for energy sources varied drastically according to uniquely different cooking processes and the unique socioeconomic limitations of families in these cultures. The team further derived design principles, both common and unique to cultures, to help generate concepts for a global cooking platform.

**BENEFITS**

- Enables systematic analysis
- Encourages comprehensiveness
- Handles large sets of data
- Reveals patterns

**INPUT**

- User Observations Database with a critical mass of research data
- Conjectures about users' behaviors

**OUTPUT**

- Insights about user behavior patterns
- Understanding of the breadth of data collected

**WHEN TO USE**

## WHAT IT DOES

Observation Queries is a method that uses a database like the User Observations Database, a continuously updated collection of user observations and insights gathered from research projects from around the world that can be searched by keywords. In this database, user observations are organized with their related photos/videos/field notes, descriptions, quotations, activities, and insights. The observations are also tagged with keywords from frameworks such as POEMS (people, objects, environments, messages, and services). We send queries to the database based on our conjectures about possible behaviors. For example, if we have a conjecture that the presence of televisions in the kitchen affects cooking behaviors, we could enter a keyword query to search for all observations with "family members in kitchens viewing televisions and cooking" and look at the results. We can review the found observations in detail, look for patterns across these observations, test the validity of our conjectures, and gain valuable insights.

## HOW IT WORKS

### STEP 1: Capture conjectures.

Refer to the research findings from Know People and Know Context modes of the project to formulate statements about your conjectures—behaviors that you think might happen.

### STEP 2: List keywords that relate to your conjectures.

For example, if your earlier research findings lead you to conjecture that breakfast is mostly eaten on the way to school or work, your query could include keywords such as "breakfast," "eating on the go," "morning," "commuting," and other similar words.

### STEP 3: Send queries.

Open the User Observations Database and send your combinations of words as queries for searching.

### STEP 4: Review query results.

Review the search results as a spreadsheet that organizes all the found observations in rows along with their related photos/videos/field notes, descriptions, quotations, activities, insights, and tags. Look for patterns across the found observations. See if these patterns match with your conjectures. Capture your insights.

### STEP 5: Modify queries and repeat the search.

Modify your conjecture with a different set of keywords and repeat the process for additional insights. Try a new query based on another conjecture.

### STEP 6: Summarize findings and discuss.

Prepare a summary document showing the results of all queries and key insights. Share them with team members and discuss your learning. Were your conjectures verified? What behavioral patterns emerged? Does the database have enough research data to reliably reveal new insights? Is there any additional research needed?

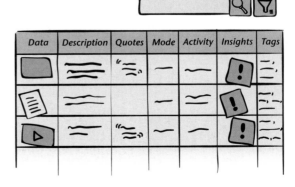

4.3 USER OBSERVATION DATABASE QUERIES

Analyzing research participants' responses to understand patterns and derive insights

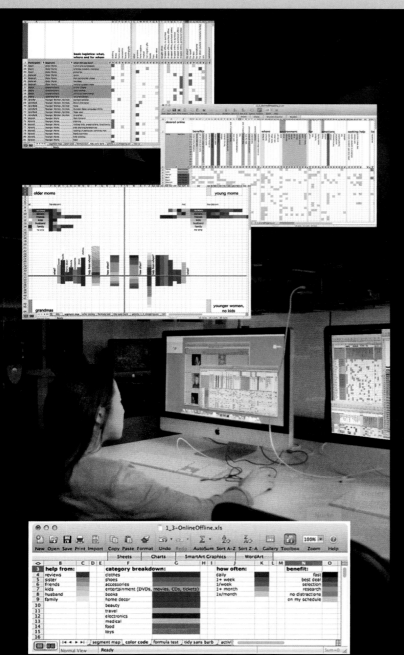

### EXAMPLE PROJECT: *Online Women Shopping (2010)*

The emergence of online user research platforms has created quick access to more data, which has translated into increased data complexity. A communication design workshop at the IIT Institute of Design explored different analytic methods for the efficient and effective management of these large data sets as well as information design principles for communicating research findings. Students worked individually using Revelation, an online research platform that collected a large qualitative data set on how working women use the Internet to care for their families.

The team downloaded the raw data from the online database into an Excel spreadsheet for doing the User Response Analysis. Each student also began by taking a point of view of what they wanted to understand from the data. One student decided to start by understanding who shops offline and online, and what and for whom they were buying. These three questions formed the first data filters in the spreadsheet. As she analyzed the responses for whom these women were making purchases, she began to color-code them in categories of "me" in green, if women were buying for themselves, and "we" in blue, if they were buying for the family. Insights about women in different life stages began to emerge showing that young wives spend equal amounts of time buying for themselves and their husbands, moms with kids preferred the flexibility of online shopping, and grandmas preferred to shop and treat others than to buy for themselves. Color-coding the responses amplified the visual picture of the "me" versus "we" shopping behaviors. This supported her design concepts for "me" shoppers developed for a mid-luxury retailer. These concepts were aimed at helping "me" shoppers connect with their families and friends, get the best quality for the best deal, and feel more in control by being an efficient and organized shopper.

**BENEFITS**

- Enables systematic analysis
- Handles large sets of data
- Keeps grounded in research
- Organizes information for easy access
- Reveals patterns

**INPUT**

- Large sets of user response data

**OUTPUT**

- Insights about patterns in user responses

**WHEN TO USE**

## WHAT IT DOES

User Response Analysis is a method that uses data visualization techniques, such as color and size, to analyze large quantities of qualitative data gathered from user surveys, questionnaires, interviews, and other ethnographic research methods. This method takes all of the qualitative, text-based data from ethnographic research—what users have said—and inputs it into a spreadsheet for data manipulation using keyword filters, data organization by arranging information in specific columns and rows, and visual coding using color to identify patterns. The visual approach helps uncover patterns from the data and find insights into what matters most to users.

## HOW IT WORKS

### STEP 1: Gather user research data into a spreadsheet.

Gather user research from questionnaires, interview transcripts, surveys, and others and enter in a spreadsheet.

### STEP 2: Reduce and organize the data.

Determine what you want to analyze, such as an entire group, a segment of a group (according to type of activity, age, gender, frequency of use), or simply individual responses. Choose topics for comparison. These could be specific questions asked in questionnaires, topics that came up in interviews, or some other dimension. Create a table to organize the data with user categories as row headings and topics of comparison as column headings.

### STEP 3: Determine the kinds of searches to conduct.

Determine if you want to conduct a broad or focused keyword search. For example, a keyword search using the word "shopping" may return results that are very general for your analysis. Additional keywords such as "grocery" or "high-end retail" may return results more suitable for your objective.

### STEP 4: Visually code the queried results.

Use visual techniques such as color, shapes, and size to highlight patterns found in your results. For example, user responses can be color-coded by age, gender, or type of user responses. The visual coding creates a macroview showing visual clusters from which new relationships can be understood.

### STEP 5: Analyze visualization for patterns and insights.

Analyze the visual map for similarities and differences such as disproportionate number of entries between two data sets. For example, a visualization comparing how different age groups of women spend time online show that more women in their 40s spend time at online banking sites than women in their 20s or 30s. Draw insights by exploring the similarities and differences in the visual data clusters and by asking probing questions about what might be influencing them.

### STEP 6: Document insights.

Summarize your analysis and insights and share them among team members. Include information that indicates the need for additional analysis.

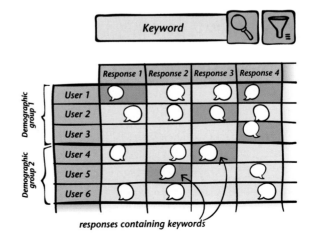

*responses containing keywords*

Diagram and analyze Entities, Relations, Attributes, and Flows

*EXAMPLE PROJECT: NHL Hockey (2008)*

What makes a sport's fan a sport's fan? What motivates a person to engage with professional sports? Asking these questions, a team of students at the IIT Institute of Design identified opportunity areas for hockey that would increase the sport's fan base.

After initial examination of the context surrounding the National Hockey League (NHL), the team recognized the impact of media and advertising on the engagement level of fans and, using the *ERAF Systems Diagram* method, evaluated the relationship between the NHL and its fans through media and advertising channels. The ERAF Systems Diagram highlighted the complex system of interactions among hockey fans, the league, the physical environment, advertising, media, and merchandising. Although it was evident that each of the entities played a significant role in all parts of the NHL fan journey, the ERAF Systems Diagram helped the team develop insights such as the disconnect between the NHL and its fans resulting from their indirect and mediated interactions. Insights about this disconnect led the team to develop two key design principles: indoctrinate fans as early as possible in their lives and highlight the positive elements of hockey's exclusivity and dispel cultural misconceptions.

**BENEFITS**

- Captures current conditions
- Creates overview
- Promotes shared understanding
- Reveals relationships
- Structures existing knowledge
- Visualizes information

**INPUT**

- Context and user research data

**OUTPUT**

- Diagrammatic visualization of the context being studied

**WHEN TO USE**

## WHAT IT DOES

The ERAF Systems Diagram is a method for creating high level–systems views of the context being explored. It helps us think about all elements of a system and their interactions with one another. Regardless of the project, any system can be basically understood by studying it as a set of entities, relations, attributes, and flows.

*Entities* are the definable parts of the system. They can be viewed as the "nouns" present in the system, such as people, places, and things. Examples of physical entities might be students, schools, or books. Conceptual entities can include abstractions such as projects, problems, or goals.

*Relations* describe how the entities connect with one another. Relations can be thought of as the "verbs" describing the nature of connection. A diagram of the retail industry might indicate the relation between fashion designers and retail buyers, with the relation defined as "fashion designers inspire buyers." Relations can be measured in that a value can be put on it.

*Attributes* are defining characteristics of any entity or relation. Because they are descriptive, they function as the "adjectives" in the system. Qualitative attributes include names, brand, or perceptions such as favorable or unfavorable. Quantitative attributes are age, size, cost, duration, or other dimensions that can be measured as quantities.

*Flows* are the directional relations between entities. They are like "prepositions" in that they indicate "to and from," "before and after," or "in and out." Flows take two forms: temporal flows, which indicate sequence and are linked to time, and

process flows, which show inputs and outputs, feedback loops, or parallel processes that indicate how things move through the system.

The ERAF Systems Diagram works on two levels: It is synthetic in that the information gathered through research is brought together in a single systems diagram, and it is analytic in that the study of the diagram points to existing, emerging, or potential problems, imbalances, missing entities, and other gaps.

## HOW IT WORKS

### STEP 1: Identify entities of the system.

Include only those entities that have a significant impact on your project. While identifying entities, keep in mind the analogy that they are the nouns of the system. List people, places, things, organizations, and the like that comprehensively cover the context you want to analyze. Draw circles to represent these entities and label them.

### STEP 2: Define relations and flows among entities.

Draw lines to show relations and arrows for flows in the diagram. Add text labels to describe these relations and flows.

### STEP 3: Define attributes of entities.

Identify attributes that are important to know for the project. Represent them as smaller circles and add labels. For detailed analysis, enter the attribute values as well; for example, income, age, and so forth.

### STEP 4: Refine the network diagram.

The resulting general diagram will show you context as a set of entities, relations, attributes, and flows. Review the diagram as a team to ensure that all these elements are comprehensively captured and described in this systems diagram.

**4.5 ERAF SYSTEMS DIAGRAM**

## STEP 5: Analyze the diagram.

Study the ERAF Systems Diagram to diagnose the current state of the context. As you review the system diagram, look for gaps, disconnects, missing entities, missing relations, or other aspects of the system that are a problem or have potential to become one. Generate a list of these deficiencies.

## STEP 6: Discuss the diagram and extract insights.

Are there big disconnects? Are there opportunities for creating new entities? Can new relations be established for creating additional value? Are there weak entities that need attention? Share these visualizations and insights with your team members and develop an action plan for next steps.

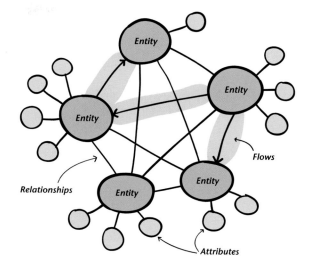

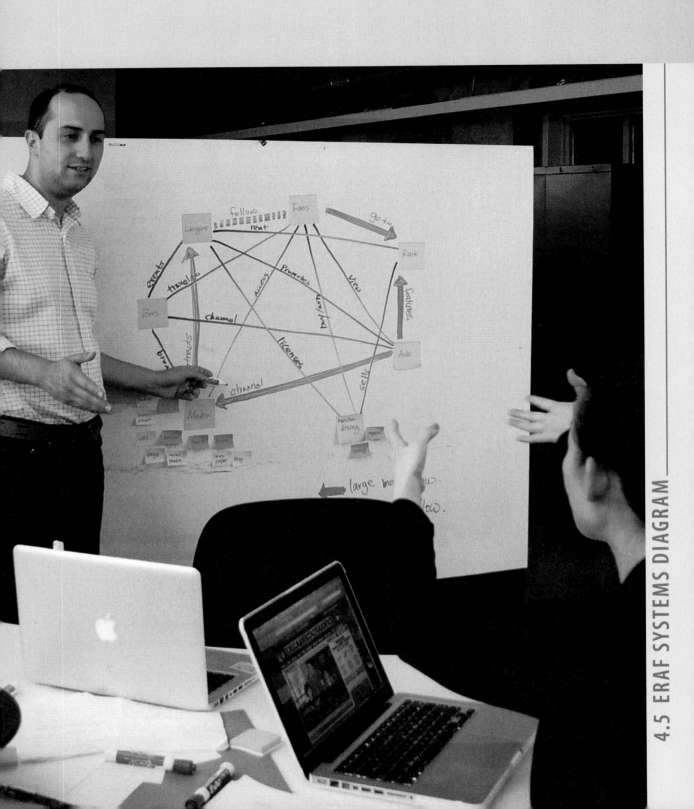

4.5 ERAF SYSTEMS DIAGRAM

# 4.6 Descriptive Value Web

Constructing a network diagram showing how value is created and exchanged in the context

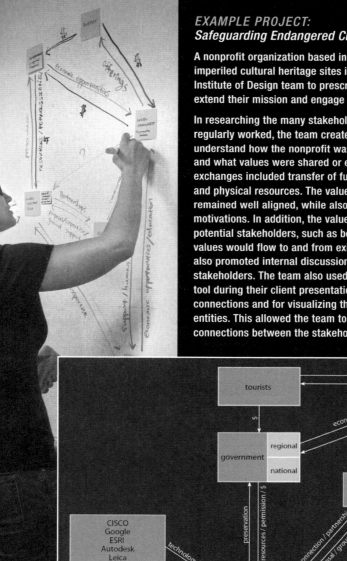

**EXAMPLE PROJECT:**
*Safeguarding Endangered Cultural Heritage Sites (2008)*

A nonprofit organization based in California that seeks to protect imperiled cultural heritage sites in the developing world tasked an IIT Institute of Design team to prescribe new strategic opportunities to extend their mission and engage new visitors.

In researching the many stakeholders with whom the organization regularly worked, the team created a *Descriptive Value Web* to better understand how the nonprofit was connected to the various players and what values were shared or exchanged between them. These exchanges included transfer of funds, different offerings, knowledge, and physical resources. The value web helped show entities that remained well aligned, while also exposing underlying stakeholder motivations. In addition, the value web helped the team explore new potential stakeholders, such as book publishers, and visualize how new values would flow to and from existing entities. In doing so, the team also promoted internal discussion about these newly identified potential stakeholders. The team also used the Descriptive Value Web as a central tool during their client presentation; both for showing stakeholder value connections and for visualizing the proposed solution with the new entities. This allowed the team to quickly convey all of the complex connections between the stakeholders in a meaningful, digestible way.

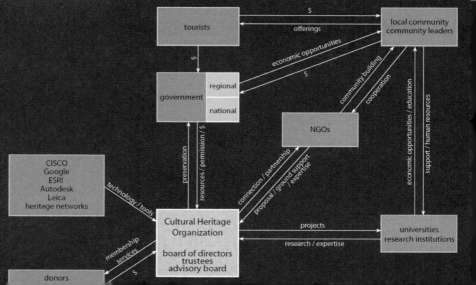

## WHAT IT DOES

A Descriptive Value Web visualizes the existing set of relationships among stakeholders in a given context, showing how value is exchanged and flows through the system. Most frequently it is represented as a network diagram in which stakeholders are presented as nodes connected by links with descriptions of what value is flowing from node to node. Common value flows include: money, information, materials, and services. Descriptive Value Webs should be viewed as snapshots of a dynamic system and, therefore, should be revisited and built upon as new information becomes available. A *descriptive* value web is used in the analysis mode to understand the state of current conditions, while a *prescriptive* value web is created in the synthesis mode to describe possible future states.

## HOW IT WORKS

### STEP 1: List all relevant stakeholders in the given context.

The stakeholders should include competing organizations, complementary organizations, suppliers, distributors, customers, relevant government agencies, and other entities that derive value from the present conditions.

### STEP 2: Determine relevant value flows.

Keep in mind that money is not always a given value flow. Consider flows of information, materials, services, and other intangible values like reputation. For example, projects designed for social good have different values such as opportunity, access to social services, or socially uplifting influences.

### STEP 3: Draw an initial value web.

Combine information from Steps 1 and 2 into a preliminary network diagram that represents your understanding of the current conditions. This initial web should serve as a sketch for further discussion and analysis.

Make sure all nodes and links are clearly labeled so that someone seeing the web for the first time can quickly grasp the nature of values being exchanged.

### STEP 4: Analyze the value web.

Ask questions to fully understand the dynamics of the value web. Where is the value fundamentally created? Which stakeholders have dominance? Which control customer interface? Which control intellectual property? Where are inefficiencies in the system? Where are the gaps? Are there imbalances in the way value flows? Discuss these and other questions as a team and document your insights.

### STEP 5: Review and refine the value web.

Through discussions among team members and outside experts, refine the value web until you reach consensus that it reflects the current state. Be sure to save all iterations so that anyone coming into the discussion at a later point can follow the rationale that underlies your depiction. Since current conditions change all of the time, plan to review the value web regularly throughout the project, as you are made aware of additional information.

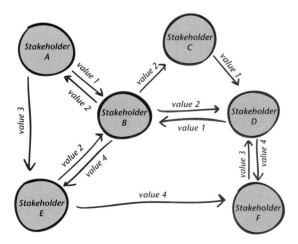

4.6 DESCRIPTIVE VALUE WEB

Plotting entities on a position map to analyze their distribution and grouping patterns

Large

climbers

rich

Utility

Indulgence

large utility sedans

strivers

indulgent compacts

seekers

Small

▲ Compact 3-Box   ● Wagon/Minivan   ▬ Truck   ◆ 4-door sedan   ● Sports/Coupe   ★ SUV

## EXAMPLE PROJECT:
### Car Buying in India (2008)

In 2008, a team at the IIT Institute of Design worked on a project to understand the car-buying motivations of people in India buying their primary car and identify ways to facilitate and improve the car-buying process.

One aspect that the team examined was the availability of cars in the Indian market. To evaluate potential innovation opportunities, the team used an *Entities Position Map* with axes that represented the size of car (large versus small) and the type of car (utility versus indulgence). By positioning each car within these extremes, the team saw how the cars related to each other.

They then related the distribution and grouping patterns to McKinsey's customer groups model based on household income in Indian market that included buyer groups like rich, climbers, strivers, and seekers. The team uncovered insights for each of these four buyer groups. For example, the grouping analysis showed that strivers had limited selection in the size and type of car, leaving them with only the choice of compact cars. This revealed an opportunity area in the market for striver-focused, larger, utility sedans. Another insight was the lack of a prominent presence for indulgent compacts. If pervasively introduced, these cars could find buyer potential in strivers, climbers, and the rich. The team gained better focus from these insights and conducted further research to identify car buyers' motivations, buying process flaws, and opportunity areas for innovation in the Indian car market.

**BENEFITS**

- Creates overview
- Facilitates comparison
- Identifies opportunities
- Improves communication
- Visualizes information

**INPUT**

- List of entities to be compared

**OUTPUT**

- Map of entities positioned according to two attribute scales revealing insights and opportunity areas

**WHEN TO USE**

## WHAT IT DOES

The Entities Position Map is a method for analyzing how entities group together in relation to two intersecting attribute scales. Each entity is plotted within the boundaries of the position map. The method helps illuminate not just where entities fall within this defined space, but their relative position to one another. Once entities have been plotted, mainly five kinds of analysis could be performed.

## HOW IT WORKS

### STEP 1: Identify entities for comparison.

Most commonly analyzed entities are products, services, technologies, users, activities, places, innovation cases, brands, and organizations.

### STEP 2: Determine attributes for comparison.

Select two attributes related to the entities that you think would be most useful for analysis. For example, for a study on cars you might choose "size" and "usage" as attributes. Turn these attributes into scales, for example, "small versus large" and "utility versus indulgence." Create a position map using these two scales.

### STEP 3: Create a position map and plot entities.

First find those entities that are likely to occupy the most extreme corners of the position map and plot them. These entities, therefore, set the boundary conditions for the context. Place the remaining entities onto the position map. The resulting constellation becomes the basis for analysis.

### STEP 4: Analyze the position map.

*Extreme analysis:* Study the entities positioned at the extreme edges and corners of the map. Look for any patterns and search for insights.

*Grouping analysis:* Groupings will be concentrations of entities on the map that suggest commonalities or affinities among them. Represent groupings by drawing a circle around them and write insights.

*Gap analysis:* It is just as important to analyze where entities do not cluster. Do the gaps represent unmet needs or areas of potential opportunity? What if anything about existing conditions makes them inhospitable to entities?

*Migration analysis:* Identify those entities that may occupy a different position on the map over time. Use arrows to indicate this migration on the map. How do these migrations affect other entities and the overall context?

*Quadrant analysis:* What are the common characteristics of the entities that fall within each quadrant? How do they differ from the entities in other quadrants? Do the entities positioned in a quadrant point to any unique characteristics of that quadrant, besides what is known from the attribute scales?

### STEP 5: Share insights and discuss.

Gather insights and findings and prepare summary documents. Share with team members and discuss.

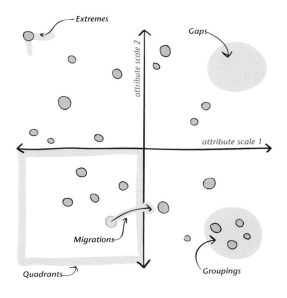

**4.7 ENTITIES POSITION MAP**

Diagramming to analyze clusters of entities that overlap

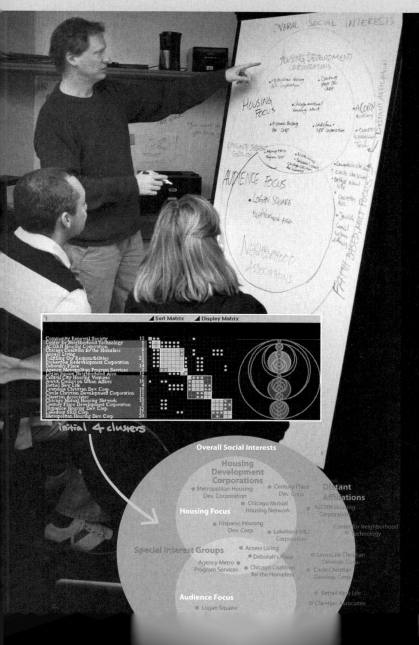

initial 4 clusters

**Overall Social Interests**

**Housing Development Corporations**

Housing Focus

Special Interest Groups

Audience Focus

Distant Affiliations

## EXAMPLE PROJECT: *Rehab Network (2001)*

A team of students in a Design Analysis project at the IIT Institute of Design sought to analyze a Midwest alliance of community-based development organizations that provides safe and affordable housing. The objective of this project was to analyze and understand the interactions, structures, and motivations of these social service organizations. The team wanted to conclude the project with some defined opportunity areas and insights about techniques to achieve them.

They performed a membership analysis of the alliance to better understand the types of organizations that comprised it. The analysis revealed four initial organization clusters: Housing Development Corporations, Faith-Based Organizations, Special Interest Groups, and Distant Affiliations. Using these clusters, the team created a ***Venn Diagram*** around the organizations in the alliance. While developing the diagram the team discussions led to the identification of an additional cluster, the Neighborhood Associations. The team determined that Neighborhood Associations were more audience-focused, while Housing Development Corporations were more housing-focused. The housing and audience focal points became the main overlapping circles in the Venn diagram with Special Interest Groups falling into the overlap between them. Distant Affiliations and Faith-Based organizations fell outside of these circles, but within the umbrella category covering social interests. The team didn't simply fit the clusters to the Venn diagram circles, but rather formed the diagram from the bottom up around the clusters. The Venn Diagramming method provided the team with a simple, visual way to organize and make connections of the different types of organizations they were analyzing.

**BENEFITS**
- Facilitates comparison
- Identifies opportunities
- Improves communication
- Reveals relationships
- Visualizes information

**INPUT**
- Sets of entities based on research findings

**OUTPUT**
- A diagram showing overlapping clusters of entities

**WHEN TO USE**

## WHAT IT DOES

Venn Diagramming is an effective method to analyze the overlaps between two or more clusters of entities. The most common context in which the method is used is for industry-level analysis. For example, if examining innovations in the video game industry, understanding overlaps between developments in the electronics, entertainment, and computer industries would be beneficial. Venn diagrams use visualizations with overlapping circles. The interior of a circle represents the entities in that cluster, while the exterior represents entities that are not members of that cluster. Venn diagrams typically support not more than three or four overlapping clusters; beyond this, the diagram becomes difficult to read and complicated to understand.

## HOW IT WORKS

### STEP 1: Identify entities for grouping and overlapping.

Although the type of entities that you want to cluster and overlap depends on the project, entities that usually benefit from seeing overlaps are products, services, technologies, users, places, brands, and organizations.

### STEP 2: Cluster entities and overlap clusters.

As you start clustering entities one by one, place the entities related together as groups and draw circles around them. If you find that some entities are common to two or more clusters, place them at the intersection of those clusters by drawing overlapping circles. When you add a new entity to the set, decide if they need to be placed outside the circles, inside the circles, or inside the intersections between circles, based on their relationship. Build the entire Venn diagram this way so that patterns of groupings and overlaps emerge.

### STEP 3: Analyze the clusters and overlaps.

*Analyze clusters:* Understand the entities in the clusters and label them.

*Analyze overlaps:* Focus on entities in the overlaps and understand their meaning.

*Analyze outliers:* Understand the meaning of disjointed entities that are outside clusters.

### STEP 4: Share insights and discuss.

Gather insights and prepare summary documents. Share with team members and discuss. How critically significant are the entities in the overlaps since they affect multiple clusters? Are there opportunities for increasing or reducing overlaps?

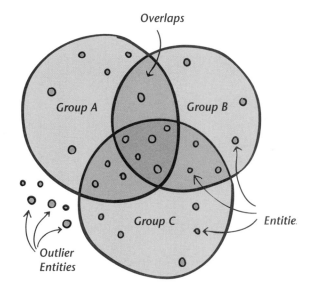

4.8 VENN DIAGRAMMING

# Tree/Semi-Lattice Diagramming

## Diagramming to analyze entities related in hierarchies

### Social Development

- Civic Involvement
- Community Participation
- Family Support

**Organizing**
14. Adapt to Community Standards
15. Liaise Public Information
16. Delineate Ownership Boundaries
17. Conserve Community Resources
18. Map Community Assets

**Community Building**
19. Innovate Land Use
20. Develop Public Spaces
21. Cultivate Shared Reference Material
22. Support Local Economic Drivers
23. Allow Interdependence
24. Contribute to Public Safety
25. Build Community Trust

**Nurturing**
26. Support Parenting
27. Encourage Expression
28. Support Family Communications
29. Encourage Socially Healthy Practices
30. Support Elder Care
31. Provide Creative Environment

**Assisting**
32. Detect Anomalies in Routine
33. Integrate Physical Assistance
34. Respond to Elder/Child Care Cues
35. Support Spacial Reconfiguration
36. Guide Emergency Response
37. Promote Autonomy
38. Coordinate Schedules
39. Ease Tension

**Entertaining**
40. Adapt Space for Social Rituals
41. Provide Space for Family Activities
42. Afford Entertainment Options
43. Provide Access to Community Activities
44. Decorate Space for Celebration

## EXAMPLE PROJECT: *Future of Living (2009)*

The convergence of trends in population growth, climate change, and resource depletion will undoubtedly have an impact on our living habits. Using principles of structured planning, students at the IIT Institute of Design developed self-sufficient dwellings for the future that integrate support for human aspirations.

In the first phase of the project, student teams worked on five segments (resource provision, environmental management, biological support, personal development, and social development) that the new housing system should address. Through contextual research, each team working on a segment identified their segment's critical issues and established the different users, activities, and functions occurring in that segment. Analysis of all activities resulted in a function structure comprising different modes under which different activities and functions were represented.

Each team used a *Semi-Lattice Diagram* to construct its function structure. For example, the social development team constructed theirs showing family support, community participation, and civic involvement as three main modes in which social development will be crucial to the housing system. The team then determined the critical activities happening in each mode. For the family support mode, the key social development activities were nurturing, assisting, and entertaining under which they defined the specific functions that people would perform. They identified that those engaged in the nurturing activity would need to perform specific functions such as support parenting, family communications, and elder care as well as encourage personal expression.

The function structures for all five segments served as the input for phase two of the project that used two proprietary computer programs to establish the links between the different activities and elements for proposed solutions.

**BENEFITS**
- Creates overview
- Improves communication
- Reveals relationships
- Visualizes information

**INPUT**
- Set of entities and an understanding of their relations based on research findings

**OUTPUT**
- A diagram visualizing entities related together in hierarchies

**WHEN TO USE**

## WHAT IT DOES

The Tree and Semi-Lattice Diagrams are good for analyzing the hierarchical nature of relationships among entities. In a tree diagram, one child entity can have only one parent entity and, therefore, the branches are distinctly separate. In a semi-lattice diagram, one child can have more than one parent and, therefore, the branches can cross over. For example, a company's "organizational chart" is normally represented as a tree diagram that presents peoples' role structures from the CEO to senior management to directors to middle managers, and so on. But, if individual middle managers report to more than one director, then the representation is a semi-lattice diagram. In a Tree/Semi-Lattice Diagram, dots or circles represent entities and lines show connections between them. For easy readability, Tree/Semi-Lattice Diagrams usually show not more than five levels in the hierarchy.

The Tree/Semi-Lattice Diagram method is most useful for data in which entities have hierarchies, and understanding the level differences is important for getting insights about the context.

## HOW IT WORKS

### STEP 1: Identify entities at various levels.

List all lower-level entities. These are the most fundamental components in the system. For example, if diagramming people's shopping behaviors, their specific tasks (e.g. making a grocery list) will be at the lowest level, their activities (e.g. making payments) next, and their mode/s (e.g. shopping) at the highest level.

### STEP 2: Construct the tree diagram.

Build the tree diagram either bottom-up by starting with the lowest level of entities or top-down starting with the highest level of entities. Represent entities as dots or circles, and connect the child entities to parent entities with lines.

### STEP 3: Analyze the diagram.

What can we learn from the shape of the tree/semi-lattice with its branching patterns? Are there branches that are distinctly denser or leaner than others? Or is the tree/semi-lattice balanced? Are there any missing entities or relations? Are entities distinct enough to be in those levels? If there are many cross-links in the semi-lattice, what do they mean? Does the tree/semi-lattice reflect your understanding of the context? Capture these insights and show them in relation to the tree/semi-lattice diagram.

### STEP 4: Share insights and discuss.

Prepare documents summarizing insights learned through analysis. Share with team members and discuss how the existing hierarchy affects the context and where opportunities for concepts may be found.

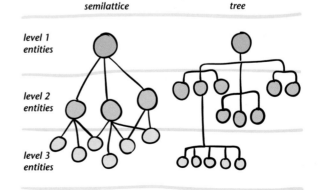

## 4.9 TREE/SEMI-LATTICE DIAGRAMMING

# 4.10 Symmetric Clustering Matrix

## Clustering entities in a set based on relations among them

**Quality:**
The quality cluster pertains to customer perceptions regarding the general store condition and product offering.

**Specialty items:**
The specialty items cluster connect motivations about specificity of offering and staff expertise.

**Urgent need:**
The urgent need motivations revolve around getting exactly what you need when you need it.

**Local flavor:**
These motivations refer to relationships that customers form with the store owners and the neighborhood.

In this project, a team of students set out to analyze corner stores defined as small, independently owned and operated convenience stores in urban environments. Their goals were to understand the motivations of customers' choice in choosing particular stores and to help a group of independent corner store owners increase revenue by aligning with customer needs and increasing loyalty among shoppers.

To understand shopper motivations, the team surveyed 100 convenience store shoppers and extracted 23 key motivations driving them to different stores. To understand how these different motivations related to one another and the higher-level drivers behind them, the team ran the list through a *Symmetric Clustering Matrix*, scoring each relationship between motivations on a scale from 0 to 3, with 0 having the weakest relationship and 3 the strongest. For example, "Sense of loyalty" and "Quality of products and store" were scored as 3, since the quality of products and the store cultivated stronger loyalty for shoppers. On the other hand, "Price" and "Customizability" were scored at 0, since these two motivations usually were not related to each other in a customer's choice. After scoring each relationship, the matrix was sorted, making visible the motivation clusters. Then, the team discussed these clusters, defined them, and named them according to the commonalities among them. The resulting motivation clusters were: Quality (perceptions of store condition and product offerings), Specialty Items (the nature of offering and staff expertise), Urgent Need (customers' ability to get what they want when they need it), and Local Flavor (relationships of customers with store owners and the neighborhood.) This process gave the team enough understanding to begin aligning these

**INPUT**
- Set of entities based on research findings
- A matrix tool for scoring and sorting

**OUTPUT**
- Entity clusters based on strengths of individual relations
- Insights about patterns among entities

**WHEN TO USE**

## What It Does

This method allows us to take a set of entities gathered during research and see how they are grouped based on their relationships. Seeing these grouping patterns from unstructured lists of entities is useful because they reveal high-level order and help us develop frameworks to drive concept exploration.

For example, a project on "personal finance" might begin by looking at peoples' activities around money. Through research we may have identified that people set different financial goals, for example, "investing in a retirement program" or "buying a house." The question becomes what relationship do these goals have to one another and are there higher-level patterns that tell us something useful? To understand this we need to compare each goal to others and see clusters. This is where the Symmetric Clustering Matrix helps. Using the matrix, goals can be compared to assess their similarity. They can be clustered and sorted to clarify how they are similar. The clusters of goals will indicate a larger framework for "personal finance," revealing insights, bringing clarity, and helping us find innovation opportunities.

## How It Works

### STEP 1: List entities for clustering.

List the kind of entities you want to compare to one another to find clustering patterns. Examples of possible listings are: (1) Peoples' activities, experiences, roles, needs, problems, challenges, goals, motivations, or other similar lists from the Know People mode; (2) Context elements like products, services, places, func-

tions, features, problems, challenges, and other similar lists from the Know Context mode.

List the entities from research findings, for example, a list of "peoples' goals in personal finance." Ensure that all elements in your list belong to the same level. For example, "investing in retirement plan" and "buying a home" are at the same level, but "issuing check for purchasing books" might be too detailed to be included in this level. Normalize the whole list this way, working as a team. Confirm that the list is also comprehensive and representative of the whole context.

### STEP 2: Determine the relation between entities.

One most commonly used relation is similarity that measures how one entity in the list is similar to another. Other examples of relations to consider are complementary (how one entity complements another), support (how one entity supports another), and frequency (how frequently one entity occurs with another).

### STEP 3: Determine a scoring scale to measure relations between entities.

The most commonly used scale has four steps: 0 means no relation between entities, 1 means minimum relation, 2 means medium relation, and 3 means maximum relation. Depending upon the scoring sensitivity needed, the scale can vary from a binary scale (0 or 1) to even one with nine steps ($-4, -3, -2, -1, 0, +1, +2, +3, +4$). It is a good idea to color-code matrix cells according to the corresponding scores. For example, lighter grays for lower scores and darker grays for higher scores.

4.10 SYMMETRIC CLUSTERING MATRIX

## STEP 4: Create a symmetric matrix.

Create a spreadsheet with a square symmetric matrix. For this, enter the same list of entities as both row and column headings. Each cell in this matrix represents a relation between two corresponding entities.

## STEP 5: Score the relations.

Enter a relation score in each matrix cell. Scoring is best done as a group to reduce biases and get to as objective a score as possible. At a minimum, spend the first hour as a group to do trial scoring so that all team members gain a shared understanding of the scoring logic and range. After this trial, restart and do the actual scoring. Scoring activity can be time-consuming and may need to be split up as the size of the matrix increases.

## STEP 6: Sort the matrix.

For small matrices (up to 30 × 30), you can do a manual sort of the matrix by shifting the position of columns and rows in the matrix so that two rows or columns having similar scores are kept next to each other. After a few shifts of columns and rows this way, you can see that the entities are reordered to reveal clusters. For larger matrices (more than 30 × 30) it is better to use available statistical algorithms to sort the matrix for efficiency.

## STEP 7: Identify clusters.

After sorting the matrix, take a step back and look at the whole matrix and see how many entity clusters can be visually identified. In a symmetric matrix, remember that the matrix is symmetric along the diagonal of the matrix. Therefore, clusters are going to form along the diagonal of the matrix. Identify a manageable and meaningful number of clusters. For a 100 × 100 matrix, it is a good idea to define 10 to 15 clusters. If needed, you could also recognize 3 to 6 higher-level clusters.

## STEP 8: Define and name clusters.

Ask questions like: What makes the entities in this cluster belong together as a group? Why is this cluster different from other clusters? Discuss as a group and define each cluster based on the similarity between entities. Appropriately label each cluster.

## STEP 9: Capture insights and make frameworks.

Capture insights out of the clustering patterns. Are the clusters of the same size and density? If their density and size varies a lot what does that mean? What can be learned from the different levels of clusters? If there are big overlaps between clusters, what does that mean? Discuss the clustering patterns, and refine them as useful frameworks for concept generation.

## STEP 10: Share insights and discuss.

Summarize findings and share them with team members and other stakeholders. Discuss the frameworks and use the feedback to revise your analysis. Document your process and results.

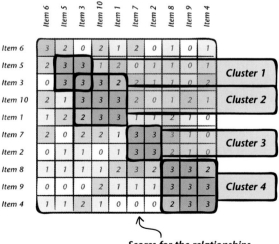

*Scores for the relationships between items from the same list*

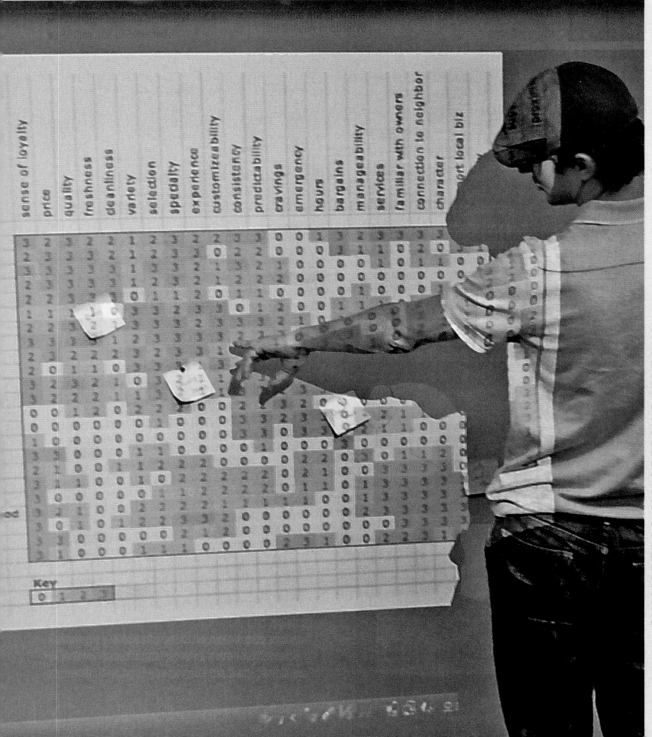

4.10 SYMMETRIC CLUSTERING MATRIX

# 4.11 Asymmetric Clustering Matrix

Clustering two entity lists based on relations between entities in one list to the other

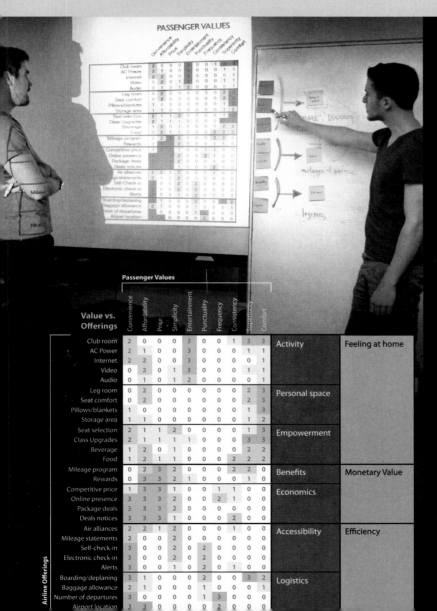

**Passenger Values**

| Value vs. Offerings | Convenience | Affordability | Price | Simplicity | Entertainment | Punctuality | Frequency | Consistency | Superiority | Comfort | | |
|---|---|---|---|---|---|---|---|---|---|---|---|---|
| **Club room** | 2 | 0 | 0 | 0 | 3 | 0 | 0 | 1 | 3 | 3 | Activity | Feeling at home |
| **AC Power** | 2 | 1 | 0 | 0 | 3 | 0 | 0 | 1 | 1 | | | |
| **Internet** | 2 | 2 | 0 | 0 | 3 | 0 | 0 | 0 | 0 | 1 | | |
| **Video** | 0 | 2 | 0 | 1 | 3 | 0 | 0 | 0 | 1 | 1 | | |
| **Audio** | 0 | 1 | 0 | 1 | 2 | 0 | 0 | 0 | 0 | 1 | | |
| **Leg room** | 0 | 2 | 0 | 0 | 0 | 0 | 0 | 0 | 2 | 3 | Personal space | |
| **Seat comfort** | 0 | 2 | 0 | 0 | 0 | 0 | 0 | 0 | 2 | 3 | | |
| **Pillows/blankets** | 1 | 0 | 0 | 0 | 0 | 0 | 0 | 0 | 1 | 3 | | |
| **Storage area** | 1 | 1 | 0 | 0 | 0 | 0 | 0 | 0 | 1 | 2 | | |
| **Seat selection** | 2 | 1 | 1 | 2 | 0 | 0 | 0 | 0 | 1 | 3 | Empowerment | |
| **Class Upgrades** | 2 | 1 | 1 | 1 | 0 | 0 | 0 | 0 | 3 | 3 | | |
| **Beverage** | 1 | 2 | 0 | 1 | 0 | 0 | 0 | 0 | 2 | 2 | | |
| **Food** | 1 | 2 | 1 | 1 | 0 | 0 | 0 | 2 | 2 | 2 | | |
| **Mileage program** | 0 | 2 | 3 | 2 | 0 | 0 | 0 | 2 | 2 | 0 | Benefits | Monetary Value |
| **Rewards** | 0 | 3 | 3 | 2 | 1 | 0 | 0 | 0 | 1 | 0 | | |
| **Competitive price** | 1 | 3 | 3 | 1 | 0 | 0 | 1 | 1 | 0 | 0 | Economics | |
| **Online presence** | 3 | 3 | 3 | 2 | 0 | 0 | 2 | 1 | 0 | 0 | | |
| **Package deals** | 3 | 3 | 3 | 2 | 0 | 0 | 0 | 0 | 0 | 0 | | |
| **Deals notices** | 3 | 3 | 3 | 1 | 0 | 0 | 0 | 2 | 0 | 0 | | |
| **Air alliances** | 2 | 2 | 1 | 2 | 0 | 0 | 0 | 1 | 0 | 0 | Accessibility | Efficiency |
| **Mileage statements** | 3 | 0 | 0 | 2 | 0 | 0 | 0 | 0 | 0 | 0 | | |
| **Self-check-in** | 3 | 0 | 0 | 2 | 0 | 2 | 0 | 0 | 0 | 0 | | |
| **Electronic check-in** | 3 | 0 | 0 | 2 | 0 | 2 | 0 | 0 | 0 | 0 | | |
| **Alerts** | 3 | 0 | 0 | 1 | 0 | 2 | 0 | 1 | 0 | 0 | | |
| **Boarding/deplaning** | 3 | 1 | 0 | 0 | 0 | 2 | 0 | 0 | 3 | 2 | Logistics | |
| **Baggage allowance** | 2 | 1 | 0 | 0 | 0 | 1 | 0 | 0 | 0 | 1 | | |
| **Number of departures** | 3 | 0 | 0 | 0 | 1 | 3 | 0 | 0 | | | | |
| **Airport location** | 3 | 3 | 0 | 0 | 0 | 2 | 0 | 0 | | | | |

*Airline Offerings*

**EXAMPLE PROJECT: *Air Travel— Design Analysis (2007)***

As part of a Design Analysis project at the IIT Institute of Design, a team of students explored the current air travel experience, looking at airline offerings and the needs of various travelers. The team began by conducting primary and secondary research on air travelers and the airline industry. From this research, they derived a list of airline offerings, such as competitive pricing, mileage program, and self-check-in; and passenger values such as convenience, punctuality, and comfort.

To understand the relationships between airline offerings and passenger values, the team built an *Asymmetric Clustering Matrix*, where they compared the elements of one list to the other. After sorting the matrix, the team analyzed the output and arrived at seven clusters. Through further analysis, three higher-level clusters emerged that equated with how passengers valued airline offerings: feeling at home, monetary value, and efficiency. By taking a step back, looking at the patterns in the asymmetric matrix, and discussing them, the team was also able to identify many insights that related to the clusters they found. For example, one insight related to the cluster feeling at home was: "Flying is considered more luxurious the more it resembles concepts of home, dining, and cinema." Another insight was: "Airline passengers value the ability to personalize their travel experiences." The asymmetrical clustering matrix proved an invaluable analysis tool for deriving such insights related to travelers, their values, and the airline offerings.

## BENEFITS

- Enables systematic analysis
- Encourages comprehensiveness
- Facilitates comparison
- Handles large sets of data
- Makes process transparent
- Reveals patterns
- Reveals relationships
- Visualizes information

## INPUT

- Two sets of entities based on research findings
- A matrix tool for scoring and sorting

## OUTPUT

- Entity clusters based on strength of relations among them
- Insights about relations between two sets of entities

## WHEN TO USE

## WHAT IT DOES

The Asymmetric Clustering Matrix works just like the Symmetric Clustering Matrix, but instead of analyzing a single set of entities, it compares two entities. This method allows us to take two sets of entities gathered during research and see how each set breaks down into clusters based on its relation to the other set. For example, this method could be used to better understand the relationship between peoples' activities and places where they happen. In the results we can see activities are clustered based on similar places where activities happen. We can also see that places are clustered because of similar activities they support.

Seeing these clustering patterns from unstructured lists of entities is useful because they reveal high-level order and help us develop frameworks to drive concept exploration.

## HOW IT WORKS

### STEP 1: List entities for clustering.

List the two *kinds of entities* you want to compare against each other to find clustering patterns. For example, comparing a list of activities against a list of places reveals clusters of common activities happening in common places. Examples of other lists that can be used to form interesting combinations are experiences, roles, needs, problems, challenges, goals, motivations, products, services, places, functions, and features.

### STEP 2: Determine the relation between entities.

Define a relation you want to measure between elements of one list to the elements of another. For

example, if your lists are activities and places, then a possible relation to measure will be *frequency*—how frequently does that activity happen in that place? Another example is if your lists are *offerings* and peoples' *motivations*, the relation could be *support*—how well do the offerings support peoples' motivations for using them?

### STEP 3: Determine a scoring scale to measure relations between entities.

The most commonly used scale has four steps: 0 means no relation between entities, 1 means minimum relation, 2 means medium relation, and 3 means maximum relation. It is a good idea to color-code matrix cells according to the corresponding scores. For example, lighter grays for lower scores and darker grays for higher scores.

### STEP 4: Create an asymmetric matrix.

Create a spreadsheet with a rectangular or asymmetric matrix. For this, enter the entities from the first list as row headings and from the second list as column headings. Each cell in this matrix represents a relation between two corresponding entities.

### STEP 5: Score the relations.

Enter a relation score in each matrix cell. Scoring is best done as a team to reduce biases and get to as objective a score as possible.

### STEP 6: Sort the matrix.

For small matrices you can do a manual sort of the matrix by shifting the position of columns and rows in the matrix so that two rows or columns having similar

4.11 ASYMMETRIC CLUSTERING MATRIX

scores are kept next to each other. After a few shifts of columns and rows this way, you can see that the entities are reordered to reveal clusters. For larger matrices it is better to use available statistical algorithms to sort the matrix for efficiency.

### STEP 7: Identify clusters.

After sorting the matrix, take a step back and look at the whole matrix and see how many clusters can be visually identified. Both lists will be clustered in the case of this asymmetric matrix. Identify a manageable and meaningful number of clusters for each list.

### Step 8: Define and label clusters.

Ask questions like: What makes the entities in this cluster belong together as a group? Why is this cluster different from other clusters? Discuss as a group and define each cluster based on the similarity between entities. Appropriately label each cluster.

### STEP 9: Capture insights and make frameworks.

Capture insights out of the clustering patterns shown in the matrix. Are the clusters of the same size and density? If their density and size varies a lot, what does that mean? What can be learned from the different levels of clusters? If there are big overlaps between clusters, what does that mean? Discuss the clustering patterns and refine them as useful frameworks for concept generation.

### STEP 10: Share insights and discuss.

Summarize findings and share with team members and other stakeholders. Discuss the insights and frameworks, and use the feedback to revise your analysis. Document your process and results.

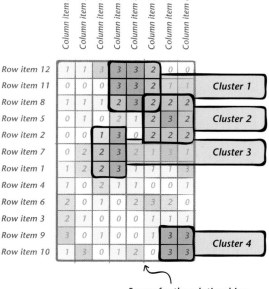

Scores for the relationships between items from different lists

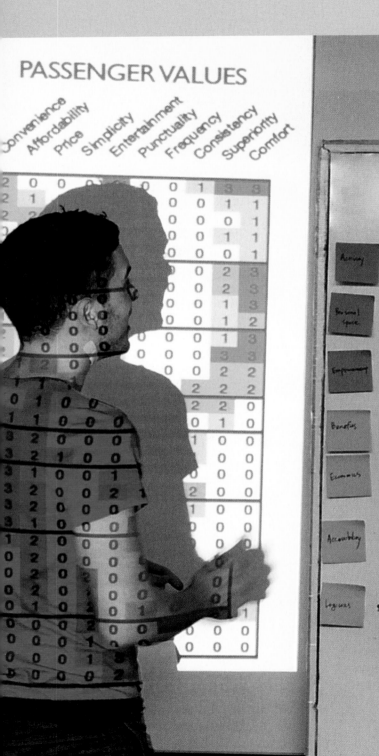

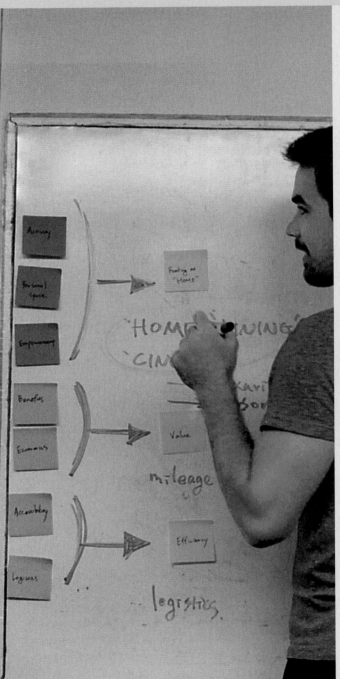

**4.11 ASYMMETRIC CLUSTERING MATRIX**

Structuring activities of stakeholders and showing how they relate to one another

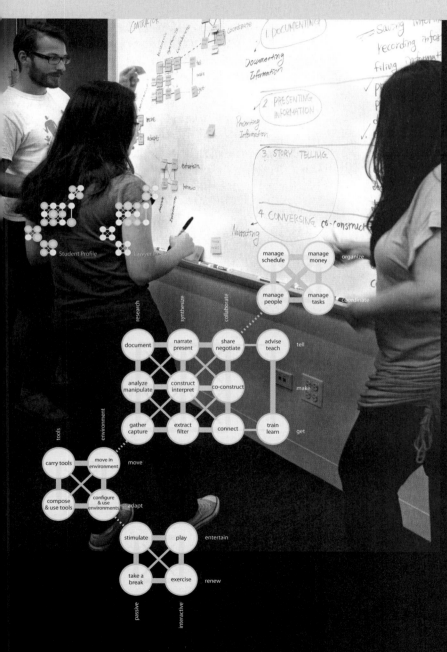

*EXAMPLE PROJECT:*
## Mobile Computing (1995)

Doblin, the innovation strategy consulting firm, conducted research on mobile computing to explore the use of mobile devices across different occupations. Using the Research Participant Mapping (a method for mapping people in a 2 × 2 map and selecting candidates for research), the team identified four occupations for in-depth research—doctor, lawyer, student, and landscaper. The team performed ethnographic research on a number of individuals from these occupations.

To understand the mobile computing activities, the team used the *Activity Network* method. They compiled a list of activities each occupation regularly engaged in, from writing to brainstorming to billing. The team combined these occupation-specific lists into a single master list of more than one hundred activities. They clustered these activities into twenty-three abstracted activity clusters. They placed them in an Activity Network diagram. For each of the four occupations, the team highlighted the activities in the network that occurred most frequently for users in that occupation. This helped the team compare the specific activities of different occupations. The team spotted patterns of similarities and differences across occupations very quickly. The Activity Network served as a prime tool for exploring the activities and needs of various occupations and helped the team reach reliable conclusions about mobile computing activities.

## What It Does

This method allows us to take a list of activities gathered during research and see how they are grouped based on their relationships. The method uses a Symmetric Clustering Matrix to relate activities of all the stakeholders (users, providers, maintainers, etc.) in the context we are studying and clusters them together. The results of clustering are then turned into a network diagram that visualizes all the activities together, showing their overall interrelationships. The diagram shows how activities constitute larger clusters of activities and how, in turn, these clusters connect to higher-level ones in a hierarchical pattern. The method is particularly effective for constructing a big picture of peoples' activities and their needs that, in turn, can help reveal opportunities for innovation.

Finding a broad definition for any cluster is a key part of the method. For example, a Symmetric Clustering Matrix on activities in an organization might cluster the activities "bringing people together," "coordinating tasks," "leading discussions," "providing support," and "monitoring projects." This cluster can be named "coordinating people." We can repeat this process to form even higher-level clusters in the hierarchy. "Coordinating people" might be just one of the clusters under the higher-level cluster, "managing people."

## How It Works

### STEP 1: List activities for structuring.

List people's *activities* that you want to compare and structure. This can be extracted from your previous research on people. The activities could include those of all stakeholders for the study—users, providers, maintainers, and so forth.

### STEP 2: Determine the relation between activities.

The most commonly used relation is *similarity*, which measures how one activity is similar to another.

### STEP 3: Determine a scoring scale to measure relations between entities.

The most commonly used scale has four steps: 0 means no relation between entities, 1 means minimum relation, 2 means medium relation, and 3 means maximum relation. It is a good idea to color-code matrix cells according to the corresponding scores. For example, lighter grays for lower scores and darker grays for higher scores.

### STEP 4: Create a symmetric matrix.

Create a spreadsheet with a square symmetric matrix. For this, enter *activities* as both row and column headings. Each cell in this matrix represents a relation between two corresponding activities.

### STEP 5: Score the relations.

Enter a relation score in each matrix cell. Scoring is best done as a team to reduce biases and get to as objective a score as possible.

### STEP 6: Sort the matrix.

For small matrices (up to 30 × 30), you can do a manual sort of the matrix by shifting the position of columns and rows in the matrix so that two rows or columns having similar scores are kept next to each other.

After a few shifts of columns and rows this way, you can see the entities getting reordered to reveal clusters. For larger matrices (more than 30 × 30), it is better to use available statistical algorithms to sort the matrix for efficiency.

### STEP 7: Identify clusters.

After sorting the matrix, take a step back and look at the whole matrix and see how many activity clusters can be visually identified and defined. For a 100 × 100 matrix, it is a good idea to define 10 to 15 clusters. If needed, you could also recognize 3 to 6 higher-level clusters.

### STEP 8: Define and label clusters.

Ask questions like: What makes the activities in this cluster belong together as a group? Why is this cluster different from other clusters? Discuss as a group and define each cluster based on the similarity between activities. Appropriately label each cluster.

### STEP 9: Create a network diagram.

Build an Activity Network Diagram with each node representing a defined activity cluster. Draw lines connecting related nodes. Rearrange the nodes in the diagram for shortest line lengths and minimum line crossings. Organize the nodes in such a way that higher-level clusters of nodes, if any, are clearly visible. The result is a diagrammatic representation of all the activities that indicate their relations and hierarchies.

### STEP 10: Capture insights and make frameworks.

Capture insights out of the clustering patterns shown in the matrix and network diagrams. Are the clusters of the same size and density? If their density and size varies a lot, what does that mean? What can be learned from the different levels of clusters? If there are big overlaps between clusters, what does that mean? Discuss the clustering patterns and refine them as useful frameworks for concept generation.

### STEP 11: Share insights and discuss.

Summarize findings and share them with team members and other stakeholders. Discuss the insights and frameworks and use the feedback to revise your analysis. Document your process and results.

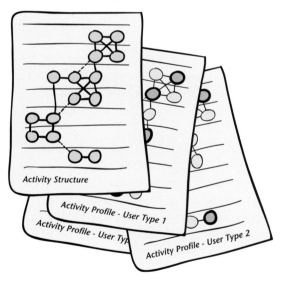

Activity Structure

Activity Profile - User Type 1

Activity Profile - User Typ

Activity Profile - User Type 2

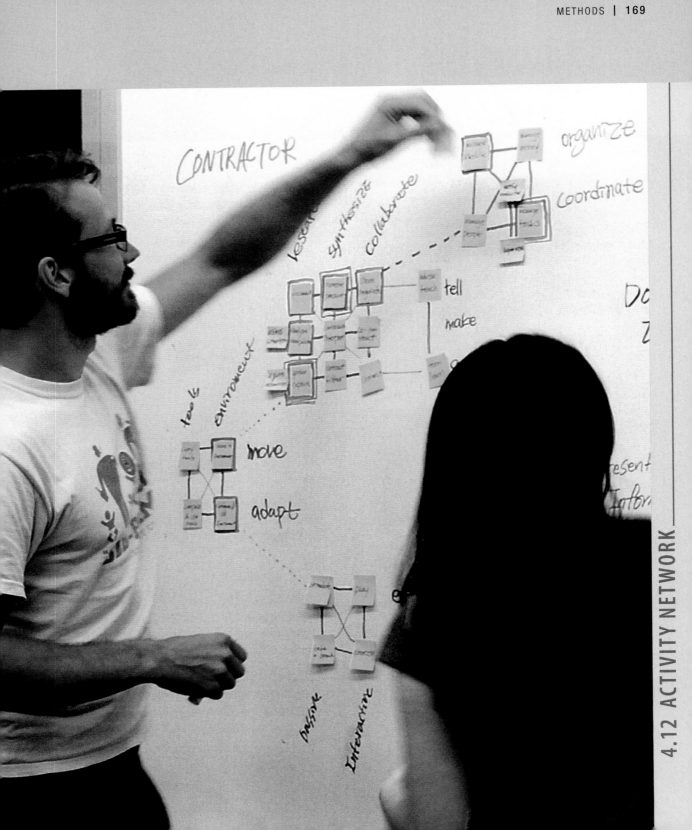

Insights Clustering Matrix

Clustering insights and showing their relations and hierarchies

99 Insights

99 Insights

1. Social Support

2. Creating Shared Experiences

3. Emotional Upkeep and Ritual

4. Kids' Special Relationship with Pets

5. Influencing Child's Good Choices

6. Balancing Measure for Choices

7. Shopping as Family Entertainment

8. Eating on the Go

9. Managing Health

**EXAMPLE PROJECT:**
*Cooking at Home (2006)*

One of the world's leading food manufacturers sought to define opportunity areas for future innovations. Leveraging the design innovation process and principles described in this work, the company shifted its focus from products to activities. This represented a significant departure from how the company normally approached its strategic initiatives. Broadening the scope to activities gave more breadth and depth to the possibilities for innovative solutions. An analysis of the company's product portfolio led the team to focus on cooking at home, since it was an activity that included a large number of their products.

After conducting primary research through a user pictures study, the project team collected all photos taken by participants and annotated observations in a database called the User Observations Database. They then generated an exhaustive list of 99 insights about the participants' lives and behaviors around cooking at home. They used the *Insights Clustering Matrix* to analyze these insights and find patterns. For this, the insights were entered into a matrix where, one by one, each relationship between insights was scored from 0 to 3 according to their similarity. Scoring the degree of similarity between two insights was highly valuable, because it allowed the team to focus on lowest-level connections that, when put together, revealed high-level patterns.

The matrix of insights was then sorted to reveal clusters and patterns that were previously indiscernible. Nine clusters of related insights were identified with the largest clusters pointing to social support, creating shared experiences, and managing health. The understanding of these clusters and patterns gave the team a strong foundation to start developing prescriptive statements to suggest objectives for concept generation.

**BENEFITS**

- Enables systematic analysis
- Encourages comprehensiveness
- Facilitates comparison
- Handles large sets of data
- Makes process transparent
- Reveals patterns
- Reveals relationships

**INPUT**

- List of insights generated from research findings

**OUTPUT**

- A central diagram representing how insights are interconnected and clustered

**WHEN TO USE**

## WHAT IT DOES

This method allows us to take a list of insights generated from the research on people and context and see how they are grouped together based on their relationships. The method uses a Symmetric Clustering Matrix to relate these insights. The results of clustering are then turned into a clustering diagram that displays all the insights together, showing their clustering patterns and overall interrelationships. The diagram shows how insights constitute larger clusters of insights and how, in turn, these clusters connect to higher-level ones in a hierarchical pattern. The method is particularly effective for constructing a big picture of insights from research that, in turn, can help us develop frameworks to drive concept exploration.

## HOW IT WORKS

### STEP 1: List entities for clustering.

List the *insights* captured from research findings that you want to compare against each other to find clustering patterns.

### Step 2: Determine the relation between entities.

The most commonly used relation is *similarity*, which measures how one insight in the list is similar to another.

### Step 3: Determine a scoring scale to measure relations between entities.

The most commonly used scale has four steps: 0 means no relation between entities, 1 means minimum relation, 2 means medium relation, and 3 means maximum relation. It is a good idea to color-code matrix cells according to the corresponding scores. For example, lighter grays for lower scores and darker grays for higher scores.

### STEP 4: Create a symmetric matrix.

Create a spreadsheet with a square symmetric matrix. For this, enter *insights* as both row and column headings. Each cell in this matrix represents a relation between two corresponding insights.

### STEP 5: Score the relations.

Enter a relation score in each matrix cell. Scoring is best done as a team to reduce biases and get to as objective a score as possible.

### STEP 6: Sort the matrix.

For small matrices (up to 30 × 30), you can do a manual sort of the matrix by shifting the position of columns and rows in the matrix so that two rows or columns having similar scores are kept next to each other. After a few shifts of columns and rows this way, you can see the entities getting reordered to reveal clusters. For larger matrices (more than 30 × 30), it is better to use available statistical algorithms to sort the matrix for efficiency.

### STEP 7: Identify clusters.

After sorting the matrix, take a step back and look at the whole matrix and see how many insights clusters can be visually identified and defined. For a 100 × 100 matrix, it is a good idea to define 10 to 15 clusters. If needed, you could also recognize 3 to 6 higher-level clusters.

### STEP 8: Define and label clusters.

Ask questions like: What makes the entities in this cluster belong together as a group? Why is this cluster different from other clusters? Discuss as a group and define each cluster based on the similarity between entities. Appropriately label each cluster.

**4.13 INSIGHTS CLUSTERING MATRIX**

### STEP 9: Capture insights and make frameworks.

Capture insights from the clustering patterns shown in the matrix. Are the clusters of the same size and density? If their density and size vary a lot, what does that mean? What can be learned from the different levels of clusters? If there are big overlaps between clusters, what does that mean? Discuss the clustering patterns and refine them as useful frameworks for concept generation.

### STEP 10: Share insights and discuss.

Summarize findings and share with team members and other stakeholders. Discuss the insights and frameworks and use the feedback to revise your analysis. Document your process and results.

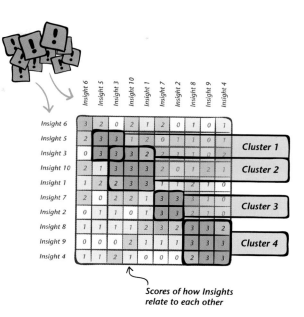

*Scores of how Insights relate to each other*

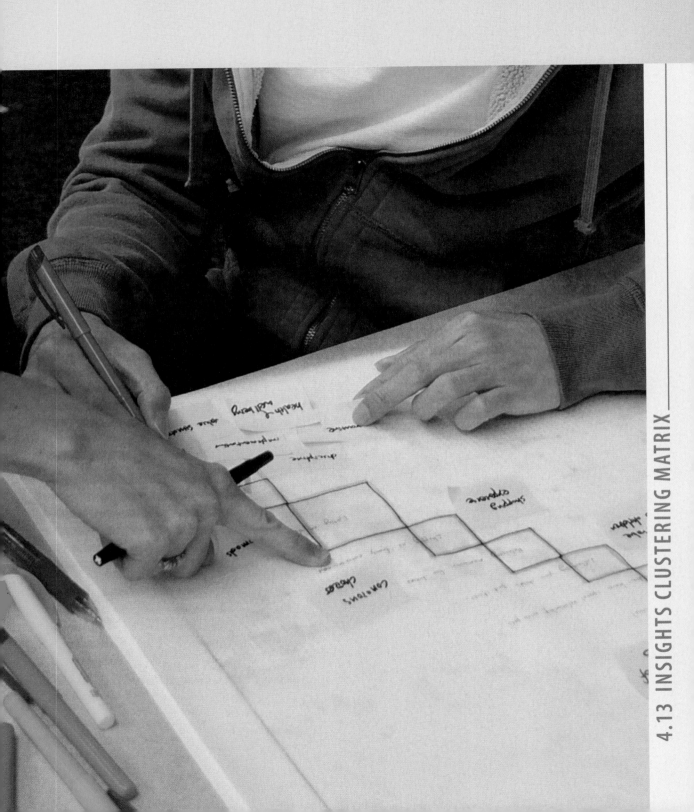

4.13 INSIGHTS CLUSTERING MATRIX

Making profiles of entities based on a set of semantic scales and comparing those profiles

*EXAMPLE PROJECT:*
*Analyzing Corner Stores (2009)*

In analyzing corner stores (small, independently owned and operated convenience stores in an urban environment), an IIT Institute of Design team asked the question: "What makes people loyal to their corner stores?" Their main mission was to help a group of independent corner-store owners increase revenue by aligning with customer needs and increasing loyalty among shoppers. After segmenting the four main customer types as neighborhoodie, specialty seeker, happenstance, and desperate shopper, they isolated the specialty seekers and neighborhoodies as the most promising in building a strong clientele and loyalty.

To understand what differentiates loyal from disloyal customers, the team used a *Semantic Profile* to map the various attributes responsible for the differences. They constructed the map using eight distinct semantic scales—price, proximity, consistency, character, offering, quality, experience, and added services. Using research data, they plotted the attitudes of the loyal customers (neighborhoodie and special seeker) versus the disloyal customer (happenstance and desperate shopper) along the scales from important to not important. Insights began to emerge. One of the insights was that loyal customers cared about store character, experience (ambiance and people interactions), and also highly valued additional, unique services. Overall, the team found that for corner stores to maintain and

## WHAT IT DOES

Semantic Profile is a method based on Osgood's Semantic Differential used in social sciences that measures peoples' attitudes about products, services, experiences, concepts, and similar entities. The method uses a set of semantic scales for measurement defined by two opposite adjectives, such as "simple" and "complicated," "weak" and "strong," or "important" and "not important." The entities, such as products, are scored on a set of such scales and each entity gets its own profile based on its scores. These profiles are then compared, and patterns of clusters and gaps are analyzed for insights and opportunities for innovation.

Most frequently, research participants are asked to score their attitudes on scales. Sometimes, design teams do the scoring based on their user perspectives.

Frequently, Semantic Profiles are used to compare how different user groups think and feel about entities. For example, attitudes of young and old people toward mobile devices.

## HOW IT WORKS

### STEP 1: Select entities to compare.

The most commonly used entities are products, services, activities, brands, and user groups. Limit the list to ten most relevant entities for easy comparisons.

### STEP 2: Define key attribute scales.

Determine the most relevant attributes that are likely to comprehensively define the profile of entities selected. Less than ten attribute scales is usual.

### STEP 3: Create a Semantic Profile diagram.

Set up attribute scales with adjective pairs as end labels, for example, "cheap" and "expensive." Set up the scales in random order to avoid implied priority. Reverse the polarity of scales to randomness; avoid preordering or aligning of negative and positive labels.

### STEP 4: Create entity profiles.

Score each entity by placing markers on the semantic scales. Connect the markers vertically to form a zig-zag line profile for each entity. Use color-coding to visually differentiate the profiles.

### STEP 5: Analyze patterns.

Compare entity profiles and recognize if there are similar ones forming clusters. Are there profiles that are diametrically opposite to each other in terms of their scores on the scales? Are there gaps between groups of profiles? What do these patterns mean?

Reorder the polarity of the scales so that end labels are aligned, based on negative and positive meanings, if relevant. In this diagram, if profiles lean toward one side of the scales, what does that mean? Look for insights.

### STEP 6: Capture insights and share them.

Document all the insights gained for the analysis and show them next to their respective places on the Semantic Profile diagram for easy readability and sharing among team members. Discuss patterns and insights.

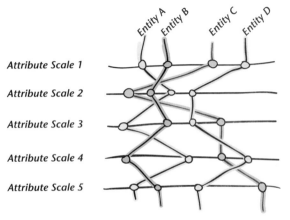

Active Explorers

- The Exerciser
- The Pick-up Artist
- The Outdoorsman

Recreational

Affectionate Enthusiasts

- The Fashionista
- "Buddy"
- Show Business
- The Empty Nester
- The Spoiler
- The First Timer
- The Lifer

Animal / Human

Canine Commanders

- The Dominator
- The Hunter
- Business Breeders
- "The Boss"
- The Paranoid

Occupational

Dependents

- The Dog Whisperer
- The Breeder (Dog/Cat Lover)
- The Rescuer
- Special Needs

## EXAMPLE PROJECT:
### Dog Ownership (2007)

The relationship between pets and their owners has changed drastically since the beginning of the last century. No longer are pets relegated to the outdoor doghouse or fixtures in suburbia. They have become an integral part of urban environments, and the pet-owner relationship has become more familial; dogs are now regarded as companions, partners, and family members.

With more households in the United States owning a pet dog, the IIT Institute of Design project team leading the research used the *User Groups Definition* method to better understand the types of dog owners and the characteristics that exist among them due to emerging trends. The team identified a list of dog owner types that was organized on a 2 × 2 map. The first axis of the map measured recreational versus occupational, referring to the primary role of the dog in the owner's life. The second measured animal versus human, referring to how owners perceive and treat their dogs. After plotting all the owner types (e.g., first-time owners, empty nesters), the team defined each of the four quadrants into user groups: Active Explorers, Affectionate Enthusiasts, Canine Commanders, and Dependents. For example, Affectionate Enthusiasts comprised the user types empty nesters, first timers, spoilers, and fashionistas. This group shared, as common characteristics, a deep-rooted love for animals, willingness to make significant investment to pamper and care for their pets, and a desire for a playful, low-stress relationship. The team also chose to focus on this particular group because they make up the majority of the market and represent those who are willing to spend money on new products, services, and experiences that enhance their relationship with their dog.

## WHAT IT DOES

User Groups Definition is a method that maps different types of users according to a set of key attributes related to the project topic. It creates a 2 × 2 map based on two important attribute scales and represents users in relation to one another on that map. This helps us look at the different user types in each quadrant of the map and define them as a user group. Then, we determine the common characteristics of these user groups, define concise descriptive user group names, and write detailed descriptions for each group. This yields a more nuanced portrait of the user landscape.

## HOW IT WORKS

### STEP 1: List user activities and user types.

Review user researcher findings. Distill findings into a list of user types with similar activities and behaviors. For example, in a research study of peoples' reading habits, the user types vary from casual readers to thesis students to language critics.

### STEP 2: Identify attribute scales.

Generate a list of attributes that apply to all user types. Sort the list to determine which attributes are most relevant to your topic. For example, a study of peoples' reading habits might lead to the generalization that readers differ according to two important attributes— the purpose of what they read and the frequency with which they read. The two attribute scales can be *recreational* versus *purposeful* and *periodic* versus *daily*.

Keep in mind that several attributes may be equally important, and if this is the case, you can create multiple user definition maps.

### STEP 3: Create a 2 × 2 map and plot user types.

Use the two attribute scales identified to create the 2 × 2 map. Plot the user types identified earlier on this map. Refine the map working with team members.

### STEP 4: Define user groups.

Study the user types in each quadrant. Identify the commonalities among their activities and their characteristics. Define each quadrant of the map as a user group and give it a descriptive name. In the example on the study of peoples' reading habits, the user group names might be *Professional Advancers, Spiritual Seekers, Self-Educators,* and *Active Escapists.*

### STEP 5: Describe common characteristics of user groups.

Study the users represented in each user groups. Describe the commonalities among their characteristics.

### STEP 6: Discuss and extend.

Can this map help describe the core user needs for concept exploration? Can these user groups be the core audience for concept development? Is it possible to focus on one or two user groups for further concept development?

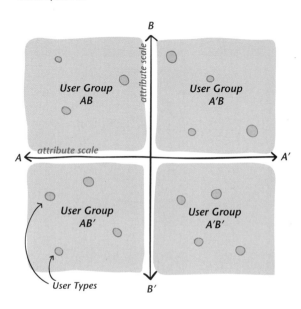

4.15 USER GROUPS DEFINITION

Mapping the entire user experience with five stages—attraction, entry, engagement, exit, and extension

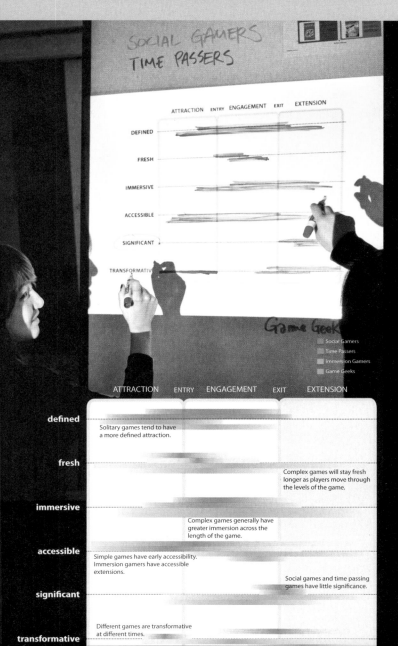

ATTRACTION ENTRY ENGAGEMENT EXIT EXTENSION

DEFINED

FRESH

IMMERSIVE

ACCESSIBLE

SIGNIFICANT

TRANSFORMATIVE

Game Geek

Social Gamers
Time Passers
Immersion Gamers
Game Geeks

ATTRACTION ENTRY ENGAGEMENT EXIT EXTENSION

**defined**

Solitary games tend to have a more defined attraction.

**fresh**

Complex games will stay fresh longer as players move through the levels of the game.

**immersive**

Complex games generally have greater immersion across the length of the game.

**accessible**

Simple games have early accessibility. Immersion gamers have accessible extensions.

Social games and time passing games have little significance.

**significant**

**transformative**

Different games are transformative at different times.

## EXAMPLE PROJECT:
### The Future of Gaming (2007)

The gaming industry has undergone rapid innovation in the last 50 years. A design team posed questions about how the industry's growth has changed both games and gamers and the implications for the future of gaming. The project focused on understanding this industry by exploring aspects like different types of gamers, their activities, and game consoles, computers, boards, Internet, and card games.

The team began by performing an era analysis to understand the evolution of gaming and how current industry trends had developed over time. Then, the team created a position map of types of gamers, and after distilling them into four gamer profiles, they assigned a prototypical game to each profile: Social Gamer to CatchPhrase, Immersion Gamer to World of Warcraft, Time Passer to Sudoku, and Game Geek to Flight Simulator. The team then created a *Compelling Experience Map* by plotting all four representative games along a range in the Attraction-Entry-Engagement-Exit-Extension experience map. This was done across all six attributes: defined, fresh, immersive, accessible, significant, and transformative. This visual representation provided a clear overview of the four game types, making disparities and similarities more immediately apparent. The Compelling Experience Map helped uncover valuable insights such as: More complex games, those most typically played by Game Geeks, have higher levels of immersion throughout the entire experience, whereas simpler games (favorites of Social Gamers) are more accessible throughout. The Compelling Experience Map provided clues to the opportunities of each gamer type, which the team extrapolated to predict possible directions for the future of gaming in the areas of gaming with more realism, gaming through mobile devices, and gaming for extreme gamers.

**BENEFITS**

- Broadens mindset
- Focuses on experience
- Identifies opportunities
- Creates overview
- Encourages comprehensiveness
- Inspires ideation

**INPUT**

- Data from context and user research

**OUTPUT**

- Understanding of strengths and weaknesses of the user experience at different stages of interacting with an offering

**WHEN TO USE**

## WHAT IT DOES

The Compelling Experience Map is a framework developed at Doblin that takes a comprehensive view of any experience looking beyond the main focus of the experience to understand what happens before, during, and after. The framework divides any experience into five stages: Attraction, Entry, Engagement, Exit, and Extension. Experiences are mapped in a linear fashion beginning with interactions prior to the experience that attract users, what happens when they arrive at the experience, engagement with the core offering, how the experience concludes, and what, if anything, is done to extend it. This broader view expands the number of touch-points that may influence users' overall perceptions of an experience and, therefore, can be designed for the best possible outcomes.

The Compelling Experiences Map also has six attributes, according to Doblin, that make any experience compelling:

*Defined*—Can you describe it? Is it bounded?

*Fresh*—Is it novel? Does it startle, amuse, amaze?

*Immersive*—Can you feel it? Can you lose yourself in it?

*Accessible*—Can you try it? Can you get it to do what you want?

*Significant*—Does it make sense? Does it make you remember, connect, think, grow?

*Transformative*—Do you feel different? Do you have something to show for it?

Each of the stages of the framework can be measured against each of these attributes to assess how compelling an experience is.

## HOW IT WORKS

**STEP 1: Select an experience to analyze and create a worksheet for analysis.**

Create a five-column worksheet with Attract, Enter, Engage, Exit, and Extend as column headings. Identify an experience that you want to analyze and discuss it among your team.

**STEP 2: Describe the Attract stage.**

Think about all of the interactions prior to an experience that generate interest in it. Trailers for upcoming films, print ads, billboards, online discussions, blogs, and other modes of communication all can be mechanisms for attracting users to an offering. Record all of the activities currently being done in the column of the worksheet.

**STEP 3: Describe the Enter stage.**

Consider what happens when the user arrives at the experience. What if anything is done to welcome the user to the experience? A chaotic ticket line in an event can affect a user's overall sense of the experience.

**STEP 4: Describe the Engage stage.**

This is the core offering. In a personal banking setting, it is the interaction that takes place between employees and customers, the ease with which transactions are done, and the information provided.

**STEP 5: Describe the Exit stage.**

This stage corresponds with the Enter stage, but refers to what happens when the user prepares to depart from the experience. It is the check-out line in a grocery store. It is the payment process in place at an online shop.

4.16 COMPELLING EXPERIENCE MAP

### STEP 6: Describe the Extend stage.

This stage is similar to the Attract stage, but it refers to anything that happens after the experience that keeps the user engaged. Amazon's online recommendation system employs an Extend stage strategy by suggesting other book titles or products that have some connection with your purchases.

### STEP 7: Rate the six attributes across the stages.

Each of the stages of the experience is measured against the six attributes (defined, fresh, immersive, accessible, significant, and transformative). Frequently the attributes are shown as horizontal lines running across all the five stages, and they are measured by changing the line thickness (or changing the color) on whichever stage attribute is relevant.

### STEP 8: Analyze the experience map.

Review the map and consider why each stage is structured as it is. What about the existing conditions cause them to be this way? Is the experience compelling in all the stages? Which attributes are strongest where? Where are the opportunities for making the experience better? Write up your analysis and share it with team members.

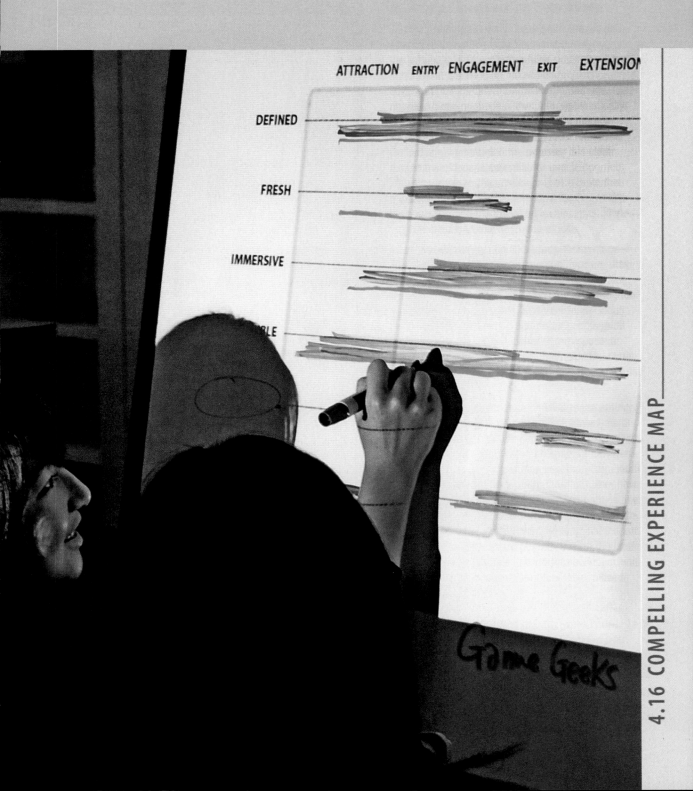

ATTRACTION ENTRY ENGAGEMENT EXIT EXTENSION

DEFINED

FRESH

IMMERSIVE

Game Geeks

Mapping the user's journey through the context

*EXAMPLE PROJECT:*
*Social Kitchen (2010)*

With more than one-half of the meals served in the United States today eaten outside of the home, a trend that shows no sign of reversing due to lack of time, a design team in an ethnographic research study set out to understand and define key motivators and constraints for current young and urban working adults' cooking experiences in their kitchen environments.

After conducting in-home observations, the research team clustered the observed kitchen activities of each participant by time and space. They began looking for patterns, from which four macrostages of the journey, which applied to all participants, emerged: Preparation, Cooking, Rewarding, and Finishing. The team then populated the *User Journey Map* chronologically with each participant's home-cooking process, using space and time as dimensions. Call-outs at certain stages of the journey indicated pain-points for the participants. One such pain-point was that users don't exactly know what they have or what they should buy before beginning the cooking process.

The team used this User Journey Map to outline each participant's steps and helped generate insights about the cooking experience as a whole. It also provided a way to identify problems and opportunity areas that led to design solutions centered on the social nature of kitchens.

**BENEFITS**

- Focuses on experience
- Reveals relationships
- Structures existing knowledge
- Visualizes information

**INPUT**

- List of all user activities happening in the context of study

**OUTPUT**

- Visualization of activity clusters over time representing the journey users go through in a particular process/experience
- Pain-points, insights, and opportunities along the user's journey

**WHEN TO USE**

## WHAT IT DOES

The User Journey Map is a flow map that tracks users' steps through an entire experience. This method breaks down users' journey into component parts to gain insights into problems that may be present or opportunities for innovations.

Activities users perform (rinse, mix, heat, serve) are shown as nodes in this map. These activities are also shown in groups as higher-level activities (preparation, cooking, finishing). Problems and insights are called out on this map to highlight areas where attention is needed and where opportunities exist.

## HOW IT WORKS

### STEP 1: Generate a list of all the activities.

Identify all the specific activities that occur throughout an experience (for example, rinsing, chopping, and disposing for cooking experience).

### STEP 2: Cluster activities.

Cluster related specific activities into higher-level activities (for example, rinsing, chopping, and disposing forming the higher-level activity precooking).

### STEP 3: Show activity clusters as nodes on a timeline.

Represent high-level activities as nodes and place them on a timeline as a flowchart. List the related specific activities under each of these nodes. Show arrows connecting the nodes to show the flow direction. If needed, include arrows showing feedback loops.

### STEP 4: Call out problems and pain-points.

Identify pain points while activities are happening during the process. Highlight these problems or pain-points as call-outs attached to the appropriate node(s) or arrows.

### STEP 5: Extend the map with extra information.

Extend the journey map with additional layers of information such as video clips of user activities, quotations from user studies commenting on process stages, or layout diagrams showing where activities take place.

### STEP 6: Look for insights.

Study the whole User Journey Map as a team, refer to your research findings, discuss them, and look for insights. For example, an insight might be stated as: "While rinsing and chopping ingredients during precooking is enjoyable, disposing of waste is universally perceived as unpleasant."

### STEP 7: Summarize the findings and share them.

Highlight these insights as overlay descriptions on the User Journey Map. Discuss the biggest opportunities for making the user journey compelling and delightful for users?

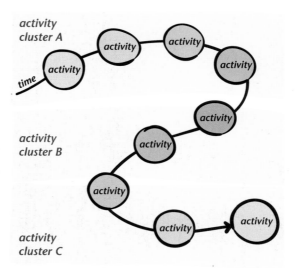

# 4.18 Summary Framework

Creating a framework summarizing key insights from analysis

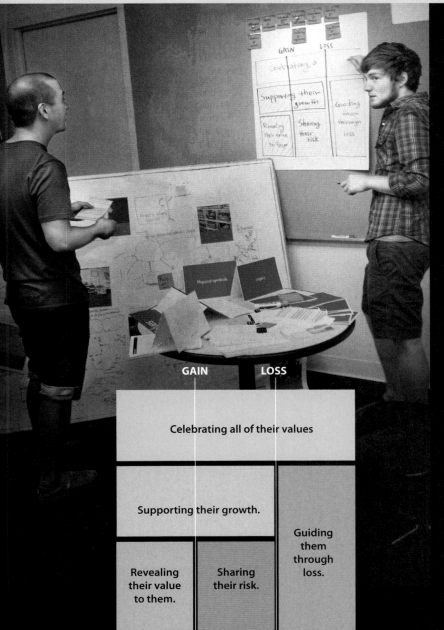

GAIN    LOSS

Celebrating all of their values

Supporting their growth.

Guiding them through loss.

Revealing their value to them.

Sharing their risk.

**EXAMPLE PROJECT:**
*Changing the Customer Experience in the Insurance Industry (2009)*

The perceptions of value that people attach to intangible possessions are dramatically changing, and how could insurance companies respond to these emerging perceptions? This was the question posed by a design team looking to suggest changes to a large insurance provider's position in the insurance industry. The team explored how this provider could shift industry expectations and enhance the entire customer experience.

After performing research, the team derived a *Summary Framework* from their key findings, insights, and design principles that fit into five pillars of focus: revealing value, supporting growth, celebrating value, sharing risk, and guiding through loss. This summary framework encompassed the whole lifespan of an insured good, from before it was even purchased, to after it was lost. By looking at the experience from beginning to end using this Summary Framework, the team identified opportunity areas for further exploration. They synthesized concepts within each opportunity area aimed at improving the customer experience. For example, in the sharing risk opportunity area, the team recommended implementing an identity gatekeeper, meant to protect private records by requiring two sets of virtual "keys," one held by the user, another held by the insurance provider. With these various concepts, the team aimed to differentiate the organization from the rest of the insurance industry by providing customers with more personalized services at each stage of the insurance journey.

**BENEFITS**
- Improves communication
- Keeps grounded in research
- Makes process transparent
- Supports transition

**INPUT**
- All research and analysis data generated

**OUTPUT**
- A table organizing key findings, insights, and principles
- Summary Framework with main ideas to be carried forward

**WHEN TO USE**

## WHAT IT DOES

The Summary Framework is a structured method used at the end of analysis to bring together key findings, insights, and design principles into an integrated whole. The framework provides a concise summary of what activities took place, the insights gained from each one, and what these findings indicate about opportunities for the future. In addition, the Summary Framework shows how user/context insights lead to design principles that then can be used to guide the development of innovation concepts. The Summary Framework is a critical transition for analysis to synthesis, from a full understanding of people and context to exploring what offerings can support them. In some way, the Summary Framework presents the rationale for a design team's point of view.

Any framework can be defined to have characteristics like:

- It is a complete and comprehensive representation of a topic.
- It is an overview showing only the high-level information; details are hidden.
- It shows a structure, the relations among parts of a topic.
- It is a single representation, usually with diagrams representing the framework.
- It is a sharable representation used to support conversations.

## HOW IT WORKS

### STEP 1: Review the key findings from research and analysis.

Review the results from the many methods you have used during the project. Write a brief statement summa-rizing your major findings as your initial point of view. The statement should describe your assumptions at the start of the project and how it led you to frame the research and analysis.

### STEP 2: Create a reference table.

Create a four-column table to summarize your work so far. Beginning with the left column, use the follow-ing headings: "Methods," "Findings," "Insights," and "Design Principles." For each method that you used write a brief description of it, a brief statement as to why you chose to use it, any key findings and insights derived from it, and any resulting design principles. Review the summary table. The summary should be exhaustive, but concise. This means that it should include all relevant research, but in the fewest words possible so that it can be scanned easily to get a sense of what was done and learned, and what should be done next.

### STEP 3: Create a Summary Framework.

Often the insight clusters or design principles clusters are used to build the Summary Framework. As a team, review the clusters of insights or design principles, and start to build your Summary Framework as diagrams: a network diagram showing relations between clusters, a tree diagram with clusters in hierarchy, or a position map diagram showing distribution of clusters. Align them with your team's point of view. Match them with your innovation intent.

### STEP 4: Describe the Summary Framework.

Write brief statements, descriptions, or stories that bring together the main ideas you want anyone to take away from the Summary Framework.

4.18 SUMMARY FRAMEWORK

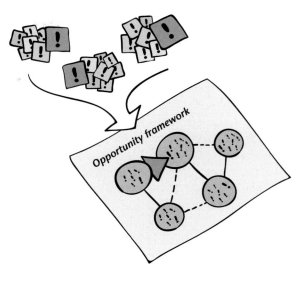

# 4.18 Summary Framework *(continued)*

**STEP 5: Share the results with the team, and discuss possible extensions.**

Review the framework with team members and key stakeholders. Discuss how to further develop the framework. Is it comprehensive enough to guide the concept exploration activities? Does it capture the team's point of view? Does it sufficiently reframe the current situation? How promising is the framework for developing successful innovations?

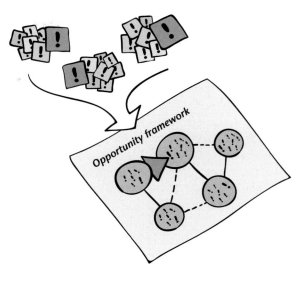

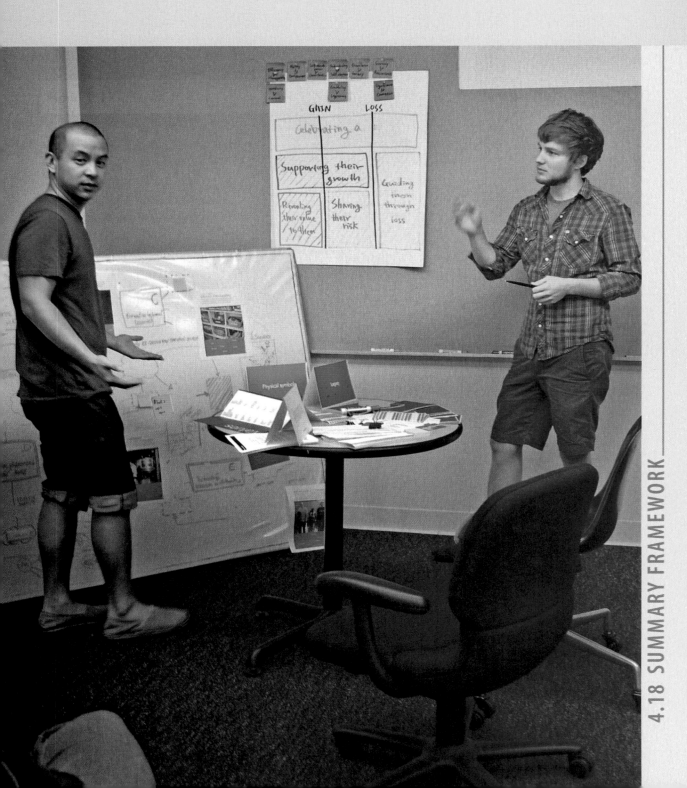

Transforming insights from research into actionable, forward-looking statements to guide ideation

## EXAMPLE PROJECT: *Reducing Violence—CeaseFire Chicago (2009)*

CeaseFire Chicago, an anti-violence program, worked with a design team to create a communications campaign to reduce the gun violence epidemic in Chicago that has afflicted the city's most disadvantaged neighborhoods. For primary research, CeaseFire helped the team broker conversations and interviews with neighborhood residents to understand their beliefs, values, and behaviors. They aimed to understand the emotional divide between the low risk in the community, those who felt besieged by the violence, and the high risk who were involved in the game of perpetuating the violence. From these conversations, the team produced an extensive list of insights that clustered into higher-level themes that defined main campaign goals.

Going from insights to *Design Principles Generation* was both a crucial and time-consuming part of the process. It required many hours and active discussion among all team members, some of them playing devil's advocate to challenge the thoughts behind each of the insights generated. The goal was to ensure that these insights were thoroughly examined, understood, and clustered into actionable design principles. The team defined four design principles that supported their "levers for change" framework: (1) Raise spirits by detoxifying the emotional environment and progress toward a healthy neighborhood. (2) Dispel myths by changing the rules of the game for the high risk and breaking the siege imposed on the low risk. (3) Guide the highest risk by establishing credibility to earn their trust and celebrating progress toward legitimacy. (4) Involve the low risk by fostering communication to gain their attention and encouraging involvement in the community.

**BENEFITS**
- Improves communication
- Keeps grounded in research
- Makes process transparent
- Supports transition

**INPUT**
- All research and analysis data generated

**OUTPUT**
- A table organizing key findings, insights, and principles
- Summary statements of main ideas to be carried forward

**WHEN TO USE**

## WHAT IT DOES

Design principles fill the "intuition gap" that exists in most innovation projects between understanding needs and having a "magical" leap of intuition about solutions that meet those needs. This method is a way to purposefully transition from the insights that we have framed to begin to explore concepts in a disciplined manner, so that concepts we develop are fully grounded in objective research data rather than biased by subjective assumptions. This method helps us turn our descriptive insights into actionable, forward-looking prescriptive statements. Design Principles help build alignment among the team as well in that they become steppingstones to move to the ideation process.

## HOW IT WORKS

### STEP 1: Gather all the insight clusters generated from many methods.

Review the methods you have previously used, especially while in this Frame Insights mode, and gather all the insights, even the detailed ones related to particular observations.

### STEP 2: Normalize them into a finite list of insights.

Review the list of insights. Eliminate duplicates. Combine similar ones. Avoid redundancy. If insights sound too detailed, consider them as part of higher-level insights. Write short descriptions for each insight for establishing shared understanding among team members.

### STEP 3: Generate design principles.

Use the insights as reference to brainstorm among your team members and generate design principles. Design principles are actionable, forward-looking prescriptive statements. Use a verb phrase to write a design principle. For example, "Raise spirits by detoxifying the emotional environment and progress toward a healthy neighborhood." Design principles should be statements that can support easy concept exploration.

### STEP 4: Find three to ten high-level design principles.

In a bottom-up approach your team might generate a large number of specific design principles from a large number of insights. If that is the case, it is a good idea to cluster them and narrow them down to three to ten high-level design principles to drive concept generation.

### STEP 5: Summarize the design principles.

As a group, look at all the design principles and discuss how to refine them to be a comprehensive starting place for exploring concepts. Describe each design principle and list the related insights under them. It will help the team trace back and understand which user need each design principle is supporting.

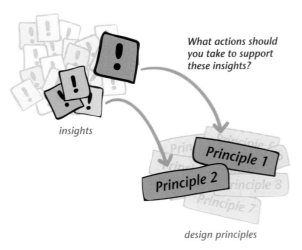

*What actions should you take to support these insights?*

*insights*

Principle 1

Principle 2

*design principles*

**4.19 DESIGN PRINCIPLES GENERATION**

Conducting a work session to understand insights, find patterns, and make frameworks for ideation

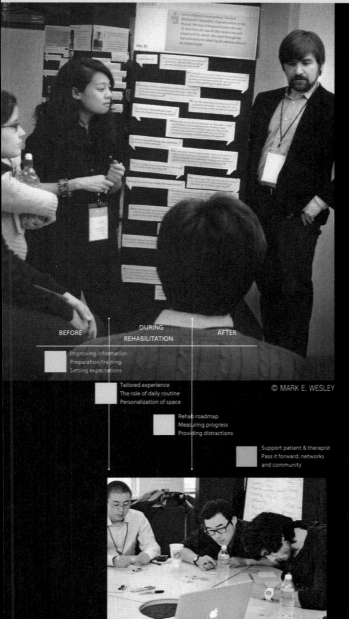

© MARK E. WESLEY

BEFORE | DURING REHABILITATION | AFTER

Improving information
Preparation/training
Setting expectations

Tailored experience
The role of daily routine
Personalization of space

Rehab roadmap
Measuring progress
Providing distractions

Support patient & therapist
Pass it forward: networks
and community

*EXAMPLE PROJECT: Improving the Outpatient Experience (2011)*

A cancer treatment center was in the process of developing a new facility that would accelerate patient recovery and improve patient experience. They worked with a design team to conceive of an environment enhancing the experience of postsurgical bone marrow transplant patients.

Primary and secondary research set the stage to understand the industry and the experience of multiple stakeholders, including clinicians, patients, patients' families, and nonclinical caregivers. After four weeks of in-depth immersion research, the project team assembled an *Analysis Workshop* to analyze the data and stories collected from research participants. The workshop was organized in three separate groups with representatives from the center and the design team. Each group observed a series of interview videos before examining individual stakeholder pedestals that provided direct quotations from each research participant. The groups then collaborated to identify patterns and insights from the research. To assist in generating insights, a statement format (e.g., I need. . ., I wish. . .) was used to allow workshop members to frame their observations around the user experience.

After developing initial insights, each group created an experience map and refined their initial insights across three basic phases of the rehab experience: Before, During, and After release from the center. For example, the insights included preparation and training in the Before stage, personalization of space in the During phase, and patient and therapist support after the rehab experience.

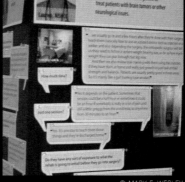

© MARK E. WESLEY

© MARK E. WESLEY

## BENEFITS

- Brings in new perspectives
- Builds higher-level systems
- Facilitates discussion
- Identifies opportunities
- Promotes collaboration
- Reveals patterns

## INPUT

- Key research findings and insights
- List of potential participants

## OUTPUT

- Identification of key insights and high-level clusters of insights
- Understanding of what those indicate about the context

## WHEN TO USE

## WHAT IT DOES

The Analysis Workshop is a method used to gain shared understanding about what is happening in a context and to build analytic frameworks useful for concept generation. The method brings together a team of people with the purpose of using the observations and the insights already developed by the design team to align around the emerging patterns. They then can be turned into a set of Summary Frameworks that can later be used for concept generation. The workshop also provides a forum for generating new insights that arise as the result of discussion among participants.

The Analysis Workshop is analogous and complementary to any of the clustering matrices used in this mode. But, instead of using a matrix or map to identify patterns in insights, this method calls for a group of people to find them through discussion and engagement in sorting and clustering activities. Conversations among team members who hold different perspectives about the insights can become sources of insight, too. Interaction and the free exchange of ideas and differing points of view can lead to higher-level insights that add depth to an analysis. In some cases, teams may choose to go further and use their insights to develop design principles that can be used later to guide ideation sessions.

## HOW IT WORKS

### STEP 1: Plan for the workshop.

Create a workshop goal statement and outline. The objective is to gain a shared understanding about what is happening in a context and to build analytic frameworks that can be useful for concept generation later. Make a schedule that divides the workshop into an initial assimilation phase to understand the defined insights and a later analysis phase to find patterns in insights. Create guidelines describing the rules of engagement. Choose participants with a variety of expertise.

### STEP 2: Gather insights already defined.

Review your research documents and gather all the insights you have developed, using many methods in this mode. Create a document describing each insight. Share it with participants to be used as a basis for the workshop session.

### STEP 3: Facilitate the workshop.

Establish an environment that is conducive to openly sharing insights and having conversations. Provide a space where many teams of three or four can work comfortably. Make sure the basics are covered, such as sticky notes, pens, paper, and even snack foods. Include graphic organizers or worksheets that will enable teams to capture their insights and organize their work. Provide adequate horizontal and vertical spaces for teams to work in and conduct sorting and clustering activities. Provide guidelines that describe the rules of engagement and how teams should interact, structure the time, and complete assigned tasks.

### STEP 4: Review insights and generate more if needed.

Use the first part of the workshop to review all the previously generated insights. Gain a shared understanding among all workshop participants. Allocate a short period for participants to reflect on the insights and generate more insights or revise existing ones. Time constraints can foster efficiency. Record all new insights. Review insights with a critical eye. Rank them according to how well they represent user and context needs.

4.20 ANALYSIS WORKSHOP

## STEP 5: Cluster insights.

Identify complementary insights and combine them to form clusters. Write brief descriptions that highlight key features of these clusters. Prepare brief write-ups to explain why you consider them to be a cluster of insights or what makes them a cluster. Use worksheets for filling in information: evocative titles for insight clusters, short descriptions, diagrams explaining the clusters, user-needs supported, context-needs supported, or other useful tags.

## STEP 6: Organize the insight clusters into analytical frameworks.

As a team review the clusters of insights and organize them in relation to each other. The clusters of insights may be organized as a network diagram or in different hierarchical levels like a tree diagram, or relatively position them in a position map diagram.

## STEP 7: Debrief participants and summarize the workshop output.

Debrief at the conclusion of the workshop. Have different teams share their findings with one another. Allow time for discussion and for the possibility of higher-level insights that might arise as the result of dialog. Compile the write-ups into output documents that can be shared with stakeholders. Discuss how these clusters will be further refined and evaluated. Discuss how design principles and concepts can be developed using these frameworks.

© MARK E. WESLEY

ER

Janet was a caregiver for 3 years. Her mother was sick with breast cancer, had surgery twice, chemotherapy and radiation treatment.

Janet started out as a part-time caregiver for her mother and became the full-time caregiver during the 6 months before her mother passed away.

"Basically talking was a good point for her and showing her that when she was sick people would come and visit her. And that's a very helpful thing at this point because they don't seem to be all alone."

tooth so her desires were to eat some cake or some things so we would go buy them and bring them ould eat it. Even though she couldn't but that's you have to sometimes take—not take the orders es them to you so they can feel better."

weeks, she would bring her mom to the complete a reatment. There was nothing special about the facility, d a TV, but I would bring my book sometimes."

tips and hints and she told us even try to but it on her before and after the radiation smooth and all that stuff. My experience y that due to the fact of that nurse, it was

earched information and I had a friend that her mother er and she had explained some times to me but it's not thing as they explain as when you see it in person."

"My little girl was three years old then and she was my mother's light. She would keep motivated my mother and myself. Because afterwards taking care of my mother then I would take care of her, my baby. So you keep on going and you try and do your best."

pital or somwhere, would have a talk and give feedback or give—like seminar or whatever to let the caregiver that they have support too. Sometimes

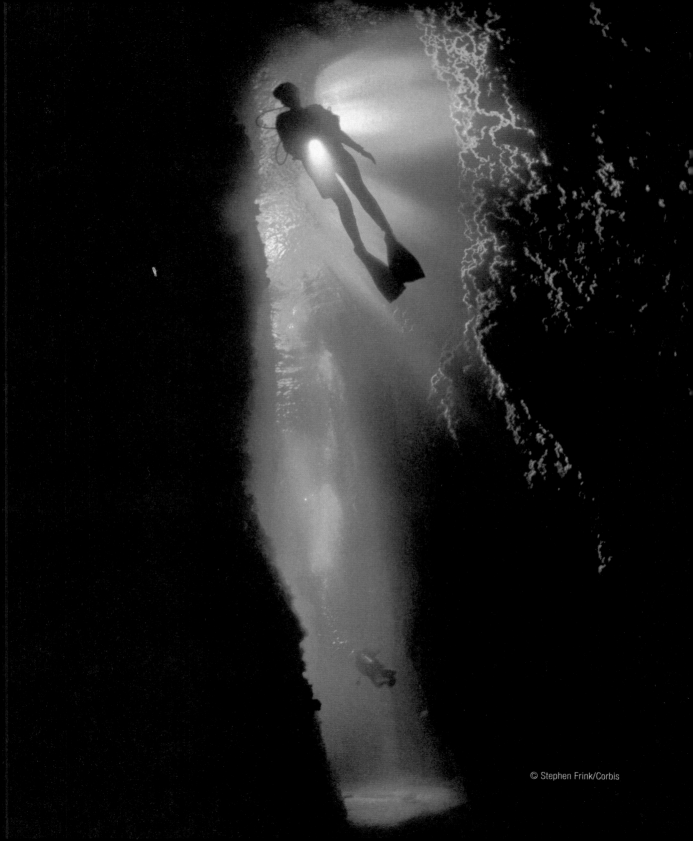

# mode 5
# EXPLORE CONCEPTS

Energized by powerful insights about people and the context, it is time to jump from the world of inquiries into the world of possibilities for the future. What are the ways to move into that world, imagine that future, and envision possibilities that enrich all participants? How can today's assumptions be questioned and reframed for tomorrow? Where are the pathways leading to a variety of ideas that will help build the future?

When venturing out into a new territory and exploring it, open-mindedness, a sense of adventure, and a spirit of creativity are naturally important. However, teams also need to maintain focus and sense of direction so as not to lose course. Rigorous processes and structured methods are essential as well.

The starting activities in this mode build on the patterns and insights gained from the previous modes. We take a strong point of view about how innovations ought to be built for the user and context needs. Exploring new concepts inherently involves "envisioning the future" through brainstorming, sketching, prototyping ideas, and storytelling. Explorations happen in nonlinear, continuous, and iterative cycles until new and valuable solutions and strategies are generated.

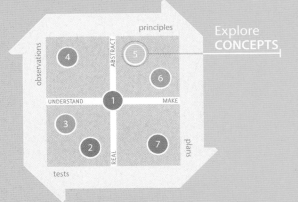

# EXPLORE CONCEPTS *mindsets*

The mindset for Explore Concepts is to be creative and open to new, perhaps radical ideas and ways of thinking; but at the same time, keeping sight of human-centered and context-driven principles for success that were identified in earlier modes. The concept explorer is primarily concerned with challenging prevailing assumptions about where solution concepts will be found; then with reframing the boundaries to a new solution space; exploring ideas most relevant to the insights from earlier modes, yet paying attention to the periphery and the fringes; generating concepts of clear value in that space; and continually communicating those explorations both internally and externally through effective storytelling.

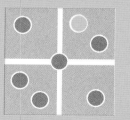

**Mindsets**

- Challenging Assumptions
- Standing in the Future
- Exploring Concepts at the Fringes
- Seeking Clearly Added Value
- Narrating Stories about the Future

## Mindset: Challenging Assumptions

Innovation teams are eager to quickly move to building concepts based on insightful findings from previous modes. When entering the mode of Explore Concepts, teams naturally follow their instincts to jump in immediately and get started on brainstorming ideas. What they might miss is uncovering the organization's or the industry's hidden assumptions and orthodoxies that prejudice the project in a given direction. The current "frame" around the area where solutions might lie may well have to be reframed. Innovators must first ask themselves, "Are we coming up with the right solutions?"

It is normal for organizations to follow the norms that their industry has established for years. But is it possible to recognize those norms as assumptions and find out if they are still relevant in these rapidly changing times? Are there other ways, new ways, to provide something new, even if they mean disrupting the industry behaviors? And is it possible to do it without losing sight of the core fundamental objectives of meeting peoples' needs and fitting well with the context?

| Organization | From assumptions... | To new ways... |
|---|---|---|
| Amazon | Mass-market book advertising | Personalized reading recommendations based on your navigation history |
| Apple | MP3 players | Managing personal music collections |
| Netflix | Brick-and-Mortar movie rentals on daily rates | Online managed library and home delivery (mailing DVD and instant streaming) on a subscription basis. |
| Nike | Shoes | Supporting runners in meeting goals |

*Organizations that create disruptive innovations and become successful are often leaders in exercising this mindset – abandoning conventional models and adopting new ways of thinking. The table shows a few examples of organizations that challenged assumptions in a timely manner and reframed their solution space, opening up drastically new opportunities for products and services.*

## Mindset: Standing in the Future

When you're planning the next phase of your career, a common approach is to ask yourself: "What am I good at now? And what can I do next?" But often a better approach is to ask: "Where do I want to be ten years from now? And what would it take to get there?"

There are two ways of thinking about the future: In one, we stand in the present, looking forward at some desired future, and plan the steps that will take us to it. This way of thinking about the future is quite common, and usually leads to incremental innovation. Another way is to imagine ourselves standing in the future, after our innovations have already taken root, and to look back at how we must have gotten there. This way of thinking is somewhat akin to the approach of science fiction authors, who create fantasies of the future that inspire us in the present, and is more likely to help us create breakthrough, disruptive innovations.

Courtesy of Steelcase Inc.

*"100 Dreams, 100 Minds, 100 Years," is Steelcase's 100th anniversary celebration project that will explore how the world will be 100 years from today. In this extraordinary collaborative project, peoples' dreams about that future are collected, analyzed for patterns, and shared. The project is built on the idea of standing in the future, imagining a world, and then using those visions as a way to guide us. It is also inspired by the notion that children instinctively imagine about the future that way.*

## Mindset: Exploring Concepts at the Fringes

Even as we seek radical ideas standing in the future, we should never forget to explore ideas adjacent to, but outside of, our normal domain. These areas at the fringes of the business can contain opportunities for new offerings that actually strengthen core concepts, systems, and market positions, which are often overlooked. The fringes of an industry's concept space, by their nature, contain unexplored and often undeveloped opportunities that can lead to disruptive innovations and competitive advantage.

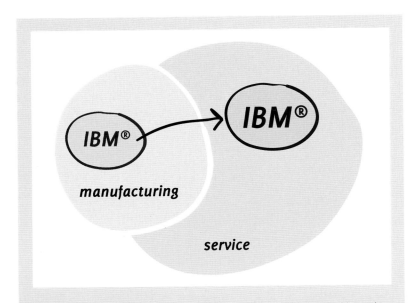

*A well-known example of exploring the fringes is IBM, which shifted its entire strategy under Lou Gerstner [early 2000] from selling technology products, to selling the much higher-value services and support of business technology—moving IBM from the increasingly competitive computer "manufacturing" sector, where companies like Dell and HP were playing, into the high-margin "service" sector, where IBM's scale and scope of expertise gave them an advantage. This kind of peripheral thinking about what innovation can involve—possibly even a leap from one sector to another—is a bold mindset to have for exploring new frontiers.*

## Mindset: Seeking Clearly Added Value

Anyone who has ever been part of a brainstorming exercise can probably remember how hard it is to get someone to let go of a favorite, flawed idea. The discussion often devolves into a test of wills rather than a test of concepts. In particular, when multidisciplinary teams brainstorm, the outcome can be strongly influenced by the biases and preferences held by the different disciplines. Technologists will prefer ideas based on the latest gizmo; marketers will want to pursue ideas that are easy to explain and sell. But often these sorts of "pet" concepts create value for only one set of stakeholders: the people who came up with them.

When exploring new concepts, innovators should always be seeking ideas that create or add value—whether for the user, the business, the economy, society, the environment, or any combination of these. This mindset is about always being alert to objectively identify and explore the concepts that deliver value more comprehensively than others. This leads to a higher proportion of focused, context-sensitive concepts rather than scattershot brainstorming.

How valuable a concept is to the stakeholders can be well recognized if organizations promote frequent team-based exploration sessions with team members from diverse disciplines. They bring different perspectives about the value of concepts and collectively can help recognize the most significant ones to pursue.

*In the world of brainstorming, probably no company is as well known as Palo Alto–based design firm IDEO. The company's ideation methods have made headlines from BusinessWeek and Fast Company to ABC's Nightline, and helped launch a slew of iconic products. Most importantly they are famous for working in multidisciplinary teams that, having experts from different areas, are able to generate and recognize which concepts are the most valuable to all stakeholders in a project.*

## Mindset: Narrating Stories about the Future

While we may have lots of great ideas in our heads, they are only useful if we communicate them effectively, and at all stages and modes of the innovation process, not merely at the end when a final presentation or report is often required. Storytelling is an effective way to express ideas that didn't previously exist or ideas that are abstract. Telling stories about the future, particularly while concepts are being explored, can trigger more concepts and help speculate on how they will be valuable in future scenarios. As useful as storytelling is for generating new ideas, the mindset ought to be about telling stories that matter. Stories need to be built on what we have already analyzed and understood about people and the context. Moreover, concepts must be clear and compelling to ourselves, to our team members, to our users, and to our client(s) if they are to succeed.

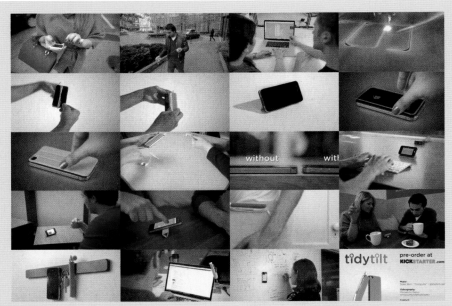

Tidytilt™ by TT Design Labs, LLC.

*Kickstarter is a Web-based service organization creating a platform for helping individuals with creative projects in mind to get funding. Selected projects are published on Kickstarter for people (as investors) to pledge money to and help the project get funded. One of the key funding success criteria is how best the project creators can tell stories about their innovations through a short video.*

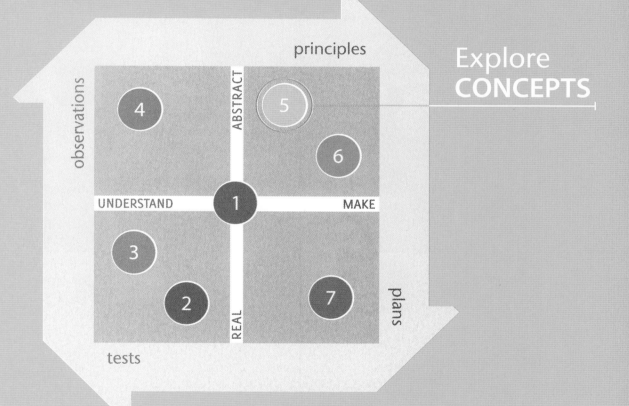

observations

principles

ABSTRACT

UNDERSTAND 1 MAKE

REAL

tests

plans

Explore
**CONCEPTS**

# EXPLORE CONCEPTS *methods*

# 5.1 Principles to Opportunities

Transitioning from analysis to synthesis: exploring opportunities
based on defined design principles

**EXAMPLE PROJECT:** *Residential and Commercial Renovation (2010)*

One of the world's leading 3D design and architecture software companies collaborated with a design team to better understand product selection in the context of residential and commercial construction and renovation projects among homeowners, professionals, and manufacturers. After performing ethnographic and secondary research, the team uncovered key insights from their observations that were clustered in four categories: external influences, mindsets, interactions, and processes.

From these insights, and understanding the needs and challenges of the key stakeholders, the team formulated design principles to guide concept development. To use the *Principles to Opportunities* method, the team first clustered the design principles revealing six higher-level principles. For example, one of the design principles under the higher-level principle Making It Real was "support discovery and decision making with tools that reflect real-world situations." Through discussions, sketches, and written descriptions, the team explored what underlying opportunities could exist to address each design principle. For example, for principles like Making It Real and Project Transparency, one opportunity identified was to create a café, a physical room that would serve as an "experimentation lab" and "discussion platform" for architects and their clients to communicate, sketch, and discuss renovation projects.

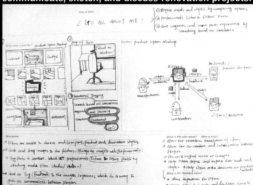

**BENEFITS**

- Broadens mindset
- Identifies opportunities
- Structures ideation
- Supports transition

**INPUT**

- Insights and design principles from research and analysis

**OUTPUT**

- List of potential opportunities at the individual offering, system, and strategic levels

**WHEN TO USE**

## WHAT IT DOES

Design principles fill the "intuition gap," giving us a good structure to move from understanding needs to defining principles to exploring opportunities to generating concepts. This method is a way to purposefully transition from the Frame Insights mode to the Explore Concepts mode in a disciplined manner, so that concepts are fully grounded in objective research data rather than biased by subjective assumptions. Exploring opportunities before jumping into generating concepts is an important step that helps us first identify areas that can be more fertile than others. Design principles also help build alignment among the team. Using them in teams as steppingstones helps bring focus to the process and avoid misunderstandings and unproductive debates.

## HOW IT WORKS

### STEP 1: Create a table to explore opportunities.

Collect all the insights and principles developed in previous modes. Create a table with your insights in the first column and the corresponding design principles in the second column. Create additional columns for exploring opportunities—single offering opportunities, system opportunities, and strategy opportunities.

### STEP 2: Generate single offering opportunities.

Focus on each design principle and think of possible single offerings and enter them in the proper column. Depending upon the nature of the project, the single offering might be a product, service, process, message, or the like. Enter as many single offering opportunities as possible for each design principle. Add sketches if needed to better express the opportunities. At this level, opportunities can feel very similar to "concepts"; the key difference is the level of detail you need to give to them—opportunities are less detailed and concrete, just indicating possibilities as a concept space.

### STEP 3: Generate system opportunities.

In the same way that you generated single offering opportunities, take each of the design principles and think of system opportunities in the next column. System-level opportunities indicate possibilities for a set of components like people, things, and environments, all working together for a common purpose.

### STEP 4: Generate strategy opportunities.

Think of strategy opportunities as well, and enter them in the column for the corresponding design principles. Thinking of strategic opportunities early in the process, and not at the end, is a good way to ensure broader conversations among the team members.

### STEP 5: View all opportunities together and gain insights.

Think through all cells in your table. Study the table as an overview and discuss all opportunities in relation to one another—single offerings, systems, and strategies. Discuss how to build on these opportunities. What are the possibilities for further developing some of these single offerings, systems, and strategies together? Are there any prominently preferable opportunities visible?

| insights | principles | individual opportunities | system opportunities | strategy opportunities |
|---|---|---|---|---|
| insight insight insight | principle 1 | | | |
| insight | principle 2 | | | |
| insight insight | principle 3 | | | |

**5.1 PRINCIPLES TO OPPORTUNITIES**

# 5.2 Opportunity Mind Map

Organizing aspects of the project and mapping areas of opportunities for innovation

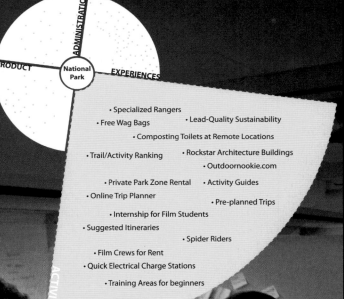

ADMINISTRATION

PRODUCT

National Park

EXPERIENCES

- Specialized Rangers
- Free Wag Bags
  - Lead-Quality Sustainability
  - Composting Toilets at Remote Locations
- Trail/Activity Ranking
  - Rockstar Architecture Buildings
  - Outdoornookie.com
- Private Park Zone Rental  • Activity Guides
- Online Trip Planner
  - Pre-planned Trips
- Internship for Film Students
- Suggested Itineraries
  - Spider Riders
- Film Crews for Rent
- Quick Electrical Charge Stations
- Training Areas for beginners

ACTIVITIES

## EXAMPLE PROJECT: *National Parks System (2005)*

The National Parks System (NPS) of the United States is a treasure, experiencing a myriad of problems, from a rise in popularity to understaffed parks to stressed ecosystems and funding cuts. A design team was charged with discovering opportunities and ways to improve the NPS.

Early in their concept exploration, the team developed an *Opportunity Mind Map* to look at the experiences that individuals have with the NPS. The team's research defined four aspects: the experience within the park, products created by the park for patrons, activities done in the park, and administrative functions of the NPS. These four key aspects were represented in the map radially around the core. By relating previously determined insights and principles to the four key aspects, the team generated concepts on the map. For example, opportunities for the activities aspect included composting toilets at remote locations, quick electrical charge stations, and training areas for beginners. Opportunities based on products for patrons included a lottery system for NPS access, tree-planting excursions, pet permits, and Good Samaritan awards. All opportunities that related to the four key aspects were distributed within the Opportunity Mind Map at the same level to show that they had the same relevance. The Opportunity Mind Map enabled the team to concentrate their efforts on improving and protecting the NPS by asking two key questions: How can these concepts be combined to generate systems of complementary ideas? What greater concept systems may exist that are not readily obvious?

**BENEFITS**
- Creates overview
- Identifies opportunities
- Reveals relationships
- Structures existing knowledge

**INPUT**
- Attributes for topic of interest

**OUTPUT**
- Collection of concepts/opportunities organized around a common attribute

**WHEN TO USE**

## WHAT IT DOES

This method is used at the beginning of concept exploration. Using frameworks from previous methods such as the Summary Framework or Design Principles Generation, teams start to create visual depictions of where innovation opportunities may reside. These visual depictions start with the core topic in the center, and possible opportunities are explored from this center, to the periphery. Opportunities are shown in relation to the various project aspects depicted on the map. The map, showing relationships and hierarchies, becomes a tool for teams to have early conversations about where it is more interesting for potential solutions to be developed. The method helps guide further exploration and concept development.

## HOW IT WORKS

### STEP 1: Define the core topic and related aspects.

Looking at the insights and frameworks developed during the Frame Insights mode, define the core topic that's most interesting to explore opportunities. Identify from previous research the key aspects related to this topic. For example, for a core topic "healthy living," the related aspects might be "health products/services," "food choices," and "education."

### STEP 2: Map the core topic and related aspects.

Build the basic structure for the mind map: position the core topic as the center, define a scale represented by concentric circles to determine the different levels of relationship to the core topic, and lastly, divide the area around the topic and show them as the key aspects you want to explore. If the project included robust research and analysis, use the categories from a framework to represent them around the core topic.

### STEP 3: Explore opportunities around the core topic and its aspects.

Based on the insights and principles developed in the Frame Insights mode, explore possible opportunities for each of the aspects mapped. Capture them in the map, positioning them according to the aspects they relate to and how they are related. Discuss ideas in teams and build on each other's ideas.

### STEP 4: Refine the map according to the attributes.

Discuss attributes that are important to track in the early stages of exploration. For example, a useful common attribute is the "relevance to the core topic." Represent the most relevant opportunities closer to the center of the radial opportunity map, and place the least relevant ones toward the periphery.

### STEP 5: Analyze the map and recognize areas for further exploration.

Analyze and evaluate the potential of the mapped opportunities. Discuss and determine which areas on the map are most interesting for further development.

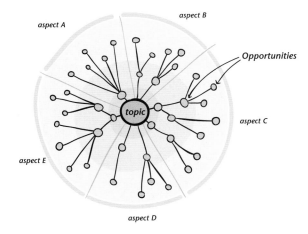

aspect A · aspect B · Opportunities · aspect C · aspect D · aspect E · topic

5.2 OPPORTUNITY MIND MAP

# 5.3 Value Hypothesis

Clearly defining what value the intended solution will create for users and providers

For: Retiring people

who: IN TRANSITON TO NEW LIFE STYLE

AAPR is: a platform

THAT: enables them to have more active and meaningful Life.

UNLIKE: other Competative platforms

VIDES: both Retired & pre-retiring Individuals w/ different options acquiring new skills or hobbies. (LEARNING), sharing the skills they have (TEACHING) & partaking in other activities (DOING)

Differentiating from others by offering advantage Connect all AAPR members into a Collaborative + othe biz partners who can participate in

A design team developed concepts for a leading American nonprofit advocate for people aged 50 and above. By exploring retirement and framing it as a process, and not a specific point in time, the team built on the organization's key strategic strength, its website, to affect the changing perception of retirement. The team generated concepts based on the potential of the website to have a greater impact on the organization's members. In addition, concepts were based on insights and design principles that were developed by exploring existing product and service platforms, and understanding retirement through primary and secondary research. Their key findings showed that the aging generation wants to keep active, many of them have not yet thoroughly thought about their retirement, and the organization's existing infrastructure could be leveraged to build a new platform to aid its members throughout the retirement process.

Based on these findings, the team developed a *Value Hypothesis* that described the intended value of a new offering, named Peer, for the organization. Peer's Value Hypothesis targeted pre-retired and retired individuals who need help transitioning to retirement with the goal of helping them lead an active and meaningful life. Peer would assist them to acquire new skills or hobbies and share the skills they already have within a well-connected, virtual and real, collaborative community. The Value Hypothesis was crucial in the concept exploration phase as it helped guide features and attributes of the proposed concepts and ensured alignment with the innovation intent of the project.

## WHAT IT DOES

Rather like an "elevator pitch," which succinctly describes the value of a new offering after it has been developed, a Value Hypothesis is a definition of the intended value for a possible new offering and is used at the beginning of development to frame the exploration area. A Value Hypothesis is created after a thorough investigation of the topic—based on a strong analysis of findings and insights from previous modes and on the generated design principles. The hypothesis should be a well-crafted synthesis of those principles and a clear representation of the team's point of view on the opportunity at hand.

There can be unlimited ways of stating a Value Hypothesis, just as there are ways of crafting any pitch. A commonly used structure, very similar to Geoffrey Moore's Value Proposition Statement, has five parts:

1. Who are the target *users*?
2. What are their unmet or underserved *needs*?
3. What are the proposed new *offerings*?
4. What are their *benefits* to users?
5. Why will users choose these offerings over those of the *competition*?

After creating an initial Value Hypothesis, keep returning to it throughout the project to ensure developments are aligned with core values. Always feel free to modify and update the Value Hypothesis as the team identifies and explores new opportunities.

## HOW IT WORKS

### STEP 1: Study the findings from previous modes.

Particularly focus on the insights, opportunities, and principles developed. Discuss these in teams, define the priorities for your project, and try to arrive at a shared point of view for crafting a hypothesis.

### STEP 2: Align on a structure for your Value Hypothesis.

There are innumerable ways in which a Value Hypothesis can be structured. The five-part model described above is a common and comprehensive structure. Think about the context of your project, and identify the key elements that should be defined to focus concept development.

### STEP 3: List options and iterate.

Based on your research and insights, list as many options as possible for each of the parts in your hypothesis. Iterate between potential combinations among those parts and create a list of possible Value Hypotheses to follow.

### STEP 4: Evaluate options and define your Value Hypothesis.

Discuss these combinations among your team and evaluate which can deliver the most value to both client and users. Select one combination and craft a cohesive and clear statement to communicate the value your team will be aiming to deliver. Share this statement with important stakeholders in the project.

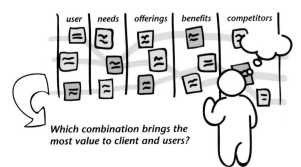

*Which combination brings the most value to client and users?*

5.3 VALUE HYPOTHESIS

Defining user personalities for exploring concepts around them

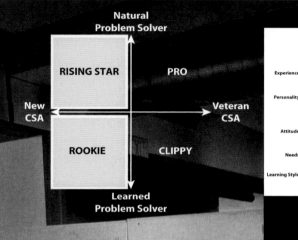

**Natural Problem Solver**

| RISING STAR | PRO |
| --- | --- |

**New CSA** ←→ **Veteran CSA**

| ROOKIE | CLIPPY |
| --- | --- |

**Learned Problem Solver**

**Sarah, 39** ROOKIE
Lives in Bridgeview with husband
Earned a GED from Truman College

*"I like my job but it's too overwhelming to try and learn all the products and to help customers with questions I don't understand."*

| | |
| --- | --- |
| **Experience** | • 15 months as Phone CSA<br>• Currently prefers to stay on Phone Sales<br>• Formerly worked in data processing in the Company's Int'l Shipping Department |
| **Personality** | • Introvert<br>• Relational, enjoys spending time with co-workers<br>• Likes to go out with husband, crochet, and dish with friends at the bar<br>• Has a feature phone but is considering switching to a smartphone |
| **Attitude** | • Grateful for job because of stability<br>• Enthusiastic but lacks support<br>• Lacks confidence in her abilities<br>• Rigid about rules and procedures |
| **Needs** | • Accessible tutorials with clearly written instructions and how-to's<br>• A sense of permission to learn and study |
| **Learning Style** | • Is a "tell me & show me" learner where she learns through visual aids and needs clear instructions for daily tasks and responsibilities |

**Ben, 45** RISING STAR
Lives in Jefferson Park with wife and 2 kids
High school degree from Lane Tech High School

*"I enjoy customer service. It's rewarding when you are the person to single-handedly solve the customer's problem quickly and efficiently."*

| | |
| --- | --- |
| **Experience** | • 11 months as Phone CSA<br>• Wants to help out wherever he is needed<br>• Formerly worked in customer service for computer hardware sales company<br>• Looking forward to transitioning to help with Counter Sales and growing in the company |
| **Personality** | • Extrovert<br>• Relational, enjoys spending time with co-workers but often can't because of family<br>• Likes to take kids to zoo, try new foods, and fix up his home in his free time<br>• Has an iPhone |
| **Attitude** | • Thrives on solving customer questions<br>• Enthusiastic and proud<br>• Looks forward to growing in the company<br>• Confident in his abilities<br>• Relies heavily on intuition and has the philosophy of 'do first, ask later' |
| **Needs** | • A reference guide for his mental shortcuts/tricks.<br>• Positive reinforcement and recognition of his work |
| **Learning Style** | • Is a "let me try" learner where he learns through practice and handling customer's questions himself.<br>• Relies heavily on experience and customer cues to field questions and problem-solve |

## EXAMPLE PROJECT: BOLT (2011)

As a consumer, a conversation with customer support is often the most influential interaction that determines a positive or negative experience with a product or service. Customer support agents (CSAs), however, are constantly faced with a complex set of problems as part of their daily jobs that affect interactions with customers. A design team worked with a manufacturing, repair, and operations company to assess the role of CSAs and understand the issues they face. The team began their research by conducting in-context interviews with phone CSAs and managers, behavioral observations during customer support calls, and in-store intercept interviews with customers. Based on their insights, the team developed attributes (natural problem solver, learned problem solver, new CSA, and veteran CSA) to help cluster common characteristics and define a manageable number of personas that represent the company's phone CSAs.

The team then used the ***Persona Definition*** method and developed four different personas for phone CSA types labeled: the rising star, rookie, pro, and clippy. Each persona was defined based on the attributes of experience, personality, attitude, needs, and learning style. The persona definition was further described with the first name, age, direct quote, and short description of an individual representative of the persona. The team strategically selected two personas that would benefit most from solutions that would address the most common pain points suffered by CSAs. By focusing on the rising star and the rookie, the team developed an application called BOLT, a problem diagnosis tool that empowers customer support by enabling support staff to expertly handle customers' needs

**BENEFITS**

- Broadens mindset
- Builds empathy
- Defines direction
- Facilitates storytelling
- Inspires ideation
- Structures existing knowledge

**INPUT**

- Findings from ethnographic research
- List of potential users and user attributes

**OUTPUT**

- Set of personas based on different user attributes to inform concept exploration

**WHEN TO USE**

## WHAT IT DOES

In this method, user personalities—personas related to the intended innovation—are defined and documented first. Analyzing the types of potential users and organizing them according to sets of shared attributes define the personas. It is helpful to think of a persona as a personality type. A finite number of such personas are created and considered as representing the target users for the project. This range of selected personas frames the opportunity space so that innovation teams can focus on them for building concepts. Concepts are built to address the needs of these personas and to fit with their context.

## HOW IT WORKS

### STEP 1: Generate a list of potential users.

Generate a list of potential users for your innovation. This should be based on your insights, design principles, Value Hypothesis, findings from ethnographic research, or results from other methods like Semantic Profile and User Groups Definition.

### STEP 2: Generate a list of user attributes.

Generate a comprehensive list of user attributes relevant to your project. These attributes may be demographic (age, gender, employment, or home ownership), psychographic (values, attitudes, interests, or lifestyles), or behavioral (motivations, intelligence, or emotions).

### STEP 3: Define a finite number (three to ten) of user types.

Cluster users based on the common attributes they have. If you don't already have a sense of what attributes are shared by different types of users you could use an Asymmetric Clustering Matrix to find groupings. Label these clusters; they represent user types. Aim at having a manageable number of user types (three to ten) to build focus and more effective communication.

### STEP 4: Create personas around user types.

For each user type, create a specific persona, a specific character. Create this persona as a combination of attributes defined earlier. Personas should be true to the findings of research and easy to empathize, give them descriptive and memorable titles. For example: Jane, the city gardener, 28 years old, lawyer, art enthusiast, and so on. Complement the persona profiles with quotes and anecdotes when possible.

### STEP 5: Build a visual profile for each persona.

Create visualizations for the personas and define a standard format to organize the attributes, quotes, and anecdotes for each of them. The resulting documents should be highly visual, well communicated, and quick to read. Share them among team members to drive concept exploration.

Insights and research data

Persona name
Persona name
Persona name
Persona name

5.4 PERSONA DEFINITION

Conducting structured sessions to generate concepts based on
defined insights and principles

## EXAMPLE PROJECT: Car-Sharing Service (2010)

In design planning, ideation sessions provide ways to create experiences
for participants to help them elicit what they feel, think, and do. A
design team conducted an *Ideation Session* with a group of users to
generate ideas about how a popular car-sharing service could strengthen
its customer relationships using a five-stage customer relationship
framework. The framework encapsulated the progression from the unaware
customer, one who has not considered the car-sharing service as an
alternative option, to the evangelist, who speaks publicly about the service
and is seen as a major influencer. The stages in between comprised the
prospective, current, and loyalist customer.

From their research findings, the team shared the key motivations that
would drive a customer to move from one stage to another, as well as the
barriers that would prevent a customer from moving to the next stage,
with the participants. These motivations ranged from practical (e.g., need
transportation) to emotional reasons (e.g., drive cool car), and some of the
barriers included high cost and lack of convenience.

Nearly one hundred concepts were developed to address specific barriers.
Some of these included a car-trading service providing customers the ability
to trade a rented car with other customers who needed it without having to
first return it to the car-sharing lot, and a rent-my-car service that would
allow people to rent their own cars for a nominal fee. The session and the
generated ideas enabled participants to realize that organizations have
different types of relationships with their constituents and should seek to
understand and support the unique nature of each stage.

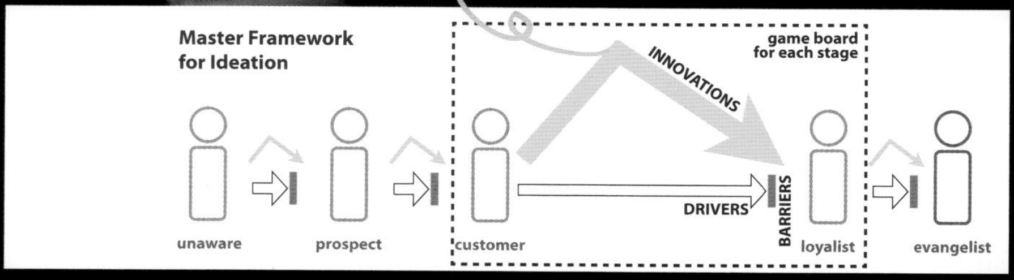

### Master Framework for Ideation

INNOVATIONS

game board for each stage

DRIVERS

BARRIERS

unaware    prospect    customer    loyalist    evangelist

**DRIVERS**
- seek reliability
- want positive experience
- want to have fun
- enjoy expressing personality

**BARRIERS**
- infrequent use
- narrow view of offering
- lack of flexibility
- cost
- two-way

**BENEFITS**

- Brings in new perspectives
- Promotes collaboration
- Structures ideation

**INPUT**

- Insights, design principles, and/or opportunity frameworks

**OUTPUT**

- Numerous concepts (around the project's research findings)

**WHEN TO USE**

## What it Does

Compared to traditional free-form brainstorming, an Ideation Session is more structured. Concepts are generated using preorganized sets of insights, principles, and frameworks that teams have already developed. The method encourages generating as many concepts as possible without making judgments and is done in a short amount of time. The session brings together people with multidisciplinary backgrounds and encourages building on each other's ideas.

Teams agree on a number of protocols that make these ideation sessions productive. Be proactive in generating "bold" ideas. Generate a lot of them. Build on each other's ideas using the "Yes…and…" approach, in which a member builds on another's idea by acknowledging it and then adding more value to it. Always stay focused on the topic for ideation and be engaged throughout the session. No idea is a bad idea in this session; therefore, capture every idea that comes up. Evaluate ideas later.

## How it Works

### STEP 1: Plan for the ideation session.

Define what you hope to achieve through the Ideation Session, how many concepts you hope to gather, and how well they can be organized and refined in the given time period. Prepare guidelines describing rules of engagement, how teams should interact, structure their time, and complete assigned tasks. Create a plan with a goal statement, a compact schedule, an inspiring space, and multidisciplinary participants.

### STEP 2: Select participants with a variety of expertise.

Involve the right combination of people for the session. For example, include people with different job functions and levels of seniority, with different points of view, different experiences and of ages, and those who will have a willingness to play along.

### STEP 3: Organize insights, principles, and frameworks to guide ideation.

Gather all insights, principles, and frameworks that your team has produced during the earlier modes. Define how to present them and how they will be used during the concept-generating activities. Organize them as reference materials for the Ideation Session. Many times an organized list of design principles is used to directly generate concepts. In such a case, decide whether or not you want participants to address all of them or only a subset.

### STEP 4: Create a comfortable environment for the session.

Create an environment that is conducive to creativity. Provide a space where many teams of three or four can work comfortably. Make sure the basics are covered, such as sticky notes, pens, paper, and even snack foods. Prepare the necessary support materials. Include graphic organizers or worksheets that will enable teams to easily capture their ideas.

### STEP 5: Start the session and facilitate activities.

Facilitators play an important role in making these sessions successful. Their role should include: engaging the whole group at all times, keeping participants focused on ideation, encouraging clear conversations, stimulating and maintaining a good energy level, encouraging contribution from shy participants, promoting enjoyment and humor, asking evocative questions, and introducing idea stimulators when activities slow down.

5.5 IDEATION SESSION

### STEP 6: Generate concepts.

The focus should be on producing as many concepts as possible. Time constraints can foster efficiency. Confine ideation to 45 minutes to 2 hours. Allow time for both individual idea generation and group discussions where team members can build off of another person's idea. Use open-ended ways to think, like: "How might we…?" and "What if…?" Have templates or worksheets to capture concepts. When slowing down, take an in-room break. Avoid the following: filtering or editing, discussing ideas too much, comments that constrain, judgments, criticizing or even complimenting ideas, and expert evaluation.

### STEP 7: Capture and summarize ideation output.

Make sure that each concept is captured or summarized in a one-page template, with a concept description, sketches, and other relevant aspects such as user values, provider values, concept strategy, capabilities, partners, and risks. Compile all concepts into output documents that can be shared with the team members and stakeholders who weren't in the session. Discuss how these concepts will be further refined and evaluated, and which of them should be further developed for prototyping.

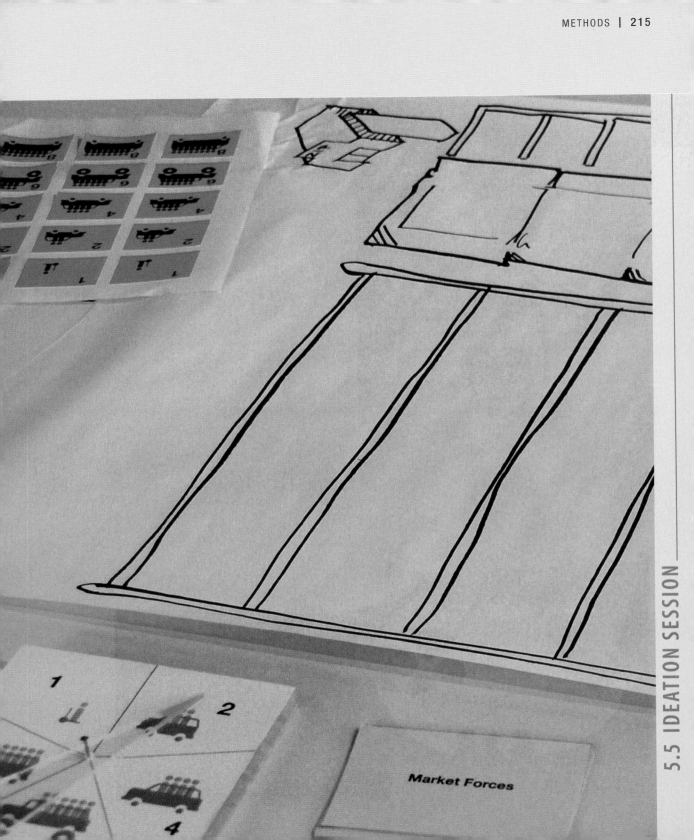

# 5.6 Concept-Generating Matrix

Generating a comprehensive and well-grounded set of concepts based on research insights

*EXAMPLE PROJECT: Bringing Relevance to Newspaper Company (2011)*

With the decline of print media showing no sign of slowing, a local Ohio newspaper tasked a design team with identifying new ways to attract and engage its readers. The newspaper wanted recommendations for short-, mid-, and long-term actions it could undertake to remain relevant in the rapidly changing industry.

The team began by performing ethnographic interviews with current subscribers, past subscribers, nonsubscribers, and subject matter experts. They identified six opportunity spaces to further explore: emergent journalism, connecting communities, personalization, channel fit, advertising, and redefining "local." From here, the team began forming ideas with a *Concept-Generating Matrix* using the six opportunity spaces against the most relevant user types (e.g., empty nesters, young families, advertisers) that emerged from research. The team then brainstormed specific concepts that addressed each of the user types across the six opportunity spaces. These concepts filled the intersections of the matrix. For example, one concept for the young professional that addressed channel fit was an audio version of the newspaper for use during daily commutes. Some intersections yielded few or no concepts, while others had multiple. The team then hosted a concept evaluation workshop with the client, where these newly generated ideas were refined and prototyped.

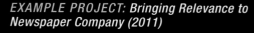

PASS IT FORWARD NETWORK

CROWDSOURCING

## BENEFITS

- Broadens mindset
- Reveals opportunities
- Encourages comprehensiveness
- Identifies opportunities
- Keeps grounded in research
- Structures ideation

## INPUT

- Two sets of factors or frameworks from research and analysis

## OUTPUT

- Collection of targeted/ relevant concepts

## WHEN TO USE

## WHAT IT DOES

A Concept Matrix takes two sets of important factors from analysis and creates a two-dimensional matrix to help explore concepts at their intersections. The key to this method is to determine which set of factors to use. Each set should be comprehensive and complementary to the other so that the intersections are coherent with the goals of the project. Often, a list of activities or needs discovered in research is an important set of factors that can be used as one axis of the matrix. A second set of factors may come from another method, for example, the stages from the Compelling Experience Map.

This method gives a simple structure to ideation while keeping it strongly grounded in research. It's also helpful to bring alignment and focus to team discussions as it defines concrete frames to explore concepts.

## HOW IT WORKS

### STEP 1: Select two sets of factors to build the matrix

Revisit the insights and frameworks that resulted from the work in Frame Insights mode. Discuss them in teams, speculate on how they can lead to valuable concepts, and choose two sets of factors for interaction. These should be complementary to each other and create interesting frames for concept exploration. For example, a commonly used combination of sets is user types and the compelling experience framework. Create a table with one set as column headings and the other as row headings.

### STEP 2: Populate the matrix cells with concepts.

Brainstorm around the intersection of pairs of factors. Some cells may be more fruitful than others; this is fine, but make sure each cell is at least considered. Give each concept a compelling and memorable name. Write a brief description about the concept. Optionally, create thumbnail sketches or diagrams of each concept. Visualizing concepts to support the description is helpful for easy communication and sharing.

### STEP 3: Use the method to further explore concepts.

Use the matrix as an overview to recognize and fill gaps, recognize critical areas in the matrix to do deeper brainstorming, compare concepts, or do initial evaluation of concepts as a team. Make other matrices with other sets of factors from the research as a way to explore more concepts.

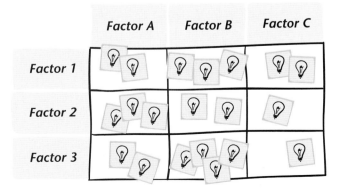

5.6 CONCEPT-GENERATING MATRIX

# 5.7 Concept Metaphors and Analogies

Generating concepts in new ways by thinking of them as something else that is familiar

FINANCIAL SURVIVING MAP

## EXAMPLE PROJECT: Better Budget (2010)

A design team sought to explore home budgeting for young people. The team was tasked with developing a platform to help young people improve their lives through home budgeting. While existing solutions focused primarily on the mechanics of money management, this platform needed to provide continuous support and motivation for young people to help them grow into healthy budgeting adults. The team conducted ethnographic research on nine participants that included young adults, experienced budgeters, and a financial expert. They derived insights from these interviews that fell into five clusters: motivation, monitoring, creative savings, money management, and guidance. To generate concepts that addressed these insight clusters, the team used the *Concept Metaphors and Analogies* method in an ideation workshop with young people.

Participants were divided into groups and given worksheets and analogies cards. The cards contained brands and services that had qualities similar to what the solutions should have. Using these brands, such as Weight Watchers, as analogies helped participants to quickly make connections to the underlying meaning of the insights. As an example, one of the cards stated: "Weight Watchers motivates people to lose weight by counting points for food. How might we keep young people connected to their budget goals on a daily basis?" The groups generated concepts in the same vein as the analogies cards, leading to ideas for each of the five clusters of insights. By framing concept generation around these familiar analogous offerings, the team was able to inspire workshop participants to generate concepts with focus, without compromising scope.

**BENEFITS**

- Challenges assumptions
- Improves communication
- Inspires ideation

**INPUT**

- Insights, value hypothesis, or design principles from research and analysis

**OUTPUT**

- Collections of interrelated concepts surrounding each metaphor or analogy

**WHEN TO USE**

## WHAT IT DOES

Framing concepts in terms of familiar metaphors or analogies can be a powerful way to inspire creativity during brainstorming. In this method, a metaphor is used to generate a concept by means of a vivid comparison but is not meant literally. For example, a mobile phone is a wallet; a tablet computer is a pad of paper. Analogies are more direct when making comparison; concepts are thought of as something similar in some ways to something else. For example, considering personal budgeting to be like managing weight loss. Analogies require reasoning to understand and they are self-evident, whereas metaphors require some interpretation. Ultimately, this method, by the very nature of its definition, leads to concepts that reframe conventional thinking.

It is easy to think of an idea around something that is familiar. Ask questions like: How can my concept be like _____ [something familiar]? Choose metaphors/analogies that can tie everything together as one central and memorable idea to guide concept generation. Moreover, use metaphors/analogies as a way to provide focus and energy for the brainstorming team.

## HOW IT WORKS

### STEP 1: Determine a starting place for using metaphors and analogies.

Any insight about an innovation opportunity identified in the earlier modes is a good starting place to explore concepts using this method. Perhaps a Value Hypothesis Statement, with its early definitions of potential "new offerings," can be used as a base to create concepts. The design principles generated in the Frame Insights mode is another starting place.

### STEP 2: Identify interesting metaphors and analogies.

As a team, take up the design principles (or other findings pointing to innovation opportunities) and use metaphors/analogies to conceive of ideas in interesting, inspiring, and unexpected ways. Think about the values that you aim to deliver and seek examples of how similar values are currently delivered. A simple yet powerful way is to use comparisons such as "acts like, looks like, or works like." For example, ask questions like: Could a portable computing device act like a secretary? Could the rental car service work like the bike rental system?

A common approach to think about analogies is called synectics. It posits four types of analogy:

*Direct analogy:* Compare the concept to something that already exists in the real world, for example, a mobile phone that's like a wallet.

*Fantasy analogy:* Compare the concept to something that doesn't exist in the real world, but is imaginable, for example, a kitchen that cooks.

*Symbolic analogy:* Compare some aspect or quality of the concept to an aspect or quality of something else, for example, a project is like a symphony.

*Personal analogy:* The innovator imagines herself to personify the concept, for example, "If I were [my concept], what would I be like?"

### STEP 3: Generate concepts.

For each metaphor and analogy uncovered in the previous step, generate concepts around the possibilities they elicit. These concepts should aim at exploring the "how" or the "what if" questions. Build on the initial concepts by further considering the insights from the Know People and Know Context modes.

### STEP 4: Document, discuss, and refine concepts.

Document all the concepts generated, add descriptions, share them with the team, and discuss how they could be evaluated and further developed.

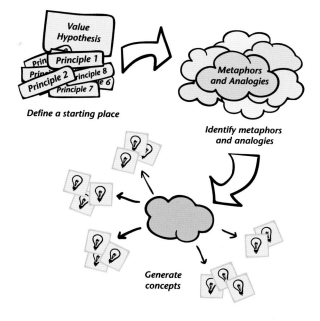

Define a starting place

Identify metaphors and analogies

Generate concepts

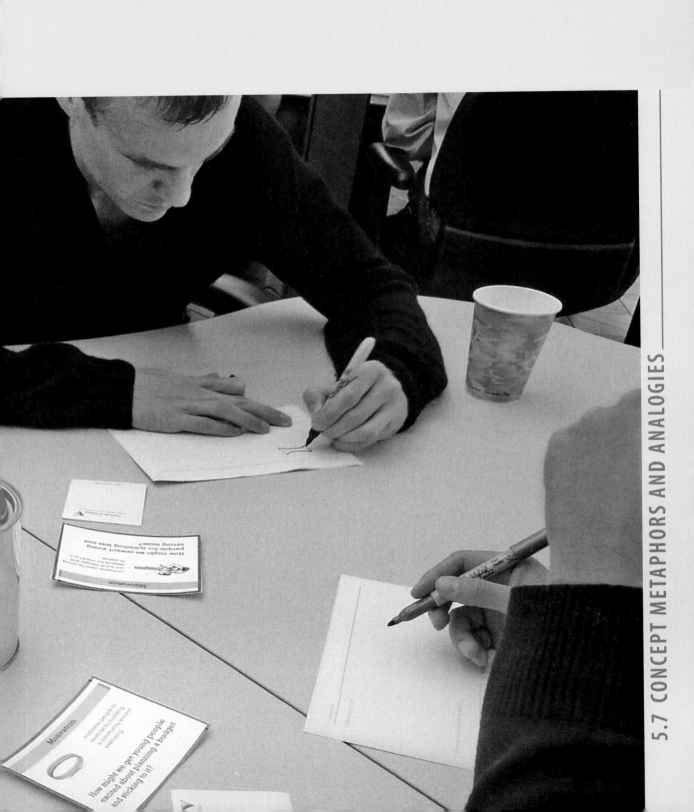

5.7 CONCEPT METAPHORS AND ANALOGIES

### EXAMPLE PROJECT: Homebuilder – Addressing the Needs of Underserved Market (2006)

In 2005, one of the nation's largest homebuilders struggled to stay competitive in an industry experiencing significant decline, increased mortgage interest rates, and fewer new housing starts. The company was the subject for a design team to explore new market opportunities and secure its position in the homebuilding industry. By employing innovation planning methods, the team arrived at a recommendation to target the relatively untapped Latino community, giving the company a first-mover advantage to grow its customer base.

The team held a Concept-Generation workshop to brainstorm ideas for targeting this underserved market. One round of this session involved *Role-Play Ideation*, where each individual was assigned the role of one of the potential stakeholders (Papá, Mamá, a Contractor, and a Concierge). The team distributed cards to each participant that provided background details on their stakeholder, such as their status, workplace, where they live, what languages they speak, what they hope to achieve, and their worries. For example, Mamá moved to the United States in her 20s, works as a shift leader in a dry-cleaning plant, lives in a mostly Latino neighborhood, speaks some English, hopes to have a big family, but worries about having enough money. From these stakeholder personas, each participant developed concepts from the perspective of their assigned role that reflected the contextual intricacies of each stakeholder. The team then scored and clustered the concepts, ranking them on likelihood of providing return on investment and how successfully each addressed the design requirements. This method helped the participants to challenge their assumptions and move past mental blocks they may have had in order to generate concepts. This exercise also enabled the team to better develop a comprehensive strategy that addressed the needs of the various stakeholders.

- Builds empathy
- Challenges assumptions
- Facilitates discussion
- Inspires ideation

**INPUT**

- Innovation opportunities from analysis

**OUTPUT**

- Collection of concepts rooted in empathy and understanding of stakeholder needs

**WHEN TO USE**

## WHAT IT DOES

Role-playing is an approach to brainstorming in which each member of the team plays the role of a different stakeholder in the concept area. Stakeholders include end users, designers, engineers, executives, marketers, suppliers, partners, and others. Brainstorming using this method can take individual team members out of their usual mindsets and assumptions, and greatly enrich the quality and quantity of ideas and generate useful discussions. The method promotes user-centered thinking and discussions on empathy, since the focus is on generating concepts that are of potential value to someone else. This can be a particularly useful preparatory exercise for team members unfamiliar with user-centered innovation. It can also be a good technique for individual ideation in the absence of a team. The solo innovator simply makes sure to spend some amount of time brainstorming concepts from the point of view of each stakeholder involved, until all stakeholders are covered.

## HOW IT WORKS

### STEP 1: Identify important topics or concept areas for brainstorming.

These topics might be based on the innovation opportunities suggested by the analysis frameworks, design principles, opportunity mind map, value hypothesis, or other sources.

### STEP 2: Identify stakeholders.

Make a list of all the stakeholders in the concept area you are considering. Identify the most important stakeholders for the purpose of brainstorming, if time is limited.

### STEP 3: Generate concepts through role-playing.

Assign each team member a stakeholder role to play during brainstorming around the topic for a period of time. Using concept sketching as part of role-playing can be very powerful. Vary the role-play periodically to sustain creative energy, in one of three ways:

> ***Role Round Robin:*** Reassign team members to different roles in a "round robin" and repeat role-play ideation.

> ***Concept Round Robin:*** Have team members sketch ideas on paper in the character of their role, and then pass the sketch to the next player, for them to add to or refine based on their own role.

> ***Concept Improv:*** Act out concepts as a group.

### STEP 4: Discuss and share the concepts among stakeholders.

The concepts generated during the session are documented, including sketches and descriptions. Share these with actual stakeholders for feedback and conversations about potential refinements and buildup.

# 5.9 Ideation Game

Engaging stakeholders in game-like activities to generate concepts

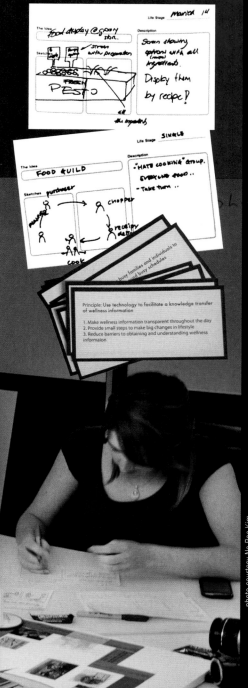

photo courtesy Na Rae Kim

**EXAMPLE PROJECT:** *Convivial Food Platform (2010)*

Convivial is a comprehensive, integrated food and wellness platform conceptualized by a design team advised by the author. During their immersive exploration to understand the concept of platforms and demonstrate its application in a home-life project, the team selected the topic of connecting family and friends together around food.

As a platform, Convivial needed to be attractive to a wide range of people in different stages of life. For this reason, the team chose an *Ideation Game* designed around Milton Bradley's Game of Life® that simulates a person's progression through different life stages. The game board was organized using the food preparation framework that they had developed from the insights gleaned from their research and that combined four distinct steps: planning, shopping, preparation, and collaboration. Organizing the board in this arrangement enabled the team to see how the transitions of life would spur the platform's growth over time.

In addition to the board game, the team also incorporated an analysis exercise to help organize the concepts. A star diagram was used as the canvas for each four-person team to cluster their ideas. Once each cluster came together, teams would work to develop themes. Teams were also encouraged to draw connections or relationships across the board to demonstrate how a platform might come together. After this exercise, teams completed the value proposition worksheet and were also asked to create an ad spot that would showcase how to sell the platform to the potential audience. At the end of the workshop, participants generated more than 75 initial concepts that were used as input in the concept development stage.

photo courtesy Na Rae Kim

## BENEFITS

- Brings in new perspectives
- Broadens mindset
- Inspires ideation
- Promotes playfulness

## INPUT

- Insights, design principles, and/or opportunity frameworks

## OUTPUT

- Numerous concepts (around the project's research findings)

## WHEN TO USE

### WHAT IT DOES

Classic games like Monopoly® and chess not only engage players in enjoyable ways, but also help them learn about topics like transaction, strategy, growth, and success. These games improve the player's skills in problem solving, decision making, strategic thinking, tactical actions, creative thinking, and the like. The casual, fun, engaging, skill-building, and educational interactions games offer are used in this method as an opportunity for generating fresh concepts. Designing and playing the game elevates participants to a new level of nonconventional thinking. Such game-building and game-playing mindsets allow participants to cut through barriers of creativity and think more openly about the future. Moreover, engaging participants in ways that are informal, fun, and relaxed makes the concept exploration process more valuable than direct methods.

The team first develops a game that a group can play in which ideation challenges are thoughtfully embedded. These challenges are created based on insights, principles, and user-centered frameworks defined in previous modes.

### HOW IT WORKS

**STEP 1: Define the intent of the game and gather the necessary input data.**

The intent is to build concepts for your project through game-playing. Concepts are generated based on inputs such as design principles, insights, and frameworks that your team has generated in the earlier modes. Collect these input data to be built into the game.

**STEP 2: Understand the players.**

Understand the audience so that the game can be designed for their interaction. Consider the number of players, their backgrounds, and how they are going to engage.

**STEP 3: Define the type of game to be built and played.**

Decide on the appropriate game options for generating concepts. Choose a type of game that is familiar to most people. Decide if it should be a board game, memory game, card game, construction game, role-playing game, or some other type. Consider how much time will be needed.

**STEP 4: Determine the key elements and build the game.**

Brainstorm to design the game. First, key elements (goal, competition, rules, interventions, tasks, rewards, and game pieces) of the game need to be defined. The goal of playing the game is to generate as many concepts as possible. Provide an appropriate level of competition to make the game exciting and engaging. Determine and describe the rules for all players to understand. Build in interventions that can help or hinder players when they encounter them. Determine the tasks or activities players need to do as the game progresses. Incorporate rewards and penalties to make the game interesting. Make physical and visual artifacts as game pieces, adding to the experience.

**STEP 5: Play the game and collect output.**

Involve the right combination of players for the game. Arrange for a comfortable space for groups to engage in the game and generate concepts.

5.9 IDEATION GAME

Establish time limits. Brief all participants before the game starts about rules, task, rewards, and other details. Facilitate the game-playing session and reward participants. Capture all concepts generated during the game and organize them in documents.

### STEP 6: Share the concepts and discuss refinements and prioritization.

Gather all the concepts generated during the game-playing session, including sketches and descriptions. Review concepts and remove unsubstantive and irrelevant ones. Share the remaining concepts with team members and discuss prioritization, refinements, and buildup.

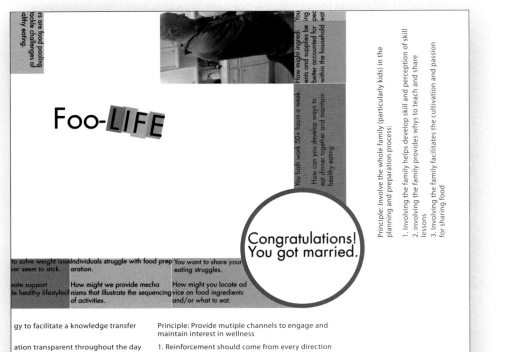

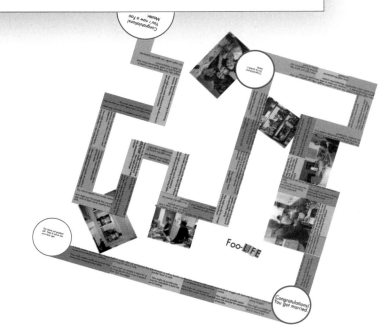

# 5.10 Puppet Scenario

Collaboratively creating current and future scenarios and enacting them with puppets as actors

Senior Interaction 2009–2012.

**EXAMPLE PROJECT:** *Senior Interaction, Supporting the Elderly (2009)*

Danish Design School students together with public and private sector partners collaborated on a co-design project aimed at addressing the challenges faced by the aging population. The goal was to design new services and technology to support and strengthen their daily social interactions and networks in the urban environment. Facilitated through a series of workshops, the project started by exploring the meaning of everyday life for senior citizens. Separated in several small groups, the seniors were first asked to represent "a good day" in a collage with material given to them for inspiration, and their stories were shared in front of the larger group. From this current view of daily life, the groups were then asked to imagine a new future using what-if cards as thought starters, such as: What if the old and young people meet on a tour? The seniors were asked to imagine these future states and themselves as active participants. Groups then coalesced the stories from the current and future states to create a new scenario using puppet dolls.

The *Puppet Scenarios* were crafted as a story in three stages: the current state, a new change, and an outlook of the near future (25 years). Because these scenarios required the seniors to dress up the dolls using materials prepared in a kit, they were able to embody their chosen actors. The workshop ended with each group enacting their new scenarios such as, "A shared movie and shopping trip" and "A nice trip to the park." These enacted scenarios made a good starting point for opening up a space of possible service concepts for the future.

Senior Interaction 2009–2012.

Senior Interaction 2009–2012.

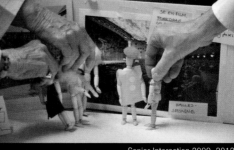

Senior Interaction 2009–2012.

**BENEFITS**

- Brings in new perspectives
- Facilitates storytelling
- Inspires ideation
- Promotes collaboration
- Promotes playfulness

**INPUT**

- Everyday-life findings and insights from ethnographic research

**OUTPUT**

- A collection of future scenarios and related concepts

## WHAT IT DOES

The Puppet Scenario is an idea-generation game used to encourage participation and collaboration among different stakeholders. It has three elements: collective exploration, design, and games. The exploratory element brings together participants with diverse backgrounds, expertise, and competencies to ideate on possible future scenarios. The design element helps participants make their ideas tangible according to their needs and interests and provides options for future design. The game element presents a protocol for engaging participants in a mutually challenging, fun, and collaborative environment beyond the confines of the participant's everyday life.

## HOW IT WORKS

### STEP 1: Prepare design cards, what-if cards, and construction kit before the workshop.

Prepare about ten design cards containing glimpses from ethnographic encounters presented as pictures, illustrations, short statements, or questions. The content of the cards should be evocative and relate to specific situations that the participants can recognize from their own everyday life. Prepare what-if cards with an illustration and a question beginning with "what if" that evokes a new idea, service, or product. Prepare a separate construction kit that will be used for scenario staging. The kit should contain a foam base for the stage, foam boards for the stage backdrop, pictures to use as a backdrop setting, colored markers, paper, felt, scissors, glue, and four to six small wooden puppets.

### STEP 2: Share everyday stories using design cards.

Participants in this method are potential users chosen through other methods. They form groups of four to six and each group should have an identical deck of design cards. Every participant chooses one or two cards and explains to the rest of the group why they have chosen that specific card and why it is interesting. They place the selected cards on a whiteboard to build a shared space of stories. When a card is placed on the whiteboard, the relations to adjacent cards on the board are explained. As clusters of stories begin to emerge, participants prioritize themes and issues that are important to them.

### STEP 3: Evoke possible directions for your project using what-if cards.

On the shared board of stories ask participants to identify (with green and red markers, for example) areas of best design possibilities and most challenging problems. Introduce what-if cards, ask participants to place them on the board, and encourage discussions about future possibilities for your project. Allow participants to share their feelings and thoughts about the what-if cards, and continue to capture them on the board. The design cards and markers on the board frame what the Puppet Scenario could be. The what-if cards evoke conceptual directions for your project.

### STEP 4: Produce and stage a Puppet Scenario.

After thinking of both current and what-if stories, allow each group to choose elements from the board to construct a cohesive story. Using the construction kit, they should produce a Puppet Scenario by dressing puppets as actors with specific charac-

ters, preferably themselves. They should cover three main scenes: the current state, a new element or action introduced, and the near future (25 years). The groups must negotiate their way to a coherent story based on their previous discussions.

**STEP 5: Enact scenario, document, and discuss.**
Rehearse and perform scenarios for other groups. As groups are enacting their final scenarios, designate a member from your team to take video and photos. Capture video one scene at a time, and record only what is enacted in front of the backdrop. Share the video scenarios with team members, participants, and other stakeholders for discussions.

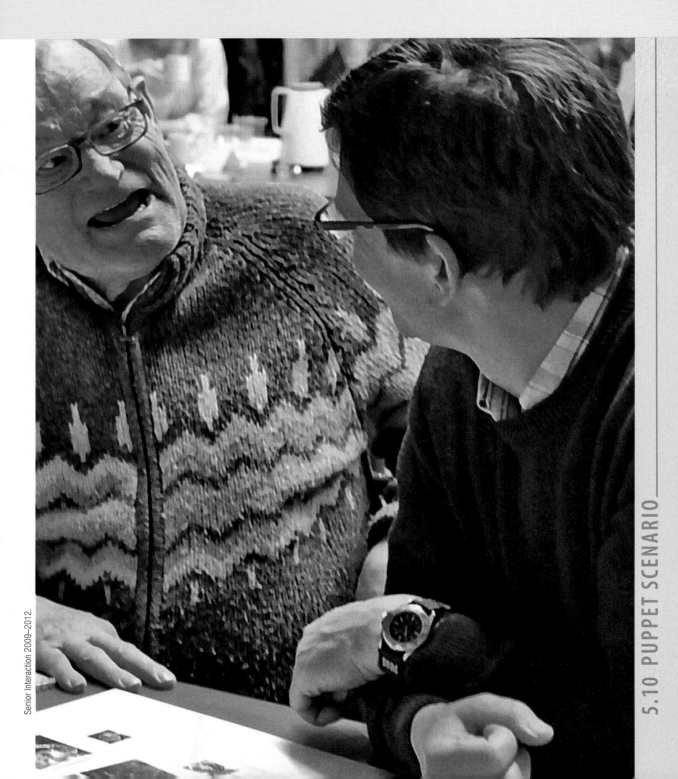

Senior Interaction 2009–2012.

5.10 PUPPET SCENARIO

# 5.11 Behavioral Prototype

Simulating situations of user activity to understand user behaviors
and build early concepts

### EXAMPLE PROJECT: ThinkeringSpaces (2006)

ThinkeringSpaces are interactive environments
that encourage school-aged children to tinker with
things in both physical and virtual spaces, reflect
upon what they discover, and share their ideas
with others. Using libraries as its main distribution
channel, ThinkeringSpaces aims to nurture and
support children's skills in creative thinking, systems
understanding, innovative problem solving, information
management, and interdisciplinary teamwork.
ThinkeringSpaces was conceived from ideas taken from
primary and secondary research in educational learning
theory, best examples of learning environments, new
technologies, flexible structures, and social trends.
These, in turn, became the foundation for defining the
project's eight design principles.

The successful design of ThinkeringSpaces depended
heavily on having a clear understanding of kids'
informal, exploratory behaviors and how they actually
perceive, interpret, use, and extend the opportunity
for open-ended tinkering. *The Behavioral Prototype*
approach provided an effective way to witness
their learning styles and experience with objects,
information, tools, and the environment. A design
team developed three behavioral prototypes that
targeted different sensory modalities, including
visual, auditory, and motor sensory modes. The first
prototype, Materials and Mind Sets, was designed to
support kids' reflective expression and exploration
using inspirational, associative, and functional
objects on a surface on which they could arrange the
materials. The prototype juxtaposed very abstract
objects with very detailed ones to analyze the child's
understanding of materials, including shape, color,
pattern, thickness, texture, and the like. The team
developed four iterations of the prototype each
time making modifications as they observed key
behaviors in how the kids interpreted the materials
to their personal interests. The key learning from
this prototype helped to inform the next steps for the
team, which included exploring more ways to achieve
tactile appeal in digital applications.

**BENEFITS**

- Builds empathy
- Encourages iterations
- Makes abstract ideas concrete
- Promotes collaboration

**INPUT**

- Key behaviors and related concepts to be studied

**OUTPUT**

- Refined concepts adjusted for user behaviors

**WHEN TO USE**

## WHAT IT DOES

A Behavioral Prototype is a method used in the Explore Concepts mode (before physical prototypes are made) in which, based on early concepts, teams plan a situation with simulated artifacts, environments, information, or processes and involve users in it. Through observation and conversation, user behaviors to help the team further build on the concepts. In particular, this method is used to understand the five human factors (physical, cognitive, social, cultural, or emotional) around behaviors and create new value added concepts to support and improve those behaviors. Information is gathered while observing interactions and recorded with video or note-taking, and observations are analyzed to assess if new insights can be supported by these new concepts.

Behavioral Prototype, unlike Concept or Solution Prototype, is primarily focused on simulating and understanding peoples' behaviors and is not focused on the function of the concept itself.

## HOW IT WORKS

### STEP 1: Identify the situation to be simulated.

Review your concepts to identify a specific situation in which a better understanding of user behaviors will be valuable for developing concepts. Determine what key behaviors you want to study. Plan a simulated situation. Include the necessary elements—actors, artifacts, props, and so forth in the simulated situation.

### STEP 2: Prepare the environment for simulation.

Find or build a physical or virtual environment where participants can engage freely in the activity and exhibit the key behaviors you seek to understand. Use props to represent your concepts and to support participants' interactions with them.

### STEP 3: Engage users in the simulated situation.

Invite participants to the simulation, determine if you want them to engage individually or in groups, and guide them through interacting with the environment.

### STEP 4: Observe, document, and query.

Observe participants engaged in the activity. Note the physical, cognitive, social, cultural, and emotional factors that affect participants' engagement. Record their behaviors with video and note taking. Conduct a post-activity interview with participants to clarify questions you may have about why they chose to act in a certain way or how they felt about certain aspects of the situation.

### STEP 5: Analyze and iterate.

Gather observations from video or notes, and analyze them for patterns of behavior. Review the findings in light of your concept. Consider adjustments to your concepts that encourage or support certain kinds of behaviors. Then, repeat the steps above until key user behaviors are supported well by your concepts.

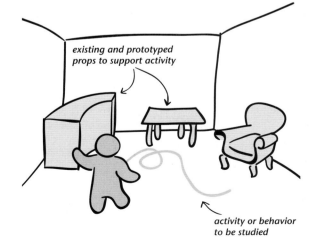

*existing and prototyped props to support activity*

*activity or behavior to be studied*

**5.11 BEHAVIORAL PROTOTYPE**

# 5.12 Concept Prototype

Embodying concepts in tangible forms to get feedback from users

**EXAMPLE PROJECT:** *Airline Medical Emergencies (2009)*

Responding to airborne medical emergencies is a serious issue for airlines with significant design implications for airline manufacturers. Medical emergencies on flights cause diversions up to 35 times per day, totaling millions of dollars in losses per year. A team of designers developed concepts that addressed five core principles: patient transport, aid treatment, tools management, process clarification, and communication with ground crew.

The team examined the frequency of common medical incidents onboard and their respective danger levels, treatment tools required, and optimal body positions for treatment. They also performed a spatial audit of treatment tools that were typically scattered across the plane, making it difficult for airline crew to get all of the necessary equipment to the patient quickly and easily. Interviews with flight attendants, volunteers, and EMTs uncovered a convoluted process for dealing with medical emergencies.

The five core principles served as the foundation for concept development. The team explored many concepts but determined that an ambulance cart was the best option. A standalone unit that fit into standard airline food cart bays, the cart can be rolled to the patient's seat for easy transport to a galley area, and can then be folded into a gurney for treatment. All of the medical supplies are located in the base of the cart. The team built many *Concept Prototypes* using materials like foam core for appearance prototypes and plywood for performance prototypes. The prototypes helped the team assess the feasibility of their concept and perform rapid exploration of different aspects and features. They also provided the team with revelations that were unforeseen until the concept was brought into physical form.

**BENEFITS**

- Encourages iterations
- Makes abstract ideas concrete
- Promotes collaboration

**INPUT**

- Concepts that can benefit from testing in tangible form

**OUTPUT**

- Refined concepts adjusted around how potential users interact with prototypes

**WHEN TO USE**

## WHAT IT DOES

A Concept Prototype is used to assess the adoptability of an early concept among teams and with potential users by giving it physical form that can be experienced. Concept Prototypes embody the principle of "building to learn" in that the process of giving a physical form to a concept facilitates discoveries about it that often cannot be foreseen until it is made tangible. By giving people something tangible to react to, Concept Prototypes can trigger thinking about alternatives or necessary revisions to initial concepts or can help inspire alternative concepts. They also provide fertile grounds for conversations about future possibilities. Concept Prototypes address both the appearance (what it looks like) and the performance (how it works) of the offering.

What emerges from the method is a kind of "reality check" that helps teams make well-informed decisions about the direction a concept needs to evolve."

## HOW IT WORKS

### STEP 1: Identify concepts to be prototyped.

Review concepts to identify those that will benefit most from testing in tangible form. Determine the kinds of readily available materials you will need to create a rough embodiment of the concept. Determine what kind of prototype—appearance prototype, performance prototype, or a combination of both—will be most useful at that stage of the process.

### STEP 2: Create a prototyping space and build to learn.

It is a good idea to identify or create a space where your team can build and test Concept Prototypes. Assemble the kinds of materials and tools you will use for building, modifying, and testing prototypes.

### STEP 3: Review prototypes, test, and discuss.

Present Concept Prototypes to your team in a review session and to a group of users. Test these prototypes and discuss each one in light of the stated design principles, user needs, form factors, human factors, and other dimensions. How does it feel to hold the prototype? Is it intuitive? Comfortable? Does it make sense?

Generate insights about refinements to the core concept. The review is also an opportunity to explore alternative concepts, consider combinations of features from different prototypes, and get guidance for iteration.

### STEP 4: Modify prototypes and iterate.

Build on existing prototypes, modify them, or create new ones to reflect input gathered through the review process. Iterate and continue to incorporate feedback into the prototype.

### STEP 5: Summarize key learning.

Use the conclusion of the review sessions to record the key learning and results from testing. Summarize how the prototype evolved from an initial manifestation to a final desired state. Share this information among team members and stakeholders to reinforce decisions about further development.

5.12 ACTIVITY NETWORK

# 5.13 Concept Sketch

Visualizing concepts as sketches to show how they work in abstract terms

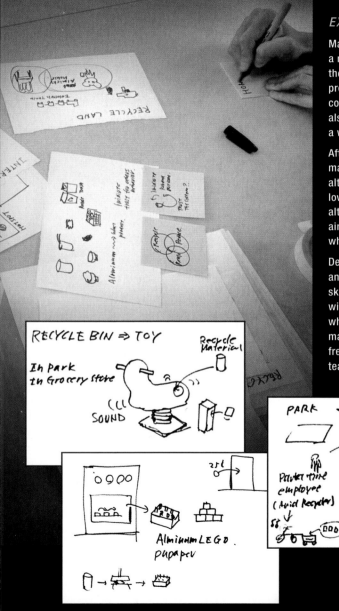

*EXAMPLE PROJECT: Recycling in Farmer's Markets (2011)*

Many cities across the United States are embracing recycling as a major initiative to promote green and sustainable practices for their residents. A design team determined that successful recycling programs are those that convert non-recyclers to recyclers, build community, and create an enjoyable and simple experience. They also recognized a valuable opportunity area in farmers' markets as a way to connect people and build community around recycling.

After conducting primary research on current recyclers, the team mapped them on a 2 × 2 space, measuring their motivations from altruistic to self-centered, and their recycling habits from high to low. They defined their opportunity space as comprising those with altruistic motivations spanning non-recyclers to avid recyclers. They aimed to give an outlet for the passionate, further engage those who are already recycling, and motivate those who are not.

Design principles covering the areas of engagement, awareness, and community, guided the *Concept Sketch* method. The team sketched many ideas that included a neighborhood recycling fair with toys for kids that create a game of the recycling process and where residents buy recycled goods, a pop recycle store, a bench made from recycled items, and modular recyclable furniture. The free-form exploratory nature of the Concept Sketching pushed the team to consider ideas beyond what currently exists.

## BENEFITS

- Facilitates discussion
- Helps refine ideas
- Makes abstract ideas concrete
- Reveals relationships

## INPUT

- Concepts that can be explained by sketches

## OUTPUT

- Visualizations that show what concepts look like and how they work

## WHEN TO USE

### WHAT IT DOES

Concept Sketches convert ideas into concrete forms that are easier to understand, discuss, evaluate, and communicate than abstract ideas that are described in words. Sketches powerfully augment written descriptions and help ideas be communicated more rapidly and effectively. Since sketching is about making an abstract idea concrete, it makes us think through the issues of embodying the idea in reality, and it gets us closer to refined concepts. Moreover, in doing so, it often sparks more ideas for further exploration. Sketching is most often done in team brainstorming sessions to clearly communicate, discuss, and steer participants in promising directions. Iterating and reacting to a teammate's sketch often leads to many more new concepts, subconcepts, or concept improvements than just ideation based on only abstract thinking.

### HOW IT WORKS

#### STEP 1: Assign sketching tasks to team members.

To ensure a smooth work process, assign some team members as designated sketchers, while others focus on verbal ideation and communication.

#### STEP 2: Gather early descriptions of concepts already generated.

Collect the description of concepts suggested by the analysis frameworks, design principles, opportunity mind map, value hypothesis, ideation session, and other methods. Sketches may be prepared beforehand and distributed as a prop for discussion or drawn live as an augmentation to discussion. Often both approaches are used.

#### STEP 3: Sketch out the core idea.

One idea, one sketch. Force yourself to capture the idea in a single representative image. Communicate only the core idea under discussion through this sketch. A high degree of artistry or realism is rarely necessary. Sketches can be very rough at this stage and can be drawn by anyone; no drawing skills are needed. In fact, if sketches have too many features or details present, it may hinder communication at this early stage.

#### STEP 4: Move from rough figurative sketches to more detailed ones.

Initially make rough figurative sketches that are good for quick visualization ("What if we did something like this?"). Later on you can move on to detailed figurative sketches that are good for seeing the concept as more real ("What would that idea really look/feel like?").

#### STEP 5: Capture every sketch and discuss.

Capture every sketch, from paper or from the whiteboard. Document every sketch with small descriptions. A concept sketch that may seem unimportant at this stage may have more value later in the process when concepts are combined into solutions. Review all sketches in teams, discuss their qualities, identify issues, iterate the concepts, and gain an initial sense of where further attention is needed.

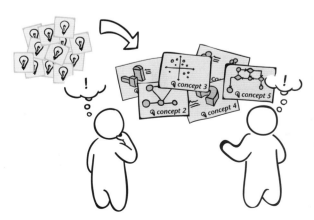

5.13 CONCEPT SKETCH

# 5.14 Concept Scenarios

Illustrating concepts as real-life stories featuring users and context

**EXAMPLE PROJECT: *Improving the Coffee Shop Experience (2011)***

How might a major coffee shop chain maintain its competitive edge against fierce competition offering a similar customer experience? A team of designers sought to explore innovations that could offer the company new ways to attract and maintain loyal customers.

After researching existing and potential customers, the team developed a five-stage experience map outlining the customers' journey from entering to leaving the coffee shop. Within each stage of the journey, the designers filled in activities of the coffee chain's customers. For example, customers assess the length of the line as they enter, utilize WiFi while they work, and check their rewards points balance on the company's website after they leave. The activities revealed a number of customer needs such as being able to easily recognize their drink on the barista counter and simplify repeat drink orders.

They clustered these needs and activities along 2 × 2 maps and generated an extensive list of concepts aligned with the research findings. They selected five of the strongest concepts around which they sketched ***Concept Scenarios*** about how they would work in real life. One concept was the integration of a mobile location-aware app with an express pickup counter. In the scenario, a man who is late for work preorders his coffee via an app, which tracks his location. Before he gets to the coffee house, his order is already prepared. He bypasses the long line and walks to the express counter, gives his name to the barista who hands him his coffee. He arrives at work right on time without foregoing his morning coffee. These scenarios communicated the essence of their concepts to others and helped the team identify hurdles and prototypes for further refinement.

## BENEFITS

- Facilitates discussion
- Facilitates storytelling
- Helps refine idea
- Improves communication
- Inspires ideation

## INPUT

- Concepts generated in Ideation Sessions

## OUTPUT

- A set of scenarios illustrating how concepts will exist in real-life situations

## WHEN TO USE

## WHAT IT DOES

While exploring concepts it is useful to visualize them working in the real world. One way to do this is through visualizing real-life scenarios or stories. Teams generate short scenarios as a series of sketches, illustrations, or photo collages to express how that concept will be used by potential users in proposed situations. These scenario sketches are great places to have discussions among team members. Seeing a concept as a scenario helps teams identify problems that would not have been obvious in the beginning stages of conceiving that idea. Concept Scenarios work like an early field test for the concept. Moreover, scenarios communicate ideas well and support good conversations.

## HOW IT WORKS

### STEP 1: Select concepts for scenario making.

Go through a set of already generated concepts and identify ones that you think will get better clarity by "imagining" them in real-life situations.

### STEP 2: Imagine a scenario to show how a concept works.

Take your concept, understand it well, and then think of possible situations in which that concept will work. Imagine the people involved and the context. Imagine the key interactions or instances that you want to show as a strong demonstration of the selected concept. Figure out what happens in between. Tie together all instances into a story.

### STEP 3: Rethink the concept during scenario making.

While imagining the users and the context you might realize that the original concepts need to be rethought. Modify or enhance the concepts.

### STEP 4: Illustrate the scenarios.

Make a series of illustrations to show the imagined situations. Include users and other people related to the concept in these illustrations. Ensure that the illustrations just touch on the main aspects of the concept only. Avoid extraneous details that could confuse or take away from the main flow of the story.

### STEP 5: Discuss the scenarios and build on the concepts.

Express the concept scenarios to one another in team sessions as well as to other stakeholders. Discuss how the concept is adding value to the imagined situations—its users and the context. Think about ways to enhance that value and move to further concept building.

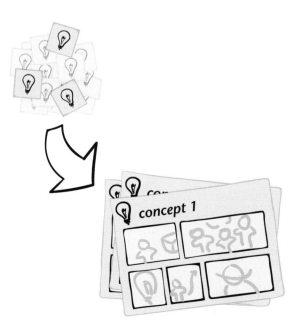

## 5.14 CONCEPT SCENARIOS

# 5.15 Concept Sorting

## Combining, normalizing, and organizing concepts into related groups

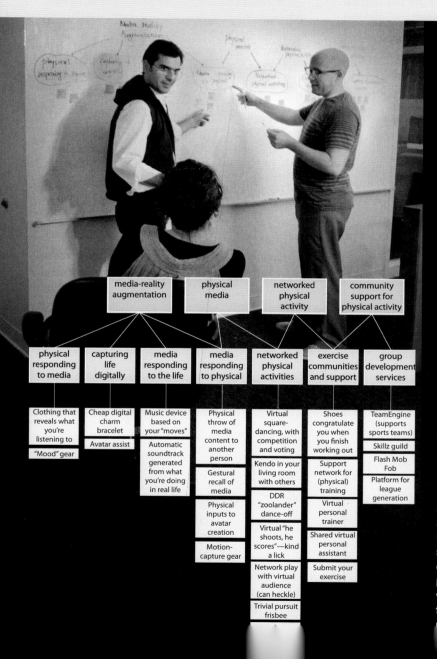

media-reality augmentation | physical media | networked physical activity | community support for physical activity

physical responding to media | capturing life digitally | media responding to the life | media responding to physical | networked physical activities | exercise communities and support | group development services

Clothing that reveals what you're listening to

"Mood" gear

Cheap digital charm bracelet

Avatar assist

Music device based on your "moves"

Automatic soundtrack generated from what you're doing in real life

Physical throw of media content to another person

Gestural recall of media

Physical inputs to avatar creation

Motion-capture gear

Virtual square-dancing, with competition and voting

Kendo in your living room with others

DDR "zoolander" dance-off

Virtual "he shoots, he scores"—kind a lick

Network play with virtual audience (can heckle)

Trivial pursuit frisbee

Shoes congratulate you when you finish working out

Support network for (physical) training

Virtual personal trainer

Shared virtual personal assistant

Submit your exercise

TeamEngine (supports sports teams)

Skillz guild

Flash Mob Fob

Platform for league generation

**EXAMPLE PROJECT:** *Kids Media (2006)*

Tweens, a demographic that includes children between the ages of ten and twelve, have unique social needs that are often supported through interactions with media and media devices. A design team conceived solutions that satisfied tweens' needs for fun, immersive, and connected experiences, as well as parents' desires for active, educational, and creative experiences for their kids. Using insights and principles developed during their analysis, the team created guidelines for how concept systems might be built around the project's three main areas of focus: co-creation, networking, and getting physical.

After generating more than 75 concepts, the team used *Concept Sorting* to organize concepts into first-level clusters, giving each cluster a title. Some examples of clusters included physical objects responding to media, capturing life digitally, networked physical activities, exercise communities and support, and group development. These first levels of clusters were further sorted by affinity. The result had concepts organized into higher-level clusters that included media-reality augmentation, networked physical activity, and community support for physical activity. Concept Sorting not only allowed the team to organize and manage all of the generated concepts, but it also led the team toward developing concept systems that extended across all concept clusters. These Concept Systems would provide tweens with compelling, integrated, virtual, and physical concepts that inspire them to learn, create, share, and author the next generation of media.

**BENEFITS**

- Builds higher-level systems
- Encourages comprehensiveness
- Facilitates discussion
- Gives focus to the process
- Reveals relationships
- Structures existing knowledge

**INPUT**

- All concepts generated to this point

**OUTPUT**

- Groupings of concepts organized around commonalities

**WHEN TO USE**

## WHAT IT DOES

Concept Sorting is a disciplined effort to go through a collection of concepts, rationally organize them, and categorize them into groups. The concepts are most often generated during focused ideation sessions. But, concepts may also originate during any point in the innovation process, during Frame Insights, Know People, Know Context, or Sense Intent. By the time we reach concept exploration, we have probably already begun to build up a collection of concepts. All of these concepts, not just the concepts generated during focused ideation sessions, should be part of the Concept Sorting exercise.

## HOW IT WORKS

### STEP 1: Collect generated concepts.

Collect all concepts, originated from ideation sessions and all other methods and modes in one place.

### STEP 2: Normalize the concepts.

Since concepts come from many methods and modes they will be differently conceived and expressed. Some concepts may be about a fine detail and some others about a complex system.

Normalize different types of concepts by restating them to be at the same level of complexity or abstraction. Combine concepts that seem similar but are stated slightly differently. Take your best judgment about which ones to be included in a set for sorting. Rephrase concept titles and descriptions in a grammatically uniform way; for example, state all of them as noun phrases. If necessary, express each concept with a short description, a diagram, or a sketch for easy reference during sorting.

### STEP 3: Sort the concepts.

Decide if you want to make a list and sort them using software or if you want to use sticky notes and sort them on a wall surface. Sort the concepts based on a

rationale agreed upon by the team. Similarity between concepts is the most common rationale. Start with sorting concepts into a large number of smaller groups. Then, combine these smaller groups into larger groups forming the next level in the hierarchy.

### STEP 4: Refine concepts and/or generate new concepts.

As discussions take place during sorting, new concepts surface. Capture these new concepts, describe them as others, and include them in the sort. Refine the existing concepts too as discussions suggest.

### STEP 5: Review concept groups and discuss.

Name the groups in such a way that the name reflects the true essence of the grouped concepts. Use jargon-free words so the names are easily understood by all team members. Discuss the resulting groups, and think of ways to refine the groups by moving concepts around or adding new ones. Are the groups independent or codependent? What are the themes emerging from the groups? Are there obvious themes missing?

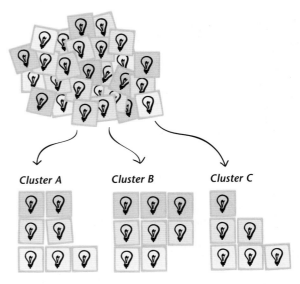

*Cluster A*     *Cluster B*     *Cluster C*

# 5.16 Concept Grouping Matrix

## Scoring relationships between concepts and revealing concept groups

| Group | Concept |
|---|---|
| Owner Companionship | Dog Vacation Travel Agency |
| | Dog Restaurant / Bar |
| | Dog Resorts & Destinations |
| | Dog Dating Service |
| Dog Inspired Activities | Dog Festivals & Events |
| | Dog Walk City Tours |
| | Dog Park 2.0 |
| | Dog Playground |
| Linked In | Dog Owner Social Network |
| | User Supported Info. Network |
| Party Poopers | Dog Party Service |
| | Waste Recycling |
| City Support | Dog-Friendly Building Services |
| | Indoor Waste Management |
| Sit! Stay home! | Puppy Starter Kit |
| | Virtual Owner System |
| | Indoor Dog Walking |
| Minimal Responsibility | Virtual Dog System |
| | Work Adoption System |
| | Dog Sharing System |
| Dog Tracking | Remote Gaming System |
| | Remote Monitoring System |

## EXAMPLE PROJECT:
### Dog Ownership (2007)

Many people regard the dog as "man's best friend," a member of the family, and a companion for recreational activities. However, the relationship between owner and dog can suffer as owners increasingly become strapped for time.

By examining this relationship, a design team recognized that owners have feelings of guilt when they are unable to spend time with their dogs. Guilt is often relieved when owners are able to bond with their dogs, especially in social and recreational settings. With these insights, the team developed concepts that explored product, information, and service systems that shape new experiences for owners and their dogs. Concepts such as dog vacation travel agencies, dog walk city tours, and virtual owner systems created new experiences that would provide social and active recreation and convenient opportunities for dog owners to include their dogs in daily activities.

Using software tools for the *Concept Grouping Matrix*, the team scored the similarity relationship of more than 20 concepts by using a scoring scale of 0 to 3. A score of 0 reflected no similarity between the concepts, while a score of 3 reflected very high similarity. Each concept was scored against all other concepts, one pair at a time. After scoring, the statistical algorithm sorted the matrix and revealed grouping patterns. The team identified and named both higher- and lower-level concept groups such as owner companionship, making life easier, and dog-inspired activities. The resulting groups of concepts were then used to formulate solutions that would energize and maintain the relationship between owners and their dogs.

**BENEFITS**

- Enables systematic analysis
- Encourages comprehensiveness
- Handles large sets of data
- Reveals patterns
- Reveals the unexpected

**INPUT**

- A list of all previously generated concepts
- A matrix tool for scoring and sorting

**OUTPUT**

- Concept groups based on individual relationship strengths

**WHEN TO USE**

## WHAT IT DOES

A Concept Grouping Matrix is a method for scoring relationships between concepts and sorting them into groups based on the collective strength of one-to-one relationships. It is a Symmetric Matrix with the same list of concepts plotted on both axes. Cells in the matrix represent the interaction between two corresponding concepts. Teams assign scores in these cells that represent the strength of the relation between the two concepts. The most frequently used relation for grouping concepts is "similarity"—how similar one concept is to another. The whole matrix is sorted based on the collective strength of these relations to reveal grouping patterns. The resulting concept groups represent concepts that are similar to each other.

## HOW IT WORKS

### STEP 1: Compile a list of concepts.

Gather all the concepts generated from various activities and compile them into a single list. They should be named in a standardized way and should be at about the same level of scale and scope.

### STEP 2: Set up the matrix and score relations between concepts.

Create an interaction matrix with the same list of concepts on both axes. Score each concept against all the others in the matrix by entering a relationship strength value in the corresponding cell. This involves giving each pair of concepts either a low score (not similar) or a high score (very similar). The granularity of the scoring scale is important. If a "neutral point" is desired, use an odd-number scale (e.g., 1 to 3), so there is a middle, neutral option. If more nuances are desired, use a seven-point scale; otherwise a three-point or even two-point (yes/no) scale is probably sufficient.

### STEP 3: Sort the matrix and identify groups of concepts.

For small matrices (up to 30 × 30), you can do a manual sort of the matrix by shifting the position of columns and rows in the matrix so that two rows or columns having similar scores are kept next to each other. After a few shifts of columns and rows this way, you can see that the entities are reordered to reveal groups. For larger matrices (more than 30 × 30), it is better to use available statistical algorithms to sort the matrix for efficiency.

### STEP 4: Define and label the concept groups.

Discuss the logic behind the visible groups in the matrix. Define and describe these groups as a team. Are there overlaps? Are there gaps? Are they comprehensive? Think of good titles for each of the concept groups. Document them with descriptions and sketches for sharing among stakeholders for feedback and further development.

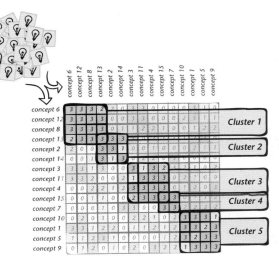

Organize key information about concepts in a central location for searching and browsing

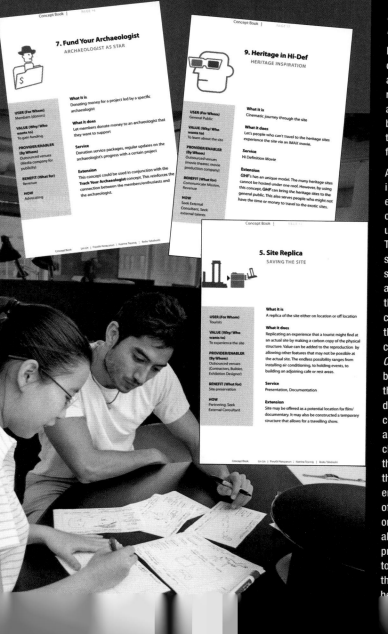

### 7. Fund Your Archaeologist
#### ARCHAEOLOGIST AS STAR

**What it is**
Donating money for a project led by a specific archaeologist

**USER (For Whom)**
Members (donors)

**What it does**
Let members donate money to an archaeologist that they want to support

**VALUE (Why/ Who wants to)**
To gain funding

**PROVIDER/ENABLER (By Whom)**
Outsourced venues (Media company for publicity)

**Service**
Donation service packages, regular updates on the archaeologist's progress with a certain project

**BENEFIT (What for)**
Revenue

**Extension**
This concept could be used in conjunction with the **Track Your Archaeologist** concept. This reinforces the connection between the members/enthusiasts and the archaeologist.

**HOW**
Advocating

---

### 9. Heritage in Hi-Def
#### HERITAGE INSPIRATION

**What it is**
Cinematic journey through the site

**USER (For Whom)**
General Public

**What it does**
Let's people who can't travel to the heritage sites experience the site via an IMAX movie.

**VALUE (Why/ Who wants to)**
To learn about the site

**PROVIDER/ENABLER (By Whom)**
Outsourced venues (movie theater, movie production company)

**Service**
Hi Definition Movie

**BENEFIT (What for)**
Communicate Mission, Revenue

**Extension**
GHF's has an unique model. The many heritage sites cannot be hosted under one roof. However, by using this concept, GHF can bring the heritage sites to the general public. This also serves people who might not have the time or money to travel to the exotic sites.

**HOW**
Seek External Consultant, Seek external talents

---

### 5. Site Replica
#### SAVING THE SITE

**What it is**
A replica of the site either on location or off location

**USER (For Whom)**
Tourists

**What it does**
Replicating an experience that a tourist might find at an actual site by making a carbon copy of the physical structure. Value can be added to the reproduction by allowing other features that may not be possible at the actual site. The endless possibility ranges from installing air conditioning, to holding events, to building an adjoining cafe or rest areas.

**VALUE (Why/ Who wants to)**
To experience the site

**PROVIDER/ENABLER (By Whom)**
Outsourced venues (Contractors, Builder, Exhibition Designer)

**BENEFIT (What for)**
Site preservation

**Service**
Presentation, Documentation

**HOW**
Partnering, Seek External Consultant

**Extension**
Site may be offered as a potential location for film/documentary. It may also be constructed a temporary structure that allows for a travelling show.

---

*EXAMPLE PROJECT: Safeguarding Endangered Cultural Heritage Sites (2008)*

Protecting, preserving, and sustaining endangered cultural sites around the world through education and community involvement is a mission that requires widespread support, collaboration, and awareness. To fulfill this mission, a California-based nonprofit organization worked with a design team to plan and design a strategic set of concepts for the organization.

A descriptive value web detailing the interactions between the organization and existing stakeholders, as well as between the organization and potential new stakeholders, was used as a foundation for developing concepts. These concepts were based on fostering and strengthening these interactions to increase support, encourage collaboration, and spread awareness for the organization. Concepts were then clustered into seven groups, covering categories like potential partnerships, ways to save the site, and heritage as inspiration. The generated concepts and named clusters were annotated in a *Concept Catalog* in the form of a book. The concept book contained a table of contents, a concept guide that detailed the standard format for each page, a description of each concept cluster, and individual concepts pages. Each concept was tagged using an icon, concept name, concept number, and cluster name. Additionally, specific attributes of the concept, including the user of the concept, the value created by the concept, the provider or enabler that made the concept possible, the benefit of the concept for the organization, and how the organization can make the concept actionable was also detailed on each page. The Concept Catalog provided a means for members of the organization to easily access generated concepts or to influence the direction of other projects in the future. It also became a knowledge artifact from which solution

**BENEFITS**

- Builds knowledge base
- Builds for future reference
- Handles large sets of data
- Organizes information for easy access
- Promotes shared understanding
- Supports transition

**INPUT**

- Set of refined concepts (generated in previous methods)

**OUTPUT**

- Organized and searchable archive of concepts

**WHEN TO USE**

## WHAT IT DOES

The Concept Catalog is a central repository that collects and organizes all relevant information of concepts generated during a project in one location. For small projects, the catalog could be thought of as a simple spreadsheet in which the concepts and the key information are organized in rows and columns, respectively. For more complex and large-scale projects that require inputs from innovation teams at multiple locations, the catalog would be a sophisticated web-based relational database. This repository becomes an important resource in later phases of the project and can also be used as reference for other projects.

## HOW IT WORKS

### STEP 1: Set up a base for creating a catalog.

Set up a base for recording key information about concepts, depending on the size and scope of the project—for example, a spreadsheet for small projects and a relational database for more complex projects.

### STEP 2: Gather and enter basic information.

Gather all the concepts generated from ideation sessions and other activities. Input all basic information about the concepts, including name, description, source, illustrations, annotations, links, and any other relevant tactical details.

### STEP 3: Select and apply tags for each concept.

It is generally best to select tags from a predetermined list that is relevant to the project, team, or organization, so that tags are consistent within and between projects. The tags may be project-specific such as design principles, user value, business value, or user activities supported. The tags may also be generic such as the Ten Types of Innovation.

### STEP 4: Search and recall concepts during the project.

Use the catalog throughout the project to search for and recall details about specific concepts, or for groups of concepts related to a specific project task or team exercise (e.g., "Show us all the concepts related to the user activity 'Finding information about the National Parks'"). Use the catalog as a reference for other projects as well.

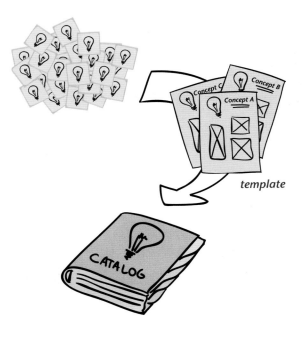

template

CATALOG

5.17 CONCEPT CATALOG

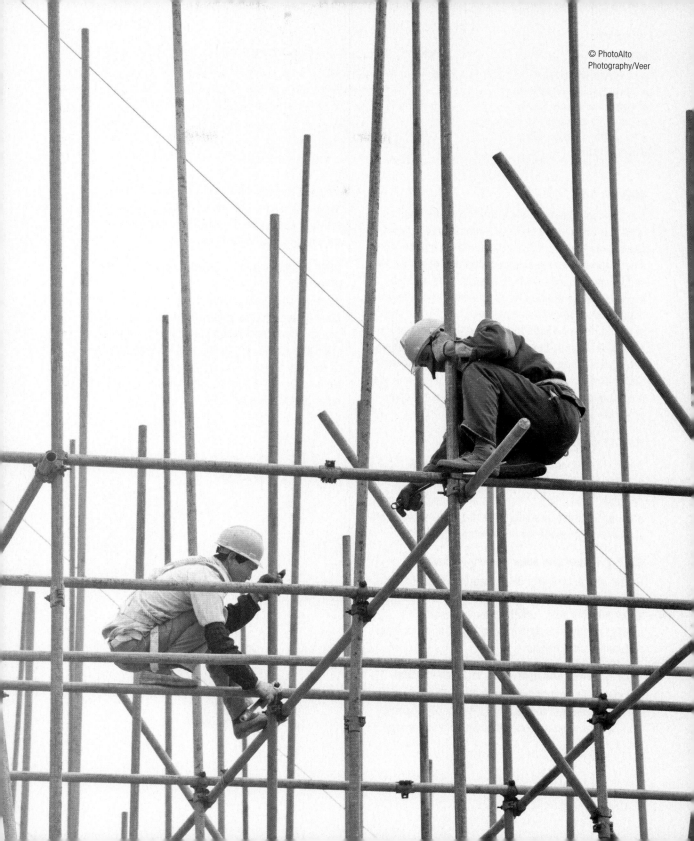
© PhotoAlto
Photography/Veer

# mode 6
# FRAME SOLUTIONS

Concept explorations produce a rich set of concepts. **The next challenge is to combine compatible and valuable concepts into reliable and systemic solutions that are actionable for future successful implementation**. It is clear that a single concept generated during the exploration mode alone is unlikely to satisfy all principles or design criteria. Potentially valuable concepts need to be integrated with one another for arriving at synergic solutions. Careful evaluation is critical to find out which concepts are promising and worth pursuing. Strengths and weaknesses of each concept need to be weighed against a set of defined criteria that is important to the project. Moreover, the synergic nature of selected solutions needs to be rationalized and communicated well to move forward with their realization. In short, the Frame Solutions mode is about assessing concepts, combining them, and constructing rationales and stories for why they should be pursued.

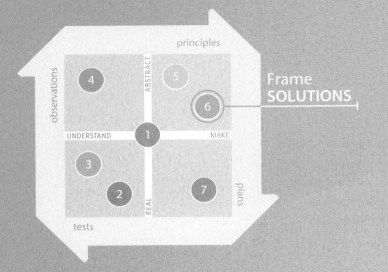

# FRAME SOLUTIONS *mindsets*

The Frame Solutions mindset is about building on the concepts created in the Explore Concepts mode, connecting them with each other to make systems-level solutions that meet desired design criteria or principles. In this mode, the mindset is also about integrating concepts into synergic solutions, compared to Explore Concepts in which the mindset is about creating new concepts independent of each other. The focus is also on making judgments about which concepts and combinations of concepts bring most value to the insights and principles generated in the previous modes.

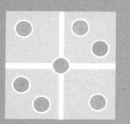

**Mindsets**
- Conceiving Holistic Solutions
- Conceiving Options
- Making Value Judgments
- Envisioning Scenarios
- Structuring Solutions

## Mindset: Conceiving Holistic Solutions

Just as a painter working on a detail of a canvas steps back to gauge its effect on the whole, innovation teams often step back from individual concepts and begin to look for holistic systems-level solutions. In this mindset, the focus of the team shifts from parts to the whole. Looking holistically at the pool of individual concepts, generated during the earlier modes, the team begins to think about how some of those individual concepts might be combined to form systems or constellations of complementary offerings. The mindset is to see the value of the whole synergic system as opposed to what individual concepts entail. Teams talk through different possible configurations of concepts and evaluate which systems of concepts are optimal for the given context. It is like experiencing the whole painting as a work of art, a full expression, compared to seeing what the individual brush strokes have done on the canvas.

© Boeing

*Boeing Company, one of the largest aircraft manufacturers in the world, excels in practicing synergic and coordinated teamwork in building their aircrafts. Researchers, engineers, designers, information technologists, psychologists, interior architects, fuel technologists, economists, instrumentation engineers, and meteorologists, all come together to build Boeing aircrafts as holistic solutions. While the attention to detail is crucial to the safe functioning of aircrafts, the synergy with which all the parts fit together is as crucial. Boeing employs thoughtful practices to bring together a multidisciplinary team to design, build, test, and maintain such a complex product like an aircraft.*

## Mindset: Conceiving Options

In the Explore Concepts mode, innovation teams are primarily focused on generating concepts, whereas in the Frame Solutions mode, teams start to pay attention to the space in between concepts, the relationships, or the connections that tie them together. The mindset is about sensing affinities among concepts and thinking of those connected concepts as a cohesive group. A manageable number of such cohesive groups are created, and each of them meets the defined innovation intent in a different way. Such cohesive groups, when combined, become a set of options to choose from for further refinement. The objective is to form a rich set of options, each option being a specific synergic combination based on complementary relationships. It is also about recognizing the right set of options that fits well within the context and meet peoples' needs.

architectural tours        local culture tours        activity-based tours

*Peoples' travel and vacation expectations are no longer place-driven. Travel behaviors are changing, evidenced by the rapid growth in personalized tours, cultural tours in local areas, activity-based vacations like skiing, interest-based tours like cooking, and extreme experiences. The travel industry has been responding to these changing behaviors well by providing a variety of option packages for their customers tailored to their preferences.*

## Mindset: Making Value Judgments

Thinking about important measures for evaluation is closely entwined with conceiving options. At the same time that individual concepts are being combined into solutions, it is natural to consider their pros and cons in light of various criteria. The key is to identify criteria that have the most bearing on the given situation and to judge how different solutions align across those criteria. For example, someone working on concepts for a fast food restaurant might develop solutions that optimize speed of service at the expense of ambiance. A different solution for an intimate dining restaurant might reflect an inversion of such criteria, with ambiance emphasized over speed of offering. Therefore, calibrating and analyzing the relative benefits of solutions in light of important criteria can help in conceiving optimized solutions.

Courtesy of IDEO.

*OpenIDEO is a platform built on the idea of open innovation and it takes up social reform challenges and opens them out widely for ideas and participation. Anyone can post their inspirations, ideas, and opinions about how to solve these challenges. People can build on each other's ideas and develop their own solutions and post them. Making judgments about the value of these solutions is also done in an open way in which people rate and comment on the solutions that they think best solve the problem according to the given criteria. Value judgments come from people, and collectively they become a reliable measure to select and further develop promising solutions.*

## Mindset: Envisioning Scenarios

While trying to find out the best possible solutions, a big part of the mindset in this mode is about envisioning what an overall solution might look like or how it might operate in the world. Creating stories about the future is also about translating systems-level solutions into narratives that can help others understand how the different components will work together. For doing this, innovators are always trying to enhance their ability to narrate possible future scenarios in compelling ways. Envisioning the future is often most effectively imagined through visualizations expressed in diagrams, comic strips, animations, videos, slide stacks, and similar media. Even thinking about how to enact possible future scenarios helps here. The stories that innovators conceive ought to be different for different audiences like clients, outside experts, end users, and investors. Thinking about what to emphasize in stories for different audiences is useful for making the solutions actually work for them.

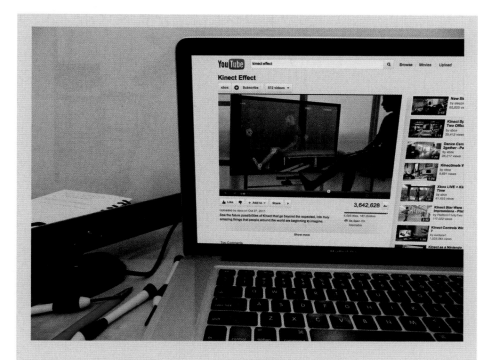

*Creating vision videos is one way for organizations to envision future scenarios. Kinect is a gaming device that works with Microsoft's Xbox 360® and uses sensors to turn peoples' voice and motion to actions on the screen. The team went beyond perfecting the gaming solution, to getting to know how people are creatively using the device—helping children with autism, supporting doctors in their surgery rooms, helping people play music without instruments, and in other unexpected ways. Calling this "Kinect Effect," the team created vision videos based on such evidence to show future scenarios, to help teams conceive new possibilities, and to communicate Kinect's potential to the world.*

## Mindset: Structuring Solutions

In the Explore Concepts and Frame Solutions modes, teams generate a number of ideas at varying levels of organization—from granular concepts to systemic solutions. This mindset is about gathering all these ideas and creating organizing structures, most often, arranged in hierarchies. Another way to imagine this organizing structure is using matrix thinking in which selected systemic solutions are on one dimension and a number of their attributes are on the other. Examples of attributes include intended users, user needs, related principles, user value, provider value, and strategic importance, among others. Looking at the interactions in the matrix, we can start to see how similar attributes cause solutions to group together. The organizing structure for imagining the system of solutions could also be in the form of catalogs, in which solutions are classified under categories just as books are organized in libraries. A third way is to imagine solutions being organized in relational databases, where browsing, searching, sorting, and other interactive sessions are possible. Giving an integrated structure to all solutions is at the core of this mindset and it becomes a good basis for further actions in the innovation process like prototyping, detailing, strategizing, storytelling, and implementing.

*Understanding that it is difficult for innovators, do-it-yourselfers, artists, inventors, and designers to source materials, Inventables built an innovative online store to support their needs. Inventables does this by selling a wide variety of materials in small quantities in well-organized retail channels. Color-coding and labeling systems have let the organization structure their offerings in engaging and compelling ways.*

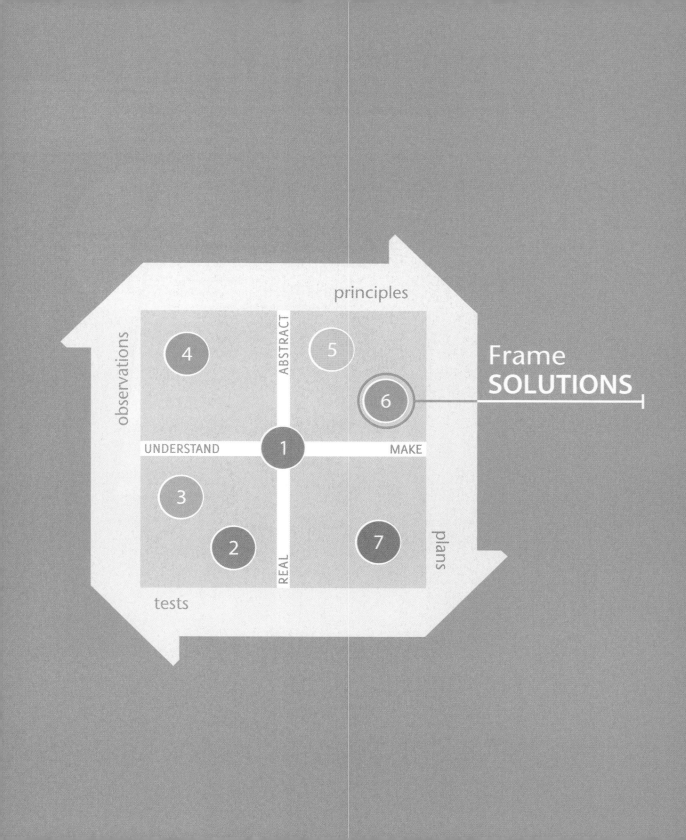

principles

observations

ABSTRACT

UNDERSTAND     1                    MAKE

REAL

tests

plans

4

5

6

Frame
**SOLUTIONS**

3

2

7

# FRAME SOLUTIONS *methods*

# 6.1 Morphological Synthesis

Organizing concepts under user-centered categories and combining concepts to form solutions

| Preparation | Finding | Connecting | Follow up |
|---|---|---|---|
| Makeover | Dual Browsing | Dinner for 8 | Relationship Warranty |
| Flirting Coach | Matchmaker | Lunch at Museum | Photo Business Cards |
| Reservation Making Service | Kiosk | 7 Courses for 7 People | Pen Pal Postcards |
| Clothing Shopping | Cell Phone/Palm-Based Browsing | Grant Park Activities | |
| | Scented Profiles | Speed Dating Bar | |
| | | Airline Seating | |
| | Singles Travel Agent | Elder Hostel | |
| | Singles Auction | Talent Night | |
| | Recommend a Friend | Chuck E. Cheese's Single Parent's Night | |
| | | Single's Cooking Class | |

**solution 1**

**Shy & Cautious**
Some people need more help than others; this set combines guidance throughout the process with low-pressure situations.

**solution 2**

**Busy Lifestyle**
This solution leverages new technology and takes care of the details for busy people. It also helps people remember who they meet.

**solution 3**

**Elders**
Many elders enjoy travelling, but do not want to go alone. This set fits with those existing behaviors, and provides some more 'low-tech' options for keeping in touch.

**solution 4**

**Single Parents**
By creating an event that is based on kids' activities, single parents are able to find others who share their situation.

## EXAMPLE PROJECT:
### Urban Dating (2003)

Over the last several years, online dating has become an increasingly popular channel for starting a relationship and finding a mate, especially given peoples' busy lives. Although online dating has shown significant growth, a team of IIT Institute of Design students recognized an opportunity for innovation in the area of urban dating. After initial analysis, the team identified the four main activities of the dating process as preparing, finding, connecting, and follow-up from which they explored, generated, and categorized individual concepts, both physical and virtual, using several design methods. To further strengthen these concepts, the team used *Morphological Synthesis* to combine these individual concepts to work together as a system of solutions.

The four dating activities served as the main categories in the morphological chart where individual concepts were organized. The team then combined complementary concepts across the four categories, or columns, resulting in holistic solutions that showed how the team's ideas mapped to different urban daters and their lifestyles. For example, the team designed a system of solutions that combined the concepts Flirting Coach, Matchmaker, Dinner for Eight, and Relationship Warranty for the shy and cautious urban daters, those who require guidance and assurance throughout the dating process. The team generated similar holistic solutions for the other types of urban daters like elders, single parents, and those who lead a busy lifestyle.

**BENEFITS**

- Builds higher-level systems
- Creates options
- Encourages comprehensiveness
- Structures existing knowledge

**INPUT**

- User-centered categories to organize concepts
- Previously generated concepts

**OUTPUT**

- Holistic solutions composed of complementary concepts

**WHEN TO USE**

## WHAT IT DOES

Morphological Synthesis is a method for solution generation that comes from the engineering discipline. As a design method it starts with a set of categories under which concepts are organized. You can use this method to organize already generated concepts or generate new ones. Normally the categories selected for organizing concepts are either a set of activities, user needs, product functions, or even design principles. All the concepts together form a menu of concept options. Many complementary concepts from this menu of options are combined to form solutions. A solution is a set of concepts that work together as a complete system.

## HOW IT WORKS

### STEP 1: Select user-centered categories to organize concepts.

Make a list of user-centered categories that you want to organize your concepts. These categories could be a list of user needs, user activities, product functions, or even a list of design principles.

### STEP 2: Create a morphological chart with concepts filled in.

List the categories in the first row. Show the related concepts below each category.

### STEP 3: Combine complementary concepts into solutions.

Select concepts from each category, or column, and combine them with complementary concepts from other columns to form combined concepts, called solutions. Write a brief description of how the solutions are systemic in nature.

### STEP 4: Compare and evaluate the different solutions.

Rank and order your solutions according to their ability to meet as many of your user-centered criteria as possible.

### STEP 5: Move to evaluation and refinement of solutions.

Document the solutions and discuss them. How can these solutions be evaluated for further development? How can they be refined as a complete solution?

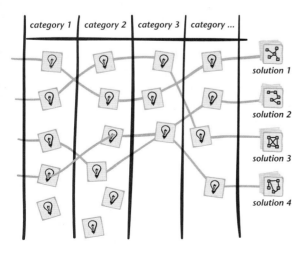

6.1 MORPHOLOGICAL SYNTHESIS

Rating concepts according to their value to users, providers, and other stakeholders

## EXAMPLE PROJECT: *Medical Tourism (2007)*

Medical tourism, defined as the act of traveling outside of one's country to obtain medical care, represents a viable alternative to U.S. healthcare. A team of designers from a strategic planning course at the IIT Institute of Design explored the booming medical tourism industry as an opportunity area for a major online travel company. Medical tourism represented a new potential market for the company that would give it first-mover advantage to this segment.

The team began by researching the travel industry and medical tourism. They analyzed the travel company's offerings, competitors, and core competencies, then performed user research by tracing the journey of three medical tourist types—practical, wellness, and cosmetic—through all stages of their experience. The team translated the research insights into design principles and held a workshop with multiple participant groups to generate concepts. They scored each concept methodically for its user and provider values in a *Concept Evaluation* map. Concepts addressing the design principles more positively received more value. The team then plotted these concepts as individual points on a scatterplot, with provider value on the Y-axis and user value on the X-axis. The team noticed that the highest-ranking concepts involved the emotional aspect of the experience that focused on increasing trust, communication, and cultural awareness and formed the pillar of their strategic recommendation. One of the recommendations the team developed was a Web-based platform called MedTripAdvisor that aids individuals in experiencing medical treatment overseas.

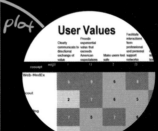

## WHAT IT DOES

Concept Evaluation is a method for evaluating concepts according to how much value they bring to users and providers. Concepts are evaluated with a user-value and a provider-value score. The two scores are translated into coordinates so that the concepts could be plotted on a scatterplot diagram. This provides a basis to compare concepts and make decisions about which concepts to develop and which could be combined with complementary concepts to form balanced combinations.

## HOW IT WORKS

### STEP 1: Assemble a list of concepts to be evaluated.

It is not uncommon to generate hundreds of concepts through ideation. Through discussions, careful considerations, combining, and recombining concepts, it is possible to define a finite number of concepts for evaluation.

### STEP 2: Create your user-value and provider-value criteria.

Refer to insights and principles from user research to determine what benefits matter most to your targeted users. Examples of user value include statements such as easy to use, reduces carbon footprint, or promotes community. Refer to findings from context research to determine what benefits matter most to the provider. Examples of provider's value criteria include profitability, brand equity, competitive advantage, and strategic growth.

### STEP 3: Create a concept evaluation matrix.

Create a spreadsheet with your concepts listed in the first column and your user-value and provider-value criteria listed in columns to the right as two separate sections. Add a total value column for each user-value and provider-value sections.

### STEP 4: Score concepts.

Select a scale to score each concept against the two different criteria—user value and provider value. In most cases, a 5-point scale will be sufficient. Add up the scores for each concept and record it in the "Total" columns at the end of each criterion.

### STEP 5: Plot concepts onto a map.

Create a map with user value and provider value as the vertical and horizontal axes. Plot the concepts in this map based on each concept's total user-value and provider-value scores.

### STEP 6: Analyze the concept distributions.

Draw a diagonal line connecting the high end points of the two scales. This diagonal divides the map into two triangular areas. The concepts in the high user-value and high provider-value triangular area are to be considered high priority. These are concepts that need more attention for further development.

### STEP 7: Share these findings and discuss the next steps.

Discuss the next steps based on these evaluations. Although the immediate focus for further development should be on high-value concepts, the concepts in the low-value triangle in combination with high-value concepts will also be desirable to pursue for further development.

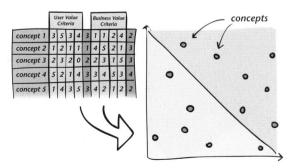

**6.2 CONCEPT EVALUATION**

# 6.3 Prescriptive Value Web

Showing how value will flow among stakeholders as new concepts are introduced in a system

Motorola, Nokia, Samsung, etc.
*Provide device to experience service and content*

potential Opportunity

$$$ HANDSETS

CONTENT
CONTENT

$$$
PHONE / SERVICE

PIPELINE
CONTENT

**content provider**
I-Tunes, YouTube, Flickr, etc.
*Making content available*

$$$
CONTENT

DEVICES

$$$

CONTENT

PLATFORM
CONTENT

Sony, Apple, Dell, Canon, etc.
*Providing means to experience content*

## EXAMPLE PROJECT: *The Future of Mobile Communications (2008)*

What is the future of voice service, especially while simultaneously accessing data? How and when do people choose certain communication methods with their mobile devices? Answering these questions was the main goal for the IIT Institute of Design team. The project team designed a Web-based communication platform named Concourse for a wireless voice and data communications services provider. Concourse empowers young and social mobile device users to communicate their intentions, and recognize the intentions of others.

By first mapping out the value exchange within the provider's existing business model, the team better understood its role as a gatekeeper to communication devices and services where content on mobile devices is only available through selected channels. The **Prescriptive Value Web** visualized the new ways in which Concourse would help the provider connect with customers by harnessing the power of social networks through customer communities and user-generated content. The introduction of Concourse on the Prescriptive Value Web showed the effect of two new links. One was between the company and the user communities where the Concourse concept was conceived to play a major role. The Concourse concept also had a role in connecting the content providers with the end users.

**BENEFITS**

- Facilitates discussion
- Makes abstract ideas concrete
- Promotes shared understanding
- Reveals relationships

**INPUT**

- Concepts and list of all stakeholders in the system

**OUTPUT**

- Visualizations of new value exchanges caused by concepts

**WHEN TO USE**

## WHAT IT DOES

A Prescriptive Value Web is a network diagram showing all the stakeholders in the system as nodes. The values that are exchanged through the system are shown as links connecting the nodes. It shows new relationships among stakeholders if a possible concept is to be implemented. Unlike Descriptive Value Webs, Prescriptive Value Webs show how the value will flow when new nodes or links are introduced or existing nodes or links are modified or delinked. The Prescriptive Value Web is a generative tool that helps us think of possible future states in the system. Similar to Descriptive Value Webs, Prescriptive Value Webs use money, information, materials, and services as common value flows. They can also be used to track other intangible values such as goodwill, customer loyalty, and emotional connections.

## HOW IT WORKS

### STEP 1: List stakeholders and key concepts.

List all the stakeholders that would be affected by the implementation of key concepts that you want to visualize. The stakeholders include customers, your organization, partnering organizations, competing organizations, suppliers, distributors, retailers, relevant government agencies, and any other entity that may be introduced by the new concept you are considering.

### STEP 2: Describe the relevant value flows.

Consider the full range of values that will be exchanged as the result of your concepts. Beyond common values like money, information, materials, and services, consider other values that you want to track, such as goodwill and customer loyalty.

### STEP 3: Create a draft Prescriptive Value Web.

Draw a network diagram with nodes representing stakeholders and links (arrows) representing value

flows. If new nodes are introduced as part of your key concepts, show them too. If a current link is deleted from the value web, indicate that on the diagram. Show line thickness variations for the links to show the intensity of value flow. If quantities of the value flow are known, for example money, write those numbers next to the link. This initial web should serve as the basis for further discussion and changes.

### STEP 4: Compare Prescriptive and Descriptive Value Webs.

Refer to your Descriptive Value Web created in the Know Context mode and juxtapose it with this Prescriptive Value Web to see how your concepts will alter the existing system by adding new value.

### STEP 5: Review and refine the value web.

Discuss the value web with team members and experts to test and challenge the underlying assumptions. Does the Prescriptive Value Web rightly reflect the impact of your concepts on the system? What are the implementation challenges to achieve the new value flows in the system?

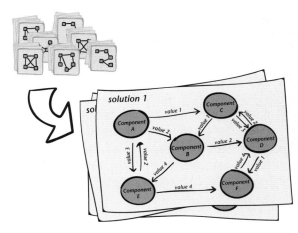

# 6.4 Concept-Linking Map

## Linking and combining complementary ideas to form a concept system or solution

### EXAMPLE PROJECT:
### Video Gaming (2007)

An IIT Institute of Design team set out to amplify the gaming experience for avid gamers by exploring the opportunity space in the video gaming industry. The team was asking questions like how video games can offer greater experiences for creating, learning, and playing as well as developing gamers' emotional and intellectual capacities.

Using four key themes about video gaming, which included co-creation with fun, strategic value of games, new gaming interactions, and lifestyle training, the team developed nine core gamer values such as connectivity, collaboration, self-expression, as the criteria for generating concepts and solutions. The team generated concepts and scored them against all nine gamer values and three provider values (low risk, profit potential, and ease of implementation). Using each concept's total score, a scatterplot was created to visualize where each concept fell in relation to user value and provider value. From this visualization, the team created a *Concept-Linking Map* that combined complementary concepts to form five concept systems or solutions. One such solution was the MobileOM, composed of the high-value concepts while the Home Meditation solution combined both high-value and lower-value concepts. Each solution was documented using a sketch, brief description, and key attributes. The Concept-Linking Map also helped the team refine their solutions by merging them into higher-level solutions. For example, MobileOM and Home Meditation were further linked into OM, a complete meditation system providing gamers stress-reducing solutions both in the virtual space and on the go. Two other solutions merged into a second higher-level solution called BurningRAM.

## WHAT IT DOES

Concepts generated through ideation address specific aspects of a topic, but rarely does one concept meet all requirements. Moreover, the concepts explored bring different levels of value to the project. Complementary and high-value concepts need to be combined to form desirable systemic solutions. The Concept-Linking Map is a method for identifying high-value concepts and combining those that complement each other. The resulting solutions meet a broader set of needs and principles in a holistic way. This method uses scored concepts as the base for systemizing them into holistic solutions. Therefore, the initial steps of this method are similar to those of building a Concept Evaluation Map.

## HOW IT WORKS

### STEP 1: Score user and provider values of concepts.

Based on the results from users and context research, determine a list of important user- and provider-value criteria that your concepts should have. Create a spreadsheet with the concepts listed in the first column and the user-value and provider-value criteria listed in columns to the right as two separate sections. Add a total value column for each user-value and provider-value sections. Score each concept against all the criteria and enter the total scores.

### STEP 2: Plot concepts onto a map.

Create a map with user values and provider values as the vertical and horizontal axes. Plot the concepts in this map based on each concept's total user- and provider-value scores.

### STEP 3: Observe patterns on the map.

Compare the relative positions of concepts. For this, draw a diagonal line connecting the high end points of the two scales. This diagonal line divides the map into two triangular areas. The concepts in the high-user-value and high-provider-value triangular area are to be considered high priority. These are concepts that high priority and need more attention.

### STEP 4: Combine concepts into solutions.

Start with the high-value concepts. Pick each concept and see if it can be combined with other complementary concepts. Even though it is logical to focus on the high-value concepts, pick even the concepts in the low-value side of the map because they might be more valuable in combination with others.

### STEP 5: Describe each solution, share, and discuss.

Write a brief description of how the various concepts work together as a unique solution. Sometimes it is helpful to think of solutions as themes that can be summarized with a brief descriptive title. Discuss further explorations. How can these solutions be improved or extended? Will prototype-testing help decide which solutions to pursue? How do these solutions align with this project's value hypothesis? What is the best means of communication for stakeholder feedback?

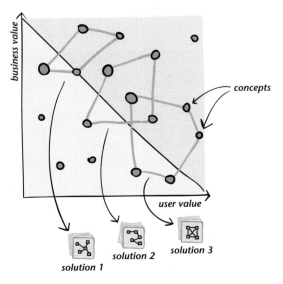

solution 1

solution 2

solution 3

Creating solutions by foreseeing possible alternative future situations

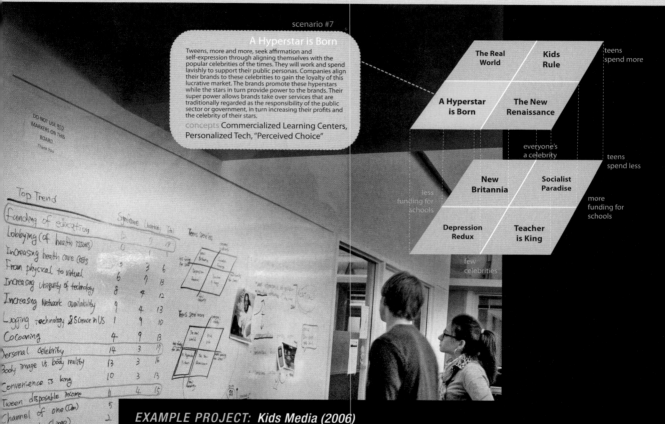

scenario #7

**A Hyperstar is Born**

Tweens, more and more, seek affirmation and self-expression through aligning themselves with the popular celebrities of the times. They will work and spend lavishly to support their public personas. Companies align their brands to these celebrities to gain the loyalty of this lucrative market. The brands promote these hyperstars while the stars in turn provide power to the brands. Their super power allows brands take over services that are traditionally regarded as the responsibility of the public sector or government, in turn increasing their profits and the celebrity of their stars.

concepts **Commercialized Learning Centers, Personalized Tech, "Perceived Choice"**

| | |
|---|---|
| The Real World | Kids Rule |
| A Hyperstar is Born | The New Renaissance |

teens spend more

everyone's a celebrity

teens spend less

| | |
|---|---|
| New Britannia | Socialist Paradise |
| Depression Redux | Teacher is King |

less funding for schools

more funding for schools

few celebrities

DO NOT USE RED MARKERS ON THIS BOARD. Thank You

Top Trend

Funding of education
Lobbying (of health issues)
Increasing health care costs
From physical to virtual
Increasing ubiquity of technology
Increasing network availability
Lagging technology & science in US
Cocooning
Personal celebrity
Body image vs body reality
Convenience is king
Tween disposable income
Channel of one (Om)
Shared media (Longo)
Getting older, younger

## EXAMPLE PROJECT: *Kids Media (2006)*

The Kids Media project focused on creating solutions that satisfy the unique social needs of tweens by examining their interactions with media and media devices, while addressing the desires of parents. The tween demographic describes children between the ages of 10 and 12. The team generated concepts by looking to future trends that would affect tweens across politics, economics, society, and technology. These emergent trends became the base for *Foresight Scenarios*.

The three top-ranking trends used to craft a Foresight Scenario included funding of education, personal celebrity, and tween disposable income. The team felt that the trend tween disposable income directly affected the other two trends and was used to create two separate 2 × 2 position maps titled "Tweens Spend Less" and "Tweens Spend More," respectively. The two position maps had axes labeled "Everyone's a celebrity versus few celebrities" and "Less funding for schools versus more funding for schools." The team developed eight foresight scenarios. One of them, titled "A Hyperstar is Born," represented "Tweens Spend More" and was from the quadrant "Less funding for schools" and "Few celebrities." Concepts were generated for this scenario in which tweens sought self-expression by aligning themselves with popular celebrities of the times. Like this, the team went on to develop a number of physical and virtual solutions driven by several of the imagined scenarios.

## BENEFITS

- Broadens mindset
- Builds higher-level systems
- Considers future context
- Facilitates discussion
- Gives focus to the process
- Inspires ideation

## INPUT

- List of emergent trends critical to projects
- Previously generated concepts

## OUTPUT

- Holistic solutions that address multiple future scenarios

## WHEN TO USE

## WHAT IT DOES

Foresight Scenario is a method for considering hypothetical futures based on emergent trends and then formulating alternative solutions designed to meet those possible situations. In this method, we often use 2 × 2 position maps to write about scenarios, possible future situations. The two dimensions of the position map are based on the emergent trends (social, cultural, technological, economic, and business) identified to be critical for the project and to have maximum impact on users and the context. Then, we write scenarios for each quadrant of the position map. Based on these scenarios, concepts are generated, if not already developed in the earlier modes, and then plotted onto the map. The plotted map can then be used to combine complementary concepts to form holistic solutions.

## HOW IT WORKS

### STEP 1: List trends and select the most important.

These trends may come from earlier efforts through a Trend Matrix or other methods. Score each trend on the basis of its importance to your project. Select the two most important trends.

### STEP 2: Make a 2 × 2 map using selected trends.

Consider the selected trends and interpret future possibilities. Think of extremes that could happen based on these trends and convert these extremes into a set of scales. Create a 2 × 2 map using these scales.

### STEP 3: Write a scenario in each quadrant of the map.

Each scenario describes the conditions of a possible future state if the two extremes happen. Write a descriptive title for each scenario.

### STEP 4: Plot concepts in each scenario.

If your team has already developed concepts using other methods like Concept Matrix, just plot those concepts according to their fit with the four scenarios in the four quadrants. Otherwise, generate concepts in each quadrant by paying attention to all the trends that you have listed at the beginning of this method. Title each of your concepts.

### STEP 5: Combine concepts within quadrants.

Combine concepts in each scenario to form synergic solutions. Generate permutations and then select the strongest combinations.

### STEP 6: Write brief summaries for each solution.

Describe how solutions work in the possible future scenarios and how the various concepts complement one another. Share these stories with the team. Which scenarios are most likely to happen in the future? How will we adapt our solutions when scenarios actually happen differently? What optional solutions do we have to respond to those eventualities?

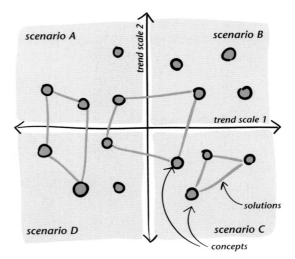

6.5 FORESIGHT SCENARIO

Travel Experience

5 Feedback

Traveler

Cultural Travelers

CityFriends. com
$$

CityFriends Corporation

CityFriend

CityFriends Pool

Certification and Training

1. Traveler selects Experience, City and CityFriend Guide
2. CityFriends.com contacts selected CityFriend guide
3. CityFriend communicates with Traveler and arranges meeting
4. Together, Traveler and CityFriend enjoy experience
5. Traveler and CityFriend provide feedback to CityFriends network

## EXAMPLE PROJECT:
### Cultural Tourism—CityFriends (2007)

Has traveling become a commonplace activity that is void of discovery, authenticity, and exploration? Based on insights developed from their research, a group at the IIT Institute of Design found an opportunity to serve a significant segment of cultural travelers that search for unique, local experiences when traveling. Rather than visit the obvious traveler attractions, cultural travelers want insider experiences and points of views that are usually only offered by local friends or family members. After thoroughly examining the current travel market, conducting user analysis, holding a workshop, and synthesizing concepts, the team framed an offering based on a system solution they called CityFriends. CityFriends engages carefully selected and trained locals, or guides, to share authentic experiences with travelers.

To better understand how the CityFriends system would work, the team developed a *Solution Diagram* that depicted the process and flow of the system, including the solutions like the CityFriends website and the different interactions between travelers and the local guides. Furthermore, the diagram helped the team align their vision of the proposed solution. The strength of the Solution Diagram was its clarity, and it helped the team develop a competitive strategic plan and roadmap to appraise implementation issues, impact on the market, and required next steps.

**BENEFITS**

- Helps refine ideas
- Improves communication
- Makes abstract ideas concrete

**INPUT**

- Solutions that can benefit from structured visualizations

**OUTPUT**

- Diagrams of refined solutions and accompanying descriptions

**WHEN TO USE**

## WHAT IT DOES

Diagrams are visual tools to explain and communicate information in rational and universally understandable ways. They are neither as abstract as the words that we use in our language system nor as real as a photograph or a scale model that we use to represent something realistically. It is because of this that diagramming is a very powerful tool to work with your concepts and solutions.

Solution Diagramming translates solutions into visual representations. The type of diagram to use depends on the aspect of the solution you want to highlight. Diagrams can effectively clarify structural relationships, describe processes, show how value flows through the system, show how the system evolves over time, map interactions between components, or work with other similar aspects of the system. Diagramming is an effective tool not only to illustrate solutions but also to generate them. The process of translating your ideas into diagrams helps reduce ambiguity.

## HOW IT WORKS

### STEP 1: Determine the type of diagram.

Determine what aspects of the solutions will benefit most from what type of diagram. For example, to show complex relationships among components of the solution, a network or map diagram is most relevant.

A few examples of how various aspects of the solution can be matched with diagram types:

*Relations* among the components of the solution: **network, matrix, map**

*Groupings* showing how components are distributed: **Venn, tree, matrix, map**

*Hierarchies* showing how solution components are structured: **tree, Venn**

*Process* or *sequence* showing how solutions work: **flow, time series**

*Locations* showing physical arrangement of components: **map**

*Quantities* showing numbers related to solutions: **bar, pie, time series**

### STEP 2: Make diagrams and refine solutions.

Make diagrams to visualize those aspects of the solution you want to show. For example, if you are showing how your solution is going to work as a compelling user experience, sketch out a flow diagram with events shown as nodes (graphic elements like circles or icons) and flows shown as arrows (with attached descriptions).

Improve your solutions as new insights emerge from the diagramming activity.

### STEP 3: Document and share.

Construct a well-thought-out and concise narrative to accompany diagrams. Do the diagrams fully explain the solution? Do the diagrams tell engaging stories? Are the visualizations universally understandable? Do you want it to be permanent or temporary, central or supplemental to your overall project?

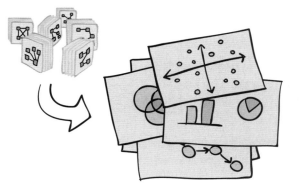

Constructing narratives that explain how system solutions work

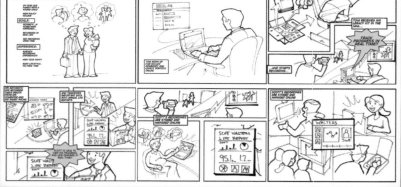

**EXAMPLE PROJECT:**
### Legacy Planning—Opportunity for a Life Insurance Company (2007)

The life insurance industry is experiencing overcrowding, homogeneous offerings, and efficiency maximization. A team of design planners from the IIT Institute of Design recognized an opportunity for a major insurance provider in the area of legacy planning, a burgeoning industry, in which the company could satisfy unmet customer needs and develop long-lasting customer relationships.

The team began by defining the opportunity space—nonfinancial services straddling the line between tangible and intangible. Legacy planning falls into this area, encompassing a range of passed-down values, possessions, and assets. After performing concept generation and evaluation, the designers combined the concepts into solutions. The team created **Solution Storyboards** for two solutions that addressed both a short and long-term company strategy. The short-term solution storyboard told the story of a 60-year-old, empty-nester married couple. They wanted to connect with their family, be remembered, share their memories, and connect with their own pasts in the process. The designers storyboarded the couple meeting with their insurance agent, receiving a "legacy kit" and depositing information, memorabilia, and experiences into it. The storyboard ends with the couple's memories being shared with grandchildren many years later.

**BENEFITS**

- Encourages iterations
- Facilitates discussion
- Facilitates storytelling
- Makes abstract ideas concrete

**INPUT**

- Solutions that can benefit from being explained as a story

**OUTPUT**

- Stories that show how the parts of a solution work together

**WHEN TO USE**

## WHAT IT DOES

The Solution Storyboard is a set of sketches (in both image and words), arranged in sequence, outlining the scenes of a story describing how all the parts of the concept system work together in situations. A solution storyboard uses narrative elements of character, action, and plot to build stories about what a user's experience might be as the user moves through an imagined situation. It begins by mapping a hypothetical journey. The narrative describes not just what happens but how various concepts are going to add value during the journey.

Stories have the fundamental ability to translate abstractions like a "system" into human terms that can be easily grasped. That is why stories can connect with audiences on emotional and experiential levels in a way that diagrams or charts simply cannot.

Design teams use the Solution Storyboard not just to communicate concepts but to improve the concepts. A storyboard can be thought of as prototyping through language.

## HOW IT WORKS

### STEP 1: Start with a good understanding of the solution to be illustrated.

Review your system solutions and related concepts. Discuss and have a clear understanding of how all the concepts in the system ought to work together.

### STEP 2: Create characters and describe their experiences.

Create characters that represent typical users. Describe their experiences as they go through the journey. Describe the change in their state of mind as a result of their experiences and engagements with your solution.

### STEP 3: Map out journeys.

Map out user journeys through imagined situations. Indicate on the map, the points along the journey where the user will encounter your concepts. Write short descriptions about what will happen at each encounter. Write about the nature of the interactions. Describe how value is being created by your concepts during those interactions. Introduce an element of drama into your narrative to hook your audience and draw them into your vision of a possible future.

### STEP 4: Create Solution Storyboards.

Illustrate scenarios with frame-by-frame storyboards. Distill narratives to the minimum number of words to convey the story. Use sketches to visualize concepts embedded in the solution.

### STEP 5: Review and rehearse the story.

Share and review these stories with stakeholders for feedback and use this feedback to further refine your concepts. Are the stories compelling enough? How are the embedded concepts helping the characters and the overall story? How can the solution be modified or improved for better uptake?

6.7 SOLUTION STORYBOARD

# 6.8 Solution Enactment

Acting out solutions to demonstrate how they work and create value

## EXAMPLE PROJECT: *Recycling in Farmers' Markets (2011)*

What's happening with recycling is similar to what has happened with food: There is more choice, convenience, and reward programs associated with recycling than ever before. But a team of design students at the IIT Institute of Design recognized the community-building aspect of recycling as an important piece missing from the recycling process and experience. Design principles derived from their user research guided concept development. The goals were to provide an outlet for the avid recycler, further engaging those who are already recycling, and motivating those who are not.

They conceptualized a system of several products intended to be used at farmers' markets, including Groupbin, a recycling station that rewards the entire community when filled; Swapbin, a place to exchange recyclables; and Fill & Sit, a pop-up recycling canister that doubles as a seat to crush cans. To communicate the concepts and immerse the city representatives in understanding how the products would work in real life, the team used *Solution Enactment* as a skit in a farmers' market. Bringing the story to life entailed staging an environment reflective of a farmers' market with tables and baskets of food and dressing as market vendors. The city representatives were able to not only provide immediate feedback, but also discuss specific product refinements that helped to craft a

**BENEFITS**

- Builds empathy
- Focuses on details
- Focuses on experience
- Improves communication
- Makes abstract ideas concrete

**INPUT**

- Interaction points of solutions that can benefit from being acted out

**OUTPUT**

- Stakeholders' feedback on how the solutions can be improved

**WHEN TO USE**

## WHAT IT DOES

Solution Enactment is a method for presenting design solutions to an audience in order to demonstrate how they work and how they create value for the stakeholders. Enactment, like storytelling, is a powerful communication tool for translating abstract ideas into terms that connect with audiences on a human level. Enactments are most often used in conjunction with Solution Storyboards to show how the various components of the solution work together. The method is most effective in demonstrating details of a system solution rather than the system as a whole. While a storyboard quickly takes an audience on a journey through an entire system, enactment is focused on specific scenes of what might happen along that journey.

## HOW IT WORKS

### STEP 1: Envision the user's journey.

Imagine a future situation in which your solution exists. Visualize the user's experience at various interaction points. Focus on those interactions where there is the clearest indication of value being created and exchanged. Sketch out the journey with the user as the key character for the enactment. What is the user's state of mind? What is the user's disposition during the interaction experience? Can actual users be involved in the enactment?

### STEP 2: Explore a range of possible encounters.

Once the basic journey and the interaction points are defined, explore a range of scenes to consider different experiences that could arise. Record the alternative scenes. Discuss and decide which ones you want to focus on for enactment. Emphasize your solution's user value, engaging interactions, and other benefits that you want stakeholders to focus on. Humor or

drama is also helpful to engage the audience.

### STEP 3: Rehearse your dramatization.

As you practice, keep in mind the target audience. Anticipate and prepare alternative dialog to address audience member concerns. Video tape the session to study later and refine.

### STEP 4: Present your enactment to stakeholders.

Enact the future scenarios to emphasize the value the solutions bring. Keep dramatizations brief and document key points. If necessary, reenact the scene inserting audience suggestions.

### STEP 5: Capture feedback and discuss next steps.

Capture feedback from the audience during the enactment. Extract insights from audience responses about the relevance of various concepts embedded in the scenes. Which specific interactions or concepts are more valuable based on audience feedback? Which concepts worked well in the scenes and which did not? What are the opportunities for reconceiving the concepts based on audience responses? How could the concepts be improved to be more valuable to users and providers?

*user's journey*

# 6.9 Solution Prototype

Simulating experiences around proposed solutions to explore how people engage in them

### EXAMPLE PROJECT: *ThinkeringSpace (2008)*

ThinkeringSpace is a system of both physical and virtual environments that aims to promote creative and critical thinking skills in school-aged kids. Implemented in libraries, ThinkeringSpace offers opportunities for collaborative work, sharing of ideas, and authoring in new ways. In-depth research and analysis of educational learning and libraries, as well as insights gleaned from behavioral and Solution Prototyping, informed the design of a flexible architectural system that is adaptable in scale and configuration with a self-contained infrastructure.

Following the insights gathered from concept prototyping, the project team used the **Solution Prototype** method and sketched 13 prototypes, each containing a description, key features and functions, and design criteria. The prototypes were further categorized into four areas that addressed systems, objects, information, and environments. One of the information prototypes, the Journey Wall Information Display, represented an interactive touch-screen panel containing a short collection of images and facts that kids can access to gain deeper related content. This Solution Prototype incorporated the design criteria to appeal to kids by providing different learning styles, creating a unique experience, and connecting them to existing knowledge. The final solution presented to the Foundation funding the project was a system of freestanding, independent, platform-based installations that define unique activity areas within libraries or other content-rich institutions.

**BENEFITS**

- Encourages iterations
- Focuses on experience
- Helps refine ideas
- Makes abstract ideas concrete
- Supports decision making

**INPUT**

- Selection of solutions to prototype that can benefit from user feedback

**OUTPUT**

- Refined solutions based on direct user feedback and observations of their experience

**WHEN TO USE**

## WHAT IT DOES

A Solution Prototype is a method in which users are observed engaging in planned activities around prototypes of proposed solutions. Two types of Solution Prototypes are used in this method: (1) Appearance Prototype, which simulates the appearance of the intended offerings, and (2) Performance Prototype, which primarily simulates the functions of the intended offerings. Through observations on these prototypes, user experiences are revealed to validate or invalidate assumptions about proposed solutions. Solution Prototypes are tested and validated in simulated environments. Information is gathered through observing the interactions and is recorded with video or note taking. The observations are then analyzed to understand users' experiences and the impact they might have on proposed solutions.

## HOW IT WORKS

### STEP 1: Identify proposed solutions and experience to be prototyped.

Review design solutions to identify those you want to prototype and study. Determine which combinations of concepts and experience of the solution you seek to learn through the prototype.

### STEP 2: Build prototypes and prepare an environment to test.

Build prototypes of the many concepts that make up solutions. These prototypes could be appearance or performance prototypes. Find a space where participants can engage freely with these prototypes and exhibit the key behaviors you seek to understand about the experience.

### STEP 3: Engage users in interacting with prototypes.

Invite users as participants to the simulation. Explain what they will be doing and why they have been invited to participate. Have the participants engage individually or in groups as needed. Guide participants in going through the prototypes and the experience.

### STEP 4: Observe and document interactions with prototypes.

Observe participants' interaction with the prototypes. Note the cognitive, physical, social, cultural, and emotional factors that affect participants' engagement with the prototypes. Record activities with video and note taking. Conduct a post-activity interview with participants to clarify questions you may have about why they interacted with the prototype in a certain way or how they felt about certain aspects of the experience.

### STEP 5: Analyze and iterate prototypes.

Gather observations from notes or video and analyze them for patterns of behaviors. Discuss and review observations in light of your findings from the simulation. Consider adjustments to the concepts embedded in your solution based on the feedback from participants. If necessary, conceive additional activities to further explore experiences. Repeat the above steps until you have confidence that your solution system will offer positive experiences for all stakeholders.

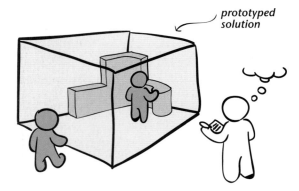

*prototyped solution*

**6.9 SOLUTION PROTOTYPE**

# 6.10 Solution Evaluation

Rating solutions according to their value to users, providers, and other stakeholders

## SOLUTIONS

**Key**
- ⬤ =(3) Strongly satisfies
- ◓ =(2) Satisfies
- • =(3) Somewhat satisfies

**USER VALUES**

| | Diabetic Gym | Food Management System | The Whole Diabetic | Health Education Program | Public Education Initiative | Medication System | Emergency Alert System | The Sweet Kitchen | Maple Grove |
|---|---|---|---|---|---|---|---|---|---|
| Provide ways to correct the effects of bad choices. | | | | | | | | | |
| Give patients & supporters more cues and feedback to indicate effects of actions. | | | | | | | | | |
| Provide method or tools for tracking data and following protocols. | | | | | | | | | |
| Involve medical support people in disease management. | | | | | | | | | |
| Increase frequency of interactions with high-impact activities. | | | | | | | | | |
| Leverage high-impact entities to increase quality of interactions with other entities. | | | | | | | | | |
| Develop new types of interactions with high-impact activities. | | | | | | | | | |

16    11    11    10

EXAMPLE PROJECT:
*Managing Diabetes (2006)*

Diabetes is one of the leading causes of death in the United States, but also one of the most controllable diseases with basic lifestyle changes. Through in-depth research and analysis, a design team derived three key insights about people with diabetes that include lack of support in making the right choices, difficulty in following maintenance protocols and tracking activities, and difficulty in drawing connections between actions and outcomes. With these insights, the team developed design principles rooted in the user values learned from their research.

A concept matrix was constructed to facilitate concept generation by listing the four components of the diabetic experience (education, diagnosis, prevention, and management) against the primary activities of managing the disease. Concepts were generated and distinguished by patient, friends and family, and medical personnel. The team then clustered and grouped the concepts into nine solution systems. To further tighten the list of solutions, the team performed a *Solution Evaluation*, scoring each solution system against the primary user values by whether it strongly satisfies, satisfies, or somewhat satisfies each of the primary user values. Values were tallied and the most effective systems were identified: Health Education Program, a series of classes, materials, and events that support diabetics and their families; Whole Diabetic, information and network technology to help the diabetic medicate more accurately and monitor exercise and diet; Emergency Alert System, an alert device on the diabetic that indicates the need for help; and Maple Grove, a managed care community for elderly diabetic patients.

**BENEFITS**

- Balances user and business needs
- Facilitates comparison
- Gives focus to the process
- Keeps grounded on research
- Supports decision making

**INPUT**

- Prototyped solutions
- User and business criteria

**OUTPUT**

- Map of solutions based on the assessment of user and business value

**WHEN TO USE**

## WHAT IT DOES

The Solution Evaluation method helps evaluate solutions once they have taken a tangible form. Solutions are plotted on a map with a user value score and a provider value score. The map reveals patterns of distribution and helps us evaluate prototypes based on their combined user and provider values. The method provides comparisons that can help us decide which prototypes to pursue and which to modify.

## HOW IT WORKS

### STEP 1: Create your user-value and provider-value criteria.

Refer to principles and insights from user research to determine the features and benefits that matter most to your targeted users. Examples of user value criteria include easy to use, easy to store, and aesthetics. Refer to findings from context research to determine what benefits matter most to the solution provider. Examples of provider value criteria include profitability, ease of implementation, and brand embodiment.

### STEP 2: Create a Solution Evaluation matrix.

Create a spreadsheet with the solutions listed in the first column and user-value and provider-value criteria listed in columns to the right as two separate sections. Add a total value column for each user-value and provider-value sections.

### STEP 3: Score solutions.

Select a scale to score each solution against the two different criteria—user value and provider value. In most cases, a five-point scale will be sufficient. Add up the scores for each solution and record it in the TOTAL columns at the end of each criterion.

### STEP 4: Plot solutions onto a map.

Create a map with user value and provider value as the vertical and horizontal axes. Plot the solutions in this map based on each solution's total user-value and provider-value scores.

### STEP 5: Analyze the solutions distributions.

Draw a diagonal line connecting the high end points of the two scales. This diagonal divides the map into two triangular areas. The solutions in the high user-value and high provider-value triangular area are high-priority solutions that need to be paid more attention to for further development.

### STEP 6: Share these findings and discuss next steps.

Discuss the next steps based on these evaluations. Although the immediate focus for further development should be on high-value solutions, the solutions in the low-value triangle in combination with high-value solutions can also be good to pursue.

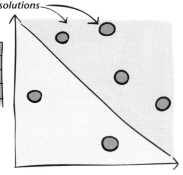

**6.10 SOLUTION EVALUATION**

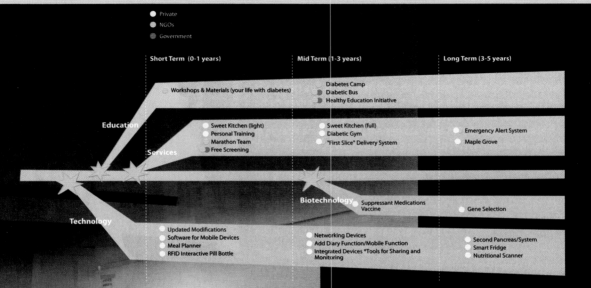

- Private
- NGOs
- Government

| | Short Term (0-1 years) | Mid Term (1-3 years) | Long Term (3-5 years) |
|---|---|---|---|
| Education | Workshops & Materials (your life with diabetes) | Diabetes Camp <br> Diabetic Bus <br> Healthy Education Initiative | |
| Services | Sweet Kitchen (light) <br> Personal Training <br> Marathon Team <br> Free Screening | Sweet Kitchen (full) <br> Diabetic Gym <br> "First Slice" Delivery System | Emergency Alert System <br> Maple Grove |
| Biotechnology | | Suppressant Medications <br> Vaccine | Gene Selection |
| Technology | Updated Modifications <br> Software for Mobile Devices <br> Meal Planner <br> RFID Interactive Pill Bottle | Networking Devices <br> Add Diary Function/Mobile Function <br> Integrated Devices *Tools for Sharing and Monitoring | Second Pancreas/System <br> Smart Fridge <br> Nutritional Scanner |

## EXAMPLE PROJECT: *Managing Diabetes (2006)*

In 2006, Diabetes was the seventh leading cause of death in the United States. Although it is one of the most controllable diseases, diabetics have difficulty making basic changes to their lifestyle to decrease the disease's effects. A team of design students worked toward developing design solutions for diabetics to facilitate and maintain a lifestyle change. Three leading insights emerged from the team's research: diabetics make bad choices because they lack support, following maintenance protocols and tracking activities are difficult, and the relationship between actions and outcomes is difficult to see.

The team developed concepts using prevention, diagnosis, education, and management as the four major functions of the diabetes experience. Concepts were then grouped into systems based on similarities in offering and implementation. With concept systems (solutions) such as diabetes camp, sweet kitchen, and smart fridge defined, the team created an initial *Solution Roadmap* to visualize how they could be implemented in the short, mid-, and long term. Solutions were organized by type of initiative fulfilled (education, services, biotechnology, technology) as well as the type of entity (private, NGOs, government) that would implement the solution.

**BENEFITS**

- Builds alignment in the organization
- Creates plans
- Helps select options
- Promotes shared understanding

**INPUT**

- All generated solutions

**OUTPUT**

- Timeline for implementation of solutions

**WHEN TO USE**

## WHAT IT DOES

The Solution Roadmap shows how to plan for implementing solutions. The roadmap helps explore how solutions are to be built up, with short-term initiatives serving as a foundation on which long-term solutions are based. It also shows which solutions are more suitable for short-term implementation compared to the ones that are more appropriate further ahead in the future. In addition, the roadmap indicates how individual solutions may evolve autonomously, sometimes branching off into two different solutions, evolving in parallel.

## HOW IT WORKS

### STEP 1: Develop an initial timeline.

Estimate the length of time required to implement your various solutions. Tactical short-term solutions tend to be those that happen within the next 12 to 24 months, strategic mid-term solutions take place 2 to 5 years out, and long-term visionary solutions occur more than 5 years from now.

### STEP 2: Plot solutions onto the timeline and create visualization.

Review your entire collection of solutions and plot them onto the timeline. Give thought to the full range of activities that must happen in order for a solution to be implemented. Think about required lead times and initial steps that are required to "seed" an idea beforehand for implementation down the line. Create a roadmap in the form of a branching tree diagram.

### STEP 3: Align the solutions with the organization's overall goals.

Review your initial ordering of solutions. Does the sequence reflect the organization's stated goals?

Do the solutions align with the organization's capabilities, finances, and resources? Do they align with the required sequence of activities to begin implementation? If not, reorder the solutions on the timeline to improve their alignment with goals and activities.

### STEP 4: Describe the roadmap.

Describe the nature of the relationship among various solutions. Do solutions build upon one another in a logical order? Write a brief summary explaining the logic of the order and why certain solutions precede or follow other ones and why it is the preferred path. Describe the various branches off the main timeline. Explain how these branches contribute to the overall system of solutions and create value.

### STEP 5: Share the map, discuss, and move to implementation details.

Share the roadmap visualization and the descriptions among stakeholders. Discuss the viability of the roadmap based on the goals of the organization. Which solutions are to be detailed out for near-term implementation? Determine how to allocate resources based on the roadmap. Who might be partners along the way?

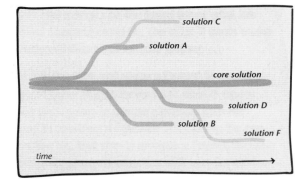

6.11 SOLUTION ROADMAP

# 6.12 Solution Database

Organizing all concepts and solutions in a searchable relational database

| | A | B | C | D | E | F |
|---|---|---|---|---|---|---|
| 1 | Solution Names | Shor Description | Cluster | Team | Author | Related solutions/ possible overlap |
| | **Team 3:** | | | | | |
| 24 | 1. Privacy Partitions | Privacy Partitions utilize light pools, fog walls, and physical partitions to indicate the status of spaces limiting interruptions during important activities like studying and working. | Learning Process | 3 | Tanu Bhat | (team 5) flexiwalls |
| 25 | 2. Nexus | Cloud provides reliable data storage and processing outside of the home and independent of personal resources. Some of these capabilities should remain within the home to insure basic functionality during service outages and privacy of sensitive data. In either case it provide access to data anywhere. | Learning Process Safety and Security | 3 | Tanu Bhat | Team 3 will discuss this in relation to being able to access data anywhere within the home. |
| 26 | 3. Visualizer | Visualizer translates raw data from the house and residents' learning progress into a visual form to enhance understanding. The visualizer does not make decisions, but it can enhance the residents' ability to make informed decisions. | Learning Process | 3 | Tanu Bhat | |
| 27 | 4. Simulated Scapes | Simulated Scapes generate synthetic experiences for multi-sensory exploration within a safe environment, and for escape to highly controlled virtual spaces for studying and other activities. | Learning Process | 3 | Nikhil Mathew | Team 3 owns it. |
| 28 | 5. Interactive Exploration Surfaces | Interactive Exploration Surfaces utilized a fully multi-modal approach that allows for data entry and retrieval, as well as communication between people on any surface and device in the home. | Learning Process Creation Process | 3 | Nikhil Mathew | team 2 will discuss the office applications. Team 3 will discuss the messy applications in the workshop and kitchen? |
| 29 | 6. Biographer | Biographer is a repository of resident generated ideas and collected inspirational material. Biographer combines tracking of personal goals with organizational tools to help achieve them. | Creation Process | 3 | Nikhil Mathew | Team 2 will discuss capturing and saving family memories. Team 3 will discuss how it applies to the learning and creation process. |
| 30 | 7. Workshop | Workshop is a group of support elements which allow one space to be utilized for a variety of dissimilar activities. These spaces are characterized by fully adjustable sturdy furniture and full atmospheric control with integrated waste collection. | Creation Process | 3 | Owen Schoppe | Make reference to Team 4 wireless charging. |
| 31 | 8. Tool Caddy | Tool Caddy is a robotic assistant that helps the resident in the creation process by collecting and delivering tools required by the user. Utilizing RFID technology, the caddy is able to track the location and maintain the inventory of objects within the home. | Creation Process | 3 | Owen Schoppe | (team 5) know it all |

system elements ▾   Team C   Sheet12   Sheet14   team 2-5 scoring - team 2   team 2-5 scoring   ◀ ▶   team 3 - Privacy Partitions

*EXAMPLE PROJECT:*
*Future of Living (2009)*

In the next few decades, population growth, climate change, and resource depletion are conditions that will change our living habits. The Systems Workshop provided IIT Institute of Design students the opportunity to tackle this complex, system-level problem, using a structured planning methodology and design a housing system that supports these new future changes.

The project was conducted in two phases. In the first phase, five student teams worked on five segments (resource provision, environmental management, biological support, personal development, and social development) that should be addressed by the new housing system. Each team identified their segment's critical issues and specific directions the project should follow. Through secondary research, each team established the different users and activities occurring in each segment. Analysis of all activities resulted in a set of insights and preliminary ideas called solution elements.

The second phase entailed using two proprietary computer programs that took all the information and organized it into a new hierarchical tree structure. With this new system structure, the teams began to develop system-level solutions. Because the newly developed system spanned five teams, a **Solution Database** was created to manage the information. Created in a spreadsheet, the database captured the name of the solution, name of the creator, key features, a description, and to which cluster it belonged. It served as a powerful tool to organize, manage, monitor, and analyze data.

**BENEFITS**

- Builds knowledge base
- Handles large sets of data
- Organizes information for easy access
- Reveals patterns
- Supports transition

**INPUT**

- All material from generated concepts and solutions

**OUTPUT**

- Searchable database of concepts and solutions

**WHEN TO USE**

## WHAT IT DOES

The Solution Database method is a disciplined and systematic approach to organizing, archiving, and reviewing the system solutions generated during the Frame Solutions mode. The method takes all of the key information accumulated during this mode—descriptions, narratives, sketches, diagrams, evaluations, and so forth—and inputs them into a database that can be searched by keyword. The method results in a comprehensive archive for the project. It also helps compare concepts or solutions by their attributes like strategic intent, user type, user value, or provider value. Though labor-intensive at the front end, the database is a valuable reference for both current and future projects.

It is not unusual during concept development to generate hundreds of ideas for system solutions. Even if concept evaluation and concept systemization reduce the total number to only a handful of solutions, the remaining concepts should not be discarded. The Solution Database method is a way of preserving all of your work for archival purposes and creating a growing repository that can be revisited later.

## HOW IT WORKS

### STEP 1: Gather key information generated during synthesis modes.

Gather all concepts and solutions developed along with descriptions, narratives, sketches, diagrams, and evaluations related to them. Review all digital and physical files to pull together a comprehensive and exhaustive list of everything that you have generated related to your concepts and system solutions.

### STEP 2: Define a set of attributes for organizing information.

Determine a set of attributes that you want to use to organize concepts and solutions in the database. Sample attributes include: design principles; user types; user value; provider value; short-term, mid-term, and long-term solutions; partners; complementors; and strategic intent. You may also use existing frameworks like the Doblin's Ten Types of Innovation to organize the concepts and solutions.

### STEP 3: Build a database.

Use readily available and user-friendly software to construct a searchable database. It could be as simple as a spreadsheet with search functions. Organize concepts under their related solutions. Enter information about your concepts and solutions into the database. Scan and upload sketches or other hand-drawn documents into the database. Assign relevant keyword terms to tag concepts and solutions to the related attributes. Conduct searches and review the results. If necessary, revise and insert additional keywords to further refine the types of searches that can be done.

### STEP 4: Search the database from different perspectives.

Using keywords, retrieve specific sets of concepts or solutions. Review and explore the relationships among various concepts and solutions. Compare them for reference, reevaluation, and inspiration. Be sure to note any large patterns that may emerge that you did not recognize during the concept-generation phase. Summarize your findings to share and discuss with team members.

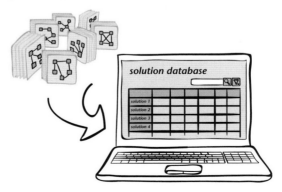

solution database

| solution 1 | | | |
| solution 2 | | | |
| solution 3 | | | |
| solution 4 | | | |

**6.12 SOLUTION DATABASE**

## Conduct short, intensive sessions to generate system solutions

**Electronic Learning Record (elr) Tablet**

The ELR is the electronic toolkit for managing a kid's educational history, goals, aptitude, and aspirations. The ELR is the interface that identifies each kid as a node on the network and allows other nodes (e.g., parents, teachers, other kids) to discover and convey the kid's achievements and needs based on learning style, aptitude, history, and personalized curriculum. The ELR also allows kids to record their portfolio of learning and work happening outside of school.

The mobile lab provides facilities to learn the expert and the kids to gather, and devices informed on they have found outside of screen.

**Mobile Genius Lab**

The Mobile Genius Lab is a place where kids can learn from real-world experts and leverage this expertise in their school projects. A genius could be a pre-eminent physicist who would set up office for one week in a city and be accessible to all the students in a school district in his mobile genius lab. The mobile lab could be moved from school to school and would act as any other node in the arcade of learning nodes.

*EXAMPLE PROJECT:*
### Schools in the Digital Age (2007)

Recognizing the challenges America's public school system is facing, a team of designers worked with educators to understand the biggest problem areas, identify opportunities, and generate new concepts. To better understand the problem of how schools could respond to the disruptive effects of recent socioeconomic and technological changes, the team conducted expert interviews and reviewed pertinent literature in the areas of organizational transformation, disruptive technology, and education. The research led to eighty-eight insights that the team clustered into sixteen problem areas, relating to four broad categories: schools' failure to respond to the current context of education, changes in the culture of the school's audience, learning environments with new technologies, and growth of bureaucracy in school structures.

The team then held two *Synthesis Workshops* with diverse groups of experts, using the clustered insights as a framework to identify a set of twenty potential research topics and three principles that should guide future work. These principles included innovations at the edges of the field, children-centered innovations rather than test-centered, and considering schools as nodes on a network. The design team also used the sixty ideas generated from the workshops to find out new opportunity areas for exploration. They sketched solutions for these opportunity areas for the final deliverable, helping to visualize the future of public schools in the Information Age.

## BENEFITS

- Brings in new perspectives
- Facilitates discussion
- Gives focus to the process
- Inspires ideation
- Keeps grounded in research
- Promotes collaboration

## INPUT

- Participants and lists of design principles and previously generated concepts

## OUTPUT

- Collection of system solutions

## WHEN TO USE

### WHAT IT DOES

The Synthesis Workshop is a method of structured brainstorming focused on generating concepts that can then be organized into systemic solutions. The method brings together a team of people with the purpose of using defined design principles to guide concept development. It is effective for producing a large number of concepts in a short amount of time. The workshop also provides a forum for synthesizing concepts into system solutions that arise as the result of discussion among participants.

The Synthesis Workshop functions as a brainstorming session, but with the added value of having an established structure. Using clearly defined design principles to guide ideation keeps teams focused on creating concepts that address user needs. The first part of the workshop is to get teams to generate as many concepts as possible for each design principle during short bursts of time. Then, the teams enter an evaluation mode in which they review concepts and rank them in relation to one another. The final phase of the workshop has teams combine complementary concepts into systemic solutions. A small number of best solutions (three to five) are identified and documented with a clear rationale for why you consider them the strongest.

### HOW IT WORKS

#### STEP 1: Plan for the workshop.

Create a workshop goal statement and outline. The objective is to generate and evaluate concepts and synthesize them into solutions. Make a schedule that divides up the workshop into an initial ideation phase, an evaluation phase, and a synthesis phase. Create guidelines describing the rules of engagement. Choose participants with a variety of expertise.

#### STEP 2: Gather design principles and concepts already created.

Gather all the design principles and concepts you have developed in the earlier modes. Create a document describing each. Share it with participants to be used as a basis for the workshop session.

#### STEP 3: Facilitate the workshop.

Establish an environment that is conducive to creativity. Provide a space where teams of three or four can work comfortably. Make sure the basics are covered, such as sticky notes, pens, paper and even snack foods. Include graphic organizers or worksheets that will enable teams to capture their ideas and organize their work.

#### STEP 4: Review concepts and generate more if needed.

Use the first part of the workshop to review all the previously generated concepts. Gain a shared understanding among all workshop participants. Allocate a short period of time for participants to reflect on the concepts and generate more concepts or revise some. Time constraints can foster efficiency. Record all new concepts.

#### STEP 5: Evaluate concepts and organize them.

Review concepts with a critical eye. Rank them according to how well they address design principles. Sort them according to user and provider value. Recognize them as short-term, mid-term or long-term solutions.

#### STEP 6: Synthesize solutions.

Identify complementary concepts and combine them to form system solutions. Write brief descriptions that highlight key features of the solutions. Identify those

**6.13 SYNTHESIS WORKSHOP**

that come closest to optimal combinations. Prepare brief write-ups to explain why you consider them to be optimal solutions.

Use worksheets for filling in: evocative title, solution description, concept sketch/diagram, user value, provider value, strategy supported, capabilities needed, partnering needed, associated risks, and other useful tags.

**STEP 7: Capture and summarize workshop output.**

Compile the write-ups into output documents that can be shared with stakeholders. Discuss how these solutions will be further refined and evaluated. Discuss how solutions can be prototyped for further development.

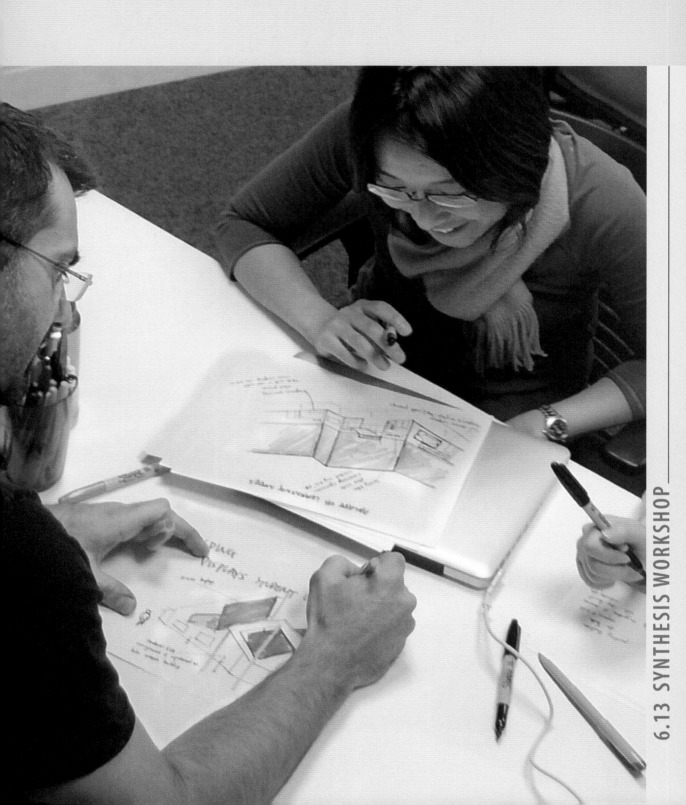

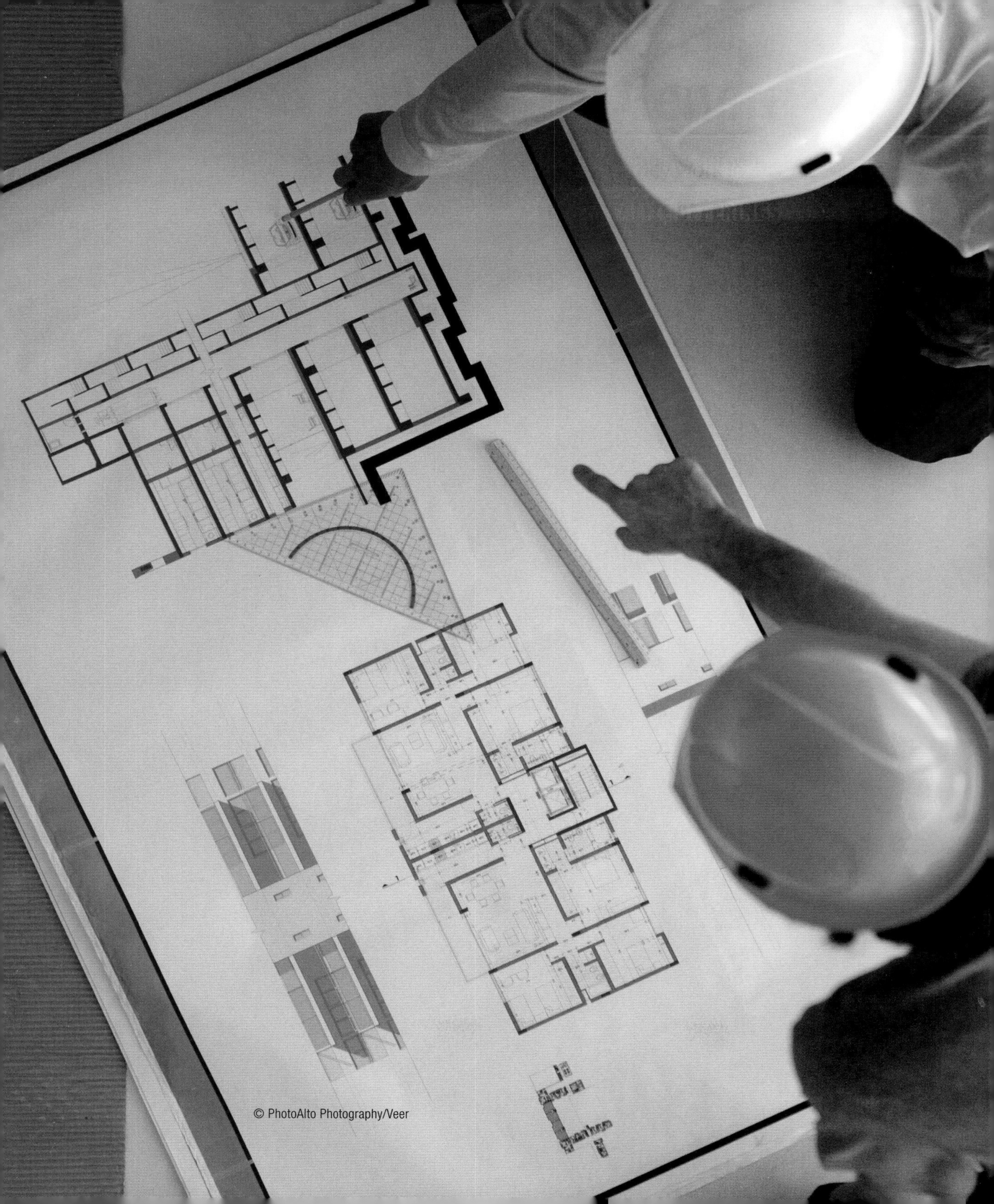

## mode 7
# REALIZE OFFERINGS

A new recipe is only an idea until a chef prepares the dish. And then, more often than not, the chef tastes it and decides if it needs to be adjusted. Through a process of testing, modifying, and retesting the right balance of taste, ingredients, and cooking time are found. If a recipe seems complex, imagine creating an entire menu. Behind every menu is a systemic approach to planning, purchasing, preparation, evaluation, and teamwork. All of the same principles hold true for innovation teams tasked with translating their concepts into actual products, experiences, and services.

**The intent in this mode is to explore how our ideas might take form in the real world and be successful.** It is about building to learn—making prototypes to understand how design solutions might work—and testing to see how users experience them. It recognizes initial failure as part of the process and iteration as fundamental to arriving at delightful solutions. Beyond simply making ideas tangible, the Realize Offerings phase of innovation embodies a series of planning activities to figure out how design solutions align with larger strategic goals. This includes estimating the kinds of resources they might require and conceiving tactical plans for implementation.

In summary, Realize Offerings is about making ideas tangible and planning how they get realized in the world.

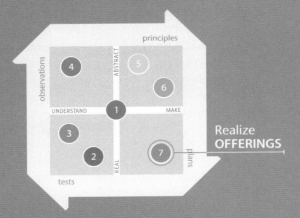

# REALIZE OFFERINGS *mindsets*

The mindset in the Realize Offerings mode is pragmatic, evaluative, and strategic. Pragmatism governs thinking about the practicality of making ideas real and devising the reliable tactics to make that happen. The evaluative mindset in this mode is concerned with doing multiple iterations of prototypes, repeatedly testing them, and demonstrating their value, and to ensure their final adoption in the real world. The mindset is also focused on choosing the right and responsive strategies and creating alternative pathways to evolve and grow. Moreover, innovators in this mode ought to champion the communication of their vision to all stakeholders. They need to bring everyone into the fold for harmonious orchestration of activities to deliver their innovation.

**Mindsets**
- Reiterating Prototypes
- Evaluating in Reality
- Defining Strategies
- Implementing in Reality
- Communicating Vision

## Mindset: Reiterating Prototypes

Turning our concepts and solutions into reality requires iterations of prototyping and evaluating until the value an offering brings to the real world can be demonstrated. Prototyping is the translation of an intangible idea into a tangible form that users can experience. During the early part of the innovation process, prototypes tend to be more abstract and may even lack physical embodiment like behavioral prototypes. As we go through the process, prototypes get more and more refined and real. Rigor and discipline are needed to repeat the process of prototyping until all the challenges have been met to ensure the successful uptake of the new offering. As a result of reiterative prototyping, we should be able to demonstrate the value our innovations bring to the real world.

*A classic example of the mindset may be seen in the efforts of Orville and Wilbur Wright to build the first fixed-wing aircraft. Unlike the prevailing theory of the time, the brothers believed that the key to flying was a reliable method of pilot control in order for an airplane to maintain its equilibrium. In the years leading up to their first flight, they created a number of gliders to learn about pilot control and how wing shapes provided optimum lift. The gliders were not ends in themselves, but acted as prototypes for learning and demonstrating the value, informing future iterations of aircraft design. In this same way, innovation teams benefit from thinking of prototyping as experimentation and demonstration in reality.*

## Mindset: Evaluating in Reality

A concept is just a captured thought until it takes the form of a prototype that can be experienced. Moreover, a prototype is nothing more than a conjecture until it can be validated through testing. Modern science is built upon the scientific method in which a hypothesis is formulated and then an experiment is designed to either confirm or disprove it. A willingness to embrace and learn from failure informs the scientific outlook that progress is achieved primarily through trial and error. Design teams benefit from embracing this same perspective when prototyping their concepts. By treating prototypes not as final implementable solutions, but as tools for learning, teams remain open-minded and receptive during user testing. Maintaining an inquisitive frame of mind allows teams to capture insights that can then serve as the basis for improving their design solutions or conceiving entirely new ones. After iterations of such testing and reconceiving, solutions can get closer to implementation. The mindset is to pursue this refinement to successfully implement the innovation.

Used with permission from McDonald's Corporation.

*McDonald's Innovation Center is a test lab that is built to implement and evaluate the concepts and solutions the company's innovators create. With highly flexible interior systems that allow the spaces in the lab to be manipulated and reconfigured quickly, the lab is able to rapidly implement concepts, for example, on new dining and ordering systems, and evaluate them, even involving potential users during the process.*

## Mindset: Defining Strategies

Realizing offerings is similar to hosting a dinner event. It can be a lot of work. Depending on the kind of tone the host wants to set, the event could be formal or informal, sophisticated or casual, or large or small. Some require more work than others, but may offer greater rewards in exchange. All of these factors must be weighed against one another when considering what to do. Like party planners, design teams envision possible desired end states, think about the effort required to get there, and then weigh each against the others to arrive at the best possible option. In its most basic sense, the Strategizing mindset is about trying to answer the question, "Where should we play?" It is about cultivating a big-picture perspective—one that encourages broad thinking about design concepts in the context of larger organizational goals. To summarize, the Strategizing mindset involves using design concepts as the basis for imagining possible directions for the organization.

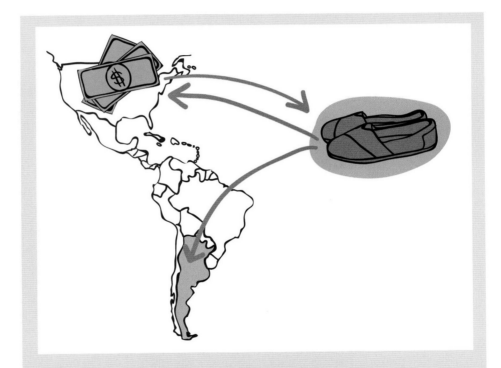

*TOMS Shoes Company has taken a philanthropic strategy to promote the organization. "Giving Pair" is a strategic program the company has initiated; when you purchase a TOMS shoe, another pair is given by TOMS to a child in need anywhere in the world. The company works with partners to determine the sizes and quantities needed for the children they serve and the shoe they give is usually a black, unisex canvas slip-on with a sturdy sole.*

## Mindset: Implementing in Reality

The success of a dinner party lies in the details: cleaning, decorations, place settings, and perhaps even making seating arrangements. A menu needs to be planned and ingredients purchased so that food can be prepared. All of these activities require effort and attention in order to ensure they come together in a coordinated fashion. The frame of mind one brings to these details is tactical in nature. The same can be said for design teams contemplating how their solutions might be implemented. If the prior Strategizing mindset is about where to play, then the Implementing mindset is about, "how to win." Thinking in this phase benefits from a narrow focus on the specific steps necessary to realize offerings. However, each one needs to work in conjunction with the others if success is to be achieved. Consideration of broad Initiatives benefits from thinking through their requirements and the available resources to meet them. Options are explored at each step in the larger implementation plan as teams are assembled, financing organized, and implementation prepared. The work culminates in the formulation of a roadmap that directs efforts toward implementation. To summarize, the thinking in the Implementing mindset is directed toward getting a clear sense of "how to get there." In this way, it is an essential transitional step from design ideas to real products and services.

*Mark Zuckerberg cocreated Facebook, an online social networking platform from his Harvard University dorm as a local personal profiling site. It soon expanded as a friends-networking tool at the university level, and to the Ivy League universities, and then to most universities in the United States and Canada. It further expanded to Europe and soon became a universally used social-networking platform. Facebook, thus, had a fairly linear but dramatic growth path driven by a strong Implementing mindset the leaders in the organization exhibited.*

## Mindset: Communicating Vision

Once solutions are conceived, strategies formulated, and plans developed, consensus and support for the initiative need to be built. This calls for creating a vision that can be shared with all stakeholders to guide activities and bring focus to the entire organization's efforts. Thinking about how to move to action is all about effective communications. It requires an empathetic frame of mind, one that seeks to understand stakeholders' values and points of view. It needs crafting messages that will inspire a wide number of people in an organization to work toward a shared goal. Cultivating foresight is important for anticipating challenges and being able to counter them with reasons for moving forward with initiatives. Ultimately, the Communicating Vision mindset is really about leadership. It is about giving consideration to how everyone involved in implementation can embrace the ideas as his or her own.

*In 1960, U.S. President John F. Kennedy announced to the world that by the end of the decade, America would put a man on the moon. The statement inspired and brought focus to the efforts of the National Aeronautics and Space Administration (NASA), so that by the end of the decade, NASA was able to realize Kennedy's vision.*

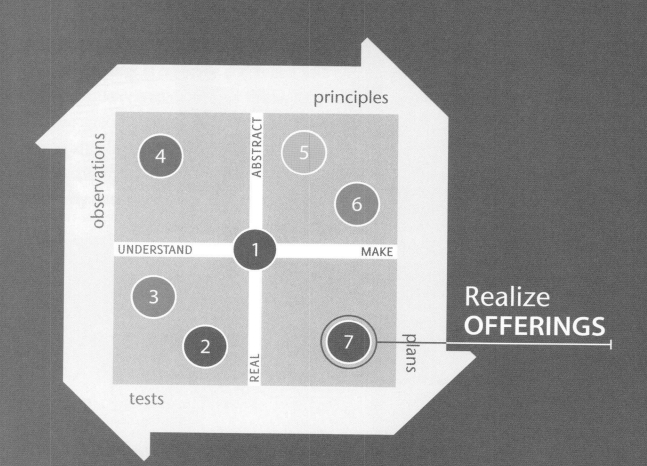

principles

observations

4

ABSTRACT

5

6

UNDERSTAND  1  MAKE

3

2

REAL

7

plans

tests

Realize
**OFFERINGS**

# REALIZE OFFERINGS *methods*

# 7.1 Strategy Roadmap

Planning innovation solutions for short-term, mid-term, and long-term strategies

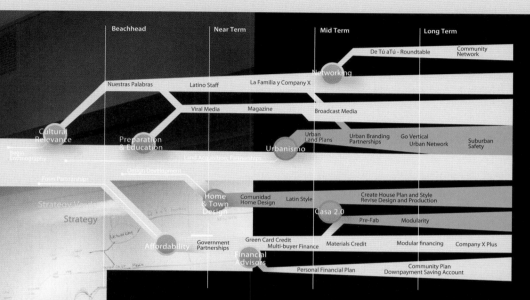

| Beachhead | Near Term | Mid Term | Long Term |
|---|---|---|---|
| | | De Tú aTú - Roundtable | Community Network |
| | | Networking | |
| Nuestras Palabras | Latino Staff | La Familia y Company X | |
| | Viral Media | Magazine | Broadcast Media |
| Cultural Relevance | Preparation & Education | Urban Land Plans | Urban Branding Partnerships | Go Vertical Urban Network | Suburban Safety |
| Begin Ethnography | | Urbanismo | |
| | Land Acquisition Partnerships | | |
| Design Development | | | |
| Town Partnerships | | | |
| Strategy Verde | Home & Town Design | Comunidad Home Design | Latin Style | Create House Plan and Style Revise Design and Production |
| Strategy | | Casa 2.0 | Pre-Fab | Modularity |
| | Government Partnerships | Green Card Credit Multi-buyer Finance | Materials Credit | Modular financing | Company X Plus |
| Affordability | | Financial Advisors | | |
| | | Personal Financial Plan | Community Plan Downpayment Saving Account |

## EXAMPLE PROJECT: Homebuilders—Addressing the Needs of an Underserved Market (2006)

One of the nation's largest homebuilders was in search of a way to boost its business amid an unsteady housing market. Recognizing that few comprehensive home-buying offerings target the Latino community, a team of designers at the IIT Institute of Design saw the penetration of this market as an attractive opportunity space to analyze and make recommendations to the firm.

The team discovered five major obstacles to typical Latino home purchases, including the lack of culturally appropriate sales methods, Latinos not being financially prepared, unaffordability of homes, Latinos being concentrated in urban areas, and the design of homes not being Latino-targeted. In response, the team formed a system of strategic recommendations, dubbed strategy Verde, which encompassed three initiatives: cultural relevance, affordability, and preparation and education. A second set of strategic recommendations that built upon Verde was called Rojo, which represented a higher-risk strategy and encompassed home design and key urban locations as its main initiatives.

After chronologically prioritizing the innovations within each strategy, the team plotted the initiatives of Verde and Rojo on a *Strategy Roadmap* detailing the foundational requirements and what needed to be implemented in the near term, mid-term, and long term. The roadmap also highlighted the points of intersection between Verde and Rojo. As an extension of the roadmap, the team also laid out issues that may arise during the implementation as well as what was required of the homebuilding firm.

**BENEFITS**
- Considers solutions over time
- Creates plans
- Defines direction
- Defines strategies
- Promotes shared understanding

**INPUT**
- Collection of solutions to be implemented

**OUTPUT**
- A plan aligning solutions to strategies and tactics over time

**WHEN TO USE**

## WHAT IT DOES

The Strategy Roadmap is a method for mapping the future strategic direction of the organization by prioritizing the order of implementation among innovation offerings. It is employed after all the solutions have been fleshed out, reviewed, compared with one another, and clustered along a timeline. Using the distribution of solutions on the timeline as guidance, distinct strategic goals for the short term, mid-term, and long term are formulated. Strategies are then developed for each of these three time periods to understand what will be their implications on the market and what is required of the organization to support these strategies.

## HOW IT WORKS

### STEP 1: Review solutions and map on a timeline.

Gather and review all the solutions generated during the Frame Solutions mode. Place each solution along a timeline that is divided into three time segments as columns—short term for those to be implemented in the next one to two years, mid-term for those planned for two to five years out, and long term for those conceived for more than five years of development and planning. Add a label that describes the set of solutions in each time segment.

### STEP 2: Write strategies for each time segment.

Understand the commonalities among the set of solutions in each time segment in terms of how they will collectively add value to the organization. Write descriptions summarizing strategies for the short-term, mid-term, and long-term segments in the first row. For example, solutions that are in the short-term segment may relate to the organization's existing brands. Their strategy could be summarized as: "Strategy focused on the core business by redesign-

ing existing products." Prepare similar statements for mid-term and long-term solutions.

### STEP 3: Describe how the organization will support the strategies.

In the second row, under each time segment, describe what your organization needs to do to support the corresponding strategies. It is useful to include your organization's strengths, weaknesses, and competencies. Discuss how to construct a business rational for the successful implementation of the strategies.

### STEP 4: Describe how the market will respond to the strategies.

In the third row, under each time segment, describe the opportunities and risks that exist in the market for the corresponding strategies. Discuss who might be the competition and how to identify partners to make the strategies work in each of the time segments.

### STEP 5: Visually communicate the strategies.

Make road map diagrams to show how strategies relate to each other. Review the Strategy Roadmap with your team and the major stakeholders of the organization.

**7.1 STRATEGY ROADMAP**

# 7.2 Platform Plan

Planning solutions as platforms using platform principles and attributes

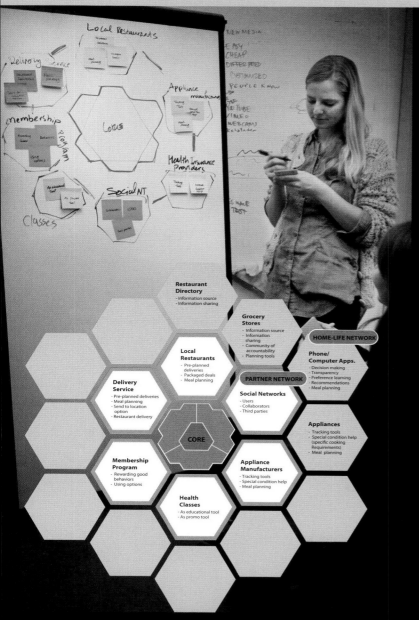

Restaurant Directory
- Information source
- Information sharing

Grocery Stores
- Information source
- Information sharing
- Community of accountability
- Planning tools

HOME-LIFE NETWORK

Local Restaurants
- Pre-planned deliveries
- Packaged deals
- Meal planning

Phone/ Computer Apps.
- Decision making
- Transparency
- Preference learning
- Recommendations
- Meal planning

PARTNER NETWORK

Delivery Service
- Pre-planned deliveries
- Meal planning
- Send to location option
- Restaurant delivery

Social Networks
- Users
- Collaborators
- Third parties

Appliances
- Tracking tools
- Special condition help (specific cooking Requirements)
- Meal planning

CORE

Appliance Manufacturers
- Tracking tools
- Special condition help
- Meal planning

Membership Program
- Rewarding good behaviors
- Using options

Health Classes
- As educational tool
- As promo tool

## EXAMPLE PROJECT: Convivial Food Platform (2010)

Convivial is a concept for a food and wellness platform developed by a team of design planners at the IIT Institute of Design. It takes a comprehensive, integrated approach to wellness, encourages and shapes healthy consumer behaviors, and creates a network of partners dedicated to healthy eating. Constructing platforms creates valuable connections and interdependencies that can respond to a variety of needs and challenges from many stakeholders.

Using the *Platform Plan*, the Convivial was constructed with three main components—core, partners, and home-life networks. The core of the platform represents a membership group of wellness consultants, health insurance providers, and software development firms that would connect with larger external partner networks including one that focuses exclusively on the home. Surrounding the platform core is the partner network and it includes local restaurants, health classes, and social networks that would expand the goods and services of the platform into the users' community. New services would offer people health-tracking tools, the ability to follow other people in the platform, as well as a reward system for healthy behaviors. The home-life component of the platform relates to the objects, services, and relationships found in and around the home, and comprises local grocery stores, appliances, phone and computer applications, and other similar components.

The Platform Plan enabled the team to map out their solutions holistically across different industries and partners and develop a strategy that could be delivered as a series of experiences connected by common standards and bringing value to all stakeholders.

| **BENEFITS** | **INPUT** | **OUTPUT** | **WHEN TO USE** |

- Considers solutions over time
- Creates plans
- Defines strategies
- Maps change over time
- Creates options
- Builds higher-level systems

- Collection of planned solutions
- Platform principles, attributes, and examples

- A plan showing reconceived solutions as platforms
- Discussions among stakeholders about how to implement the platform solutions

## WHAT IT DOES

This method allows us to frame our solution as a possible platform. A platform is an innovation strategy that provides a common base (a set of standards or an infrastructure) that enables a variety of options as offerings. A platform strategy is to build an entire constellation of offerings by allowing its users and participants to gain value in different ways. For example, Facebook is a platform that is used by people in a variety of ways: to share their activities, to make social connections, to stay in touch, to play games such as Mafia Wars or Farmville, to promote brands, or for companies to gain exposure.

Any platform will need to consider four basic principles:

- Core with options—the basic set of offerings on which things can be built, for example, the core tools, interfaces, space, account, and so forth that Facebook provides for people to build, connect, and share.

- Sticky users—peoples' use of the platform grows over time, and they become more invested in the platform. For example, in Facebook, peoples' social networking and friends circle expand over time, and this expanding collection becomes an important asset that people value.

- Distributed owners—platform providers have only part ownership of the platform, only the basic infrastructure and core support. The "owner" is widely distributed. For example, in Facebook, the company only provides basic tools, interfaces, databases, and servers to allow users to generate and share content. Other stakeholders take ownership of their own offerings.

- Open partners—the base provides an environment to attract partners to participate in the platform.

For example, in Facebook, external entities, such as companies or game developers, proactively participate and grow on the platform with benefits of their own.

Compared to individual independent offerings, platforms provide higher value to all stakeholders involved—the users, providers, and partners. Successful platforms ensure easy access to all stakeholders as well. As a strategy, a platform is self-expanding and grows over time with all stakeholders contributing to the growth. For the platform provider, the strategy is more about long-term value than immediate gains in the marketplace. All these are platform attributes that we can build into our system of solutions with the help of this method, to create greater value.

## HOW IT WORKS

### STEP 1: Discuss key attributes of successful platforms.

Discuss and reach a common understanding about platforms as an innovation strategy. Use platform examples from the real world to understand their key attributes.

### STEP 2: Identify solutions/initiatives that have a potential to be a platform over time.

Can a platform strategy work for your solution? Using your team's collective understanding about platforms and your in-depth knowledge about how you have framed your solutions, determine if your solutions have the potential to grow as a platform.

### STEP 3: Use the four platform principles to review solutions.

Use the four principles—core with options, sticky users, distributed owners, and open partners—to think

**7.2 PLATFORM PLAN**

of a platform strategy for your solutions. Model your solution system as platform with these four components. Discuss how to conceive your solutions to fit with the platform definition.

### STEP 4: Use the key platform attributes to review solutions.

List platform attributes such as potential for networking, connectivity, participation, sharing, growth, accessibility, business collaboration, trust, and loose controls among others. Think of which attributes are "must have" and "nice to have" for your solutions. Rethink your solutions by relating them to the platform attributes.

### STEP 5: Create a plan for platform implementation.

Create a plan on a timeline (with short-term, mid-term, long-term goals), and show how your reconceived solutions will grow as a platform. Describe details like strategies, actions needed, partners involved, technologies needed, key drivers, risks, and investments needed.

### STEP 6: Share the plan with stakeholders and discuss next steps.

Share and discuss this platform plan. How driven would the target users be to engage in the platform over a long time? How viable is the platform plan in the context of competitors and partners? What are the barriers for implementation of the platform? What are the most uncertain parts of the plan?

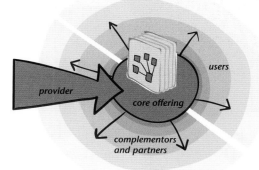

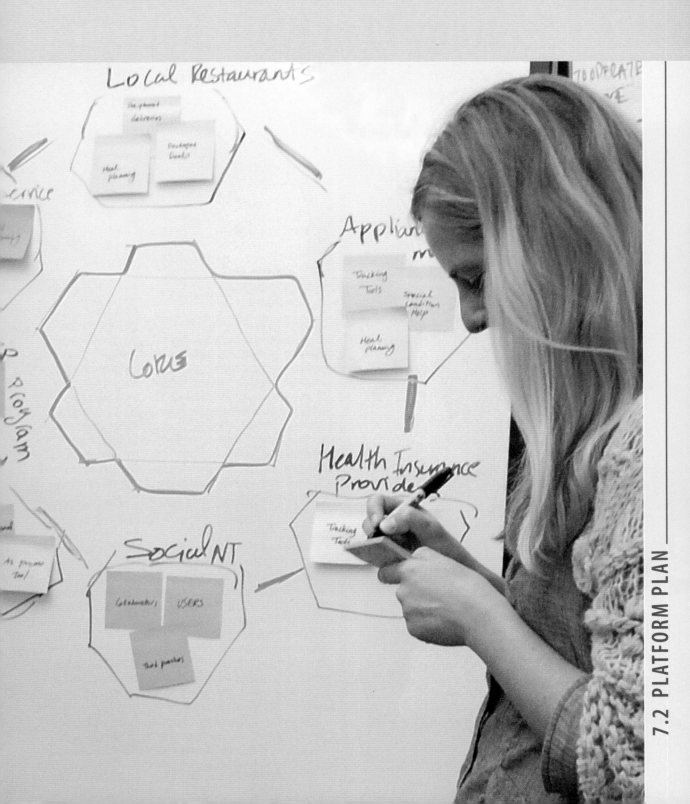

# 7.3 Strategy Plan Workshop

Creating organizational strategies and aligning around them for realizing proposed solutions

**EXAMPLE PROJECT:**
*Design Research Conference (2010)*

The Design Research Conference (DRC) is an annual conference planned and organized by students of the IIT Institute of Design and brings together leading thinkers, practitioners, and seasoned executives in design research. After each year, leadership of the conference is passed to two new DRC co-chairs. The previous year's conference is evaluated by discussing the feedback from conference attendees reviewing the overall experience. In 2010, the newly appointed co-chairs saw an opportunity to elevate the brand of the DRC. Leveraging the planning and feedback of past conferences, the co-chairs held a *Strategy Plan* Workshop with current students, members of the school's administration, and other stakeholders to discuss the goals and objectives for the upcoming DRC.

As design research is becoming more pervasive and reaching communities outside of the design industry, the Strategy Plan Workshop aimed to discuss how to diversify the roster of speakers to illuminate the extending reach the discipline is experiencing. Additionally, the workshop participants conceived ways to create new experiences for attendees at the conference, not only from provocative speakers, but also from an experiential environment that would encourage collaboration, storytelling, and connection among attendees and speakers. The strategy workshop delineated teams who would be involved in recruiting speakers, creating the brand materials, planning logistics, volunteering, and creating the experience/exhibit design (a new endeavor for this conference). After the strategic discussions, deliverables were mapped out on a calendar as short-, mid-, and long-term objectives and shared with the various teams and administration to ensure that responsibilities were properly assigned and deadlines were met.

**BENEFITS**
- Builds alignment in the organization
- Creates plans
- Defines strategies
- Identifies challenges
- Promotes collaboration

**INPUT**
- Collection of solutions to be implemented and supporting documentation
- Stakeholders key to implementation process

**OUTPUT**
- A strategic plan showing how solutions align to the organization's goals, the steps to be taken, and challenges to be faced
- Alignment among stakeholders on how to bring solutions to market

**WHEN TO USE**

## WHAT IT DOES

The workshop brings together key stakeholders from different parts of the organization to develop a strategy plan for realizing a proposed innovation. It engages participants to think through all of the potential ramifications for realizing the innovation offerings. The workshop gives people operating in different parts of the organization an opportunity to work through potential challenges and align on an overall plan. It is an effective vehicle for inviting participation in the innovation process and giving stakeholders a sense of ownership to start their initiatives. The outcome is a strategic plan that proposes innovation solutions, describes the challenges for realizing them, and discusses the organization's responses to meet those challenges.

## HOW IT WORKS

Participants review summaries of all key findings about solutions that have been pieced together earlier. They think through how the innovation solutions and strategies defined in the Frame Solutions mode might be realized and supported by different competencies within and outside the organization. Alternative approaches and paths are considered through dialog and discussion. The workshop builds consensus about a strategy plan that can be later shared with all stakeholders and leadership.

### STEP 1: Plan the workshop.

Build an outline of how the day will proceed. Decide what kind of participants will bring most value to the strategic planning. Then, pick the right people to participate in the workshop.

### STEP 2: Prepare workshop materials.

Piece together the key findings related to the innovation solutions defined in the Frame Solutions mode. Create a presentation, focused on these defined solutions, to be introduced in the workshop. Be prepared to offer supporting evidence such as concepts, principles, and insights that led to these solutions.

### STEP 3: Prepare for the workshop activity.

Establish an environment that invites dialog, critiquing, and input. Provide a space where breakout teams of three or four can work comfortably. Make sure team spaces have paper, pens, sticky notes, and any other required supplies that will enable participants to capture and share thoughts. Include templates or worksheets that will enable teams to capture their ideas and organize their work.

### STEP 4: Discuss the defined solutions and concepts.

Share the preprepared presentation on proposed solutions. If your team has already prepared a Strategic Roadmap, share that too; it will provide additional information about how solutions are distributed on a timeline. Discuss, and capture participants' comments for later review.

### STEP 5: Build a matrix to show how solutions grow over time.

Build a matrix with the solutions as row headings. Enter three time segments as column headings—short-term (one to two years), mid-term (two to five years), and long-term (five-plus years). State the strategies (e.g., launch new offerings, build brand) for each of these time segments also in column headings. In the cells, describe what needs to be done to make the solutions work in their corresponding time segments. Include strategic challenges, implementation issues, or other challenges that teams find useful for building a plan.

### STEP 6: Extend the matrix with other considerations for successful implementation.

A common framework that is most often used to extend this matrix has three parts—challenges for creating user

value, challenges for creating provider value, and the organization's responses to these challenges. Add these three as columns to the right of the matrix. Fill the cells with descriptions of user-value and provider-value challenges and list specific ways in which the organization will take action to meet those challenges. Discussions on the matrix provide a good opportunity for the stakeholders to align around what needs to be done at an organizational level to realize the innovation solutions.

### STEP 7: Review the matrix and plan for a detailed implementation plan.

Participants review the whole matrix and discuss how to schedule time and resources and begin to formulate ideas on how to make these strategies real.

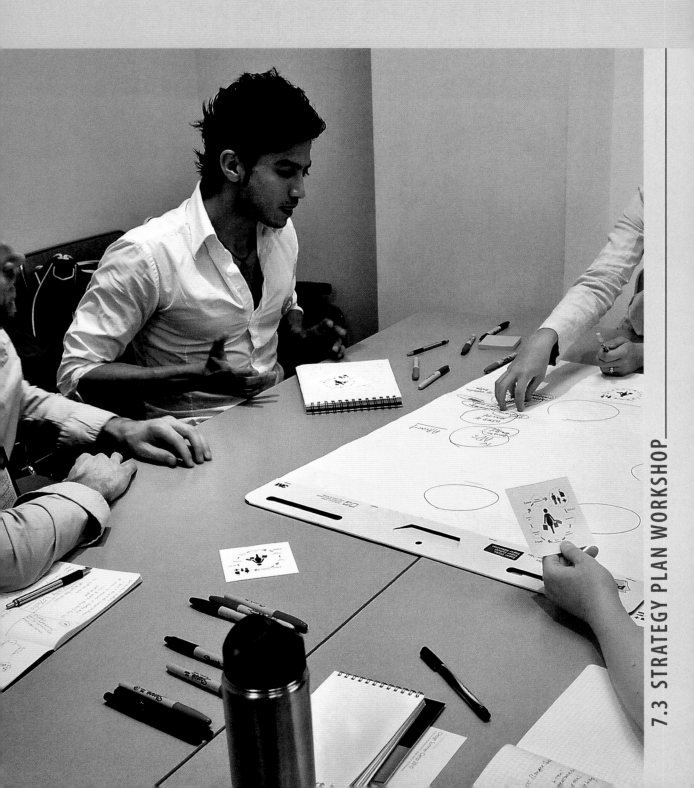

7.3 STRATEGY PLAN WORKSHOP

# 7.4 Pilot Development and Testing

Placing offerings in the marketplace to learn how they perform and how users experience them

**EXAMPLE PROJECT:** *New Options for Out-of-School Youth—Exposure Studio (2009)*

Wouldn't it make sense to try a career out before committing, much like trying on clothes before buying them? This is the question posed by an IIT Institute of Design team, looking to ease the process for those deciding on a career, while helping to avoid unnecessary and expensive career switches later in life. In conducting research, the team found that youths were typically very skeptical of career-advice organizations and wouldn't attend unless strongly incentivized. They had likely been lectured to about careers in large group settings and found little benefit. This age group tended to desire experiences outside of their neighborhood, while still seeking out familiar elements.

Working with an existing career-advice organization, one student team member did *Pilot Development and Testing* by implementing different concepts and strategies for engaging youths and providing them with valuable exposure to possible career paths. For example, the youths were brought to a bakery and fire station to talk to real people about different career options in their regular work environment. There were in-studio sessions as well, where participants conducted usability testing on a mobile application and explored various aspects of digital graphics creation. Through piloting these strategies with real people, the students were able to quickly measure what worked and what didn't and make adjustments as necessary. The students went on to develop a physical space to serve as a pilot home base for the organization's career sessions.

Photos by Seth Kutnik, IIT, Institute of Design.

## BENEFITS
- Creates plans
- Encourages iteration
- Makes abstract ideas concrete
- Provides evidence

## INPUT
- Selected solutions and their development plans
- Access to key stakeholders in the offering launch

## OUTPUT
- Results based on assessment and analysis of offerings in the pilot market

## WHEN TO USE

## WHAT IT DOES

Pilot Development and Testing is a method for testing innovation solutions by placing them in contexts where they function as real offerings. The development of a pilot requires tactical planning no different than the launch of an actual offering (product or service). It varies only in terms of scale. Instead of a new offering being piloted to an entire market, it is usually piloted in a test market so that it can be studied to inform modifications prior to full launch. Thought is given to where a pilot will be implemented and how easily findings from the pilot testing can be generalized for the larger market. Pilot testing consists of measuring marketplace acceptance (sales), user feedback, and observed engagement with the offering. Findings are analyzed and used to determine whether or not modification to the piloted offering is required or if it can be rolled out as is. The method is also particularly effective for understanding the impact of the offering on organizational resources, and what additional requirements might need to be in place prior to a full-scale roll out.

## HOW IT WORKS

### STEP 1: Select solutions to be piloted.

As a team review the set of solutions that you have developed and organized as a Strategic Roadmap. Look for the most significant solutions that you are most uncertain about regarding their potential in real markets.

### STEP 2: Prepare a pilot development plan.

Draft an initial plan that identifies all parts of the organization that need to be involved in a launch. Co-create a pilot introduction plan by involving key people from marketing, finance, engineering, sales, and other relevant departments. The plan should function much like a scaled-down product launch. Include a budget, timeline, team, and indication of required resources in the draft plan.

### STEP 3: Identify a test market and get approval.

Identify a specific target market where the offering will be piloted. Include a rationale for why the market has been chosen. Get approval from key decision makers.

### STEP 4: Establish the performance metrics.

Select qualitative and quantitative performance measures and put mechanisms in place to measure them in the test market.

### STEP 5: Launch and monitor the pilot.

Get launch approval, assemble interorganizational management team, launch, and monitor the pilot.

### STEP 6: Analyze performance and revise offerings.

Take note of the variables that may affect users' experience of the offering. These variables can include time of year, location, venue, adjacent offerings, and so forth. This information will help assess performance. Capture use/sales data, conduct intercept interviews, and gather in-depth feedback. Gather as a team to analyze findings and revise subsequent iterations of the offering.

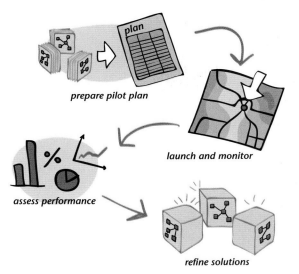

*prepare pilot plan*

*launch and monitor*

*assess performance*

*refine solutions*

**7.4 PILOT DEVELOPMENT AND TESTING**

# 7.5 Implementation Plan

## Addressing implementation issues and creating a plan to realize solutions

| CHALLENGES | INITIATIVES | | | *Strategy Verde* | *Strategy Roja* |
| --- | --- | --- | --- | --- | --- |
| | Cultural Relevance | Preparation & Education | Affordability | Home/Town Design | Urbanismo |
| **Hire** People | - Ethnographic researchers<br>- Spanish speaking marketing & design employees<br>- Spanish translators<br>- Latino trainers | - Ad agency oversight<br>- Print designers, Latino marketing employees<br>- Video producers<br>- Magazine writers, editors<br>- Latino event hosts | - Latino partner alliance/ relationship/biz dev employees<br>- Latino financial advisors | - Latino salespeople<br>- Architects with residential design experience for Latino clients or in Latin countries<br>- Architects/engineers experienced in prefab and modular homes | - Latino residential and commercial real estate agents |
| **Develop** Systems | - Training programs<br>- Events to bring home buyers together | - Education programs<br>- Community events<br>- Media production | - Open platform for financial assistance; Company X financial assistance area within bank<br>- Mortgage products for extended families<br>- Modular financing products<br>- Personal and community first home purchase savings programs<br>- Supplier network for home additions | - Prefab planning and construction systems<br>- Club membership program | - Urban and commercial land acquisition process |
| **Build** Structures | - Research facilities<br>- Discussion areas | - Company X education materials display area within local banks | | - Prototyping space for Nuestro Centro | - Urban land<br>- Urban commercial tenants |
| **Manage Relationships with** Partnerships | - Hispanic cultural organizations<br>- Latino staffing company | - Neighborhood banks (Banco Popular)<br>- Spanish TV, radio networks<br>- Ad agencies | - Neighborhood banks (Banco Popular)<br>- Local and federal governments<br>- Non-governmental agencies | - Global Homes | - City governments<br>- Urban construction companies |

## EXAMPLE PROJECT: *Homebuilder – Addressing the Needs of an Underserved Market (2006)*

Latino homeownership in the United States lags nearly 30 percent behind that of other Americans. From their research, an IIT Institute of Design team learned that Latinos have not been offered homeownership opportunities that are both culturally and economically relevant. This presented an opportunity for one of the nation's largest homebuilders to respond to the needs of the underserved Latino real estate market by providing products and services as part of a compelling, culturally appropriate, and integrated real estate buying experience.

As part of their recommendation to the homebuilding company, the IIT Institute of Design team developed a strategy with five initiatives, each drawing on existing company resources and capabilities, but with differing levels of investment. Anticipating significant growth in the Latino population in the United States by 2050, the team structured an *Implementation Plan*.

The Implementation Plan matrix served as a guide for the company to evaluate the resources required to accomplish each of the five initiatives: cultural relevance, preparation and education, affordability, home/town design, and urbanismo. Each of the five initiatives was placed as column headings while challenges brought in by people, systems, structures, and partnerships were assigned as headings for rows. The team organized the matrix in this way to assess the resources that the homebuilder would need. For example, the challenge posed by cultural relevance and people would require the homebuilder to hire ethnographic researchers to learn more about the community and to hire Spanish and Latino translators to engage the Latino community with a familiar voice. Being able to specify the requirements paved a path for the homebuilder to plan for implementation.

**BENEFITS**
- Creates plans
- Defines direction
- Encourages comprehensiveness
- Gives focus to the process
- Identifies challenges
- Promotes shared understanding

**INPUT**
- Strategy Roadmap and/or Strategic Plan from Workshop

**OUTPUT**
- Implementation Plan identifying actions, timeframe, and resources needed to overcome expected challenges/issues

**WHEN TO USE**

## WHAT IT DOES

The Implementation Plan matrix is a method for making the Strategy Roadmap actionable. With a good understanding of all the strategies defined using other methods, this method helps to avoid misalignment between organizational competencies and implementation goals. For example, it is a challenge if the organization lacks the right competencies to implement a critically important solution or a concept. The response to that challenge might be to create initiatives to grow that competency in the organization or partner with another organization that might have that competency. The Implementation Plan helps teams think through such challenges and generate appropriate responses. A well-designed plan provides a structure for implementing innovation solutions, lays out the specific actions needed, and makes the process clear to all parts of the organization.

## HOW IT WORKS

### STEP 1: Review the defined organizational strategies and the proposed solutions.

Gather the output from other methods like Strategy Roadmap and Strategy Plan Workshop. Review how solutions are planned to evolve over three time segments (short, mid-, and long term) and the broad organizational strategies planned.

### STEP 2: Write a description of the changing context.

Refer to your contextual research to find out what are the trends in the industry and adjacent ones during these three time segments. Describe at a high level how your offering will address the users' changing needs, the nature of competition in the market, and relevant changes happening in social, economic, political, and cultural aspects. Aim to make the descriptions high level and provide citations to your earlier findings.

### STEP 3: Create a matrix of innovation solutions versus challenges.

Create a matrix with innovation solutions as the row headings and the implementation challenges as column headings. The implementation challenges most often used in the matrix are market, operational, management, and financial.

### STEP 4: Think through key implementation challenges.

Discuss and describe how your organization will address key implementation challenges in the matrix cells. Make sure that you include representatives from the most appropriate departments (marketing, engineering, research, finance, etc.) in the discussions.

The following will be useful as a guide to think through implementation challenges for each innovation solution.

- Market challenges, which include strategic positioning, relations with partners, and existing and emerging competitors
- Operational challenges, which include processes, communications, structures, and culture of the organization
- Management challenges, which include leadership, champions, teams, and schedules
- Financial challenges, which include ROI, expenses and investments, revenue and profit growth, and market share

## STEP 5: Discuss and include stakeholder feedback.

As a group, view the whole matrix and discuss the biggest challenges and most significant actions that your organization needs to take. Identify areas where external expertise needs to be brought in. Use this matrix to further flesh out implementation details such as teams, schedules, resources, and others. Share this plan with the key stakeholders in your organization responsible for implementation and incorporate their feedback as part of the Implementation Plan.

## STEP 6: Create a master Implementation Plan.

Compile all of the findings from the previous steps into a single sharable document. Include a spread-sheet as a Gantt chart that lays out the master sequence and allows for the presentation of simultaneous activities. Assign implementation responsibilities to teams.

| | Initiative A | Initiative B | Initiative C |
|---|---|---|---|
| Market | (issues) | | |
| Operations | | | |
| Management | | | |
| Financial | | | |

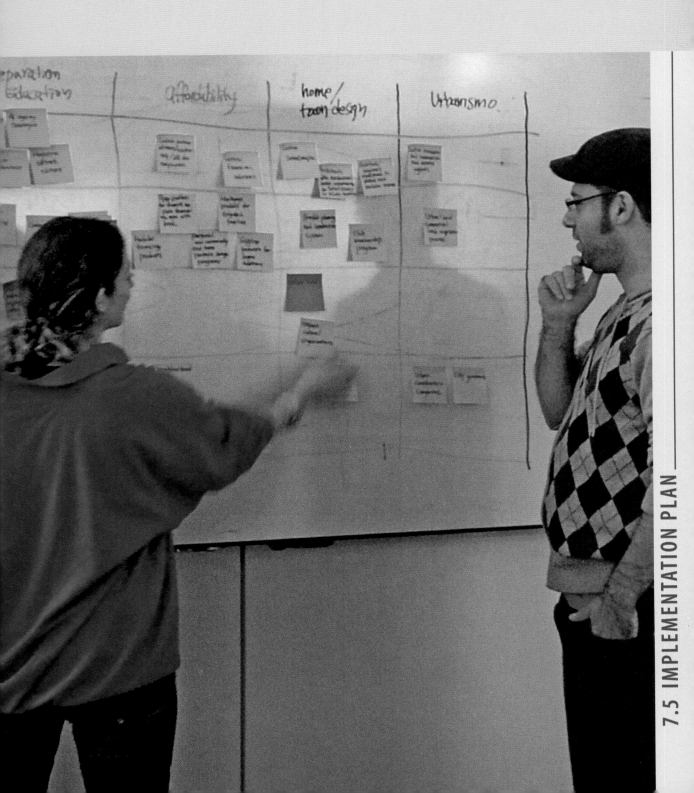

Planning for competencies needed to make innovation initiatives successful

| | Information Aggregation | | Delivery | | Content Development | |
|---|---|---|---|---|---|---|
| | IT Services | Standardization | Market Segmentation | User Identification | Subject matter Expertise | Local customs Knowledge |
| **Initiative 1:** Real Estate Investment Management | **R&D EIC** IT backbone will be necessary to collect, analyze, manage, and transmit needed data. | | | **R&D** Properties will need to be matched with appropriate investors. | **R&D** Property investment and management abilities will be crucial to successfully attracting investors. | **R&D $$** Need to be ahead of local market trends, shifting regional centers, and government policy changes. |
| **Initiative 2:** Project Management Support | **R&D EIC** IT infrastructure will be critical to ensure parties have easy and efficient access with software and online services. | **EIC** A single reliable set of tools and forms will require creating standards from a range of collected data. | | **EIC** Target different types of construction personnel with unique offerings. | **EIC** Tools and forms can be based on those commonly used in U.S. market. | **R&D $$** Subtle unique characteristics and needs of Indian market personnel may determine success or failure. |
| **Initiative 3:** Standards and Certification | **R&D EIC** IT systems will help to manage information regarding standards and certified companies. | **EIC** Content will need to be filtered and evaluated when received and processed into a common form when distributed. | **EIC** Product data will be used differently within different markets, based on different needs. | | Engineering ability to inspect and evaluate product materials is crucial for standards and advisory practices. | **R&D** Knowledge of government enforced and tacit industry standards will drive acceptance of certified products. |
| **Initiative 4:** Brand Awareness | | | **R&D** Certain market segments driving growth and investment will be most critical to target. | **R&D** Target offerings towards personnel with purchasing power and decision making abilities. | | |

**Importance to Offering**
- major importance
- minor importance

**Means for Implementation**
- **EIC** existing internal capability
- **R&D** internal development
- **$$** partnership
- acquisition capability

## EXAMPLE PROJECT: *Points of Arrival in Emerging Markets (2005)*

For an information systems company servicing the architectural and construction industries, a team of IIT Institute of Design students developed a Strategic Plan to develop new products and services for the Indian market because of the country's strong growth prospects in new construction and infrastructure development. The final recommendations move the company from an information provider into an advisory role in which it would define industry standards for building materials through certification services. The strategy would also facilitate foreign investment and development in India's real estate market.

The Competencies Plan connected the organization's existing competencies in information aggregation, delivery, and content development with the four initiatives the team recommended—real estate investment management, project management support, standards and certification, and brand awareness. The plan also suggested the means for implementing these new competencies, some of which existed within the firm and required no further development and others that required brand new development. Acquiring additional competencies entailed forming new partnerships or full acquisition of companies having complementary capabilities. Whether to develop, partner, or acquire competencies or use existing ones became clear as a result of this method. It also showed competencies of critical importance for which significantly more resources were to be allocated compared to others.

**BENEFITS**
- Creates plans
- Manages resources
- Builds alignment in the organization
- Encourages comprehensiveness
- Gives focus to the process

**INPUT**
- List of initiatives to pursue
- Understanding of current competencies of the organization

**OUTPUT**
- Organized matrix of initiatives showing how the required competencies are going to be developed

**WHEN TO USE**

## WHAT IT DOES

The Competencies Plan seeks to provide an alternative planning structure, one based on competencies needed for innovation initiatives rather than time. The competencies needed for each initiative must be mustered from internal resources of an organization, newly developed, or gained through acquisition or partnership. For planning this, a competencies matrix is used in which the initiatives are listed on the vertical axis and the required competencies are listed on the horizontal. The cells in this matrix are used to describe how organizations can ensure the competencies needed to support various initiatives—develop, partner, acquire, or use existing. The cells also show the critical importance of a competency for making an initiative successful.

## HOW IT WORKS

### STEP 1: List the initiatives to pursue.

"Initiatives" are solutions translated into initial projects for implementation. Review your previous efforts in translating solutions into initiatives for implementation. If initiatives are not yet defined, then create projects around your solutions by adding resources, schedules, people, and an overall plan for implementation. List these initiatives.

### STEP 2: Identify competencies needed.

Go through each initiative and figure out what competencies are needed for their successful implementation. For example, an initiative that offers new digital tools for interaction will need competencies like software development, user interface design, and even technology trend expertise in some cases.

### STEP 3: Set up an initiatives versus competencies matrix.

Set up a matrix and enter the names of initiatives as row headings and competencies as column headings.

### STEP 4: Describe the plan of action in the cells.

In the cells in which competencies are required for an initiative, describe how that competency will be ensured by the organization for the successful implementation of that initiative. If that competency already exists in the organization, determine whether it will be enough to support the initiative. If not, describe how that competency will be developed internally or gained through partnerships or acquisitions. Additionally, describe if the competency is of major or minor importance to the initiative. This will provide a sense of the amount of resources to be allocated for implementation.

### STEP 5: Discuss and share the plan for taking action.

Share this Competency Plan matrix among the key stakeholders in the organization to ensure that implementation actions are taken and the competencies are made available and the initiatives are launched.

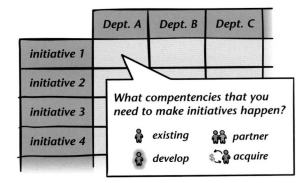

**7.6 COMPETENCIES PLAN**

Planning initiatives based on innovation solutions and forming teams around them

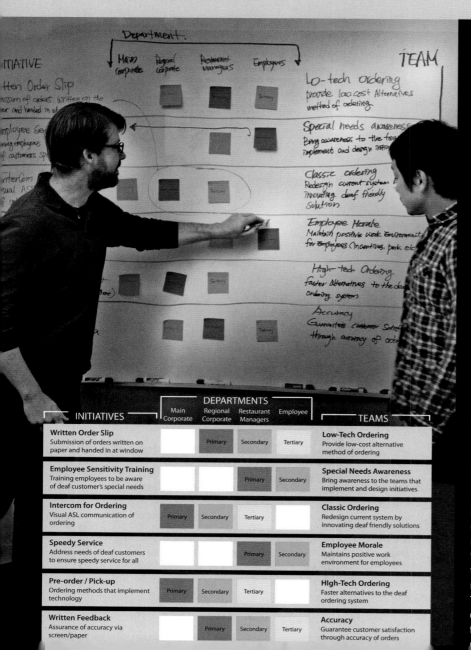

| INITIATIVES | DEPARTMENTS | | | | TEAMS |
|---|---|---|---|---|---|
| | Main Corporate | Regional Corporate | Restaurant Managers | Employee | |
| **Written Order Slip** Submission of orders written on paper and handed in at window | | Primary | Secondary | Tertiary | **Low-Tech Ordering** Provide low-cost alternative method of ordering |
| **Employee Sensitivity Training** Training employees to be aware of deaf customer's special needs | | | Primary | Secondary | **Special Needs Awareness** Bring awareness to the teams that implement and design initiatives |
| **Intercom for Ordering** Visual ASL communication of ordering | Primary | Secondary | Tertiary | | **Classic Ordering** Redesign current system by innovating deaf friendly solutions |
| **Speedy Service** Address needs of deaf customers to ensure speedy service for all | | | Primary | Secondary | **Employee Morale** Maintains positive work environment for employees |
| **Pre-order / Pick-up** Ordering methods that implement technology | Primary | Secondary | Tertiary | | **High-Tech Ordering** Faster alternatives to the deaf ordering system |
| **Written Feedback** Assurance of accuracy via screen/paper | | Primary | Secondary | Tertiary | **Accuracy** Guarantee customer satisfaction through accuracy of orders |

### EXAMPLE PROJECT:
### Drive-Thru for the Hearing Impaired (2005)

In understanding how the hearing-impaired customers are affected by the existing drive-through technology and process at fast food restaurants, a team of IIT Institute of Design students discovered four problem areas that the hearing impaired face: verbal communication, customer-employee and computer-mediated interactions, basic feedback, and lack of services. In responses to these challenges, systemized service and equipment solutions in the form of six initiatives were developed—written-order slip, employee sensitivity training, intercom for ordering, speedy service, pre-order/pick-up, and written feedback.

The project used the *Team Formation Plan* to determine the departments and the people needed to implement these initiatives. As an example, the group created a "high-tech ordering team," composed of members from main corporate department, regional corporate department, and restaurant managers department. This team was assigned to concentrate on the "pre-order/pick-up" initiative. In order of priority, the main corporate department would have the primary responsibility for implementation; the regional managers department, the second; and the restaurant managers department, the third. The teaming plan matrix provided a comprehensive picture of the roles all the implementation teams needed to play across all major initiatives.

**BENEFITS**
- Creates plans
- Encourages comprehensiveness
- Gives focus to the process
- Manages resources
- Promotes collaboration

**INPUT**
- Generated solutions
- Understanding of existing talent in the organization

**OUTPUT**
- A matrix of initiatives/solutions and the necessary capabilities across departments needed to execute them

**WHEN TO USE**

## WHAT IT DOES

This method helps to create a plan for forming teams to implement innovation initiatives. "Initiatives" are solutions translated into initial projects for implementation. Teams are formed by carefully thinking about the most appropriate knowledge and skills needed for each of the initiatives. Multidisciplinary teams are created by tapping into various existing departments of the organization such as engineering, marketing, research, and finance.

The Team Formation Plan asserts the importance of starting projects that are directly based on human-centered solutions, carefully developed using disciplined processes and thinking. The method also respects the existing function structure of the organization for forming multidisciplinary teams, without needing to create new and risky functional structures that new initiatives usually demand.

## HOW IT WORKS

### STEP 1: Translate proposed solutions as initiatives.

Translate solutions as "initiatives" by describing them as initial projects to start implementation. This translation is done to understand solutions as action items but not to reframe or change the content of solutions.

### STEP 2: Create a matrix of "initiatives" versus "departments."

Set up a matrix with the initiatives listed as the row headings. The various departments of the organizations, such as engineering, marketing, research, and finance, relevant to the initiatives, are listed as the column headings.

### STEP 3: Define capabilities needed for initiatives.

Review the solutions to be implemented in each of the initiatives, and determine what kinds of capabilities

are needed for their successful implementation—for example, engineering design, software development, financial planning, branding, and marketing.

### STEP 4: Choose appropriate people for the team.

Identify departments where the capabilities needed for each initiative may be found. Look for potential team members. Ensure that the whole team is multidisciplinary in nature. Fill the matrix with names of selected team members and describe the capabilities they bring.

### STEP 5: Assign roles and leadership.

The different departments of the organization contribute to the initiative at different levels of criticality and their roles vary in importance. Indicate each team member's contribution as primary, secondary, or tertiary in the matrix cells. If possible, indicate which team member will take the leadership role for executing the project. Describe the team goals and deliverables.

### STEP 6: Discuss and extend the plan.

As a group, discuss all the initiatives and think of ways in which they could be launched. How will teams coordinate across initiatives? How will the initiatives change over time? How will the team composition change as the project evolves? How can external capabilities be brought in?

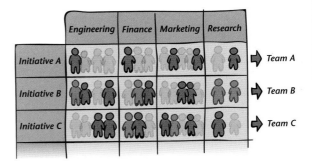

**7.7 TEAM FORMATION PLAN**

# 7.8 Vision Statement

Showing and telling what the offering will be as a comprehensive illustration

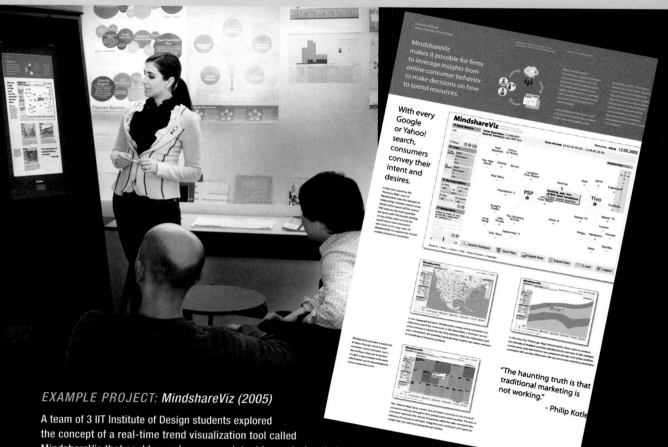

## EXAMPLE PROJECT: *MindshareViz (2005)*

A team of 3 IIT Institute of Design students explored the concept of a real-time trend visualization tool called MindshareViz that could reveal consumer intent by analyzing their online search behaviors. The team found that this concept would benefit marketers, product developers, and venture capitalists trying to learn about consumer intent and desires beyond what traditional trend forecasting and market research reports could offer. Users of MindshareViz can input a set of keywords and other search parameters related to time, demographics, and geography of some set of search activity. Users can then select dynamic "views" to look at the resulting data in various ways to gain insights into consumer search behaviors. These views are conceived as windows into consumer intent and mental models.

As part of communicating this concept, the team created a *Vision Statement* in the form of a presentational poster. They gave the concept a large title at the top along with a concise phrase describing MindshareViz, a diagrammatic description, and a short and crisp value statement. The poster also presented four key views: Relations Map, Geographic View, Timescape Map, and Volume Map—that showed how consumers conveyed their intent and desires while searching. The team used this overview Vision Statement poster to communicate their concept to various audiences for testing the concept and to do reviews with stakeholders for refinement.

**BENEFITS**

- Creates overview
- Organizes information for easy access
- Builds alignment in the organization
- Defines direction
- Improves communication
- Structures existing knowledge

**INPUT**

- Key results like insights, principles, innovations, prototypes, strategies, plans, roadmaps from project

**OUTPUT**

- Overview visualization showing the key aspects of the solution and the project

**WHEN TO USE**

## WHAT IT DOES

A Vision Statement is a method for describing the result of an innovation project as an overview, showing how the innovation offering is implemented by the organization. Part of the method is to express the innovation intent and its realization in only a minimum set of words or visuals, for example, a title statement as brief as, "We will eradicate breast cancer in the next twenty years." It contains no specifics, but grounds all innovation efforts.

The method aims to distill all of the research, analysis, and synthesis into a concise expression that summarizes the fulfillment of the innovation intent in an easy to grasp format, especially making it clear to any stakeholder. It expresses the value proposition, targeted users, key activities, performance, channels, resources, cost structure, revenue streams, strategy, and similar key factors. The Vision Statement is often developed during the process of crafting a Strategy Plan.

## HOW IT WORKS

### STEP 1: Review the project and summarize the key results.

Go through the whole innovation process (research, analysis, synthesis, realization) and summarize the key results such as insights, principles, innovations, prototypes, strategies, plans, roadmaps, and others.

### STEP 2: Create an outline for the vision statement.

Based on a good understanding of the project, outline a short Vision Statement that best communicates your innovation to the stakeholders. Distill the innovation process and the results down to just the most essential parts.

This outline may be based on a revision of the innovation Intent Statement written earlier in the process. It has parts such as customers, needs, opportunities, new values, and risks.

Alternatively, consider these three parts for the Vision Statement:

- A compelling title and a supporting phrase
- Short descriptions of challenges and solutions
- Illustration of key benefits

### STEP 3: Write a title and a supporting phrase for the innovation.

Create a distinctive and compelling title for the proposed innovation. Just as in a slogan, in a few words, write a short supporting phrase to concisely express the essence of the innovation.

### STEP 4: Write short descriptions of challenges and solutions.

Write a short description about the challenges (problems) being addressed by your project. In parallel, write about how the innovation solutions respond to these challenges and what benefits (value) they bring to face those challenges.

### Step 5: Illustrate key benefits of the solutions.

Using key images, captions, and descriptions, illustrate key benefits of your most valuable solutions. For this, create three to ten illustrations with diagrams, screen shots, research settings, prototypes, scenarios, strategies, implementation issues, and others.

**7.8 VISION STATEMENT**

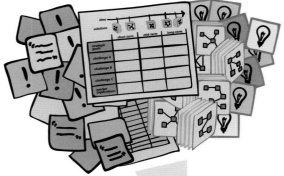

### STEP 6: Visualize as an overview.

Create an overview visualization of the Vision Statement. Embody the overview as a presentation (up to ten slides), a poster, a brochure, or a short document (one to five pages).

### Step 7: Review with stakeholders and revise.

Share the Vision Statement with stakeholders. Get feedback and revise as needed.

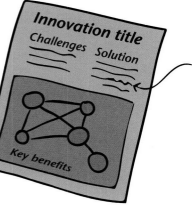

*single and concise communication piece*

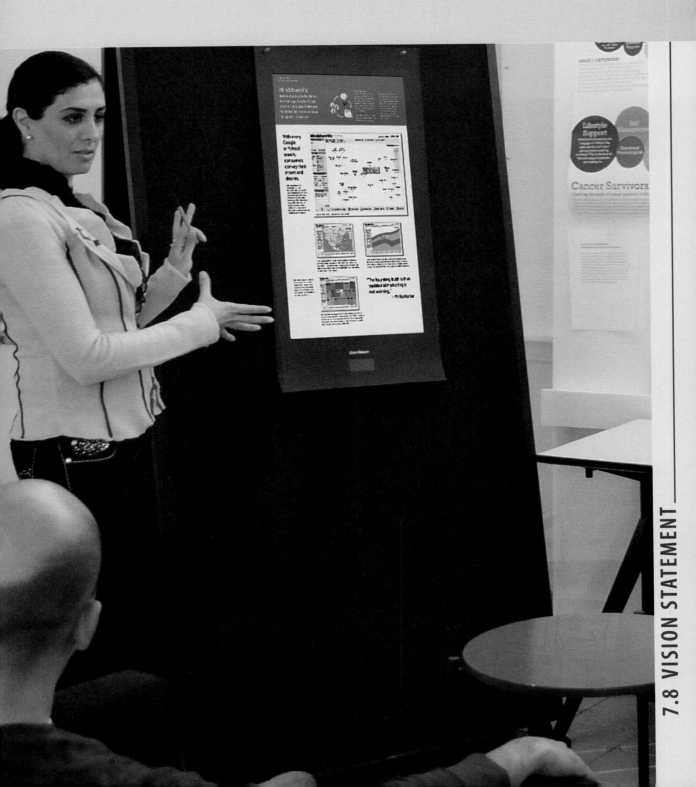

# 7.9 | Innovation Brief

Making the vision for innovation offerings understandable for all stakeholders

Although the technology boom influenced significant growth of the middle class in India, a good healthcare system is still inaccessible to many. By examining India's healthcare system and the competencies of a technology company, a team of IIT Institute of Design students developed a strategic communications plan to show how the company could enter India's healthcare industry using their proposed solutions and improve healthcare access and meet the needs of India's urban poor. The plan integrated the roles, needs, and challenges of all stakeholders (e.g., the technology company, state government, local communities) required to build an infrastructure for a sustainable national healthcare system.

Solutions were presented using the *Innovation Brief* method. The team prepared a short executive summary intended for the company leaders, a report for anyone to know about the project details, and a presentation to communicate the ideas to the stakeholders. A key part of the communication was a strategy framework made of three phases: empower, connect, and extend. In the empower phase, the plan expressed the goal of building partnerships with private sector and community-based organizations, such as private hospitals, NGOs, and health guides. Innovations would focus on implementing electronic medical records and tools for collecting, tracking, and transmitting information from health guides to private hospitals. The connect phase focused on bridging the gap between private and public hospitals and supporting them through training services and involving state government in self-sustaining communities. The final extend phase introduced a nationwide plan that would provide analytic tools to government officials to develop standards and regulations and implement information management solutions across the healthcare industry.

| BENEFITS | INPUT | OUTPUT | WHEN TO USE |
|---|---|---|---|

**BENEFITS**
- Builds alignment in the organization
- Encourages comprehensiveness
- Improves communication
- Supports transition

**INPUT**
- Strategy Plan, Strategic Roadmap, and Vision Statement
- Key audiences relevant to implementation

**OUTPUT**
- A communication plan identifying different audiences and respective communication strategies and tactics for each

## WHAT IT DOES

The Innovation Brief is a method for translating innovation plans into messages and images that make them understandable to stakeholders and end users. It divides all communications into three aspects: the message, the intended audience, and medium through which it is delivered. Empathy, metaphor, analogy, visualization, and emotional design are all employed in conjunction with planning activities to think through how we will present our offerings. The method is a structured approach to communication that promotes consistency of message in various forms. It also involves delivering messages differently to diverse audiences like finance managers, marketing researchers, engineers, or end users.

## HOW IT WORKS

### STEP 1: Review your Strategy Plan and Vision Statement.

Identify key messages presented in the Strategy Plan, Vision Statement, and other similar explorations and choose the core ideas that you need to communicate.

### STEP 2: Consider the audiences.

Think of different audiences to be addressed in order to implement your innovation solutions. In addition to key messages, determine what kind of detailed information is needed to engage the audience and engender their buy in. Consider how conversations are framed with this audience so that they understand the offerings and the role they need to play during implementation.

### STEP 3: Explore different methods of delivery for different audiences.

Think about various presentation formats for your different audiences. Will the content be presented through factual data, illustrations, visualizations, stories, or expressions that appeal to emotions? In most cases, it will consist of a combination of formats. Select modes of delivery that help emphasize points that matter most to the particular audience. For example, quantitative points of reference may give a finance-minded audience a sense of comfort and readiness to engage with your message.

### STEP 4: Develop an Innovation Brief for each audience.

Discuss the role a particular audience plays in the implementation. Identify what matters to that audience, and determine how you will engage them in your communications. Based on this understanding, review all your findings from the whole innovation process and extract the key pieces that communicate best to the audience. Compile all these pieces into an effective communication document or presentation for delivery.

### STEP 5: Test, refine, and deliver the Innovation Brief.

Review the communication documents and presentations. Test them with audience representatives, obtain feedback, and refine. Based on the feedback, deliver the Innovation Brief as a compelling communication experience.

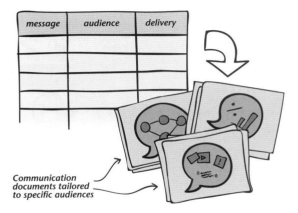

Communication documents tailored to specific audiences

**7.9 INNOVATION BRIEF**

# CREDITS FOR EXAMPLE PROJECTS

**1.1 Buzz Reports.** Example: Learning Apps—Peapod Labs; 2010; Peapod Labs. Team: Jared Allen, Guillermo Krovblit, JunYoung Yang.

**1.2 Popular Media Scan.** Example: HeartSense—Addressing Obama's Health Care Agenda; 2009; IIT Institute of Design (IIT ID). Advisor: Larry Keeley. Team: Mo Goltz, Elena O'Curry, Mike Roy, Owen Schoppe, Traci Thomas.

**1.3 Key Facts.** Example: New Options for Out-of-School Youth; 2008; IIT ID. Advisor: Vijay Kumar, Chris Conley, Jeff Harris, Ash Arnet. Team: Matt Cowen, Marie-Claude Garneau, James Heys, Jennifer Lee, Kate Pemberton, Susan Stirling.

**1.4 Innovation Sourcebook.** Example: Home-Life Strategic Platform; 2010; IIT ID. Advisor: Vijay Kumar. Team: Jin Shaun Ang, Tanushree Bhat, Young Jin Chung, Benjamin Davis, Luis Eduardo Dejo, Eunkyung Kim, Na Rae Kim, Shilpi Kumar, Joohyun Lyoo, Francesca Passoni, Zack Perry, Joseph Shields, Alok Singh, Jung Joo Sohn, Jessica Striebich, Traci Thomas, Helen Tong, John Vollmer.

**1.5 Trend Experts Interview.** Example: Convivial Food Platform; 2010; IIT ID. Advisor: Vijay Kumar. Team: Benjamin Davis, Na Rae Kim, Francesca Passoni, Zack Perry, Alok Singh.

**1.6 Keyword Bibliometrics.** Example: Innovations for a Medical Devices Company; 2007; Doblin.

**1.7 Ten Types of Innovation Framework.** Example: Innovations in Car Rental Company; 2000; Doblin.

**1.8 Innovation Landscape.** Example: Innovations in Healthcare Industry; 2006; Doblin.

**1.9 Trends Matrix.** Example: Cultural Tourism—CityFriends; 2007; IIT ID. Advisor: Vijay Kumar. Team: Andrew Buhayar, Carol Coletta, Jillian Lee, John Montgomery, Ethan Suh.

**1.10 Convergence Map.** Example: Food-Wellness-Diabetes Convergence; 2008; Doblin. Advisor: Larry Keeley.

**1.11 From … To Exploration.** Example: Reframing Education—Singapore; 2010; Innovation Methods. Advisor: Vijay Kumar.

**1.12 Initial Opportunity Map.** Example: Legacy Planning—Opportunity for a Life Insurance Company; 2007; IIT ID. Advisor: Vijay Kumar. Team: Manoj Kumar Adusumilli, Erik Crimmin, Trent Kahute, Elisabeth Martinez De Morentin, Peter Rivera-Pierola, Alexander Troitzsch.

**1.13 Offering-Activity-Culture Map.** Example: Maintaining Clothes; 2011; IIT ID. Advisor: John Pipino. Team: Shilpi Kumar, Catherine Pansard, Jaime Rivera.

**1.14 Intent Statement.** Example: Reducing Violence—CeaseFire Chicago; 2009; IIT ID. Advisor: Vijay Kumar. Team: Kristine Angell, James Barton, Apeksha Garga,Amanda Geppert, Shivani Mohan, Hye Kyung Yoo.

**2.1 Contextual Research Plan.** Example: Automobiles in India Research; 2008; Innovation Methods. Advisor: Vijay Kumar.Bhumi Gajjar, Shin Sano.

**2.2 Popular Media Search.** Example: SHIFT Platform; 2010; IIT ID. Advisor: Larry Keeley. Team: Lawrence Abrahamson, Amir Arabkheradmand, Youna Choi, Hiro Iwasaki, Hyunjoo Lee.

**2.3 Publications Research.** Example: Points of Arrival in Emerging Markets; 2005; IIT ID. Advisor: Vijay Kumar. Team: Michael Beebe, Jaime Chen, Henning Fischer, Taylor Lies, Matthew Locsin.

**2.4 Eras Map.** Example: Dog Ownership; 2007; IIT ID. Advisor: Vijay Kumar. Team: Joe Dizney, Andrea Kachudas, Trent Kahute, Suk Jun Lim, Natrina Toyong.

**2.5 Innovation Evolution Map.** Example: The Future of Play; 2006; IIT ID. Advisor: Vijay Kumar. Team: Steve Babitch, Enric Gili Fort, Andy Kim, Pam Nyberg, Albert Wan

**2.6 Financial Profile.** Example: e-Wallet—Creating Mobile Service for Financial Management; 2010; IIT ID. Advisor: David Sonder. Team: Guillermo Krovblit, JunYoung Yang.

**2.7 Analogous Models.** Example: New Options for Out-of-School Youth; 2008; IIT ID. Advisor: Vijay Kumar. Team: Kate Hanna Korel, Erin Myers, Amy Seng.

**2.8 Competitors-Complementors Map.** Example: Homebuilder—Addressing the Needs of Underserved Market; 2006; IIT ID. Advisor: Vijay Kumar. Team: Joshua Kaplan, Christine Kim, David McGaw, Waewwan Sitthisathainchai.

**2.9 Ten Types of Innovation Diagnostics.** Example: Long-term Strategy for a Professional Organization; 2008; IIT ID. Advisor: Vijay Kumar. Team: Ulrike Anders, Margaret Jung, Nanqian Xu.

**2.10 Industry Diagnostics.** Example: Club V—A Strategic Venture; 2006; IIT ID. Advisor: Vijay Kumar. Team: Joyce Chen, Hyuniee Jung, Randy MacDonald, Rishabh Singh

**2.11 SWOT Analysis.** Example: The Future of News Media; 2007; IIT ID. Advisor: Vijay Kumar. Team: Alex Cheek, Irene Chong, Sangho Lee, Ido Mor, Eric Niu, Natrina Toyong.

**2.12 Subject Matter Experts Interview.** Example: Schools in the Digital Age; 2007; IIT ID. Advisor: Patrick Whitney, Vijay Kumar, John Grimes, Kevin Denney. Team: Carol Coletta, Erik Crimmin, Kevin Denney, Suk Jun Lim, Pam Nyberg.

**2.13 Interest Groups Discussion.** Example: Learning Apps—Peapod Labs; 2010; Peapod Labs. Team: Jared Allen, Guillermo Krovblit, JunYoung Yang.

**3.1 Research Participant Map.** Example: Mobile Computing; 1995; Doblin.

**3.2 Research Planning Survey.** Example: Gen-Y and the Future of Retail; 2007; IIT ID. Advisor: Vijay Kumar. Team: Jonathan Campbell, Jennifer Comiskey, James Heys, Yoo Jong Lee, Mary Kay McCaw, Shin Sano, Gauri Verma.

**3.3 User Research Plan.** Example: Residential and Commercial Renovations; 2010; IIT ID. Advisor: Vijay Kumar. Team: Cecilia Ambros, Mehmet Cirakoglu, Tom DeVries, Jill Haagenson, Amber Lindholm, Nikhil Mathew, Elena O'Curry, Fei Qi, Kshitij Sawant, Owen Schoppe, Libby Taggart, Pinxia Ye.

**3.4 Five Human Factors.** Example: Entertaining at Home; 2005; IIT ID. Advisor: Patrick Whitney, Vijay Kumar, Anjali Kelkar. Team: Alexa Curtis, Taylor Lies, Douglas Look, Douglas Wills.

**3.5 P.O.E.M.S.** Example: Kitchen Activities; 2005; IIT ID. Advisor: Patrick Whitney, Vijay Kumar, Anjali Kelkar. Team: Linong Dai, Jillian Lee, Rachel Pluto, Abbey Ripstra.

**3.6 Field Visit.** Example: Learning through Play; 2009; IIT ID. Advisor: Martin Thaler. Team: Jared Allen, James Barton, Mehmet Cirakoglu, Benjamin Davis, Apeksha Garga, Qijing Huang, Guillermo Krovblit, Ji Sun Park, Katherine Pemberton, Dania Peterson, Joseph Shields, Jung Joo Sohn, Chao Su, Libby Taggart, Van Vuong, Kathryn Wasserman, Junyoung Yang, Pinxia Ye, HyeKyung Yoo, Gene Young.

**3.7 Video Ethnography.** Example: Air Travel Experience; 1996; Doblin.

**3.8 Ethnographic Interview.** Example: Automobiles in India; 2008; Innovation Methods. Advisor: Vijay Kumar. Team: Bhumi Gajjar, Shin Sano.

**3.9 User Pictures Interview.** Example: Eating and Drinking On-the-Go; 2010; IIT ID. Advisor: Patrick Whitney. Team: Luis Eduardo Dejo, Alla Donina, Na Rae Kim, Catherine Pansard.

**3.10 Cultural Artifacts.** Example: Comunidad Diabetes; 2009; IIT ID. Advisor: Judith Gregory. Team: Marco Cimatti, Jessamyn Haupt, Elisabeth de Kleer, Yadira Ornelas, Gladys Rosa-Mendoza, Eric Swanson, Pinxia Ye.

**3.11 Image Sorting.** Example: Reducing Violence—CeaseFire Chicago; 2009; IIT ID. Advisor: Vijay Kumar. Team: Kristine ell, James Barton, Apeksha Garga, Amanda Geppert, Shivani Mohan, Hye Kyung Yoo.

**3.12 Experience Simulation.** Example: Bus Rapid Transit; 2008; IIT ID. Advisor: Martin Thaler. Team: Ofori-Amoah David, Saurabh Gupta, Stephanie Krieger, Edwin Lee, Seung Wan Lim, Lise Lynam, Jamie Mash, Shivani Mohan, Amy Palit, Nallieli Santamaria, Amy Seng, Nanqian Xu.

**3.13 Field Activity.** Example: New Options for Out-of-School Youth; 2008; IIT ID. Advisor: Vijay Kumar, Chris Conley, Jeff Harris, Ash Arnet. Team: Matt Cowen, Marie-Claude Garneau, James Heys, Jennifer Lee, Kate Pemberton, Susan Stirling.

**3.14 Remote Research.** Example: Automobiles in India; 2008; Innovation Methods. Advisor: Vijay Kumar. Team: Bhumi Gajjar, Shin Sano.

**3.15 User Observations Database**. Example: Entertaining at Home; 2005; IIT ID. Advisor: Vijay Kumar, Patrick Whitney, Anjali Kelkar. Team: Alexa Curtis, Taylor Lies, Douglas Look, Douglas Wills.

**4.1 Observations to Insights.** Example: Transaction Account of the Future; 2011; IIT ID. Advisor: Bruce Bendix. Team: Jessica Barnes, Kevin Knapp.

**4.2 Insights Sorting.** Example: Residential and Commercial Renovations; 2010; IIT ID. Advisor: Vijay Kumar. Team: Cecilia Ambros, Mehmet Cirakoglu, Tom DeVries, Jill Haagenson, Amber Lindholm, Nikhil Mathew, Elena O'Curry, Fei Qi, Kshitij Sawant, Owen Schoppe, Libby Taggart, Pinxia Ye.

**4.3 Observation Queries.** Example: Global Cooking Platform; 2007; IIT ID. Advisor: Vijay Kumar, Patrick Whitney. Team: Joseph Dizney, Jessica Gatto, Marieke Smets.

**4.4 User Response Analysis.** Example: Online Women Shopping; 2010; IIT ID. Advisor: Kim Erwin. Team: Libby Taggart.

**4.5 ERAF Systems Diagram.** Example: NHL Hockey; 2008; IIT ID. Advisor: Vijay Kumar. Team: Matt Cowen, Jim Heys, Lise Lynam, Soo Yeon Paik.

**4.6 Descriptive Value Web.** Example: Safeguarding Endangered Cultural Heritage Sites; 2008; IIT ID. Advisor: Vijay Kumar, Patrick Whitney. Team: Lin Lin, Preethi Narayanan, Reiko Takahashi, Natrina Toyong.

**4.7 Entities Position Map.** Example: Car Buying in India; 2008; IIT ID. Advisor: Vijay Kumar. Team: Jonathan Campbell, Bhumi Gajjar, Preethi Narayanan, Shin Sano.

**4.8 Venn Diagram.** Example: Rehab Network; 2001; IIT ID. Advisor: Vijay Kumar. Team: Devesh Desai, Shivani Kothari, Holly Roeske, Karen Scanlan, Shawn Stokes.

**4.9 Tree / Semi-lattice Diagram.** Example: Future of Living; 2009; IIT ID. Advisor: Charles L. Owen, John Pipino, Amanda McKown. Team: Cornelia Bailey, Tanushree Bhat, Marilee Bowles-Carey, Anthony Caspary, Eric Diamond, Xiaonan Huang, Reenu John, Na Rae Kim, Paolo Korre, Eugene Limb, Hsin-Cheng Lin, Miguel Martinez, Nikhil Mathew,

Elise Metzger, Mahdieh Salimi, Kshitij Sawant, Owen Schoppe, Jessica Striebich, Hannah Swart, Traci Thomas, Helen Tong, Sally Wong, Yixiu Wu, Hye Kyung Yoo, Gene Young.

**4.10 Symmetric Clustering Matrix.** Example: Analyzing Corner Stores; 2009; IIT ID. Advisor: John Pipino. Team: Jamie Mash, Amanda McKown, Dania Peterson, Angela Robertson.

**4.11 Asymmetric Clustering Matrix.** Example: Air Travel—Design Analysis; 2007; IIT ID. Advisor: Vijay Kumar. Team: Liza Leif, Ido Mor, Woo Jin Park, Jihyun Sun.

**4.12 Activity Network.** Example: Mobile Computing; 1995; Doblin.

**4.13 Insights Clustering Matrix.** Example: Cooking at Home; 2006; IIT ID. Advisor: Vijay Kumar, Patrick Whitney, Anjali Kelkar. Team: Alex Cheek, Polly Greathouse, Margo Horowitz, Elisabeth M. de Morentin.

**4.14 Semantic Profile.** Example: Analyzing Corner Stores; 2009; IIT ID. Advisor: John Pipino. Team: Jamie Mash, Amanda McKown, Dania Peterson, Angela Robertson.

**4.15 User Groups Definition.** Example: Dog Ownership; 2007; IIT ID. Advisor: Vijay Kumar. Team: Joe Dizney, Andrea Kachudas, Trent Kahute, Suk Jun Lim, Natrina Toyong.

**4.16 Compelling Experience Map.** Example: The Future of Gaming; 2007; IIT ID. Advisor: Vijay Kumar. Team: Manoj Kumar Adusumilli, Brian Brigham, Valerie Campbell, Michael Solheim, Kayo Takasugi.

**4.17 User Journey Map.** Example: Social Kitchen; 2010; IIT ID. Advisor: Ben Jacobson. Team: Youna Choi, Shilpi Kumar, Derek Tarnow.

**4.18 Summary Framework.** Example: Changing the Customer Experience in the Insurance Industry; 2009; IIT ID. Advisor: Vijay Kumar. Team: Amy Batchu, Marilee Bowles-Carey, Preethi Lakshminarayanan, Amanda McKown, Shilpa Rao, Nallieli Santamaria, Gauri Verma, Nanqian Xu.

**4.19 Design Principles Generation.** Example: Reducing Violence— CeaseFire Chicago; 2009; IIT ID. Advisor: Vijay Kumar. Team: Kristine Angell, James Barton, Apeksha Garga, Amanda Geppert, Shivani Mohan, Hye Kyung Yoo.

**4.20 Analysis Workshop.** Example: Improving the Outpatient Experience; 2011; IIT ID. Advisor: Matthew Locsin, Ryan Pikkel.Young Jin Chung, Stephanie Hon, Shilpi Kumar, Hyun Joo Lee, Tuduyen Annie Nguyen, Aaron Penn, Gladys Rosa-Mendoza.

**5.1 Principles to Opportunities.** Example: Residential and Commercial Renovations; 2010; IIT ID. Advisor: Vijay Kumar. Team: Cecilia Ambros, Mehmet Cirakoglu, Tom DeVries, Jill Haagenson, Amber Lindholm, Nikhil Mathew, Elena O'Curry, Fei Qi, Kshitij Sawant, Owen Schoppe, Libby Taggart, Pinxia Ye.

**5.2 Opportunity Mind Map.** Example: National Park System; 2005; IIT ID. Advisor: Vijay Kumar. Team: Nathaniel Block, Geoff Colbath, Henning Fischer, Taylor Lies, Kristina Marich, Laate Olukotun.

**5.3 Value Hypothesis.** Example: Planning for Retirement; 2010; IIT ID. Advisor: Vijay Kumar. Team: Jin Shaun Ang, Young Jin Chung, Luis Eduardo Dejo, Jung Joo Sohn, Jessica Striebich.

**5.4 Persona Definition.** Example: BOLT; 2011; IIT ID. Advisor: Tom MacTavish. Team: Reenu John, Eugene Limb, Tuduyen Annie Nguyen, Cameron Reynolds-Flatt, Sally Wong.

**5.5 Ideation Session.** Example: Car Sharing Service; 2010; IIT ID. Advisor: Ryan Pikkel. Team: Mo Chang, Eugene Limb, Mike Roy, Peter Zapf.

**5.6 Concept Generating Matrix.** Example: Bringing Relevance to Newspaper Company; 2011; IIT ID. Advisor: Matthew Locsin, Ryan Pikkel. Team: Leticia Baiao, Tanushree Bhat, Kang-Il Chung, Luis Eduardo Dejo, Sajid Reshamwala, Rebecka Sexton, Jung Joo Sohn.

**5.7 Concept Metaphors & Analogies.** Example: Better Budget; 2010; IIT ID. Advisor: Vijay Kumar. Team: Tanushree Bhat, Joohyun Lyoo, Helen Tong, John Vollmer

**5.8 Role-play Ideation.** Example: Homebuilder—Addressing the Needs of Underserved Market; 2006; IIT ID. Advisor: Vijay Kumar. Team: Joshua Kaplan, Christine Kim, David McGaw, Waewwan Sitthisathainchai.

**5.9 Ideation Game.** Example: Convivial Food Platform; 2010; IIT ID. Advisor: Vijay Kumar. Team: Benjamin Davis, Na Rae Kim, Francesca Passoni, Zack Perry, Alok Singh.

**5.10 Puppet Scenario**. Example: Senior Interaction, Supporting the Elderly; 2009; The Royal Danish Academy of Fine Arts. Team: Maria Foverskov, Tau Ulv Lenskjold, Sissel Olander, Signe Louise Yndigegn.

**5.11 Behavioral Prototype.** Example: ThinkeringSpaces; 2006; IIT ID. Project Advisors: Dale Fahnstrom, Greg Prygrocki, Heloisa Moura. Team: Alok Chandel, Alexa Curtis, Jereme Dumm, Chelsea Holzworth, Lauren Schwendimann, Andrea Small.

**5.12 Concept Prototype.** Example: Airline Medical Emergencies; 2009; IIT ID. Advisor: Martin Thaler. Team: James Barton, Fei Gao, Fei Qi.

**5.13 Concept Sketch.** Example: Recycling in Farmer's Markets; 2011; IIT ID. Advisor: Martin Thaler. Team: Jin Shaun Ang, Yelim Hong, Hironori Iwasaki, Jung Joo Sohn.

**5.14 Concept Scenario.** Example: Improving the Coffee Shop Experience; 2011; IIT ID. Advisor: Jeremy Alexis. Team: Yelim Joanne Hong, Ted Pollari, Cameron Reynolds-Flatt, James Schuyler, Derek Tarnow.

**5.15 Concept Sorting.** Example: Kids Media; 2006; IIT ID. Advisor: Vijay Kumar. Team: Christopher Bernard, Mark King, David McGaw, Zachary Paradis, Aurora Tallacksen.

**5.16 Concept Grouping Matrix.** Example: Dog Ownership; 2007; IIT ID. Advisor: Vijay Kumar. Team: Joe Dizney, Andrea Kachudas, Trent Kahute, Suk Jun Lim, Natrina Toyon.

**5.17 Concept Catalog.** Safeguarding Endangered Cultural Heritage Sites; 2008; IIT ID. Advisor: Vijay Kumar, Patrick Whitney. Team: Lin Lin, Preethi Narayanan, Reiko Takahashi, Natrina Toyong.

**6.1 Morphological Synthesis.** Example: Urban Dating; 2001; IIT ID. Advisor: Vijay Kumar. Team: Elizabeth Akers, Tamara Bohorquez, Cinthya Urasaki, Felicia Zusman.

**6.2 Concept Evaluation.** Example: Medical Tourism; 2007; IIT ID. Advisor: Vijay Kumar. Team: Gabriel Biller, Sue Jin Kim, Jeffery Mau, Kristy Scovel, Eric Wilmot, Ming-Shan Wu.

**6.3 Prescriptive Value Web.** Example: The Future of Mobile Communications; 2008; IIT ID. Advisor: Vijay Kumar. Team: Kichu Hong, Kyungsun Kim, Min-Joong Kim, Edwin Lee, David Ofori-Amoah, Soo Yeon Paik, Pushkar Vichare.

**6.4 Concept Linking Map.** Example: Video Gaming; 2007; IIT ID. Advisor: Vijay Kumar. Team: Barry Hastings, Sue Jin Kim, Jae Hyun Park, Max Shapiro.

**6.5 Foresight Scenario.** Example: Kids Media; 2006; IIT ID. Advisor: Vijay Kumar. Team: Christopher Bernard, Mark King, David McGaw, Zachary Paradis, Aurora Tallacksen.

**6.6 Solution Diagram.** Example: Cultural Tourism—CityFriends; 2007; IIT ID. Advisor: Vijay Kumar. Team: Andrew Buhayar, Carol Coletta, Jillian Lee, John Montgomery, Ethan Suh.

**6.7 Solution Storyboard.** Example: Legacy Planning—Opportunity for a Life Insurance Company; 2007; IIT ID. Advisor: Vijay Kumar. Team: Manoj Kumar Adusumilli, Erik Crimmin, Trent Kahute, Elisabeth Martinez De Morentin, Peter Rivera-Pierola, Alexander Troitzsch .

**6.8 Solution Enactment.** Example: Recycling in Farmers' Markets; 2011; IIT ID. Advisor: Martin Thaler. Team: Jin Shaun Ang, Yelim Hong, Hironori Iwasaki, Jung Joo Sohn.

**6.9 Solution Prototype.** ThinkeringSpaces; 2008; IIT ID. Advisors: Dale Fahnstrom, Thomas J. McLeish, Greg Prygrocki, Heloisa Moura. Team: Ann Hintzman, LaLuce Mitchell, Van Vuong.

**6.10 Solution Evaluation.** Example: Managing Diabetes; 2006; IIT ID. Advisor: Vijay Kumar. Team: Joyce Chen, Enric Gili Fort, Derrick Kiker, Sarah Nelson, Sara Todd.

**6.11 Solution Roadmap.** Example: Managing Diabetes; 2006; IIT ID. Advisor: Vijay Kumar. Team: Joyce Chen, Enric Gili Fort, Derrick Kiker, Sarah Nelson, Sara Todd.

**6.12 Solution Database.** Example: Future of Living; 2009; IIT ID. Advisors: Charles L. Owen, John Pipino, Amanda McKown. Team: Cornelia Bailey, Tanushree Bhat, Marilee Bowles-Carey, Anthony Caspary, Eric Diamond, Xiaonan Huang, Reenu John, Na Rae Kim, Paolo Korre, Eugene Limb, Hsin-Cheng Lin, Miguel Martinez, Nikhil Mathew, Elise Metzger, Mahdieh Salimi, Kshitij Sawant, Owen Schoppe, Jessica Striebich, Hannah Swart, Traci Thomas, Helen Tong, Sally Wong, Yixiu Wu, Hye Kyung Yoo, Gene Young.

**6.13 Synthesis Workshop.** Example: Schools in the Digital Age; 2007; IIT ID. Advisors: Vijay Kumar, Patrick Whitney, John Grimes. Team: Carol Coletta, Erik Crimmin, Kevin Denney, Suk Jun Lim, Pam Nyberg.

**7.1 Strategic Roadmap.** Example: Homebuilder—Addressing the Needs of Underserved Market; 2006; IIT ID. Advisor: Vijay Kumar. Team: Joshua Kaplan, Christine Kim, David McGaw, Waewwan Sitthisathainchai.

**7.2 Platform Plan.** Example: Convivial Food Platform; 2010; IIT ID. Advisor: Vijay Kumar. Team: Benjamin Davis, Na Rae Kim, Francesca Passoni, Zack Perry, Alok Singh.

**7.3 Strategy Plan Workshop.** Example: Design Research Conference; 2010; IIT ID. Team: Ralph D'Amico, Gene Young.

**7.4 Pilot Development and Testing.** Example: New Options for Out-of-school Youth—Exposure Studio; 2009; IIT ID. Advisor: Chris Conley, Vijay Kumar. Team: Seth B. Kutnick.

**7.5 Implementation Issues Matrix.** Example: Homebuilder—Addressing the Needs of Underserved Market; 2006; IIT ID. Team: Joshua Kaplan, Christine Kim, David McGaw, Waewwan Sitthisathainchai.

**7.6 Competencies Plan.** Example: Points of Arrival in Emerging Markets; 2005; IIT ID. Advisor: Vijay Kumar. Team: Michael Beebe, Jaime Chen, Henning Fischer, Taylor Lies, Matthew Locsin.

**7.7 Team Formation Plan.** Example: Drive-Thru for the Hearing Impaired; 2005; IIT ID. Advisor: Vijay Kumar. Team: Elena Limbert, Griva Patel, Stacie Sabady, Papinya Thongsomjit.

**7.8 Vision Statement.** Example: MindshareViz; 2005; IIT ID. Advisor: Vijay Kumar. Team: Zachary Jean Paradis, Jason Ring, Chris Yin.

**7.9 Innovation Brief.** Example: Healthcare and Technology in India; 2005; IIT ID. Advisor: Vijay Kumar. Team: Kristina Marich, Jose Sia, Martin Zabaleta.

# INDEX